PENGUIN BOOKS

BERLIN DIARY

William L. Shirer's name was a household word for American radio-listeners in the years before World War II when he was chief of Universal News Service's Berlin bureau and a broadcaster for CBS. His other books include *End of a Berlin Diary; Midcentury Journey; The Challenge of Scandinavia: Norway, Sweden, Denmark, and Finland in Our Time; The Sinking of the* Bismarck; *The Rise and Fall of Adolf Hitler; Collapse of the Third Republic: An Inquiry into the Fall of France in 1940; Traitor; Twentieth-Century Journey;* and the monumental bestseller *The Rise and Fall of the Third Reich.*

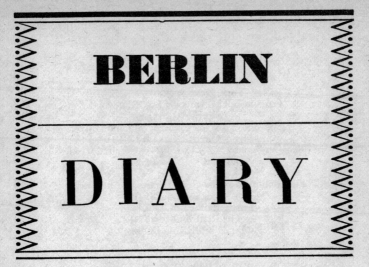

BERLIN

DIARY

The JOURNAL
of a Foreign Correspondent
1934–1941

WILLIAM L. SHIRER

PENGUIN BOOKS

Penguin Books Ltd, Harmondsworth,
Middlesex, England
Penguin Books, 625 Madison Avenue,
New York, New York 10022, U.S.A.
Penguin Books Australia Ltd, Ringwood,
Victoria, Australia
Penguin Books Canada Limited, 2801 John Street,
Markham, Ontario, Canada L3R 1B4
Penguin Books (N.Z.) Ltd, 182–190 Wairau Road,
Auckland 10, New Zealand

First published in the United States of America by
Alfred A. Knopf 1941
First published in Canada by
The Ryerson Press 1941
Published in Penguin Books 1979

LIBRARY OF CONGRESS CATALOGING IN PUBLICATION DATA
Shirer, William Lawrence, 1904–
Berlin diary: the journal of a foreign correspondent, 1934–1941.
Reprint of the 1st ed. published in 1941 by Knopf, New York.
Includes index.
1. World War, 1939–1945—Personal narratives,
American. 2. Shirer, William Lawrence, 1904–
3. World War, 1939–1945—Germany. 4. Europe—Politics
and government—1918–1945. 5. Germany—Politics and
government—1933–1945. 6. Journalists—United States—
Biography. I. Title.
D811.5s5 1979   940.54′81′73   79–11580
ISBN 0 14 00.5182 1

Printed in the United States of America by
Offset Paperback Mfrs., Inc., Dallas, Pennsylvania
Set in Scotch

To TESS

Who Shared So Much

FOREWORD

Most diaries, it may well be, are written with no thought of publication. They have no reader's eye in view. They are personal, intimate, confidential, a part of oneself that is better hidden from the crass outside world.

This journal makes no pretence to being of that kind. It was recorded for my own pleasure and peace of mind, to be sure, but also — to be perfectly frank — with the idea that one day most of it might be published, if any publisher cared to commit it to print. Obviously this was not because I deemed for one second that I and the life I led were of the slightest importance or even of any particular interest to the public. The only justification in my own mind was that chance, and the kind of job I had, appeared to be giving me a somewhat unusual opportunity to set down from day to day a first-hand account of a Europe that was already in agony and that, as the months and years unfolded, slipped inexorably towards the abyss of war and self-destruction.

The subject of this diary therefore is not, except incidentally, its keeper, but this Europe which he watched with increasing fascination and horror plunge madly down the road to Armageddon in the last half of the 1930's. The primary cause of the Continent's upheaval was one country, Germany, and one man, Adolf Hitler. Most of my years abroad were spent in that country in proximity to that man. It was from this vantage point that I saw the European democracies falter and crack and, their confidence and judgment and will paralysed, retreat from one bastion to another until they could no longer, with the exception of Britain, make a stand. From within that totalitarian citadel I could observe too how Hitler, acting with a cynicism, brutality, decisiveness, and clarity of mind and purpose which the Continent had not seen since Napoleon, went from victory to victory, unifying Germany, rearming it, smashing and annexing its neighbours until he had made the Third Reich the militant master of the Continent, and most of its unhappy peoples his slaves.

I jotted down these things from day to day. Unfortunately some of my original notes were lost; others I burned rather than risk them and myself to the tender mercies of the Gestapo; a few things I dared not write down, attempting to imprint them in my memory to be recorded at a later and safer date. But the bulk of my notes and copies of all my broadcasts, before they were censored, I was able to smuggle out. Where there are lapses, I have drawn freely upon my dispatches and radio scripts. In a few cases I have been forced to reconstitute from memory the happenings of the day, conscious of the pitfalls of such a method and the demands of ruthless honesty.

And, finally, certain names of persons in Germany or with relatives in Germany have been disguised or simply indicated by a letter which has no relation to their real names. The Gestapo will find no clues.

Chappaqua, New York
April 1941

CONTENTS

PART I

Prelude to War

WLS

LLORET DE MAR, SPAIN, *January* 11, 1934

Our money is gone. Day after tomorrow I must go back to work. We had not thought much about it. A wire came. An offer. A bad offer from the Paris *Herald*. But it will keep the wolf away until I can get something better.

Thus ends the best, the happiest, the most uneventful year we have ever lived. It has been our " year off," our sabbatical year, and we have lived it in this little Spanish fishing village exactly as we dreamed and planned, beautifully independent of the rest of the world, of events, of men, bosses, publishers, editors, relatives, and friends. It couldn't have gone on for ever. We wouldn't have wanted it to, though if the thousand dollars we had saved for it had not been suddenly reduced to six hundred by the fall of the dollar, we might have stretched the year until a better job turned up. It was a good time to lay off, I think. I've regained the health I lost in India and Afghanistan in 1930–1 from malaria and dysentery. I've recovered from the shock of the skiing accident in the Alps in the spring of 1932, which for a time threatened me with a total blindness but which, happily, in the end, robbed me of the sight of only one eye.

And the year just past, 1933, may very well have

been one not only of transition for us personally, but
for all Europe and America. What Roosevelt is doing
at home seems to smack almost of social and economic
revolution. Hitler and the Nazis have lasted out a
whole year in Germany and our friends in Vienna write
that fascism, both of a local clerical brand and of the
Berlin type, is rapidly gaining ground in Austria.
Here in Spain the revolution has gone sour and the
Right government of Gil Robles and Alexander Ler-
roux seems bent on either restoring the monarchy or
setting up a fascist state on the model of Italy — perhaps both. The Paris that I came to in 1925 at the
tender age of twenty-one and loved, as you love a
woman, is no longer the Paris that I will find day after
tomorrow — I have no illusions about that. It almost
seems as though the world we are plunging back into
is already a different one from that we left just a year
ago when we packed our clothes and books in Vienna
and set off for Spain.

We stumbled across Lloret de Mar on a hike up the
coast from Barcelona. It was five miles from the railroad, set in the half-moon of a wide, sandy beach under
the foot-hills of the Pyrenees. Tess liked it at once.
So did I. We found a furnished house on the beach —
three storeys, ten rooms, two baths, central heating.
When the proprietor said the price would be fifteen
dollars a month, we paid the rent for a year. Our ex-
penses, including rent, have averaged sixty dollars a
month.

What have we done these past twelve months? Not
too much. No great " accomplishments." We've swum,
four or five times a day, from April to Christmas.
We've hiked up and around the lower reaches of the
Pyrenees that slope down to the village and the sea,
past a thousand olive groves, a hundred cork-oak

forests, and the cool whitewashed walls of the peasants'
houses, putting off until tomorrow and for ever the
climb we were always going to make to the peaks that
were covered with snow late in the spring and early in
the fall. We've read — a few of the books for which
there was never time in the days when you had a nightly
cable to file and were being shunted from one capital
to another — from Paris and London to Delhi. Myself: some history, some philosophy, and Spengler's
Decline of the West; Trotsky's *History of the Russian
Revolution; War and Peace;* Céline's *Voyage au bout
de la nuit,* the most original French novel since the war;
and most or all of Wells, Shaw, Ellis, Beard, Heming-
way, Dos Passos, and Dreiser. A few friends came and
stayed: the Jay Allens, Russell and Pat Strauss, and
Luis Quintanilla, one of the most promising of the
younger Spanish painters and a red-hot republican.
Andres Segovia lived next door and came over in the
evening to talk or to play Bach or Albeniz on his guitar.

This year we had time to know each other, to loaf
and play, to wine and eat, to see the bull-fights in the
afternoon and Barcelona's gaudy *Barrio Chino* at
night; time to sense the colours, the olive green of the
hills, the incomparable blues of the Mediterranean in
the spring, and the wondrous, bleak, grey-white skies
above Madrid; time too to know the Spanish peasant
and worker and fisherman, men of great dignity and
guts and integrity despite their miserable, half-starved
lives; and at the Prado and Toledo just a little time
for Greco, whose sweeping form and colour all but
smote us down and made all the Renaissance painting
we had seen in Italy, even the da Vincis, Raphaels,
Titians, Botticellis, seem pale and anæmic.

It has been a good year.

PARIS, *February* 7

A little dazed still from last night. About
five p.m. yesterday I was twiddling my thumbs in the
Herald office wondering whether to go down to the
Chamber, where the new premier, Édouard Daladier,
was supposed to read his ministerial declaration, when
we got a tip that there was trouble at the Place de la
Concorde. I grabbed a taxi and went down to see. I
found nothing untoward. A few royalist *Camelots du
Roi, Jeunesses Patriotes* of Deputy Pierre Taittinger,
and *Solidarité Française* thugs of Perfumer François
Coty — all right-wing youths or gangsters — had attempted to break through to the Chamber, but had been
dispersed by the police. The *Place* was normal. I telephoned the *Herald*, but Eric Hawkins, managing
editor, advised me to grab a bite of dinner near by and
take another look a little later. About seven p.m. I
returned to the Place de la Concorde. Something obviously was up. Mounted steel-helmeted Mobile Guards
were clearing the square. Over by the obelisk in the
centre a bus was on fire. I worked my way over through
the Mobile Guards, who were slashing away with their
sabres, to the Tuileries side. Up on the terrace was a
mob of several thousand and, mingling with them, I
soon found they were not fascists, but Communists.
When the police tried to drive them back, they unleashed
a barrage of stones and bricks. Over on the bridge leading from the *Place* to the Chamber across the Seine, I
found a solid mass of Mobile Guards nervously fingering their rifles, backed up by ordinary police and a fire-
brigade. A couple of small groups attempted to advance
to the bridge from the quay leading up from the Louvre,
but two fire-hoses put them to flight. About eight
o'clock a couple of thousand U.N.C. (*Union Nationale*

des Combattants [1]) war veterans paraded into the *Place*,
having marched down the Champs-Élysées from the
Rond-Point. They came in good order behind a mass
of tricoloured flags. They were stopped at the bridge
and their leaders began talking with police officials. I
went over to the Crillon and up to the third-floor balcony overlooking the square. It was jammed with people. The first shots we didn't hear. The first we knew
of the shooting was when a woman about twenty feet
away suddenly slumped to the floor with a bullet-hole
in her forehead. She was standing next to Melvin
Whiteleather of the A.P. Now we could hear the shooting, coming from the bridge and the far side of the
Seine. Automatic rifles they seemed to be using. The
mob's reaction was to storm into the square. Soon it
was dotted with fires. To the left, smoke started pouring
out of the Ministry of Marine. Hoses were brought
into play, but the mob got close enough to cut them.
I went down to the lobby to phone the office. Several
wounded were laid out and were being given first aid.

The shooting continued until about midnight, when
the Mobile Guards began to get the upper hand. Several times the Place de la Concorde changed hands, but
towards midnight the police were in control. Once —
about ten o'clock it must have been — the mob, which
by this time was incensed, but obviously lacked leadership, tried to storm the bridge, some coming up along
the quais, whose trees offered them considerable protection, and others charging madly across the *Place*.
"If they get across the bridge," I thought, "they'll
kill every deputy in the Chamber." But a deadly fire
— it sounded this time like machine-guns — stopped

---

[1] A right-wing organization of some eight hundred thousand members. France's other four million war veterans were organized in the
Fédération des Anciens Combattants.

them and in a few minutes they were scattering in all directions.

Soon there was only scattered firing and about ten minutes after twelve I started sprinting up the Champs-Élysées towards the office to write my story. Near the President's Élysée Palace I noticed several companies of regular troops on guard, the first I had seen. It is almost a mile up hill along the Champs-Élysées to the *Herald* office and I arrived badly out of breath, but managed to write a couple of columns before deadline. Officially: sixteen dead, several hundred wounded.

LATER. — Daladier, who posed as a strong man, has resigned. He gives out this statement: " The government, which has the responsibility for order and security, refuses to assure it by exceptional means which might bring about further bloodshed. It does not desire to employ soldiers against demonstrators. I have therefore handed to the President of the Republic the resignation of the Cabinet."

Imagine Stalin or Mussolini or Hitler hesitating to employ troops against a mob trying to overthrow their regimes! It's true perhaps that last night's rioting had as its immediate cause the Stavisky scandal. But the Stavisky swindles merely demonstrate the rottenness and the weakness of French democracy. Daladier and his Minister of the Interior, Eugène Frot, actually gave the U.N.C. permission to demonstrate. They should have refused it. They should have had enough Mobile Guards on hand early in the evening to disperse the mob before it could gather strength. But to resign now, after putting down a fascist coup — for that's what it was — is either sheer cowardice or stupidity. Important too is the way the Communists fought on the same side of the barricades last night as the fascists. I do not like that.

PARIS, *February* 8

Old " Papa " Doumergue is to head the government of " national union." They've dragged him from his village of Tournefeuille, where he had retired with his mistress, whom he married shortly after stepping down from the presidency. He says he will form a cabinet of former premiers and chiefs of parties, but it will be Rightish and reactionary. Still, the moderate Left — men like Chautemps, Daladier, Herriot — have shown they can't govern, or won't.

PARIS, *February* 12

A general strike today, but not very effective, and there's been no trouble.

LATER. — Dollfuss has struck at the Social Democrats in Austria, the only organized group (forty per cent of the population) which can save him from being swallowed up by the Nazis. Communications with Vienna were cut most of the day, but tonight the story started coming through to the office. It is civil war. The Socialists are entrenched in the great municipal houses they built after the war — models for the whole world — the Karl Marx Hof, the Goethe Hof, and so on. But Dollfuss and the Heimwehr under Prince Starhemberg, a play-boy ignoramus, and Major Fey, a hatchet-faced and brutal reactionary, have control of the rest of the city. With their tanks and artillery, they will win — unless the Socialists get help from the Czechs, from near-by Bratislava.

This, then, is what Fey meant yesterday. I was struck by a report of his speech which Havas carried last night: " During the last few days I have made certain that Chancellor Dollfuss is a man of the Heimwehr. Tomorrow we shall start to make a clean breast of things in Austria." But I put it down to his usual loud-mouthedness. And what a role for little Dollfuss! It's only a little more than a year ago that I, with John Gunther and Eric Gedye, had a long talk with him after a luncheon which the Anglo-American Press Club tendered him. I found him a timid little fellow, still a little dazed that he, the illegitimate son of a peasant, should have gone so far. But give the little men a lot of power and they can be dangerous. I weep for my Social Democrat friends, the most decent men and women I've known in Europe. How many of them are being slaughtered tonight, I wonder. An'd there goes democracy in Austria, one more state gone. Remained at the office until the paper was put to bed at one thirty a.m., but feel too weary and depressed by the news to sleep.

PARIS, *February* 15

The fighting in Vienna ended today, the dispatches say. Dollfuss finished off the last workers with artillery and then went off to pray. Well, at least the Austrian Social Democrats fought, which is more than their comrades in Germany did. Apparently Otto Bauer and Julius Deutsch got safely over the Czech frontier. A good thing, or Dollfuss would have hanged them.

February 23

My birthday. Thirty. And with the worst job I've ever had. Tess prepared a great birthday ban-

quet and afterwards we went out to a concert. How the
French *slide* over Beethoven! Elliot Paul used to say
that if the French musicians would stop reading *L'In-
transigeant* or *Paris-Soir* during a performance they
would do better. Must see Shakespeare's *Coriolanus* at
the Comédie Française, which the Left people charge
has some anti-democratic lines. Heard today that Dollfuss had hanged Koloman Wallisch, the Social Democrat mayor of Bruck an der Mur. Claude Cockburn,
who should know better, came out the other day in
Week with an absurd account of the February 6 riots.
Described them as a "working class" protest. Curiously enough, his description of that night reads suspiciously like that which Trotsky has written of the
first uprising in Petrograd in 1917 in his *History of the
Russian Revolution.* The fact is that February 6 was
an attempted fascist coup which the Communists, wit-
tingly or not, helped.

PARIS, *June* 30

Berlin was cut off for several hours today, but
late this afternoon telephone communication was re-
established. And what a story! Hitler and Göring have
purged the S.A., shooting many of its leaders. Röhm,
arrested by Hitler himself, was allowed to commit suicide
in a Munich jail, according to one agency report. The
French are pleased. They think this is the beginning
of the end for the Nazis. Wish I could get a post in
Berlin. It's a story I'd like to cover.

PARIS, *July* 14

My sister is here, and the three of us celebrated Bastille Day a little tonight. We took her around

to the cafés to watch the people dance. Later we ended
up at Café Flore where I introduced her to some of
the Latin Quarterites. Alex Small was in great form.
When Alex started to fight the Battle of Verdun again,
I dragged the family away, having heard it many times
over the years.

It now develops that Hitler's purge was more drastic
than first reported. Röhm did not kill himself, but was
shot on the orders of Hitler. Other dead: Heines, notorious Nazi boss of Silesia, Dr. Erich Klausner, leader
of the " Catholic Action " in Germany, Fritz von Bose
and Edgar Jung, two of Papen's secretaries (Papen
himself narrowly escaped with his life), Gregor Strasser, who used to be second in importance to Hitler in
the Nazi Party, and General von Schleicher and his
wife, the latter two murdered in cold blood. I see
von Kahr is on the list, the man who balked Hitler's
Beer House *Putsch* in 1923. Hitler has thus taken his
personal revenge. Yesterday, on Friday the 13th, Hitler got away with his explanation in the Reichstag.
When he screamed: " The supreme court of the German
people during these twenty-four hours consisted of myself! " the deputies rose and cheered. One had almost
forgotten how strong sadism and masochism are in the
German people.

Paris, *July* 25

Dollfuss is dead, murdered by the Nazis, who
today seized control of the Chancellery and the radio
station in Vienna. Apparently their coup has failed
and Miklas and Dr. Schuschnigg are in control. I do
not like murder, and Nazi murder least of all. But I
cannot weep for Dollfuss after his cold-blooded slaughter of the Social Democrats last February. Fey seems

to have played a curious role, according to the dispatches. He was in the Chancellery with Dollfuss and kept coming to the balcony to ask for Rintelen, whom the Nazis had named as their first Chancellor. Apparently he thought the Nazi coup had succeeded and was ready to join. A bad hatchet-face, this Fey.

PARIS, *August* 2

Hindenburg died this morning. Who *can* be president now? What will Hitler do?

PARIS, *August* 3

Hitler did what no one expected. He made himself *both* President *and* Chancellor. Any doubts about the loyalty of the army were done away with before the old field-marshal's body was hardly cold. Hitler had the army swear an oath of unconditional obedience to him personally. The man is resourceful.

PARIS, *August* 9

Dosch-Fleurot rang me at the office this afternoon from Berlin and offered me a job with Universal Service there. I said yes at once, we agreed on a salary, and he said he would let me know after talking with New York.

PARIS, *August* 11

Larry Hills, editor and manager of the *Herald*, whined a bit this evening about my going, but finally overcame his ill temper and we went over to the bar of the Hotel California and had a drink. Must brush up my German.

BERLIN, *August* 25

Our introduction to Hitler's Third Reich this evening was probably typical. Taking the day train from Paris so as to see a little of the country, we arrived at the Friedrichstrasse Bahnhof at about ten this evening. The first persons to greet us on the platform were two agents of the secret police. I had expected to meet the secret police sooner or later, but not quite so soon. Two plain-clothes men grabbed me as I stepped off the train, led me a little away, and asked me if I were Herr So-and-So — I could not for the life of me catch the name. I said no. One of them asked again and again and finally I showed him my passport. He scanned it for several minutes, finally looked at me suspiciously, and said: " So. . . . You are not Herr So-and-So, then. You are Herr Shirer." " None other," I replied, " as you can see by the passport." He gave me one more suspicious glance, winked at his fellow dick, saluted stiffly, and made off. Tess and I walked over to the Hotel Continental and engaged an enormous room. Tomorrow begins a new chapter for me. I thought of a bad pun : " I'm going from bad to Hearst."

BERLIN, *August* 26

Knickerbocker tells me Dorothy Thompson departed from the Friedrichstrasse station shortly before we arrived yesterday. She had been given twenty-four hours to get out — apparently the work of Putzi Hanfstängl, who could not forgive her for her book *I Saw Hitler*, which, at that, badly underestimated the man. Knick's own position here is precarious apparently because of some of his past and present writings. Goebbels, who used to like him, has

fallen afoul of him. He's going down to see Hearst at
Bad Nauheim about it in a day or two.

BERLIN, *September* 2

          In the throes of a severe case of depression.
I miss the old Berlin of the Republic, the care-free,
emancipated, civilized air, the snubnosed young women
with short-bobbed hair and the young men with either
cropped or long hair — it made no difference — who
sat up all night with you and discussed anything with
intelligence and passion. The constant *Heil Hitler's*,
clicking of heels, and brown-shirted storm troopers or
black-coated S.S. guards marching up and down the
street grate me, though the old-timers say there are not
nearly so many brown-shirts about since the purge.
Gillie, former *Morning Post* correspondent here and
now stationed in Paris, is, perversely, spending part of
his vacation here. We've had some walks and twice have
had to duck into stores to keep from either having to
salute the standard of some passing S.A. or S.S. battalion or facing the probability of getting beaten up
for not doing so. Day before yesterday Gillie took me
to lunch at a pub in the lower part of the Friedrichstrasse. Coming back he pointed out a building where
a year ago for days on end, he said, you could hear
the yells of the Jews being tortured. I noticed a sign.
It was still the headquarters of some S.A. *Standarte*.
Tess tried to cheer me up by taking me to the Zoo yesterday. It was a lovely, hot day and after watching the
monkeys and elephants we lunched on the shaded terrace of the restaurant there. Called on the Ambassador,
Professor William E. Dodd. He struck me as a blunt,
honest, liberal man with the kind of integrity an American ambassador needs here. He seemed a little dis-

pleased at my saying I did not mourn the death of
Dollfuss and may have interpreted it as meaning I
liked the Nazis, though I hope not. Also called on the
counsellor of Embassy, J. C. White, who appears to
be the more formal type of State Department career
diplomat. He promptly sent cards, nicely creased, to
the hotel, but since I do not understand the creased-
card business of diplomacy I shall do nothing about it.
Am going to cover the annual Nazi Party rally at
Nuremberg day after tomorrow. It should provide a
thorough introduction to Nazi Germany.

N u r e m b e r g , *September* 4

Like a Roman emperor Hitler rode into this
mediæval town at sundown today past solid phalanxes
of wildly cheering Nazis who packed the narrow streets
that once saw Hans Sachs and the *Meistersinger*. Tens
of thousands of Swastika flags blot out the Gothic beau-
ties of the place, the façades of the old houses, the
gabled roofs. The streets, hardly wider than alleys, are
a sea of brown and black uniforms. I got my first
glimpse of Hitler as he drove by our hotel, the Würt-
temberger Hof, to his headquarters down the street at
the Deutscher Hof, a favourite old hotel of his, which
has been remodelled for him. He fumbled his cap with
his left hand as he stood in his car acknowledging the
delirious welcome with somewhat feeble Nazi salutes
from his right arm. He was clad in a rather worn gaber-
dine trench-coat, his face had no particular expression
at all — I expected it to be stronger — and for the life
of me I could not quite comprehend what hidden springs
he undoubtedly unloosed in the hysterical mob which
was greeting him so wildly. He does not stand before
the crowd with that theatrical imperiousness which I

have seen Mussolini use. I was glad to see that he did
not poke out his chin and throw his head back as does
the Duce nor make his eyes glassy — though there *is*
something glassy in his eyes, the strongest thing in his
face. He almost seemed to be affecting a modesty in
his bearing. I doubt if it's genuine.

This evening at the beautiful old Rathaus Hitler
formally opened this, the fourth party rally. He spoke
for only three minutes, probably thinking to save his
voice for the six big speeches he is scheduled to make
during the next five days. Putzi Hanfstängl, an immense, high-strung, incoherent clown who does not often
fail to remind us that he is part American and gradu-
ated from Harvard, made the main speech of the day
in his capacity of foreign press chief of the party. Obviously trying to please his boss, he had the crust to ask
us to "report on affairs in Germany without attempting to interpret them." "History alone," Putzi
shouted, "can evaluate the events now taking place
under Hitler." What he meant, and what Goebbels and
Rosenberg mean, is that we should jump on the band-
wagon of Nazi propaganda. I fear Putzi's words fell
on deaf, if good-humoured, ears among the American
and British correspondents, who rather like him despite
his clownish stupidity.

About ten o'clock tonight I got caught in a mob of
ten thousand hysterics who jammed the moat in front
of Hitler's hotel, shouting: "We want our Führer." I
was a little shocked at the faces, especially those of the
women, when Hitler finally appeared on the balcony
for a moment. They reminded me of the crazed expres-
sions I saw once in the back country of Louisiana on
the faces of some Holy Rollers who were about to hit
the trail. They looked up at him as if he were a Messiah,
their faces transformed into something positively in-

human. If he had remained in sight for more than a
few moments, I think many of the women would have
swooned from excitement.

Later I pushed my way into the lobby of the
Deutscher Hof. I recognized Julius Streicher, whom
they call here the Uncrowned Czar of Franconia. In
Berlin he is known more as the number-one Jew-baiter
and editor of the vulgar and pornographic anti-
Semitic sheet the *Stürmer*. His head was shaved, and
this seemed to augment the sadism of his face. As he
walked about, he brandished a short whip.

Knick arrived today. He will cover for INS and I
for Universal.

NUREMBERG, *September* 5

I'm beginning to comprehend, I think, some
of the reasons for Hitler's astounding success. Borrow-
ing a chapter from the Roman church, he is restoring
pageantry and colour and mysticism to the drab lives
of twentieth-century Germans. This morning's opening meeting in the Luitpold Hall on the outskirts of
Nuremberg was more than a gorgeous show; it also
had something of the mysticism and religious fervour
of an Easter or Christmas Mass in a great Gothic cathedral. The hall was a sea of brightly coloured flags.
Even Hitler's arrival was made dramatic. The band
stopped playing. There was a hush over the thirty
thousand people packed in the hall. Then the band
struck up the *Badenweiler March*, a very catchy tune,
and used only, I'm told, when Hitler makes his big entries. Hitler appeared in the back of the auditorium,
and followed by his aides, Göring, Goebbels, Hess,
Himmler, and the others, he strode slowly down the
long centre aisle while thirty thousand hands were

raised in salute. It is a ritual, the old-timers say, which is always followed. Then an immense symphony orchestra played Beethoven's *Egmont* Overture. Great Klieg lights played on the stage, where Hitler sat surrounded by a hundred party officials and officers of the army and navy. Behind them the " blood flag," the one carried down the streets of Munich in the ill-fated putsch. Behind this, four or five hundred S.A. standards. When the music was over, Rudolf Hess, Hitler's closest confidant, rose and slowly read the names of the Nazi " martyrs " — brown-shirts who had been killed in the struggle for power — a roll-call of the dead, and the thirty thousand seemed very moved.

In such an atmosphere no wonder, then, that every word dropped by Hitler seemed like an inspired Word from on high. Man's — or at least the German's — critical faculty is swept away at such moments, and every lie pronounced is accepted as high truth itself. It was while the crowd — all Nazi officials — were in this mood that the Führer's proclamation was sprung on them. He did not read it himself. It was read by *Gauleiter* Wagner of Bavaria, who, curiously, has a voice and manner of speaking so like Hitler's that some of the correspondents who were listening back at the hotel on the radio thought it was Hitler.

As to the proclamation, it contained such statements as these, all wildly applauded as if they were new truths: " The German form of life is definitely determined for the next thousand years. For us, the nervous nineteenth century has finally ended. There will be no revolution in Germany for the next one thousand years! "

Or: " Germany has done everything possible to assure world peace. If war comes to Europe it will come only because of Communist chaos." Later before a " *Kultur* " meeting he added: " Only brainless dwarfs

cannot realize that Germany has been the breakwater
against Communist floods which would have drowned
Europe and its culture."

Hitler also referred to the fight now going on against
his attempt to Nazify the Protestant church. " I am
striving to unify it. I am convinced that Luther would
have done the same and would have thought of unified
Germany first and last."

NUREMBERG, *September* 6

Hitler sprang his *Arbeitsdienst,* his Labour
Service Corps, on the public for the first time today and
it turned out to be a highly trained, semi-military group
of fanatical Nazi youths. Standing there in the early
morning sunlight which sparkled on their shiny spades,
fifty thousand of them, with the first thousand bared
above the waist, suddenly made the German spectators
go mad with joy when, without warning, they broke
into a perfect goose-step. Now, the goose-step has always seemed to me to be an outlandish exhibition of the
human being in his most undignified and stupid state,
but I felt for the first time this morning what an inner
chord it strikes in the strange soul of the German people. Spontaneously they jumped up and shouted their
applause. There was a ritual even for the Labour Service boys. They formed an immense *Sprechchor* — a
chanting chorus — and with one voice intoned such
words as these: " We want one Leader! Nothing for us!
Everything for Germany! *Heil Hitler!* "

Curious that none of the relatives or friends of the
S.A. leaders or, say, of General von Schleicher have
tried to get Hitler or Göring or Himmler this week.
Though Hitler is certainly closely guarded by the S.S.,
it is nonsense to hold that he cannot be killed. Yester-

day we speculated on the matter, Pat Murphy of the
Daily Express, a burly but very funny and amusing
Irishman, Christopher Holmes of Reuter's, who looks
like a poet and perhaps is, Knick, and I. We were in
Pat's room, overlooking the moat. Hitler drove by, returning from some meeting. And we all agreed how
easy it would be for someone in a room like this to toss
a bomb on his car, rush down to the street, and escape
in the crowd. But there has been no sign of an attempt
yet, though some of the Nazis are slightly worried about
Sunday, when he reviews the S.A.

NUREMBERG, *September* 7

Another great pageant tonight. Two hundred thousand party officials packed in the Zeppelin
Wiese with their twenty-one thousand flags unfurled
in the searchlights like a forest of weird trees. " We are
strong and will get stronger," Hitler shouted at them
through the microphone, his words echoing across the
hushed field from the loud-speakers. And there, in the
flood-lit night, jammed together like sardines, in one
mass formation, the little men of Germany who have
made Nazism possible achieved the highest state of being the Germanic man knows: the shedding of their
individual souls and minds — with the personal responsibilities and doubts and problems — until under the
mystic lights and at the sound of the magic words of
the Austrian they were merged completely in the Germanic herd. Later they recovered enough — fifteen
thousand of them — to stage a torchlight parade
through Nuremberg's ancient streets, Hitler taking the
salute in front of the station across from our hotel.
Von Papen arrived today and stood alone in a car behind Hitler tonight, the first public appearance he has

made, I think, since he narrowly escaped being murdered by Göring on June 30. He did not look happy.

NUREMBERG, *September* 9

Hitler faced his S.A. storm troopers today for
the first time since the bloody purge. In a harangue to
fifty thousand of them he " absolved " them from blame
for the Röhm " revolt." There was considerable tension
in the stadium and I noticed that Hitler's own S.S.
bodyguard was drawn up in force in front of him, sepa-
rating him from the mass of the brown-shirts. We
wondered if just one of those fifty thousand brown-
shirts wouldn't pull a revolver, but not one did. Viktor
Lutze, Röhm's successor as chief of the S.A., also spoke.
He has a shrill, unpleasant voice, and the S.A. boys
received him coolly, I thought. Hitler had in a few of
the foreign correspondents for breakfast this morning,
but I was not invited.

NUREMBERG, *September* 10

Today the army had its day, fighting a very
realistic sham battle in the Zeppelin Meadow. It is difficult to exaggerate the frenzy of the three hundred
thousand German spectators when they saw their soldiers go into action, heard the thunder of the guns,
and smelt the powder. I feel that all those Americans
and English (among others) who thought that German
militarism was merely a product of the Hohenzollerns
— from Frederick the Great to Kaiser Wilhelm II —
made a mistake. It is rather something deeply ingrained
in all Germans. They acted today like children playing
with tin soldiers. The Reichswehr " fought " today only
with the " defensive " weapons allowed them by Ver-

sailles, but everybody knows they've got the rest —
tanks, heavy artillery, and probably airplanes.

LATER. — After seven days of almost cease-
less goose-stepping, speech-making, and pageantry, the
party rally came to an end tonight. And though dead
tired and rapidly developing a bad case of crowd-
phobia, I'm glad I came. You have to go through one
of these to understand Hitler's hold on the people, to
feel the dynamic in the movement he's unleashed and
the sheer, disciplined strength the Germans possess.
And now — as Hitler told the correspondents yesterday
in explaining his technique — the half-million men
who've been here during the week will go back to their
towns and villages and preach the new gospel with new
fanaticism. Shall sleep late tomorrow and take the
night train back to Berlin.

BERLIN, *October* 9

We've taken a comfortable studio flat in the
Tauenzienstrasse. The owner, a Jewish sculptor, says
he is getting off for England while the getting is good
— probably a wise man. He left us a fine German library, which I hope I will get time to use. We get a
little tired of living in flats or houses that other people
have furnished, but the migrant life we lead makes it
impossible to have our own things. We were lucky to
get this place, which is furnished modernly and with
good taste. Most of the middle-class homes we've seen
in Berlin are furnished in atrocious style, littered with
junk and knick-knacks.

LATER. — On my eight o'clock call to the
Paris office tonight, they told me that the King of Yugoslavia had been assassinated at Marseille this afternoon

and that Louis Barthou, the French Foreign Minister, had been badly wounded. Berlin will not be greatly disappointed, as King Alexander seemed disposed to work more closely with the French bloc against Germany, and Barthou had been doing some good work in strengthening French alliances in eastern Europe and in attempting to bring Russia in on an Eastern Locarno.

BERLIN, *November* 15

Not much news these days. Have been covering the fight in the Protestant church. A section of the Protestants seem to be showing more guts in the face of *Gleichschaltung* (co-ordination) than the Socialists or Communists did. But I think Hitler will get them in the end and gradually force on the country a brand of early German paganism which the " intellectuals " like Rosenberg are hatching up. Went tonight to one of Rosenberg's *Bierabends* which he gives for the diplomats and the foreign correspondents once a month. Rosenberg was one of Hitler's " spiritual " and " intellectual " mentors, though like most Balts I have met he strikes me as extremely incoherent and his book *Mythus of the Twentieth Century*, which sells second only to *Mein Kampf* in this country, impresses me as a hodgepodge of historical nonsense. Some of his enemies, like Hanfstängl, say he narrowly missed being a good Russian Bolshevist, having been in Moscow as a student during the revolution, but that he ran out on it because the Bolshies mistrusted him and wouldn't give him a big job. He speaks with a strong Baltic accent which makes his German difficult for me to understand. He had Ambassador Dodd at his table of honour tonight, and the professor looked most unhappy. Bernhard

Rust, the Nazi Minister of Education, was the speaker,
but my mind wandered during his speech. Rust is not
without ability and is completely Nazifying the schools.
This includes new Nazi textbooks falsifying history —
sometimes ludicrously.

BERLIN, *November* 28

Much talk here that Germany is secretly arming, though it is difficult to get definite dope, and if
you did get it and sent it, you'd probably be expelled.
Sir Eric Phipps, the British Ambassador, whom I used
to see occasionally in Vienna when he was Minister there
(he looks like a Hungarian dandy, with a perfect poker
face), but whom I have not seen here yet, returned from
London yesterday and is reported to have asked the
Wilhelmstrasse about it. Went out to a cheap store in
the Tauenzienstrasse today and bought a comical-
looking ready-made suit of "tails" for our foreign
press ball at the Adlon Saturday night. A dinner
jacket, I was told, was not enough.

BERLIN, *December* 2

The ball all right. Tess had a new dress and
looked fine. Goebbels, Sir Eric Phipps, François Poncet, Dodd, and General von Reichenau, the nearest thing
to a Nazi general the Reichswehr has and on very good
terms with most of the American correspondents, were
among those present. Von Neurath was supposed to be
there, but there was some talk of his being displeased
with the seating arrangements — a problem with the
Germans every time you give a party — and I didn't
see him all evening. We danced and wined until about
three, ending up with an early breakfast of bacon and
eggs in the Adlon bar.

BERLIN, *January* 14, 1935

The good Catholics and workers of the Saar
voted themselves back into the Reich yesterday. Some
ninety per cent voted for reunion — more than we had
expected, though no doubt many were afraid that they
would be found out and punished unless they cast their
ballot for Hitler. Well, at least one cause of European
tension disappears. Hitler has said, and repeated in a
broadcast yesterday, that the Saar was the last territorial bone of contention with France. We shall
see. . . .

BERLIN, *February* 25

Diplomatic circles and most of the correspondents are growing optimistic over a general settlement that will ensure peace. Sir John Simon, the British
Foreign Minister, is coming to Berlin. A few days ago
Laval and Flandin met the British in London. What
they offer is to free Germany from the disarmament
provisions of the peace treaty (though Hitler secretly
is rapidly freeing himself) in return for German promises to respect the independence of Austria and all
the other little countries. The French here point out,
though, that Hitler has cleverly separated Paris and
London by inviting the British to come here for talks,
but not the French. And simple Simon has fallen for
the bait.

SAARBRÜCKEN, *March* 1

The Germans formally occupied the Saar today. There has been a pouring rain all day, but it has
not dampened the enthusiasm of the local inhabitants.

They *do* have the Nazi bug, badly. But I shall come
back here in a couple of years to see how they like it
then — the Catholics and the workers, who form the
great majority of the population. Hitler strode in this
afternoon and reviewed the S.S. and the troops. Before the parade started, I stood in the stand next to
Werner von Fritsch, commander-in-chief of the Reichswehr and the brains of the growing German army. I
was a little surprised at his talk. He kept up a running
fire of very sarcastic remarks — about the S.S., the
party, and various party leaders as they appeared. He
was full of contempt for them all. When Hitler's cars
arrived, he grunted and went over and took his place
just behind the Führer for the review.

BERLIN, *March 5*

Something has gone wrong with the drive for
a general settlement. Simon was supposed to arrive here
day after tomorrow for his talks with the Germans, but
this morning von Neurath told the British that Hitler
had a cold and asked Simon to postpone his trip. A
little investigation in the Wilhelmstrasse this afternoon
revealed it's a " *cold diplomatique*." The Germans are
sore at the publication in London yesterday of a Parliamentary White Paper initialled by Prime Minister Mac-
Donald and commenting on the growing rearmament
of Germany in the air. The Germans are especially
peeved at this passage which they say is in the paper:
" This [German air force] rearmament, if continued
at the present rate, unabated and uncontrolled, will
aggravate the existing anxieties of the neighbours of
Germany and may consequently produce a situation
where peace will be in peril. His Majesty's government
have noted and welcomed the declarations of the leaders

of Germany that they desire peace. They cannot, however, fail to recognize that not only the forces but the
spirit in which the population, and especially the youth
of the country, are being organized, lend colour to, and
substantiate, the general feeling of insecurity which has
already been incontestably generated."

All of which is true enough, but the Nazis are furious
and Hitler refuses to see Simon.

BERLIN, *March* 15

Simon, it's now announced, will come here
March 24. But all is not well. Göring has told the
Daily Mail, which through Lord Rothermere, its owner,
and Ward Price, its roving correspondent — both pro-
Nazi — has become a wonderful Nazi mouthpiece and
sounding-board, that Germany is building up a military
air force. This is the first time he has publicly admitted
it. Today it was stated here that Göring as Minister
of Air will be under von Blomberg, Minister of Defence,
thus putting the stamp of approval of the army on his
job of creating a new German air force. Tonight the
Wilhelmstrasse people protested against France's increasing the period of conscription for the French
army.

BERLIN, *March* 16

At about three o'clock this afternoon the
Propaganda Ministry called excitedly and asked me to
come at five to a press conference at which Dr. Goebbels
would make a statement of the "utmost importance."
When I got there about a hundred foreign correspondents were crowded into the conference room, all a little
high strung, but none knowing why we had been con-

voked. Finally Goebbels limped in, looking very important and grave. He began immediately to read in a loud voice the text of a new law.[1] He read too fast to take it down in long-hand but there was no need for that. Hitler had of his own accord wiped out the military sections of the Versailles Treaty, restored universal military service and proclaimed the formation of a conscript army of twelve army corps or thirty-six divisions. Louis Lochner of A.P., Ed Beattie of U.P., Pierre Huss of INS, and Gordon Young of Reuter's leaped to their feet and made for the telephones in the hall, not waiting for the rest of Dr. Goebbels's words. Finally the little *Doktor* finished. Two or three officials remained to answer questions, but it was plain they were afraid to say any more than was contained in the official communiqué. How many men would the new army have? Thirty-six divisions, they said. How many men in a German division? That depends, they said. And so on.

I walked up the Wilhelmstrasse with Norman Ebbutt of the London *Times*, by far the best-informed foreign correspondent here, and Pat Murphy of the *Daily Express*. Ebbutt seemed a little stunned by the news, but kept insisting that after all it was not new, that the Germans had been building up their army for more than a year. I hurried to my office in the Dorotheenstrasse, made some calls, and then sat down to write

[1] The text: Law for the Re-Creation of the National Defence Forces.

The Reich government has decreed the following law, which is herewith proclaimed:

1. Service in the defence forces is based on universal military service.

2. The German peace army, inclusive of police units incorporated therein, comprises twelve corps commands and thirty-six divisions.

3. Supplementary laws for regulating universal military service will be drafted and presented to the Reich Cabinet by the Reich Minister of Defence.

my head off. It was Saturday and at home the Sunday
morning papers go to bed early.

Later. — Finished my story about ten p.m.
and waited around the office to answer queries from New
York. Hitler, I learn, acted with lightning speed, apparently on the inspiration that now was the time — if
ever — to act and get by with it, and it looks as though
he will. The Paris office told me tonight that the French
were excited and were trying to get the British to do
something, but that London was holding back. Hitler
returned from his mountain retreat at Berchtesgaden early last evening and immediately convoked the
Cabinet and the military leaders. The decision was
made then, or rather communicated by Hitler to the
others. There seems, so far as I can learn, to have been
no hesitation by anyone, or if so, it was not expressed.
Experts went to work to draft the law, and Hitler and
Goebbels began to draw up two proclamations, one from
the party, the other by the Führer to the German
people.

At one p.m. this afternoon Hitler again convoked the
Cabinet and the military people and read to them the
texts of the law and the two proclamations. According
to one informant, the Cabinet members embraced one
another after Hitler's magic voice had died down. Grey-
haired General von Blomberg then led all present in
three lusty cheers for Hitler. It must have been one of
the most undignified Cabinet meetings in German history. But these Nazis don't rest on dignity — if they
can get results. And the Junkers who are running the
army will forget a lot — and swallow a lot — now that
Hitler has given them what they want. A big crowd
gathered in the Wilhelmplatz in front of the Chancel-

lery this evening and cheered Hitler until he appeared
at a window and saluted. Today's creation of a conscript army in open defiance of Versailles will greatly
enhance his domestic position, for there are few Germans, regardless of how much they hate the Nazis, who
will not support it wholeheartedly. The great majority
will like the way he has thumbed his nose at Versailles,
which they all resented, and, being militarists at heart,
they welcome the rebirth of the army.

It is a terrible blow to the Allies — to France,
Britain, Italy, who fought the war and wrote the peace
to destroy Germany's military power and to keep it
down. What will London and Paris do? They could
fight a " preventive " war and that would be the end of
Hitler. The Poles here say Pilsudski is willing to help.
But first reactions tonight — at least according to our
Paris office — are all against it. We shall see.

To bed tired, and sick at this Nazi triumph, but
somehow professionally pleased at having had a big
story to handle, Dosch being away, which left the job
to me alone.

BERLIN, *March* 17

The first paragraph of my dispatch tonight
sums up this extraordinary day: " This Heroes Memorial Day in memory of Germany's two million war dead
was observed today amid scenes unequalled since 1914
as rebirth of Germany's military power brought forth
professions of peace mixed with defiance." The Germans call the day *Heldengedenktag*, and it corresponds
to our Decoration Day. The main ceremony was at the
Staatsoper at noon and it was conducted with all the
colour which the Nazis know how to utilize. The ground

floor of the Opera House was a sea of military uniforms, with a surprising number of old army officers who overnight must have dusted off their fading grey uniforms and shined up their quaint pre-war spiked helmets, which were much in evidence. Strong stage lights played on a platoon of Reichswehr men standing like marble statues and holding flowing war flags. Above them on a vast curtain was hung an immense silver and black Iron Cross. The proper atmosphere was created at once when the orchestra played Beethoven's *Funeral March*, a moving piece, and one that seems to awaken the very soul of the German. Hitler and his henchmen were in the royal box, but he himself did not speak. General von Blomberg spoke for him, though it seemed to me that he was uttering words certainly penned by the Führer. Said Blomberg: " The world has been made to realize that Germany did not die of its defeat in the World War. Germany will again take the place she deserves among the nations. We pledge ourselves to a Germany which will never surrender and never again sign a treaty which cannot be fulfilled. We do not need revenge because we have gathered glory enough through the centuries." As Hitler looked on approvingly, the general continued: " We do not want to be dragged into another world war. Europe has become too small for another world-war battlefield. Because all nations have equal means at their disposal for war, the future war would mean only self-mutilation for all. We want peace with equal rights and security for all. We seek no more."

Clever words, and meant not only to assure the German people, who certainly don't want war, but the French and British as well. For the French, the reference to " security " — a word that haunts the Quai d'Orsay. Hitler had Field Marshal von Mackensen, the only surviving field-marshal of the old army, at his side, the old man having dressed himself up in his Death-Head Hussars uniform. Present also, I noticed, was Crown Prince Wilhelm, though Hitler was careful not to have him in *his* box. Dodd was the only ambassador present, the British, French, Italian, and Russian envoys being conspicuous by their absence. Not even the Jap showed up. Dodd looked rather uncomfortable.

After the opera " service " Hitler reviewed a contingent of troops. Not lacking was a battalion of air-force men in sky-blue uniforms who goose-stepped like the veterans they undoubtedly are — but are not supposed to be.

It is worth noting, I think, the two proclamations issued yesterday, which, on re-reading in the Sunday morning newspapers, impress me more than ever in showing Hitler's skill in presenting his *fait accompli* in the most favourable light to his own people while at the same time impressing outside world opinion not only that he is justified in doing what he has done, but that he is a man of peace. For example the pronouncement of the party: ". . . With the present day the honour of the German nation has been restored. We stand erect as a free people among nations. As a sovereign state we are free to negotiate, and propose to co-operate in the organization of peace."

Or Hitler's own proclamation to the German people. It begins with the story he has told many times: Wilson's Fourteen Points, the unfair peace treaty, Germany's complete disarmament in a world where all the others are fully armed, Germany's repeated attempt to reach an agreement with the others, and so on. And then: " In so doing [in proclaiming conscription] it proceeded from the same premises which Mr. Baldwin in his last speech so truthfully expressed: ' A country which

is not willing to adopt the necessary preventive measures
for its own defence will never enjoy any power in this
world, either moral or material.' "

Then, to France: " Germany has finally given France
the solemn assurance that Germany, after the adjustment of the Saar question, now no longer will make
territorial demands upon France."

Finally, to Germans and the whole world: ". . . In
this hour the German government renews before the
German people and before the entire world its assurance
of its determination never to proceed beyond the safeguarding of German honour and the freedom of the
Reich, and especially it does not intend in rearming
Germany to create any instrument for warlike attack,
but, on the contrary, exclusively for defence and thereby
for the maintenance of peace. In so doing, the Reich
government expresses the confident hope that the German people, having again obtained their own honour,
may be privileged in independent equality to make their
contribution towards the pacification of the world in
free and open co-operation with other nations."

Every German I've talked to today has applauded
these lines. One of the Germans in my office, no Nazi,
said: " Can the world expect a fairer offer of peace? "
I admit it *sounds* good, but Ebbutt keeps warning me
to be very sceptical, which I hope I am.

Talked to both our London and Paris offices tonight
on the phone. They said the French and British are
still trying to make up their minds. London said Garvin came out in the *Observer* with an editorial saying
Hitler's action occasioned no surprise and calling on
Simon to go ahead with his Berlin visit. Beaverbrook's
Sunday Express warned against threatening Germany
with force. Tomorrow, according to our office, the

Times will take a conciliatory line. My guess is that Hitler has got away with it.

BERLIN, *March* 18 (*at the office*)

A squadron of Göring's bombers just flew over our roof in formation — the first time they have appeared in public. They kept their formation well.

BERLIN, *March* 26

Simon and Eden have been here for the last couple of days conferring with Hitler and Neurath and this afternoon the two British envoys received us at the dilapidated old British Embassy to tell us — nothing. Simon struck me as a very vain man. Eden, who looked and acted like a schoolboy, kept pacing up and down the stage — we were in the ballroom, which has a stage — prompting his chief and occasionally whispering to him when we asked an embarrassing question. The only thing Simon said worth reporting is that he and Hitler found themselves in " disagreement on almost everything." Apparently — at least the Germans say so — Hitler put on a big song and dance against Russia and the proposed Eastern Locarno, which would bring in Russia in a defence system on Germany's eastern frontiers. The Wilhelmstrasse scarcely hides the fact that Hitler did all the talking, Simon all the listening. Eden goes on to Warsaw and Moscow; Simon home.

BERLIN, *April* 9

A gala reception at the Opera tonight on the occasion of Göring's wedding. He has married a provincial actress, Emmy Sonnemann. I received an invitation, but did not go. Party people tell me Goebbels is in a rage at his arch-enemy's lavish displays, of which tonight was only one example, and that he's told the press it can comment sarcastically. Not many editors will dare to, I think.

BERLIN, *April* 11

Dr. S., a successful Jewish lawyer who served his country at the front in the war, suddenly appeared at our apartment today after having spent some months in the Gestapo jail, Columbia House. Tess was at home and reports he was in a bad state, a little out of his head, but apparently aware of his condition, because he was afraid to go home and face his family. Tess fortified him with some whisky, cheered him up, and sent him home. His wife has been on the verge of nervous prostration for a long time. He said no charges had been preferred against him other than that he was a Jew or a half-Jew and one of several lawyers who had offered to help defend Thälmann. Many Jews come to us these days for advice or help in getting to England or America, but unfortunately there is little we can do for them.

BAD SAAROW, *April* 21 (*Easter*)

Taking the Easter week-end off. The hotel mainly filled with Jews and we are a little surprised to see so many of them still prospering and apparently unafraid. I think they are unduly optimistic.

BERLIN, *May* 1

A blizzard today pretty well spoiled the big Labour Day show at Tempelhof. Dosch insisted on

going out to cover it despite his bad health. Hitler had
nothing particular to say and seemed to be depressed.
Thousands of workers being marched to Tempelhof for
the meeting took advantage of the blizzard to slip out
of ranks and make for the nearest pub. There were a
surprising number of drunks on the street tonight —
unusual for Berlin. The talk around town is that the
British are going to negotiate a naval agreement with
Hitler, thus helping him to break another shackle of
Versailles.

BERLIN, *May* 21

  Hitler made a grandiose " peace " speech in
the Reichstag this evening and I fear it will impress
world opinion and especially British opinion more than
it should. The man is truly a superb orator and in the
atmosphere of the hand-picked Reichstag, with its six
hundred or so sausage-necked, shaved-headed, brown-
clad yes-men, who rise and shout almost every time
Hitler pauses for breath, I suppose he *is* convincing to
Germans who listen to him. Anyway, tonight he was in
great form and his program — of thirteen points —
will convince a lot of people. It's rather an amazing
program, at that; very astutely drawn up.

  Leading up to it, Hitler screamed: " Germany needs
peace. . . . Germany wants peace. . . . No one of us
means to threaten anybody." As to Austria: " Germany neither intends nor wishes to interfere in the internal affairs of Austria, to annex Austria, or to conclude an *Anschluss*."

  Then he launched into his thirteen-point program.

  1. Germany cannot return to Geneva unless the
Treaty and the Covenant are separated.

  2. Germany will respect all other provisions of the

Treaty of Versailles, including the territorial provisions.

3. Germany will scrupulously maintain every treaty
voluntarily signed. In particular it will uphold and
fulfil all obligations arising out of the Locarno Treaty.
. . . In respecting the demilitarized zone, the German
government considers its action as a contribution to the
appeasement of Europe. . . .

4. Germany is ready to co-operate in a collective system for safeguarding European peace. . . .

5. Unilateral imposition of conditions cannot pro-
mote collaboration. Step-by-step negotiations are in-
dispensable.

6. The German government is ready in principle to
conclude pacts of non-aggression with its neighbours,
and to supplement these pacts with all provisions that
aim at isolating the war-maker and isolating the area
of war.

7. The German government is ready to supplement
the Locarno Treaty with an air agreement.

8. Germany is ready to limit armaments on the basis
of aerial parity with the individual big powers of the
West, and naval tonnage equal to thirty-five per cent
of the British.

9. Germany desires the outlawing of weapons and
methods of warfare contrary to the Geneva Red Cross
convention. Here the German government has in mind
all those arms which bring death and destruction not so
much to the fighting soldiers as to non-combatant
women and children. It believes it is possible to pro-
scribe the use of certain arms as contrary to international law and to outlaw those nations still using
them. For example, there might be a prohibition of the
dropping of gas, incendiary, and explosive bombs outside the real battle zone. This limitation could then be

extended to complete international outlawing of all bombing.

10. Germany desires the abolition of the heaviest arms, especially heavy artillery and heavy tanks.

11. Germany will accept any limitation whatsoever of the calibre of artillery, the size of warships, and the tonnage of submarines, or even the complete abolition of submarines, by agreement.

12. Something should be done to prohibit the poisoning of public opinion among the nations by irresponsible elements orally or in writing, and in the theatre or the cinema.

13. Germany is ready at any time to reach an international agreement which shall effectively prevent all attempts at outside interference in the affairs of other states.

What could be more sweet or reasonable — if he means it? Hitler spoke until nearly ten o'clock. He was in an easy, confident mood. The diplomatic box was jammed, the ambassadors of France, Britain, Italy, Japan, and Poland being in the front row. Dodd sat in the third row — a typical Nazi diplomatic slight to America, it seemed to me. Filed several thousand words, and then to bed, tired and a little puzzled by the speech, which some of the British and French correspondents at the Taverne tonight thought might really after all pave the way to several years of Peace.

BERLIN, *June 3*

We've moved again, this time to Tempelhof, our studio place in the Tauenzienstrasse, which was just under the roof, proving too warm. We've taken the apartment of Captain Koehl, a German flying ace in the World War, and the first man (with two friends) to fly the Atlantic from east to west. He and his wife, pretty, dark, great friends of the Knicks. He is one of the few men in Germany with enough courage not to knuckle down to Göring and the Nazis. As a result he is completely out, having even lost his job with Lufthansa. A fervent Catholic and a man of strong character, he prefers to retire to his little farm in the south of Germany rather than curry Nazi favour. He is one of a very few. I've taken a great liking to him.

BERLIN, *June* 7

The ticker brings in this news: Baldwin succeeds MacDonald as British Prime Minister. There will be few tears for MacDonald, who betrayed the British labour movement and who in the last five years has become a vain and foolish man. Ribbentrop is in London negotiating a naval treaty which will give Germany thirty-five per cent of Britain's tonnage. The Nazis here say it's in the bag.

BERLIN, *June* 18

It's in the bag, signed today in London. The Wilhelmstrasse quite elated. Germany gets a U-boat tonnage equal to Britain's. Why the British have agreed to this is beyond me. German submarines almost beat them in the last war, and may in the next. Ended up at the Taverne, as on so many nights. The Taverne, a *Ristorante Italiano*, run by Willy Lehman, a big, bluff German with nothing Italian about him, and his wife, a slim, timid Belgian woman, has become an institution for the British and American correspondents here, helping us to retain some sanity and affording an opportunity to get together informally and talk

shop — without which no foreign correspondent could
long live. We have a *Stammtisch* — a table always reserved for us in the corner — and from about ten p.m.
until three or four in the morning it is usually filled.
Usually Norman Ebbutt presides, sucking at an old
pipe the night long, talking and arguing in a weak,
high-pitched voice, imparting wisdom, for he has been
here a long time, has contacts throughout the government, party, churches, and army, and has a keen intelligence. Of late he has complained to me in private that
the *Times* does not print all he sends, that it does not
want to hear too much of the bad side of Nazi Germany
and apparently has been captured by the pro-Nazis in
London. He is discouraged and talks of quitting. Next
to him sits Mrs. Holmes, a beak-nosed woman of undoubted intelligence. She swallows her words so, however, that I find difficulty in understanding what she
says. Other habitués of the *Stammtisch* are Ed Beattie
of U.P., with a moon-faced Churchillian countenance
behind which is a nimble wit and a great store of funny
stories and songs; Fred Oechsner of U.P. and his wife,
Dorothy, he a quiet type but an able correspondent, she
blonde, pretty, ebullient, with a low, hoarse voice; Pierre
Huss of INS, slick, debonair, ambitious, and on better
terms with Nazi officials than almost any other; Guido
Enderis of the New York *Times*, aging in his sixties but
sporting invariably a gaudy race-track suit with a loud
red necktie, minding the Nazis less than most — a man
who achieved the distinction once of working here as an
American correspondent even after we got into the war;
Al Ross, his assistant, bulky, sleepy, slow-going, and
lovable; Wally Deuel of the Chicago *Daily News*, youthful, quiet, studious, extremely intelligent; his wife,
Mary Deuel, much the same as he is, with large, pretty
eyes, they both very much in love; Sigrid Schultz of the

Chicago *Tribune*, the only woman correspondent in our ranks, buoyant, cheerful, and always well informed; and Otto Tolischus, who though not head of the bureau of the New York *Times* is its chief prop, complicated, profound, studious, with a fine penchant for getting at the bottom of things. Present often is Martha Dodd, daughter of the Ambassador, pretty, vivacious, a mighty arguer. Two American correspondents come rarely if at all, Louis Lochner of A.P. and John Elliott of the New York *Herald Tribune*, John, who is a very able and learned correspondent, being a teetotaller and non-smoker and much addicted — as we should all be — to his books.

New York, *September* 9

Home for a brief vacation, and New York looks awfully good though I find most of the good people much too optimistic about European affairs. Everyone here, I find, has very positive knowledge and opinions.

New York, *September* 16

Week-end with Nicholas Roosevelt out on Long Island. Had not seen him since he was Minister in Budapest. He was too preoccupied with Franklin Roosevelt's "dictatorship" — as he called it — to allow for much time to argue European affairs. He seemed deeply resentful that the New Deal would not allow him to grow potatoes in his garden, and went into the matter in some detail, though I'm afraid I did not follow. I kept thinking of Ethiopia and the chances of war. A very intelligent man, though. Have had a good visit — but much too short — with my family.

Mother, despite her age and recent illnesses, seemed to be looking quite pert. The office insists I return at once to Berlin because of the Abyssinian situation. Dosch is to go to Rome and I am to have the *Buro*.

BERLIN, *October* 4

Mussolini has begun his conquest of Abyssinia. According to an Italian communiqué, the Duce's troops crossed the frontier yesterday " in order to repulse an imminent threat from the Ethiopians." The Wilhelmstrasse is delighted. Either Mussolini will stumble and get himself so heavily involved in Africa that he will be greatly weakened in Europe, whereupon Hitler can seize Austria, hitherto protected by the Duce; or he will win, defying France and Britain, and thereupon be ripe for a tie-up with Hitler against the Western democracies. Either way Hitler wins. The League has provided a sorry spectacle, and its failure now, after the Manchurian debacle, certainly kills it. At Geneva they talk of sanctions. It's a last hope.

BERLIN, *December* 30

Dodd called us in today for a talk with William Phillips, Under Secretary of State, who is visiting here. We asked him what action Washington would take if the Nazis began expelling us. He gave an honest answer. He said: None. Our point was that if the Wilhelmstrasse knew that for every American correspondent expelled, a German newspaperman at home would be kicked out, perhaps the Nazis would think twice before acting against us. But the Secretary said the State Department was without law to act in such a case — a lovely example of one of our democratic weaknesses.

BERLIN, *January* 4, 1936

The afternoon press, especially the *Börsen Zeitung* and the *Angriff*, very angry at Roosevelt's denunciation of dictatorships and aggression, obviously directed mostly against Mussolini, but also meant for Berlin. Incidentally, an item I forgot to record: X of the *Börsen Zeitung* is not to be executed. His death sentence has been commuted to life imprisonment. His offence: he occasionally saw that some of us received copies of Goebbels's secret daily orders to the press. They made rich reading, ordering daily suppression of this truth and the substitution of that lie. He was given away, I hear, by a Polish diplomat, a fellow I never trusted. The German people, unless they can read foreign newspapers (the London *Times* has an immense circulation here now), are terribly cut off from events in the outside world and of course are told nothing of what is happening behind the scenes in their own country. For a while they stormed the news-stands to buy the *Baseler Nachrichten*, a Swiss German-language paper, which sold more copies in Germany than it did in Switzerland. But that paper has now been banned.

BERLIN, *January* 23

An unpleasant day. A telephone call awakened me this morning — I work late and sleep late — and it turned out to be Wilfred Bade, a fanatical Nazi careerist at the moment in charge of the Foreign Press in the Propaganda Ministry. He began: " Have you been in Garmisch recently? " I said: " No." Then he began to shout: " I see, you haven't been there and yet you have the dishonesty to write a fake story about the Jews there. . . ." " Wait a minute," I said, " you can't call me dishonest . . ." but he had hung up.

At noon Tess turned on the radio for the news just in time for us to hear a ringing personal attack on me, implying that I was a dirty Jew and was trying to torpedo the winter Olympic Games at Garmisch (which begin in a few days) with false stories about the Jews and Nazi officials there. When I got to the office after lunch, the front pages of the afternoon papers were full of typically hysterical Nazi denunciations of me. The Germans at the office expected the Gestapo to come to get me at any moment. Actually, I had written in a mail series, some time ago, that the Nazis at Garmisch had pulled down all the signs saying that Jews were un-wanted (they're all over Germany) and that the Olym-pic visitors would thus be spared any signs of the kind of treatment meted out to Jews in this country. I had also remarked, in passing, that Nazi officials had taken all the good hotels for themselves and had put the press in inconvenient *pensions,* which was true.

Every time the office boy brought in a new paper dur-ing the afternoon I grew more indignant. Most of my friends called up to advise me to ignore the whole affair, saying that if I fought it I'd probably be thrown out. But the stories were so exaggerated and so libellous I could not control my temper. I called up Bade's office and demanded to see him. He was out. I kept calling. Finally a secretary said he was out and would not be coming back. About nine p.m. I could contain myself no further. I went over to the Propaganda Ministry, brushed by a guard and burst into Bade's office. As I suspected, he was there, sitting at his desk. Uninvited, I sat down opposite him and before he could recover from his surprise demanded an apology and a correc-tion in the German press and radio. He started to roar at me. I roared back, though in moments of excitement

I lose what German I speak and I probably was most
incoherent. Our shouting apparently alarmed a couple
of flunkeys outside, because they opened the door and
looked in. Bade bade them shut the door and we went
after each other again. He started to pound on the
table. I pounded back. The door was hurriedly opened
and one of the flunkeys came in, ostensibly to offer his
chief some cigarettes. I lit one of my own. Twice again
our pounding brought in the flunkey, once with more
cigarettes, once with a pitcher of water. But I began
to realize, what I should have known, that I was getting
nowhere, that no one, and Bade least of all, had the
power or the decency ever to correct a piece of Nazi
propaganda once it had been launched, regardless of
how big the lie. In the end, he grew quiet, even sugary.
He said they had decided not to expel me as first
planned. I flared up again and dared him to expel me,
but he did not react and finally I stumped out. Much
too wrought up, I fear.

GARMISCH-PARTENKIRCHEN, *February*

This has been a more pleasant interlude than
I expected. Much hard work for Tess and myself from
dawn to midnight, covering the Winter Olympics, too
many S.S. troops and military about (not only for me
but especially for Westbrook Pegler!), but the scenery
of the Bavarian Alps, particularly at sunrise and sunset, superb, the mountain air exhilarating, the rosy-
cheeked girls in their skiing outfits generally attractive, the games exciting, especially the bone-breaking
ski-jumping, the bob-races (also bone-breaking and
sometimes actually " death-defying "), the hockey
matches, and Sonja Henie. And on the whole the Nazis

have done a wonderful propaganda job. They've greatly impressed most of the visiting foreigners with the lavish but smooth way in which they've run the games and with their kind manners, which to us who came from Berlin of course seemed staged. I was so alarmed at this that I gave a luncheon for some of our businessmen and invited Douglas Miller, our commercial attaché in Berlin, and the best-informed man on Germany we have in our Embassy, to enlighten them a little. But they told *him* what things were like, and Doug scarcely got a word in. It has been fun being with Pegler, whose sharp, acid tongue has had a field day here. He and Gallico and I were continually having a run-in with the S.S. guards, who, whenever Hitler was at the stadium, surrounded it and tried to keep us from entering. Most of the correspondents a little peeved at a piece in the *Völkische Beobachter* quoting Birchall of the New York *Times* to the effect that there has been nothing military about these games and that correspondents who so reported were inaccurate. Peg especially resented this. Tonight he seemed a little concerned that the Gestapo might pick him up for what he has written, but I don't think so. The " Olympic spirit " will prevail for a fortnight or so more, by which time he will be in Italy. Tess and I have seen a great deal of Paul Gallico. He's at an interesting cross-road. He has deliberately thrown up his job as the highest-paid sports-writer in New York, said farewell to sports, and is going to settle down in the English countryside to see if he can make his living as a free-lance writer. It's a decision that few would have the guts to make. Back to Berlin tomorrow to the grind of covering Nazi politics. Tess is going over to the Tyrol to get a rest from the Nazis and do some skiing.

BERLIN, *February* 25

Learn that Lord Londonderry was here around the first of the month, saw Hitler, Göring, and most of the others. He is an all-out pro-Nazi. Fear he has not been up to any good.

BERLIN, *February* 28

The French Chamber has approved the Soviet pact by a big majority. Much indignation in the Wilhelmstrasse. Fred Oechsner says that when he and Roy Howard saw Hitler day before yesterday, he seemed to be very preoccupied about something.

BERLIN, *March* 5

Party circles say Hitler is convoking the Reichstag for March 13, the date they expect the French Senate to approve the Soviet pact. Very ugly atmosphere in the Wilhelmstrasse today, but difficult to get to the bottom of it.

BERLIN, *March* 6, *midnight*

This has been a day of the wildest rumours. Definite, however, is that Hitler has convoked the Reichstag for noon tomorrow and summoned the ambassadors of Britain, France, Italy, and Belgium for tomorrow morning. Since these are the four Locarno powers, it is obvious from that and from what little information I could pry out of party circles that Hitler intends to denounce the Locarno Treaty, which only a year ago this month he said Germany would " scrupulously respect." My guess too, based on what I've heard today, is that Hitler will also make an end of the demilitarized

zone in the Rhineland, though the Wilhelmstrasse
savagely denies this. Whether he will send the Reichswehr in is not sure. This seems too big a risk in view
of the fact that the French army could easily drive it
out. Much friction in the Cabinet reported today, with
von Neurath, Schacht, and the generals supposedly
advising Hitler to go slow. One informant told me tonight that Hitler would not send in troops, but merely
declare the strong police force he now has in the Rhineland as part of the army, thus giving practical effect
to ending its demilitarization. Hitler's lightning move,
according to one man in the Wilhelmstrasse, came after
he'd received reports from his Embassy in Paris that
the French Senate is sure to vote the Soviet pact in
a day or two. Berlin tonight full of Nazi leaders hurriedly convoked for the Reichstag meeting. Saw a lot
of them at the Kaiserhof and they seemed in a very
cocky mood. Was on the phone several times to Dr.
Aschmann, press chief at the Foreign Office, who kept
giving the most categorical denials that German troops
would march into the Rhineland tomorrow. That would
mean war, he said. Wrote a dispatch which may have
been a little on the careful side. But we shall know by
tomorrow.

BERLIN, *March* 7

    A little on the careful side is right! Hitler on
this day has torn up the Locarno Treaty and sent in
the Reichswehr to occupy the demilitarized zone of the
Rhineland! A few diplomats on the pessimistic side
think it means war. Most think he will get by with it.
The important thing is that the French army has not
budged. Tonight for the first time since 1870 grey-
clad German soldiers and blue-clad French troops

face each other across the upper Rhine. But I talked
to Karlsruhe on the phone an hour ago; there have been
no shots. I've had our Paris office on the line all evening, filing my dispatch. They say the French are not
mobilizing — yet, at least — though the Cabinet is in
session with the General Staff. London — as a year ago
— seems to be holding back. The Reichswehr generals
are still nervous, but not so nervous as they were this
morning.

To describe this day, if I can:

At ten o'clock this morning Neurath handed the ambassadors of France, Britain, Belgium, and Italy a long
memorandum. For once we got a break on the news
because Dr. Dieckhoff, the State Secretary in the
Foreign Office, called in Freddy Mayer, our counsellor
of Embassy, and gave him a copy of the memorandum,
apparently suggesting he give it to the American correspondents, since the American Embassy rarely gives us
a lift like this of its own accord. Huss, who needed an
early report for the INS, hurried over to the Embassy,
and I walked over to the Reichstag, which was meeting
at noon in the Kroll Opera House. The memorandum,
however, along with Neurath's oral remarks to the ambassadors that German troops had marched into the
Rhineland at dawn this morning, told the whole story.

It argued that the Locarno pact had been rendered
"extinct" by the Franco-Soviet pact, that Germany
therefore no longer regarded itself as bound by it, and
that the "German Government has therefore, as from
today, restored the full and unrestricted sovereignty of
the Reich in the demilitarized zone of the Rhineland."
There followed then another beautiful attempt by Hitler — and who can say he won't succeed, after May 21
last? — to throw sand in the eyes of the "peace-loving"
men of the West, men like Londonderry, the Astors,

Lord Lothian, Lord Rothermere. He proposed a seven-point program of " Peace " in order, as the memo puts it, " to prevent any doubt as to its [the Reich government's] intentions, and to make clear the purely defensive character of this measure, as well as to give expression to its lasting desire for the true pacification of Europe. . . ." The proposal is a pure fraud, and if I had any guts, or American journalism had any, I would have said so in my dispatch tonight. But I am not supposed to be " editorial."

In this latest " peace proposal " Hitler offers to sign a twenty-five-year non-aggression pact with Belgium and France, to be guaranteed by Britain and Italy ; to propose to Belgium and France that *both* sides of their frontiers with Germany be demilitarized ; to sign an air pact ; to conclude non-aggression pacts with her eastern neighbours ; and, finally, to return to the League of Nations. The quality of Hitler's sincerity may be measured by his proposal to demilitarize *both* sides of the frontiers, thus forcing France to scrap her Maginot Line, now her last protection against a German attack.

The Reichstag, more tense than I have ever felt it (apparently the hand-picked deputies on the main floor had not yet been told what had happened, though they knew something was afoot), began promptly at noon. The French, British, Belgian, and Polish ambassadors were absent, but the Italian was there and Dodd. General von Blomberg, the War Minister, sitting with the Cabinet on the left side of the stage, was as white as a sheet and fumbled the top of the bench nervously with his fingers. I have never seen him in such a state. Hitler began with a long harangue which he has often given before, but never tires of repeating, about the injustices of the Versailles Treaty and the peacefulness of Germans. Then his voice, which had been low and hoarse at the beginning, rose to a shrill, hysterical scream as he raged against Bolshevism.

" I will not have the gruesome Communist international dictatorship of hate descend upon the German people! This destructive Asiatic *Weltanschauung* strikes at all values! I tremble for Europe at the thought of what would happen should this destructive Asiatic conception of life, this chaos of the Bolshevist revolution, prove successful! " (Wild applause.)

Then, in a more reasoned voice, his argument that France's pact with Russia had invalidated the Locarno Treaty. A slight pause and:

" Germany no longer feels bound by the Locarno Treaty. In the interest of the primitive rights of its people to the security of their frontier and the safeguarding of their defence, the German Government has re-established, as from today, the absolute and unrestricted sovereignty of the Reich in the demilitarized zone! "

Now the six hundred deputies, personal appointees all of Hitler, little men with big bodies and bulging necks and cropped hair and pouched bellies and brown uniforms and heavy boots, little men of clay in his fine hands, leap to their feet like automatons, their right arms upstretched in the Nazi salute, and scream " *Heil's*," the first two or three wildly, the next twenty-five in unison, like a college yell. Hitler raises his hand for silence. It comes slowly. Slowly the automatons sit down. Hitler now has them in his claws. He appears to sense it. He says in a deep, resonant voice: " Men of the German Reichstag! " The silence is utter.

" In this historic hour, when in the Reich's western provinces German troops are at this minute marching into their future peace-time garrisons, we all unite in two sacred vows."

He can go no further. It is news to this hysterical
" parliamentary " mob that German soldiers are already on the move into the Rhineland. All the militarism in their German blood surges to their heads.
They spring, yelling and crying, to their feet. The
audience in the galleries does the same, all except a few
diplomats and about fifty of us correspondents. Their
hands are raised in slavish salute, their faces now con-
torted with hysteria, their mouths wide open, shouting,
shouting, their eyes, burning with fanaticism, glued on
the new god, the Messiah. The Messiah plays his role
superbly. His head lowered as if in all humbleness, he
waits patiently for silence. Then, his voice still low,
but choking with emotion, utters the two vows:

" First, we swear to yield to no force whatever in the
restoration of the honour of our people, preferring to
succumb with honour to the severest hardships rather
than to capitulate. Secondly, we pledge that now, more
than ever, we shall strive for an understanding between
European peoples, especially for one with our western
neighbour nations. . . . We have no territorial demands to make in Europe! . . . Germany will never
break the peace."

It was a long time before the cheering stopped. Down
in the lobby the deputies were still under the magic spell,
gushing over one another. A few generals made their
way out. Behind their smiles, however, you could not
help detecting a nervousness. We waited in front of
the Opera until Hitler and the other bigwigs had driven
away and the S.S. guards would let us through. I
walked through the Tiergarten with John Elliott to the
Adlon, where we lunched. We were too taken aback to
say much.

There is to be an " election " on March 29, " so the
German people may pass judgment on my leadership,"

as Hitler puts it. The result, of course, is a foregone conclusion, but it was announced tonight that Hitler will make a dozen " campaign " speeches starting to-morrow.

He cleverly tried to reassure Poland in his speech today. His words were: " I wish the German people to understand that although it affects us painfully that an access to the sea for a nation of thirty-five million peo-ple should cut through German territory, it is unreason-able to deny such a great nation that access."

After lunch I took a stroll alone through the Tier-garten to collect my thoughts. Near the Skagerakplatz I ran into General von Blomberg walking along with two dogs on the leash. His face was still white, his cheeks twitching. " Has anything gone wrong? " I won-dered. Then to the office, where I pounded my head off all afternoon, stopping to telephone to Paris my story every time I had three or four hundred words. Remem-bered it was Saturday when New York came through by cable hollering for early copy for the Sunday morn-ingers. Saturday is Hitler's day all right: the blood purge, conscription, today — all Saturday affairs.

Tonight as I finished my story, I could see from my office window which looks down the Wilhelmstrasse end-less columns of storm troopers parading down the street past the Chancellery in torchlight procession. Sent Hermann down to take a look. He phoned that Hitler was taking the salute from his balcony, Streicher (of all people) at his side. The DNB claims there are torch-light processions all over the Reich tonight.

Our Cologne correspondent phoned several times to give a description of the occupation. According to him, the German troops have been given delirious receptions everywhere, the women strewing their line of march with flowers. He says the air force landed bombers and fight-

ers at the Düsseldorf airdrome and several other fields.
How many troops the Germans have sent into the
Rhineland today nobody knows. François Poncet (the
French Ambassador) told a friend of mine tonight that
he had been lied to three times by the German Foreign
Office on the subject in the course of the day. The Germans first announced 2,000 troops, then later 9,500
with "thirteen detachments of artillery." My information is that they've sent in four divisions — about
50,000 men.

And so goes the main pillar of the European peace
structure, Locarno. It was freely signed by Germany,
it was not a *Dictat,* and Hitler more than once solemnly
swore to respect it. At the Taverne tonight one of the
French correspondents cheered us up by stating positively that the French army would march tomorrow but
after what our Paris office said tonight I doubt it. Why
it doesn't march, I don't understand. Certainly it is
more than a match for the Reichswehr. And if it does,
that's the end of Hitler. He's staked all on the success
of his move and cannot survive if the French humiliate
him by occupying the west bank of the Rhine. Around
the Taverne's *Stammtisch* most of us agreed on this.
Much beer and two plates of spaghetti until three a.m.,
and then home. Must get up in time to attend another
Heroes Memorial Day service at the Opera tomorrow.
It should be even better than last year — unless the
French —

BERLIN, *March* 8

Hitler has got away with it! France is not
marching. Instead it is appealing to the League! No
wonder the faces of Hitler and Göring and Blomberg
and Fritsch were all smiles this noon as they sat in the

royal box at the State Opera and for the second time in two years celebrated in a most military fashion Heroes Memorial Day, which is supposed to mark the memory of the two million Germans slain in the last war.

Oh, the stupidity (or is it paralysis?) of the French! I learned today on absolute authority that the German troops which marched into the demilitarized zone of the Rhineland yesterday had strict orders to beat a hasty retreat if the French army opposed them in any way. They were not prepared or equipped to fight a regular army. That probably explains Blomberg's white face yesterday. Apparently Fritsch (commander-in-chief of the Reichswehr) and most of the generals opposed the move, but Blomberg, who has a blind faith in the Führer and his judgment, talked them into it. It may be that Fritsch, who loves neither Hitler nor the Nazi regime, consented to go along on the theory that if the coup failed, that would be the end of Hitler; if it succeeded, then one of his main military problems was solved.

Another weird story today. The French Embassy says — and I believe it — that Poncet called on Hitler a few days ago and asked him to propose his terms for a Franco-German rapprochement. The Führer asked for a few days to think it over. This seemed reasonable enough to the Ambassador, but he was puzzled at Hitler's insistence that no word leak out to the public of this visit. He is no longer puzzled. It would have spoiled Hitler's excuse that France was to blame for his tearing up the Locarno Treaty if the world had known that France, which after all had not yet ratified the Soviet pact, was willing to negotiate with him — indeed, had asked to negotiate.

The memorial services at the Opera this noon were

conducted in a Wagnerian setting (Wagner's influence
on Nazism, on Hitler, has never been grasped abroad),
the flood-lit stage full of steel-helmeted soldiers bearing
war flags against a background of evergreen and a huge
silver and black Iron Cross. The lower floor and bal-
conies dotted with the old Imperial army uniforms and
spiked helmets. Hitler sitting proudly in the Imperial
box surrounded by Germany's war leaders, past and
present: Field-Marshal von Mackensen in his Death-
Head Hussars uniform, Göring in a resplendent scarlet
and blue uniform of an air-force general, General von
Seekt, creator of the Reichswehr, General von Fritsch,
its present leader, Admiral von Raeder, chief of the
rapidly growing navy, and General von Krausz in the
uniform of the old Austro-Hungarian army, his face
adorned with vast side-whiskers *à la* Franz Josef. Absent only was Ludendorff, who declines to make his peace
with his former corporal and who has turned down an
offer of a field-marshalship; and the Crown Prince.

General von Blomberg delivered the address, a curious mixture of bluff, defiance, and glorification of militarism. "We do not want an offensive war," he said,
"but we do not fear a defensive war." Though everyone here — if not in Paris or London — knows that he
does, and that yesterday he was terrified that it might
come off. Blomberg, obviously on Hitler's orders, went
out of his way in a most unsoldierly way to silence
rumours that the Reichswehr generals opposed the
Rhineland occupation and have little sympathy for
Nazism. I could almost see Fritsch wince when his chief
denounced the " whispers in the outside world about relations between the Nazi Party and the army." Said the
general with some emphasis: "We in the army are
National Socialists. The party and the army are now

closer together." He went on to tell why. "The National Socialist revolution instead of destroying the old army, as other revolutions have always done, has re-created it. The National Socialist state places at our disposal its entire economic strength, its people, its entire male youth." And then a hint of the future: "An enormous responsibility rests upon our shoulders. It is all the more heavy because *we may be placed before new tasks.*"

As Blomberg spoke, Goebbels had his spotlights and movie cameras grinding away, first at the stage, then at the box where the Leader sat. After the "service" the usual military parade, but I had had enough and was hungry and went off to Habel's excellent little wine shop down the Linden and had lunch washed down by some Deidesheimer.

LATER. — Dosch-Fleurot had an interesting story tonight from the Rhineland, where he's been watching the German occupation. He reports that Catholic priests met the German troops at the Rhine bridges and conferred blessings on them. In Cologne Cathedral Cardinal Schulte, he says, praised Hitler for "sending back our army." Quickly forgotten is the Nazi persecution of the church. Dosch says the Rhine wine is flowing freely down there tonight.

And the French are appealing to Geneva! I called our London office to see what the British are going to do. They laughed, and read me a few extracts from the Sunday press. Garvin's Sunday *Observer* and Rothermere's *Sunday Dispatch* are *delighted* at Hitler's move. The British are now busy restraining the French! The Foreign Office here, which kept open tonight to watch the reaction from Paris and London, is in high spirits. No wonder!

KARLSRUHE, *March* 13

Here, within artillery range of the Maginot Line, Hitler made his first " election " speech tonight. Special trains poured in all day from surrounding towns, bringing the faithful and those ordered to come. The meeting was held in a huge tent and the atmosphere was so suffocating that I left before Hitler arrived, returning to my hotel, where over a good dinner and a bottle of wine, with most of the other correspondents, I listened to the speech by radio. Nothing new in it, though he drummed away nicely about his desire for friendship with France. Certainly these Rhinelanders don't want another war with France, but this reoccupation by German troops has inculcated them with the Nazi bug. They're as hysterical as the rest of the Germans. Later went out to a *Kneipe* with a taxi-driver who had driven me around during the day and had a few *Schnaps*. He turned out to be a Communist, waxed bitter about the Nazis, and predicted their early collapse. It was a relief to find one German here against the regime. He said there are a lot of others, but I sometimes wonder.

March 29

A fine early spring day for the " election " and according to Goebbels's figures ninety-five per cent of the German people have approved the reoccupation of the Rhineland. Some of the correspondents who visited the polling-booths today reported irregularities. But there's no doubt, I think, that a substantial majority of the people applaud the Rhineland coup regardless of whether they're Nazis or not. It's also true that few dare to vote against Hitler for fear of being found out. Learned tonight that in Neukölln and Wedding, former Communist strongholds in Berlin, the "No" vote ran as high as twenty per cent and that the people there are going to catch it in the next few days.

The new Zeppelin — to be called the *Hindenburg* — soared gracefully over our office yesterday. I was down to Friedrichshafen the other day to inspect it and it's a marvel of German engineering genius. Yesterday it was doing "election" propaganda, dropping leaflets exhorting the populace to vote "*Ja*." Dr. Hugo Eckener, who is getting it ready for its maiden flight to Brazil, strenuously objected to putting it in the air this week-end on the ground it was not yet fully tested, but Dr. Goebbels insisted. Eckener, no friend of the regime, refused to take it up himself, though he allowed Captain Lehmann to. The *Doktor* is reported howling mad and determined to get Eckener.

BERLIN, *April (undated)*

An amusing lunch today at the Dodds'. Eckener, who is off to America soon to ask Roosevelt personally for enough helium to fill his new balloon (there seems to be some opposition to this at home), was the guest of honour. He told one joke after another on Goebbels, for whom he has nothing but contempt. Someone asked him about the balloting on the *Hindenburg*, which was taken while it was still aloft. "Goebbels hung up a new record," he fired back. "There were forty persons on the *Hindenburg*. Forty-two *Ja* votes were counted." Goebbels has forbidden the press to mention Eckener's name.

BERLIN, *May 2*

The Italians entered Addis Ababa today. The Negus has fled. Mussolini has triumphed — largely with mustard gas. That's how he's beaten the Ethiopians. He's also triumphed over the League, by bluff. That's how he kept off oil sanctions, which might have stopped him. We picked up a broadcast of him shouting from the balcony of the Palazzo Venezia in Rome. Much boloney about thirty centuries of history, Roman civilization, and triumph over barbarism. Whose barbarism?

RAGUSA, YUGOSLAVIA, *June 18*

Having a glorious Dalmatian holiday. This place has everything: sea, sun, mountains, flowers, good wine, good food, pleasant people. The Knickerbockers, back from Addis Ababa, vacationing with us. Agnes to have a baby in a few months. Knick full of weird tales of how the correspondents scrapped and fought each other in Addis; of how poor Bill Barbour of the Chicago *Tribune* died and was buried there; of the bombing of Dessye; of a nightmarish disorderly house full of lepers in Jibouti, and so on. We loaf and swim and chatter and read all day, going down to the café in the old port in the evening for drink, food, and dancing. Finished Thomas Mann's *Magic Mountain*, a tremendous novel; and a book of Chekov's plays, which I much liked, as I do his short stories.

RAGUSA, *June 20*

A bad scare today. While Knick, Agnes, and I were still eating breakfast on the terrace of the hotel,

which is a half-mile or so up the coast from town, Tess
went off to town to snap some photographs. A couple
of army bombers suddenly appeared and started to do
acrobatics over Ragusa, a curious thing because they
were much too cumbersome for stunting. Then one went
into a long dive right over the centre of town. Agnes
looked away. It failed to come out of it entirely, or
rather seemed to fall apart in the air, as it was coming
out, just over the house-tops. Then there was an explosion and flames. I thought of Tess. The flames were
leaping up from just next to the Cathedral. That's
where she mentioned she wanted some " shots." I had on
only shorts and a shirt and beach shoes. I must have got
away automatically. I sprinted up the road to town.
Something told me she was in it. Several houses were
on fire when I got to the little square in front of the
cathedral. Police were carrying away blanketed forms
on stretchers. I started to look under the blankets, then
held myself back. I darted in and around the jam of
people in the streets. No sign of Tess. Hysterical I
became. I started asking for the mayor, the governor,
anyone who could tell me. In the end there was a nudge.
" Get out of my way, I want to get that." Tess was
squinting through her Leica. She had been a hundred
yards distant, she said after she finished her photographing, when the plane crashed.

LATER. — It seems that the two pilots met
a pair of dazzling girls in town last night and to further
their romantic adventure told them to be on their bal-
conies at eight this morning, promising them something " exciting." The death-roll ten, including the
pilot and observer.

RAGUSA, *June* 22

Took a steamer to a little town fifteen miles
up the coast today to see a chapel which Mestrovich
designed and in which he has placed some of the most
exciting sculptured works I've ever seen. It's a magnificent thing, the architecture, the reliefs, the figures,
blending in a beautiful harmony. Since the day I set
eyes on El Greco in the Prado in Madrid I haven't
seen a work of art which has stirred me so.

BERLIN, *July* 15

Have started, God help me, a novel. The
scene: India. I was there twice, in 1930 and 1931, during Gandhi's Civil Disobedience movement, and I cannot get India out of my system.

BERLIN, *July* 18

Trouble in Spain. A right-wing revolt.
Fighting in Madrid, Barcelona, and other places.

BERLIN, *July* 23

The Lindberghs are here, and the Nazis, led
by Göring, are making a great play for them. Today at
a luncheon given him by the Air Ministry he spoke out
somewhat, warning that the airplane had become such a
deadly instrument of destruction that unless those " who
are in aviation " face their heavy responsibilities and
achieve a " new security founded on intelligence," the
world and especially Europe are in for irreparable damage. It was a well-timed little thrust, for Göring is undoubtedly building up the deadliest air force in Europe.
The DNB was moved to remark this afternoon that

Lindbergh's remarks " created a strong impression," though I doubt it. " Annoyance " would be a more accurate word.

This afternoon the Lufthansa company invited some of us correspondents to a tea-party at Tempelhof for the Lindberghs, apparently not informing them that we would be there, for fear they would object, their phobia about the press being what it is. It was the first time I had seen him since 1927 when I covered his arrival at Le Bourget. Surprised how little he had changed, except that he seemed more self-confident. Later we went for a ride in Germany's largest land plane, the *Field-Marshal von Hindenburg*. Somewhere over Wannsee Lindbergh took the controls himself and treated us to some very steep banks, considering the size of the plane, and other little manœuvres, which terrified most of the passengers. The talk is that the Lindberghs have been favourably impressed by what the Nazis have shown them. He has shown no enthusiasm for meeting the foreign correspondents, who have a perverse liking for enlightening visitors on the Third Reich, as they see it, and we have not pressed for an interview.

B E R L I N, *July* 27

The Spanish government seems to be getting the upper hand. Has quelled the revolt in Barcelona and Madrid, Spain's two most important cities. But it's a much more serious affair than it seemed a week ago. The Nazis are against the Spanish government, and party circles are beginning to talk of help for the rebels. Tragic land! And just when there seemed such hope for the Republic. But interest here is concentrated on the Olympic Games opening next week, with the Nazis outdoing themselves to create a favourable impression on foreign visitors. They've built a magnificent sport-field, with a stadium for a hundred thousand, a swimming stadium for ten thousand, and so forth. Gallico here, and a pleasant dinner with him and Eleanor Holm Jarrett, an American swimming phenomenon with a very pretty face, who, it seems, is being thrown off the team for alleged imbibing of champagne on the boat coming over.

BERLIN, *August* 16

The Olympic Games finally came to an end today. I got a kick out of the track and field, the swimming, the rowing, and the basket-ball, but they were a headache to us as a job. Hitler and Göring and the others showed up this afternoon for the finale, which dragged on until after dark. Huss and I had to use our wits to smuggle in Mrs. William Randolph Hearst, a woman friend of hers, and the Adolphe Menjous, who arrived in town last night after all tickets had been sold. We lost Menjou in the scuffle, but he showed up after a few minutes. We had to pack them in our already crowded press cabin, but we finally prevailed on some S.S. guards to let them sit in the seats reserved for diplomats where they could get a good view of Hitler. Afterwards they seemed quite thrilled at the experience.

I'm afraid the Nazis have succeeded with their propaganda. First, the Nazis have run the games on a lavish scale never before experienced, and this has appealed to the athletes. Second, the Nazis have put up a very good front for the general visitors, especially the big businessmen. Ralph Barnes and I were asked in to meet some of the American ones a few years ago. They said frankly they were favourably impressed by the Nazi " set-up." They had talked with Göring, they said, and

he had told them that we American correspondents were
unfair to the Nazis.

" Did he tell you about Nazi suppression, say, of the
churches? " I asked.

" He did," one of the men spoke up, " and he assured
us there was no truth in what you fellows write about
persecution of religion here."

Whereupon, I'm afraid, Ralph and I unduly flared
up. But I don't think we convinced them.

BERLIN, *August* 25

     Press now quite open in its attacks on the
Spanish government. And I learn from a dependable
source that the first German airplanes have already
been dispatched to the rebels. Same source says the
Italians are also shooting planes. Seems to me if the
French had any sense they could send in a few troops,
disguised as volunteers, and some arms, and squelch the
rebellion for Madrid. But Blum, though a Socialist,
seems to be taking a non-intervention line out of fear
of what Germany and Italy may do.

BERLIN, *September* 4

     Got out of covering the party congress at
Nuremberg beginning next week. After the Olympic
crowds, don't think I could have survived it.

BERLIN, *September* (*undated*)

     Lunched with Tom Wolfe. Martha Dodd
suggested we meet, as I'd often expressed enthusiasm
about his work. We found a quiet corner table at
Habel's. An immense fellow physically, boiling with

energy, he developed a Gargantuan appetite, ordering
a second main dish of meat and vegetables, and more
bottles of *Pfälzer* wine than were good for us — or at
least for me. I liked him immediately and we had much
good talk — about American writing and why most
American writers — Lewis and Dreiser and Anderson,
for example — either stopped writing or fell off from
their best work just at the prime of their lives — a time
when the Europeans usually produce their greatest
novels and plays. A subject I'd often pondered about
and discussed once with Lewis in Vienna. Wolfe is
somewhat conscious of not being politically minded at
a time when most writers are and indeed, we agreed,
should be. He admitted the deficiency, but said he was
learning. " I'm supporting Roosevelt for re-election,"
he said. Curious thing: Wolfe translates excellently
into German and *Look Homeward, Angel* has had a big
success here, I believe. We parted, promising to meet in
New York. A very genuine person and more promising, if he can integrate himself, than any other young
novelist we have.

BERLIN, *September* 9

      Hitler at Nuremberg announces a Four-Year
Plan to make Germany self-sufficient in raw materials.
Göring to be in charge. Obviously a war plan, but of
course the Germans deny it. Party rally mostly con-
cerned this year with attacking Bolshevism and the
Soviets. There is talk of a break in diplomatic relations.

LONDON, *October*

      A pleasant week, seeing old friends, blowing
myself to two new suits in Savile Row, and, best of all,

five days at Salcombe in Devonshire with Squire Gallico, who has bought a place there. We had some fantastic fishing (Tess's first experience, and she outfished both Paul and me), superb walks along the wind-blown cliffs, and much good talk. Paul's gamble has been well worth while. He's written and sold three short stories and got a handsome movie royalty from one of them. Funny: he's scared stiff of his butler, who looks as though he had just stepped off the stage and completely runs the place.

Returning to Berlin tomorrow. Pleasant visits with the Newell Rogerses, the Strausses, Jennie Lee, who is very Scotch, very pretty, very witty, and really should be back in Parliament, from which she was ousted in the last elections, her husband, Aneurin Bevan, M.P. from a Wales mining district, himself a former miner, keen-minded, slightly impish, a grand guy. This afternoon we had tea with Bill Stoneman, who has just replaced John Gunther as Chicago *Daily News* correspondent here, and Maj Lis (his wife). Bill was terribly wrought up about something, nervous as an old hen — so much so that in a moment of exasperation I said: " Why don't you come out with it, Bill, whatever it is? Maybe you'll feel better." Whereupon he produced from his pocket a cablegram and tossed it to me. It was a ten-line dispatch to his paper this afternoon. I scanned it. It said: " Mrs. E. A. Simpson has filed suit for divorce against Mr. E. A. Simpson at the Ipswich Assizes. Case to be heard . . ." A detail or two about when the case would be heard. That was all.

It's a tremendous scoop and should blow the story sky-high. Obviously the King intends to marry the woman now and make her Queen.

BERLIN, *November* 18

The Wilhelmstrasse announced today that
Germany (with Italy) has recognized Franco. General
Faupel, who has done good work for Germany in South
America and Spain, is to be Hitler's Ambassador to
Salamanca. Apparently today's decision was timed to
offset Franco's failure to take Madrid just as he seemed
to have it in his grasp. At first, I'm told, recognition
was to coincide with Franco's entry into Madrid, which
the Germans expected ten days ago. Dodd tells me our
consulate in Hamburg reported this week the departure
from there of three German ships loaded with arms for
Spain. In the meantime the comedy of " non-intervention " goes on in London. For two years now the policies
of London and Paris have ceased making sense to me,
judged by their own vital interests. They did nothing
on March 16, 1935 and on March 7 this year, and
they're doing nothing about Spain now. Is my judgment becoming warped after two years in this hysterical
Nazi land? Is it absurd or isn't it absurd to conclude
that Blum and Baldwin don't know their own interests?

BERLIN, *November* 25

We were summoned to the Propaganda
Ministry today for an " important " announcement.
Wondered what Hitler was up to, but it turned out to
be merely the signing of an anti-Comintern pact between Germany and Japan. Ribbentrop, who signed for
Germany, strutted in and harangued us for a quarter
of an hour about the pact's meaning, if any. He said
it meant, among other things, that Germany and Japan
had joined together to defend " Western civilization."
This was such a novel idea, for Japan at least, that at

the end of his talk one of the British correspondents
asked him if he had understood him correctly. Ribbentrop, who has no sense of humour, then repeated the
silly statement, without batting an eye. It seems obvious that Japan and Germany have drawn up at the
same time a secret military treaty calling for joint action against Russia should one of them get involved in
war with the Soviets.

BERLIN, *December* 25

A pleasant Christmas dinner, and American
at that, even to mince pie, with Ralph and Esther
Barnes and their children. Ralph and I had to get up
in the middle of it, though, to check on queries from
New York about a sensational A.P. report that the
Germans had landed a large body of troops in Morocco
to help Franco. There was no one in the Wilhelmstrasse, as all officials are out of town over the holidays,
so we were unable to get a confirmation or denial.
Sounds like a fake, though.

BERLIN, *April* 8, 1937

April here and no Hitler surprise this spring
yet. This may be a year of Nazi consolidation, building up the armed forces, assuring Franco victory in
Spain, cementing relations with Italy (support for the
Duce in Spain and the Mediterranean in return for his
giving Germany a free hand in Austria and the Balkans), and giving the nerves of the German people a
little rest.

BERLIN, *April* 14

Have bought a sailboat for four hundred
marks from a broken-down boxer who needed the cash.

It has a cabin with two bunks and Tess and I can week-end on it, if we ever get a week-end free. Know nothing about sailing, but with the help of some hastily scrawled diagrams on the back of an envelope telling what to do with the wind behind you or against you or from the side which one of the Germans at the office did for me, and with much luck, we managed to sail ten miles down the Wannsee to where the Barneses have taken a house for the summer. Had some difficulty in docking it there, as the wind was blowing towards shore and I didn't know what to do. The little boat-house owner raised an awful howl, claiming I'd damaged his dock, but a five-mark piece quieted him.

BERLIN, *April* 20

Hitler's birthday. He gets more and more like a Cæsar. Today a public holiday with sickening adulation from all the party hacks, delegations from all over the Reich bearing gifts, and a great military parade. The Reichswehr revealed a little of what it has: heavy artillery, tanks, and magnificently trained men. Hitler stood on the reviewing stand in front of the Technische Hochschule, as happy as a child with tin soldiers, standing there more than two hours and saluting every tank and gun. The military attachés of France, Britain, and Russia, I hear, were impressed. So were ours.

BERLIN, *May* 3

Gordon Young of Reuter's and I ran into Lord Lothian about midnight in the lobby of the Adlon. He arrived here suddenly yesterday to confer with Nazi leaders. Young asked him why he had come. " Oh,

Göring asked me to," he replied. He is probably the
most intelligent of the Tories taken in by Hitler, Göring,
and Ribbentrop. We wanted to ask him since when he
was under orders from Göring, but refrained.

BERLIN, *May* 7

      Hillman awakened me with a phone call from
London about four a.m. today to inform me that the
Zeppelin *Hindenburg* had crashed at Lakehurst with
the loss of several lives. I immediately phoned one of
the men who designed it, at Friedrichshafen. He refused to believe my words. I telephoned London and
gave them a little story for the late editions. I had
hardly gone back to sleep when Claire Trask of the
Columbia Broadcasting System phoned to ask me to do
a broadcast on the German reaction to the disaster. I
was a bit ill-tempered, I'm afraid, at being awakened
so early. I told her I couldn't do it and suggested two
or three other correspondents. About ten she called
back again and insisted I do it. I finally agreed, though
I had never broadcast in my life.

Kept thinking all morning of how first I and then
Tess were invited to make *this* trip on the *Hindenburg*,
and almost accepted. For some reason there were several places they could not sell, so about ten days before
it was due to leave, the press agent of the Zeppelin
Reederei phoned me and offered a free passage to New
York. It was impossible for me, as I was holding down
the office alone. The next day he called up and asked
if Tess would like to go. For reasons which are a little
obscure — or maybe not so obscure, though I do not
think it is honest to say I had a *feeling* that something
might happen — I did not mention the matter to Tess
and politely declined on her behalf the next day.

Wrote out my broadcast this afternoon between dispatches to New York, Claire Trask taking it page by page to the Air Ministry for censorship. Was a little surprised to find that there was Nazi censorship of radio, as we have none as newspaper correspondents, but Miss Trask explained it was just for this time. I arrived at the studio a quarter of an hour before the time set to begin, as nervous as an old hen. With about five minutes to go, Miss Trask arrived with the script. The censors had cut out my references to Nazi suspicion that there had been sabotage, though I had cabled this early in the afternoon in a dispatch. So nervous when I began my broadcast that my voice skipped up and down the scale and my lips and throat grew parched, but after the first page gradually lost my fright. Fear I will never make a broadcaster, but felt relieved I did not have microphone fright, which I understand makes some people speechless before a microphone.

BERLIN, *May 10*

Finished the Indian novel, or at least the first draft. A great load off my mind.

BERLIN, *May 30*

I have rarely seen such indignation in the Wilhelmstrasse as today. Every official I saw was fuming. The Spanish republicans yesterday bombed the pocket-battleship *Deutschland* at Ibitza with good result, killing, according to the Germans, some twenty officers and men and wounding eighty. One informant tells me Hitler has been screaming with rage all day and wants to declare war on Spain. The army and navy are trying to restrain him.

BERLIN, *May* 31

I feel like screaming with rage myself. The Germans this day have done a typical thing. They have bombarded the Spanish town of Almería with their warships as reprisal for the bombing of the *Deutschland*. Thus Hitler has his cheap revenge and a few more Spanish women and children are dead. The Wilhelmstrasse also announced Germany's (and Italy's) withdrawal from the Spanish naval patrol and from the non-intervention talks. Dr. Aschmann called us to the Foreign Office about ten a.m. to give us the news. He was very pious about it all. I was too outraged to ask questions, but Enderis and Lochner asked a few. Perhaps today's action will end the farce of "non-intervention," a trick by which Britain and France, for some strange reason, are allowing Hitler and Mussolini to triumph in Spain.

BERLIN, *June* 4

Helmut Hirsch, a Jewish youth of twenty who was technically an American citizen though he had never been to America, was axed at dawn this morning. Ambassador Dodd fought for a month to save his life, but to no avail. It was a sad case, a typical tragedy of these days. He was convicted by the dreaded People's Court, a court of inquisition set up by the Nazis a couple of years ago, of planning to murder Julius Streicher, the Nuremberger Jew-baiter. What kind of trial it was — no American or outside representatives were present — can only be imagined. I've seen a few trials before this court, though most of them are *in camera*, and a man scarcely has a chance, four of the five judges being

Nazi party boys (the fifth is a regular judge) who do
what they're expected to do.

Actually, the Nazis had something on poor Hirsch.
A student at Prague University, he was put up to the
job either by Otto Strasser or some of Strasser's followers or supposed followers in Prague. Among Strasser's " followers " there was certainly a Gestapo agent,
and Hirsch was doomed from the outset. As far as I
can piece the story together, Hirsch was provided with
a suitcase full of bombs and a revolver and dispatched
to Germany to get someone. The Nazis claim it was
Streicher. Hirsch himself never seems to have admitted
who. The Gestapo agent in Prague tipped off Himmler's people here, and Hirsch, with his incriminating
suitcase, was nabbed as soon as he set foot in Germany.
It may well be, as Hirsch's lawyer in Prague suggests,
that the young man was merely bringing the weapons
to Germany for someone else, already here, to do the
job, and that he may not have known, even, of the contents of his luggage. We shall never know. Perhaps
he was simply framed by the Gestapo. He was arrested,
tried, and, this morning, executed. I had a long talk
with Dodd this morning about the case. He told me he
had appealed to Hitler himself to commute the sentence
and read me the text of his moving letter. The Führer's
reply was a flat negative. When Dodd tried to get a
personal interview with Hitler to plead the case in person, he was rebuffed.

This afternoon I received from Hirsch's lawyer in
Prague a copy of the last letter the young man wrote.
He wrote it in his death cell and it was addressed to his
sister, for whom he obviously had a deep attachment. I
have never read in all my life braver words. He had
just been informed that his final appeal had been re-

jected and that there was no more hope. " I am to die,
then," he says. " Please do not be afraid. I do not feel
afraid. I feel released, after the agony of not quite
knowing." He sketches his life and finds meaning in it
despite all the mistakes and its brief duration — " less
than twenty-one years." I confess to tears before I had
finished reading. He was a braver and more decent man
than his killers.

BERLIN, *June* 15

Five more Protestant pastors arrested yesterday, including Jacobi from the big Gedächtniskirche.
Hardly keep up with the church war any more since
they arrested my informant, a young pastor; have no
wish to endanger the life of another one.

BERLIN, *June* 21

Blum out in Paris, and that's the end of the
Popular Front. Curious how a man as intelligent as
Blum could have made the blunders he's made with his
non-intervention policy in Spain, whose Popular Front
he has also helped to ruin.

BERLIN, *July* 5

The Austrian Minister tells me that the new
British Ambassador here, Sir Nevile Henderson, has
told Göring, with whom he is on very chummy terms,
that Hitler can have his Austria so far as he, Henderson, is concerned. Henderson strikes me as being very
" pro."

LONDON, *July* (*undated*)

Dinner with Knick at Simpson's, and then out to his house, where Jay Allen and Carroll Binder, foreign editor of the Chicago *Daily News*, joined us. We chinned until about two a.m. Jay had said that Binder was supposed to take me aside and offer me a job on the *News* (Colonel Knox in Berlin had asked me if I wanted one), but he did nothing of the kind. Jay also gave me a card to Ed Murrow, who, he said, was connected with CBS, but I shall not have time to see him as Knick and I leave tomorrow morning for Salcombe, where Tess and Agnes already are installed at Gallico's. From there Tess and I cross to France without returning to London.

PARIS, *July* (*undated*)

The Van Goghs at the Paris Exposition well worth the price of admission. Have had little time to see anything else. Saw Berkson, chief of Universal Service in New York. He assured me there was nothing to the rumours about Universal closing down and that in fact for the first time in history it was actually making money. So, reassured about my job, we leave for the Riviera tomorrow for some sun and swimming, Tess to remain there until fall on account of — we are to have a baby!

BERLIN, *August* 14

Universal Service has folded after all. Hearst is cutting his losses. I am to remain here with INS, but as second man, which I do not like.

BERLIN, *August* 16

Norman Ebbutt of the London *Times*, by far
the best correspondent here, left this evening. He was
expelled, following British action in kicking out two or
three Nazi correspondents in London, the Nazis seizing
the opportunity to get rid of a man they've hated and
feared for years because of his exhaustive knowledge
of this country and of what was going on behind the
scenes. The *Times*, which has played along with the
pro-Nazi Cliveden set, never gave him much support
and published only half of what he wrote, and indeed
is leaving Ebbutt's assistant, Jimmy Holburn, to continue with the office here. We gave Norman a great
send-off at the Charlottenburger station, about fifty of
the foreign correspondents of all nations being on the
platform despite a tip from Nazi circles that our presence would be considered an unfriendly act to Germany!
Amusing to note the correspondents who were afraid
to show up, including two well-known Americans. The
platform full of Gestapo agents noting down our names
and photographing us. Ebbutt terribly high-strung,
but moved by our sincere, if boisterous, demonstration
of farewell.

BERLIN, *August* (*undated*)

A little depressed tonight. I'm without a job.
About ten o'clock this evening I ceased being employed.
I was in my office writing a dispatch. The office boy
came in with a cable. There was something about his
face. It was a brief wire, hot off the ticker. It was from
New York. It said — oh, something about INS being
unable to retain all the old Universal Service corre-

spondents and that I was getting the usual two weeks' notice.

I guess I was a little stunned. I guess it was a little sudden. Who was it the other night — one of the English correspondents — who jokingly observed that it was bad to be getting a baby in your family because it invariably coincided with your getting fired? Well, maybe we shouldn't have had a baby now. Maybe you shouldn't ever have a baby if you're in this business. Maybe the French girl in Paris many years ago was right. She said: " Put a baby into this world? *Pas moi!* "

I finished my dispatch (what was it about?) and went out for a breath of air, strolling along the river Spree down behind the Reichstag. It was a beautiful, warm, starlit August night, and the Spree making its soft curve just before it gets to the Reichstag, I noticed, and a launch going by, filled with noisy holiday-makers back from a Havel *Rundfahrt*. No ideas came to me, as expected. I went back to the office.

On the desk I noticed a wire that had come in ten minutes before the fatal one. It was from Salzburg, a baroque town of great charm where I used to go to hear some Mozart. It was signed: " Murrow, Columbia Broadcasting." I dimly remembered the name, but could not place it beyond his company. " Will you have dinner with me at the Adlon Friday night? " it said. I wired: " Delighted."

BERLIN, *August* 20

I have a job. I am to go to work for the Columbia Broadcasting System. That is, *if.* . . . And what an *if* it is! It is this way: It is crazy. I have the job *if* my *voice* is all right. That's the catch. Who ever heard of an adult with no pretentions to being a singer or any other kind of artist being dependent for a good, interesting job on his *voice?* And mine is terrible. I'm positive of it. But that's my situation tonight.

It has been quite an evening. I met Edward R. Murrow, European manager of CBS, in the lobby of the Adlon at seven o'clock. As I walked up to him I was a little taken aback by his handsome face. Just what you would expect from radio, I thought. He had asked me for dinner, I considered, to pump me for dope for a radio talk he must make from Berlin. We walked into the bar and there was something in his talk that began disarming me. Something in his eyes that was not Hollywood. We sat down. We ordered two Martinis. The cocktails came. I wondered why he had asked me. We had friends in common, Ferdy Kuhn, Raymond Gram Swing. . . . We discussed them. Apparently he was not here to do a broadcast, then.

" You must come sailing with me tomorrow or Sunday," I said.

" Swell. I'd like to."

The waiter gathered up the empty cocktail glasses and laid two menus before us.

" Just a minute before we order," Murrow broke in. " I've got something on my mind."

That's the way it was. He said he had something on his mind. He said he was looking for an experienced foreign correspondent to open a CBS office on the Continent. He could not cover all of Europe from London. I began to feel better, though I said nothing.

" Are you interested? " he asked.

" Well, yes," I said, trying to down my feelings.

" How much have you been making? "

I told him.

"Good. We'll pay you the same."

"Fine," I said.

"It's a deal," he said, and reached for the *Speisekarte*. We ordered dinner. We talked of America, Europe, the music at Salzburg he had just heard. We had coffee. We had brandy. It was getting late.

"Oh, there's one little thing I forgot to mention," he said. "The voice . . ."

"The what?"

"Your voice."

"Bad," I said, "as you can see."

"Perhaps not. But, you see, in broadcasting it's a factor. And our directors and numerous vice-presidents will want to hear your voice first. We'll arrange a broadcast. You give a talk, say, on the coming party rally. I'm sure it'll work out all right."

Berlin, *September 5*

Did my trial broadcast this Sabbath day. Just before it began I was very nervous, thinking of what was at stake and that all depended upon what a silly little microphone and an amplifier and the ether between Berlin and New York did to my voice. Kept thinking also of all those CBS vice-presidents sniffing at what they heard. Everything went wrong at first. Claire Trask, fifteen minutes before the start, discovered she had left the script of her introduction at a café where we'd met. She dashed madly out of the studio, returning only a few minutes before we were to begin. At the last minute the microphone which apparently had been set for a man at least eight feet tall wouldn't come down. "It is stuck, *mein Herr*," said the German engineer. He advised me to point my head towards the ceiling. I tried it, but it so constricted my vocal cords that only a squeak came out when I started to talk.

" One minute to go," shouted the engineer.

" I can't go on with that mike," I protested.

I espied some packing-cases in the corner just behind the microphone. I had an idea.

" Boost me up on those, will you? "

" *Wie, bitte?* What you say? "

" Give me a lift." And in a second I was atop the
boxes, my legs dangling nicely, my mouth just opposite
the level of the microphone. We all laughed.

" Quiet," the engineer shouted, giving us the red
light. I had no time to get nervous again.

And now I must wait for the verdict. In the meantime leaving for Nuremberg tonight to do the Party
Congress for the U.P. Webb Miller and Fred Oechsner
were rather insistent that I help them out. It's better,
at that, to have some distraction in the next few days
while I wait. Wrote Tess we probably won't starve.

NUREMBERG, *September* 11

A week now and no word from Murrow. My
voice apparently was pretty lousy. Birchall of the New
York *Times* talks of giving me a job, but won't pay
much. Returning to Berlin day after tomorrow.

NUREMBERG, *September* 13

Murrow called and said I'm hired. Start
October 1. Wired Tess. Celebrated a little tonight, I
fear, on the very potent local Franconian wine. Prentiss Gilbert, our counsellor of Embassy, has been here,
the first American diplomat to attend a Nazi Party
Congress. Ambassador Dodd, who is in America,
strongly disapproves, though Prentiss, a swell guy,

says he was forced into it by Henderson, the pro-Nazi British Ambassador, and Poncet, who used to be " pro " but is probably so no longer. The congress duller this year and many are asking if Hitler is slowing up. I hope so. Constance Peckham, a nice young lady from *Time* magazine has been here. She thinks we " veterans " are much too blasé about this party show, which appears to have given her a tremendous kick. Much good talk and drink with her, Jimmy Holburn, and George Kidd this night. Appropriate, I suppose, that I should begin and end my newspaper sojourn in Germany at this madhouse which is the party rally. Three years. They've gone quickly. Germany has gone places. What will radio be like?

BERLIN, *September 27*

Tess back, feeling fine, and we're packing. We are to make our headquarters in Vienna, a neutral and central spot for me to work from. Most of our old friends have left — the Gunthers, the Whit Burnetts — but it is always that way in this game. Go to London next week, then Paris, Geneva, and Rome to meet the radio people, renew contacts with the newspaper offices, and, in Rome, to find out if the Pope is really dying, as reported. We are glad to be leaving Berlin.

To sum up these three years: Personally, they have not been unhappy ones, though the shadow of Nazi fanaticism, sadism, persecution, regimentation, terror, brutality, suppression, militarism, and preparation for war has hung over all our lives, like a dark, brooding cloud that never clears. Often we have tried to segregate ourselves from it all. We have found three refuges: Ourselves and our books; the " foreign colony," small, limited, somewhat narrow, but *normal*, and containing

our friends — the Barneses, the Robsons, the Ebbuttses,
the Dodds, the Deuels, the Oechsners, Gordon Young,
Doug Miller, Sigrid Schultz, Leverich, Jake Beam,
and others; thirdly, the lakes and woods around Berlin,
where you could romp and play and sail and swim,
forgetting so much. The theatre has remained good
when it has stuck to the classics or pre-Nazi plays, and
the opera and the Philharmonic Symphony Orchestra,
despite the purging of the Jews and the year's disci-
plining of Fuertwängler (who has now made his peace
with Satan), have given us the best music we've ever
heard outside of New York and Vienna. Personally too
there was the excitement of working here, the " Saturday surprises," the deeper story of this great land in
evil ferment.

Somehow I feel that, despite our work as reporters,
there is little understanding of the Third Reich, what
it *is*, what it is up to, where it is going, either at home
or elsewhere abroad. It is a complex picture and it may
be that we have given only a few strong, uncoordinated
strokes of the brush, leaving the canvas as confusing
and meaningless as an early Picasso. Certainly the
British and the French do not understand Hitler's
Germany. Perhaps, as the Nazis say, the Western
democracies have become sick, decadent, and have
reached that stage of decline which Spengler predicted.
But Spengler included Germany in the decline of the
West, and indeed the Nazi reversion to the ancient,
primitive, Germanic myths is a sign of her retrogres-
sion, as is her burning of books and suppression of liberty and learning.

But Germany is stronger than her enemies realize.
True, it is a poor country in raw materials and agriculture; but it is making up for this poverty in aggressive-
ness of spirit, ruthless state planning, concentrated

direction of effort, and the building up of a mighty military machine with which it can back up its aggressive spirit. True, too, that this past winter we have seen long lines of sullen people before the food shops, that there is a shortage of meat and butter and fruit and fats, that whipped cream is *verboten*, that men's suits and women's dresses are increasingly being made out of wood pulp, gasoline out of coal, rubber out of coal and lime; that there is no gold coverage for the Reichsmark or for anything else, not even for vital imports. Weaknesses, most of them, certainly, and in our dispatches we have advertised them.

It has been more difficult to point out the sources of strength; to tell of the feverish efforts to make Germany self-sufficient under the Four-Year Plan, which is no joke at all, but a deadly serious war plan; to explain that the majority of Germans, despite their dislike of much in Nazism, are behind Hitler and believe in him. It is not easy to put in words the *dynamics* of this movement, the hidden springs that are driving the Germans on, the ruthlessness of the long-term ideas of Hitler or even the complicated and revolutionary way in which the land is being mobilized for Total War (though Ludendorff has written the primer for Total War).

Much of what is going on and will go on could be learned by the outside world from *Mein Kampf*, the Bible and Koran together of the Third Reich. But — amazingly — there is no decent translation of it in English or French, and Hitler will not allow one to be made, which is understandable, for it would shock many in the West. How many visiting butter-and-egg men have I told that the Nazi goal is domination! They laughed. But Hitler frankly admits it. He says in *Mein Kampf*: "A state which in an age of racial pollution devotes itself to cultivation of its best racial elements must some day become master of the earth. . . . We all sense that in a far future mankind may face problems which can be surmounted only by a supreme Master Race supported by the means and resources of the entire globe."

When the visiting firemen from London, Paris, and New York come, Hitler babbles only of peace. Wasn't he in the trenches of the last war? He knows what war is. Never will *he* condemn mankind to *that*. Peace? Read *Mein Kampf*, brothers. Read this: " Indeed, the pacifist-humane idea is perhaps quite good whenever the man of the highest standard has previously conquered and subjected the world to a degree that makes him the only master of the globe. . . . Therefore first fight and then one may see what can be done. . . . For oppressed countries will not be brought back into the bosom of a common Reich by means of fiery protests, but by a mighty sword. . . . One must be quite clear about the fact that the recovery of the lost regions will not come about through solemn appeals to the dear Lord or through pious hopes in a League of Nations, but only by FORCE OF ARMS. . . . We must take up an active policy and throw ourselves into a final and decisive fight with France. . . ."

France is to be annihilated, says Hitler, and then the great drive to the eastward is to begin.

Peace, brothers? Do you know what the *Deutsche Wehr*, which speaks for the military in this country, remarked two years ago? " Every human and social activity is justified only if it helps prepare for war. The new human being is completely possessed by the thought of war. He must not and cannot think of anything else."

And how will it be? Again the *Deutsche Wehr;* " Total war means the complete and final disappearance of the vanquished from the stage of history ! "

This, according to Hitler, is Germany's road. The
strain on the life of the people and on the economic
structure of the state already is tremendous. Both may
well crack. But the youth, led by the S.S., is fanatic.
So are the middle-class *alte Kämpfer*, the " old fighters " who brawled in the streets for Hitler in the early
days and have now been awarded the good jobs, authority, power, money. The bankers and industrialists,
not so enthusiastic now as when I arrived in Germany,
go along. They must. It is either that or the concentration camp. The workers too. After all, six million
of them have been re-employed and they too begin to
see that Germany is going places, and they with it.

I leave Germany in this autumn of 1937 with the
words of a Nazi marching song still dinning in my ears:

> *Today we own Germany,*
> *Tomorrow the whole world.*

LONDON, *October* 7

Murrow will be a grand guy to work with.
One disappointing thing about the job, though: Murrow and I are not supposed to do any talking on the
radio ourselves. New York wants us to hire newspaper
correspondents for that. We just arrange broadcasts.
Since I know as much about Europe as most newspaper
correspondents, and a bit more than the younger ones,
who lack languages and background, I don't get the
point.

PARIS, *October* 12

Suppered with Blanche Knopf. She urged
me to get along with the revision of the Indian novel.

GENEVA, *October* 15

The *Bise* blowing, and something dead and sad about this town.

ROME, *October* 18

Saw the Pope today and he seemed most sprightly for a man who is said to have one foot in the grave. Frank Gervasi got me into an audience at Castel Gondolfo, the summer residence. The Pope was receiving a delegation of Austrian mayors, which made it nice for me because he spoke in German and I could understand him. He fairly bubbled over with energy. Made elaborate arrangements for radio coverage in the event of the Pope's death (it will be the first time radio has ever had a chance to cover it), but did not hire Monsignor Pucci, a sly, colourful man who works for every correspondent and most of the embassies in town.

MUNICH, *October* (*undated*)

Rushed up here to get acquainted with the Duke of Windsor with instructions to stick to him, accompany him to America, and arrange for him to broadcast there. He's been touring Germany to study "labour conditions," being taken around by one of the real Nazi ruffians, Dr. Ley. Had my first view of Mrs. Simpson today and she seemed quite pretty and attractive. Randolph Churchill, who looks like his father but does not think like him — at least, not yet — has been most helpful. A curious thing for the Duke to do, to come to Germany, where the labour unions have been smashed, just before he goes to America. He has been badly advised.

BRUSSELS, *November* 11

Armistice Day, cold and grey and drizzly, but no greyer than the prospects of the Nine-Power Conference now in session here to try to straighten out Japan's war in China. This is my first actual broadcasting assignment and not very exciting. Have put on or am putting on Norman Davis, Wellington Koo, whom I like immensely, and other delegates. Litvinov refuses to broadcast and seems worried by news from Moscow that his private secretary has been arrested by the Ogpu; Eden declines too. Silly, this CBS policy that I must not do any reporting, only hire others to do it. Edgar Mowrer, Bob Pell, Chip Bohlan, John Elliott, Vernon Bartlett here to chatter with about the sad state of the world; and a pleasant evening with Anne and Mark Somerhausen, she as pretty and brilliant as ever, he quieter and much occupied in Parliament, where he sits as a Social Democrat deputy. The Nine-Power Conference so far an awful farce.

VIENNA, *December* 25

Christmased this afternoon with the Wileys; John our chargé d'affaires here now. Walter Duranty there, as always, the Fodors, etc. Chip Bohlan, on leave from the Moscow Embassy, came with me to the studio of the Austrian Broadcasting Company to help me shepherd the youngsters of the American colony through a Christmas broadcast. A childish job and one that I do not like, being too much interested in the political situation at present.

We are nicely installed in an apartment in the Ploesslgasse, next door to the Rothschild palace. The owners, being Jewish, have removed themselves to

Czechoslovakia for greater safety, though Schuschnigg
seems to have the situation fairly well in hand here.
Vienna, though, is terribly poor and depressing compared to our last sojourn here, from 1929 to 1932. The
workers are sullen, even those who have jobs, and one
sees beggars on every street corner. A few people have
money and splash it at the night-clubs and a few
fashionable restaurants such as the Drei Husaren and
Am Franziskanerplatz. The contrast is sickening and
the regime is resented by the masses, who are either re-
verting to their old Socialist Party, which is fairly
strong underground, or going over to Nazism. The
great mistake of this clerical dictatorship is not to have
a social program. Hitler and Mussolini have not made
that mistake. Still, there is more to eat here than in
Germany, and the dictatorship is much milder — the
difference between Prussians and Austrians! Next to
Paris I love this town, even now, more than any other
in Europe, the *Gemütlichkeit*, charm, and intelligence
of its people, the baroque of its architecture, the good
taste, the love of art and life, the softness of the accent,
the very mild quality of the whole atmosphere. A great
deal of anti-Semitism here, which plays nicely into the
hands of the Nazis, but then there always was — ever
since the days of Mayor Karl Lueger, Hitler's first
mentor on the subject when he was down and out in this
city. Have had much good talk with Duranty, who is
living here for a few months; the Fodors, she lovable
as before, he a walking dictionary on central Europe
and generous in telling what he knows; Emil Vadnai of
the New York *Times*, a Hungarian of great charm,
knowledge, and intelligence. Had Duranty broadcast
the other day, though New York was afraid his voice
was too high. Came a cable the same evening from Chi-

cago:" . . . your clear, bell-like voice . . ." signed by
Mary Garden, who ought to know.

We wait for the baby, due in seven weeks now, arguing the while over names.

VIENNA, *February* 5, 1938

Doings in Berlin. Today's papers say Blomberg and Fritsch, the two men who have built up the
German army, are out. Hitler himself becomes a sort
of "Supreme War-Lord," assuming the powers of the
Minister of Defence. Two new generals appear: Wilhelm Keitel as chief of the High Command, and Walther von Brauchitsch as commander-in-chief of the
army in place of Fritsch. Neurath is out as Foreign
Minister, replaced by Ribbentrop. Schacht is out, replaced by Walther Funk. Göring — strange! — is
made a field-marshal. What's back of all this? The
meeting of the Reichstag which had been set for January 30 and then postponed is now to be held February
20, when we shall probably know.

VIENNA, *February* 7

Fodor tells me a strange tale. He says Austrian police raided Nazi headquarters in the Teinfalt-
strasse the other day and found a plan initialled by
Rudolph Hess, Hitler's deputy, for a new *Putsch.* Idea
was, says Fodor, to organize a riot in front of the German Embassy in the Metternichstrasse, have someone
shoot Papen and the German military attaché, and thus
give Hitler an excuse to march in.

Vienna, *February* 13

Much tension here this Sabbath. Schusch-nigg has had a secret meeting with Hitler at Berchtes-gaden, but we don't know what happened.

Vienna, *February* 16

A terrible thing has happened. We learned day before yesterday about Berchtesgaden. Hitler took Schuschnigg for a ride, demanded he appoint sev-eral Nazis led by Seyss-Inquart to the Cabinet, amnesty all Nazi prisoners, and restore the political rights of the Nazi Party — or invasion by the Reichswehr. Presi-dent Miklas seems to have balked at this. Then yester-day Hitler dispatched an ultimatum: Either carry out the terms of the Berchtesgaden " agreement," or the Reichswehr marches. A little after midnight this morn-ing Schuschnigg and Miklas surrendered. The new Cabinet was announced, Seyss-Inquart is in the key post of Minister of the Interior, and there is an amnesty for all Nazis. Douglas Reed when I saw him today so indignant he could hardly talk. He's given the London *Times* the complete story of what happened at Berchtes-gaden. Perhaps it will do some good. I dropped by the Legation this evening. John Wiley was pacing the floor.
" It's the end of Austria," he said.

Vienna, *February* 20

Tess, Ed Taylor, and I sat glumly around the radio on this Sunday afternoon listening to Hitler thunder before his Reichstag in Berlin. Today he came out in the open with his theory that Germany will her-self protect the ten million Germans living outside the

Reich's borders — meaning, though he did not say so, the seven millions in Austria and the three million Sudeten Germans in Czechoslovakia. He even proclaimed their right to " racial self-determination." His words: " There must be no doubt about one thing. Political separation from the Reich may not lead to deprivation of rights — that is, the general rights of self-determination. In the long run it is unbearable for a world power to know there are racial comrades at its side who are constantly being afflicted with the severest suffering for their sympathy or unity with the whole nation, its destiny, and its *Weltanschauung.* To the interests of the German Reich belong the protection of those German peoples who are not in a position to secure along our frontiers their political and spiritual freedom by their own efforts."

LATER. — A New York broadcast says Eden has resigned. It almost seems as though at the bidding of Hitler, who singled him out for attack in his speech this afternoon. The Ballhausplatz very worried.

VIENNA, *February* 22

The baby is due, but has not yet come. I must leave tonight for a broadcast in Sofia. My bad luck to miss the event, but perhaps I shall get back in time.

VIENNA, *February* 26

When I stepped off the train at four p.m., Ed Taylor was on the platform and I could tell by his face it had happened.

" Congratulations! " he said, but I could see he was forcing his smile.

" And Tess? "

He hesitated, swallowed. " She had a bit of a hard time, I'm afraid. Cæsarean. But she's better now."

I told the taxi-driver to hurry to the hospital.

" Aren't you going to ask the sex? " Ed said.

" What is it? "

" A girl," he said.

It was a sweet girl I saw a few minutes later, not discoloured and deformed as in the books, but white-skinned and well-shaped and full of beans, but her birth had almost cost the life of her mother. In the nick of time, the operation, early this morning.

" The danger is past. Your wife will recover. And the baby is fine," the doctor said. A little resentful, he seemed, that I had taken so long in showing up.

A bit too excited tonight to sleep, I fear.

VIENNA, *March* 2

Tess and the baby doing well considering everything. I spending most of my time at the hospital. Tension growing here daily. Hear Schuschnigg is now negotiating with the workers, whom his colleague Doll-fuss shot down so cold-bloodedly just four years ago. They are asking for little, but the negotiations with these stupid reactionaries go slowly. Still the workers prefer what they can undoubtedly get now from Schuschnigg to the Nazis. I feel a little empty, being here on the scene but doing no actual reporting. Curious radio doesn't want a first-hand report. But New York hasn't asked for anything, being chiefly concerned with an educational broadcast I must do from Ljubl-jana in a few days — a chorus of schoolchildren or something! Göring made a nice gentle speech yester-day, according to the local press. He said: " We [the

German air force] will be the terror of our enemies. . . .
I want in this army iron men with a will to action. . . .
When the Führer in his Reichstag speech said that we
would no longer tolerate the suppression of ten million
German comrades beyond our borders, then you know
as soldiers of the air force that, if it is to be, you must
back these words of the Führer to the limit. We are
burning to prove our invincibility."

LJUBLJANA, YUGOSLAVIA, *March* 10

Here is a town to shame the whole world. It is
full of statues and not one of them of a soldier. Only
poets and thinkers have been so honoured. Put on a
chorus of coal-miners' kids for a Columbia School of
the Air program. They sang magnificently, like Welsh
coal-miners. Afterwards at the station, waiting for the
Vienna train, much good Slovene wine with the local
priests, Slovenia being a strong Catholic province.
Without news of the world for two days while here.

VIENNA, *March* 11–12 (4 *a.m.*)

The worst has happened! Schuschnigg is
out. The Nazis are in. The Reichswehr is invading
Austria. Hitler has broken a dozen solemn promises,
pledges, treaties. And Austria is finished. Beautiful,
tragic, civilized Austria! Gone. Done to death in the
brief moment of an afternoon. This afternoon. Impossible to sleep, so will write. Must write something.
The Nazis will not let me broadcast. Here I sit on one
of the biggest stories of my life. I am the only broadcaster in town. Max Jordan of NBC, my only com-
petitor, has not yet arrived. Yet I cannot talk. The
Nazis have blocked me all night. I have argued,

pleaded, fought. An hour ago they ushered me out with bayonets.

To begin at the beginning of this day of nightmare, if I can:

The sun was out and spring was in the air when my train got into the Südbahnhof at eight this morning. I felt good. Driving to Ploesslgasse I noticed the streets littered with paper. Overhead two planes were dropping leaflets.

" What is it? " I asked the taxi-driver.

" Plebiscite."

" What plebiscite? "

" The one Schuschnigg ordered." He did not trust me and would say no more.

I climbed the stairs to our apartment puzzled. I asked the maid. She handed me a stack of newspapers for the last three days. Over breakfast I caught up on the news. On Wednesday night (March 9) Schusch-nigg, speaking at Innsbruck, had suddenly ordered a plebiscite. For this Sunday. The question: " Are you for an independent, social, Christian, German, united Austria? *Ja oder Nein.*"

Breakfast over, I hurried to the hospital. Tess was not so good. Fever, and the doctor afraid of phle-bitis in the left leg. A blood clot. A hell of a thing, after the other. I stayed with her for two hours until she dozed off. About eleven a.m. I took a taxi into town and went to the Schwarzenberg Café on the Schwarzen-bergplatz to see what was up. Fodor and Taylor and some Austrian newspapermen were there. They were a little tense, but hopeful. The plebiscite would go off peacefully, they thought. And Schuschnigg, assured of the support of the workers, would win, hands down. That would hold Hitler for a while. I felt better. Some-one turned on the radio. The announcer was reading a

proclamation calling up the class of 1915 to active service. That's merely to police the election, we agreed. One
of the Austrians was called to the phone. When he came
back he said something about the Nazis having just
smashed the windows of the Monarchist offices near the
Stefansplatz. For some reason, I remember now, everyone laughed. I had in mind to phone Colonel Wolf,
the Legitimist leader, with whom I've been negotiating
for a broadcast by Otto von Habsburg. But I didn't.

Shortly before four p.m. I set out for the hospital to
see if Tess was any better. Crossing the Karlsplatz to
catch a subway train I was stopped by a crowd of about
a thousand people. They were Nazis and it was a bit
comical. One lone policeman was yelling and gesticu-
lating at them. And they were giving ground! " If
that's all the guts the Nazis have, Schuschnigg *will* win,
hands down," I mused. " And he's arming the workers.
That'll take care of the Nazi toughs." I hurried along
to my train.

About six o'clock, returning from the hospital, I
emerged from the subway to the Karlsplatz. What had
happened? Something! Before I knew it I was being
swept along in a shouting, hysterical Nazi mob, past
the Ring, past the Opera, up the Kärntnerstrasse to
the offices of the German "Tourist" Bureau, which,
with its immense flower-draped portrait of Hitler, has
been a Nazi shrine for months. The faces! I had seen
these before at Nuremberg — the fanatical eyes, the
gaping mouths, the hysteria. And now they were shouting like Holy Rollers: " *Sieg Heil! Sieg Heil! Sieg
Heil! Heil Hitler! Heil Hitler! Heil Hitler! Hang
Schuschnigg! Hang Schuschnigg! Hang Schuschnigg! Ein Volk, ein Reich, ein Führer!* " And the
police! They were looking on, grinning. What had
happened? I was still in the dark. I shouted my ques-

tion into the ears of three or four jammed against me. No response. Couldn't hear. Finally a middle-aged woman seemed to get me. " The plebiscite! " she yelled. " Called off! "

There was no need to learn more. That was the end of Austria. I extricated myself from the swirling dervishes and made my way down the Ring to the Hotel Bristol. Taylor was there. He introduced me to his wife, Vreni, pretty, brunette, intelligent-looking, who had just arrived. He confirmed the news. It had been announced an hour before on the radio, he said. We took a taxi to the American Legation. John Wiley was standing before his desk, clutching his invariable long cigarette-holder, a queer smile on his face — the smile of someone who has just been defeated and knows it.

" It's all over," he said quietly. There had been an ultimatum from Berlin. No plebiscite, or the German army marches. Schuschnigg had capitulated.

" You'll hear more on the radio shortly," John said. " Stick around."

I left to put in a call for Murrow, who's in Warsaw. Going out of the Legation I stumbled into Gedye, very excited. Home, I put in a call for Ed, my radio playing softly a Viennese waltz. Hateful, it sounded. It stopped abruptly. " Attention! Attention! " a voice said. " In a few minutes you will hear an important announcement." Then the ticking of a metronome, the Ravag's identification signal. Maddening, it sounded. Tick . . . tick . . . tick . . . tick. I turned it down. Then a voice — Schuschnigg's, I recognized — without introduction.

" This day has placed us in a tragic and decisive situation. I have to give my Austrian fellow countrymen the details of the events of today.

" The German Government today handed to President Miklas an ultimatum, with a time limit, ordering him to nominate as chancellor a person designated by the German Government and to appoint members of a cabinet on the orders of the German Government; otherwise German troops would invade Austria.

" I declare before the world that the reports launched in Germany concerning disorders by the workers, the shedding of streams of blood, and the creation of a situation beyond the control of the Austrian Government are lies from A to Z. President Miklas has asked me to tell the people of Austria that we have yielded to force since we are not prepared even in this terrible situation to shed blood. We have decided to order the troops to offer no resistance.

" So I take leave of the Austrian people with a German word of farewell uttered from the depth of my heart: God protect Austria."

Towards the end you feel his voice will break; that there will be sobbing. But he controls it to the last. There is a second silence. And then the national anthem played from an old record. It is the tune of *Deutschland über Alles,* only in the original and slightly different version as Haydn first composed it. That is all. That is the end.

The rest of this evening? A little later the rasping voice of Judas. Dr. Seyss-Inquart is saying something, saying he considers himself responsible for order, saying the Austrian army is not to offer resistance. This is the first we hear of the German invasion. The ultimatum, Schuschnigg says, said capitulate *or* invasion. Now Hitler has broken even the terms of his own ultimatum.

I cannot get Ed in Warsaw. His hotel keeps saying he's out. It is still early. I call the Austrian Broadcasting System to see about my broadcast. No answer.

I start downtown. In the Karlsplatz there's a tremendous crowd. Someone is shouting a speech from the steps of the Karlskirche. "Hess and Buerckel," a storm trooper near me whispers. His uniform gave off a stench of moth balls. "Hess and Buerckel! They're here." But I could not get near enough to see.

I fought my way out of the crowd towards the Kärntnerstrasse. Crowds moving about all the way. Singing now. Singing Nazi songs. A few policemen standing around good-naturedly. What's that on their arm? A red-black-white Swastika arm-band! So they've gone over too! I worked my way up Kärntnerstrasse towards the Graben. Young toughs were heaving paving blocks into the windows of the Jewish shops. The crowd roared with delight.

Over at the Café Louvre Bob Best of U.P. is sitting at the same table he has occupied every night for the last ten years. Around him a crowd of foreign correspondents, male and female, American, English, Hungarian, Serb. All but Best in a great state of excitement, running to the phone every five minutes to get some news or give it. The most fantastic rumours. Bob reads over to me his dispatches. He is called away to the phone. He comes back. Schuschnigg has been recalled as chancellor and the Nazis are out, he says. He is optimistic; things are not over yet. A few minutes later: it's a false report. The Nazis have taken over at the Ballhausplatz. We sprint over to the Ballhausplatz, Metternich's Ballhausplatz . . . Congress of Vienna. . . . Twenty storm troopers are standing on one another before the building, forming a human pyramid. A little fellow scampers to the top of the heap, clutching a huge Swastika flag. He pulls himself up to the balcony, the same balcony where four years ago Major

Fey, held prisoner by the Nazis after Dollfuss was shot, parleyed with the Schuschnigg people. He unfurls the flag from the balcony and the *Platz* rings with cheers.

Back to the Louvre. Martha Fodor is there, fighting to keep back the tears, every few minutes phoning the news to Fodor. Emil Maass, my former assistant, an Austro-American, who has long posed as an anti-Nazi, struts in, stops before the table. " Well, *meine Damen und Herren*," he smirks, " it was about time." And he turns over his coat lapel, unpins his hidden Swastika button, and repins it on the outside over the button-hole. Two or three women shriek: " Shame! " at him. Major Goldschmidt, Legitimist, Catholic, but half Jewish, who has been sitting quietly at the table, rises. " I will go home and get my revolver," he says. Some-one rushes in. Seyss-Inquart is forming a Nazi govern-ment. It is a little after eleven p.m. Time to go over to Broadcasting House. Five p.m. in New York.

In the Johannesgasse, before the Ravag building, men in field-grey uniforms stand guard with fixed bayo-nets. I explain who I am. After a long wait they let me in. The vestibule and corridor are full of young men in army uniforms, in S.S. and S.A. uniforms, brandish-ing revolvers, playing with bayonets. Two or three stop me, but taking my courage in my hand I bark at them and make my way into the main hall, around which are the studios. Czeja, the *General-Direktor* of Ravag, and Erich Kunsti, program director, old friends, stand in the middle of the room, surrounded by excited, chattering Nazi boys. One glance. They are prisoners. I manage to get in a word with Kunsti.

" How soon can I go on the air? " I say.

He shrugs his shoulders. " I've ceased to exist around here," he laughs. He beckons towards a scar-faced chap who seems to be the boss, for the moment anyway. I explain my wants. No impression. I do it again. He doesn't get me.

"Let me talk to your chiefs in Berlin," I say. "I know them. They'll want me to broadcast."

"Can't get through to Berlin," he says.

"But you will, some time tonight," I say.

"Well, maybe later. You can come back."

"Not a chance," Kunsti whispers. A couple of guards, fingering their revolvers, edge me out. I wait outside in the hall, barging in every so often to see if Scarface has Berlin on the phone. Around midnight a broadcast comes through from the Ballhausplatz. A new government is to be announced soon. I dash over there. Spotlights (from where?) play on the balcony. A dozen men are standing there. I make out Seyss-Inquart, Glaise-Horstenau. . . . Judas is reading his new Cabinet list. He himself is Chancellor.

Back to Ravag. Wait. Argument. Wait. Argument. They cannot get Berlin. There is no wire. No broadcast possible. Sorry. More arguments. Threats. In the end I'm escorted out. No argument with bayonets. Out in the Johannesgasse I look at my watch. Three a.m. I go up to the Kärntnerstrasse once more. Deserted now. Home then.

The phone rings. It is Ed in Warsaw. I tell him the news. And our bad news. Even if I remain here tomorrow and do get facilities, we'll be under strict Nazi censorship, I say.

"Fly to London, why don't you?" Ed suggests. "You can get there by tomorrow evening and give the first uncensored eyewitness account. And I'll come down to Vienna."

A phone call to the Aspern airport. All planes booked tomorrow. What time do the London and Ber-

lin planes leave? Seven a.m.; eight a.m. Thank you.
I forget I have not spoken to Fodor on this night. The
Nazis don't like him. Maybe. . . . I phone. " I'm all
right, Bill," he says. He's sobbing. A line to Tess explaining why she will not see me for a few days. Now
to bed. An hour of sleep.

In a Dutch plane between Amsterdam and London, *March* 12

Have just finished scrawling out a script.
Can go on the air as soon as we get into London. Went
to work on it just after we took off from Tempelhof in
Berlin, Amsterdam being the next stop and so no danger of a Nazi censor. I've had luck today. I was at the
Aspern airport at seven a.m. The Gestapo had taken
over. At first they said no planes would be allowed to
take off. Then they cleared the London plane. But I
could not get on. I offered fantastic sums to several
passengers for their places. Most of them were Jews
and I could not blame them for turning me down. Next
was the plane to Berlin. I got on that.

Vienna was scarcely recognizable this morning.
Swastika flags flying from nearly every house. Where
did they get them so fast? Another piece of news at
Aspern from a police official I had known slightly.
Schuschnigg has not fled, he insisted. Refused, though
they kept an airplane waiting until midnight for him.
Guts. The airfield at Aspern already crowded with
German war planes when we took off. We came down at
Prague and Dresden and it was noon before we arrived
in Berlin. More luck. A seat on a Dutch plane straight
through to London. I had an hour for lunch. I bought
the morning Berlin newspapers. Amazing! Goebbels
at his best, or worst! Hitler's own newspaper, the

Völkische Beobachter, on my lap here. Its screaming banner-line across page one: GERMAN–AUSTRIA SAVED FROM CHAOS. And an incredible story out of Goebbels's evil but fertile brain describing violent Red disorders in the main streets of Vienna yesterday, fighting, shooting, pillaging. It is a complete *lie*. But how will the German people know it's a lie? The DNB also has a story today that sounds phony. It claims Seyss-Inquart last night telegraphed to Hitler to send troops to protect Austria from armed Socialists and Communists. Since there were no "armed Socialists and Communists" in Vienna last night, this obviously is also a lie. But interesting to note Hitler's technique. The same which was used to justify the June 30 purge. Any lie will do. Croydon now just ahead of us.

LATER, *London*. — Broadcast at eleven thirty p.m. And now for some sleep.

LONDON, *March* 14

At one a.m. this morning (eight p.m. yesterday, New York time) we did our first European radio round-up. It came off like this.

About five o'clock yesterday afternoon my telephone rang. Paul W. White, Columbia's director of public affairs, was calling from New York. He said: "We want a European round-up tonight. One a.m. your time. We want you and some member of Parliament from London, Ed Murrow of course from Vienna, and American newspaper correspondents from Berlin, Paris, and Rome. A half-hour show, and I'll telephone you the exact time for each capital in about an hour. Can you and Murrow do it?"

I said yes, and we hung up. The truth is I didn't

have the faintest idea how to do it — in eight hours, anyway. We had done one or two of these, but there had
been *months* of fussing over technical arrangements before each one. I put in a long-distance call to Murrow
in Vienna. And as valuable minutes ticked away I considered what to do. The more I thought about it, the
simpler it became. Murrow and I have newspaper
friends, American correspondents, in every capital in
Europe. We also know personally the directors and
chief engineers of the various European broadcasting
systems whose technical facilities we must use. I called
Edgar Mowrer in Paris, Frank Gervasi in Rome, Pierre
Huss in Berlin, and the directors and chief engineers
of PTT in Paris, EIAR in Turin, and the RRG in
Berlin.

Murrow came through from Vienna; he undertook to
arrange the Berlin as well as the Vienna end and gave
me a badly needed technical lesson as to how the entire
job could be done. For each capital we needed a powerful short-wave transmitter that would carry a voice
clearly to New York. Rome had one, but its availability
was doubtful. Paris had none. In that case we must
order telephone lines to the nearest short-wave trans-
mitting station. Before long my three telephones were
buzzing, and in four languages: English, German,
French, and Italian. The first three I know fairly well,
but my Italian scarcely exists. Still, I understood
enough from Turin to get the idea that no executives
of the Italian Broadcasting Company could be reached
at the moment. Alas, it was Sunday. I still had Rome
coming in. Perhaps I could arrange matters with the
branch office there. Berlin came through. The Reichs-
Rundfunk-Gesellschaft would do its best. Only, they
explained, the one line to Vienna was in the hands of
the army and therefore doubtful.

As the evening wore on, the broadcast began to take shape. New York telephoned again with the exact times scheduled for each capital. New York's brazen serenity, its confidence that the broadcast would come off all right, encouraged me. My newspaper friends started to come through. Edgar Mowrer, Paris correspondent of the Chicago *Daily News*, was spending Sunday in the country. Much urging to persuade him to return to town to broadcast. But Edgar couldn't fool me. No man, I knew, felt more intensely than he what had happened in Austria. Gervasi in Rome and Huss in Berlin came through. They would broadcast if their New York office agreed. Not much time to inquire at the New York newpaper offices, especially on Sunday afternoon. Another call to Columbia in New York: Get permission for Gervasi and Huss to talk. And by the way, New York said, what transmitters and wave-lengths are Berlin and Rome using? I had forgotten about that. Another call to Berlin. The station would be DJZ, 25.2 metres, 11,870 kilocycles. An urgent cable carried the information to the CBS control room in New York.

Time was getting short. I remembered that I must also write out a talk for the London end of the show. What was Britain going to do about Hitler's invasion of Austria? I telephoned around town for material. Britain wasn't going to do anything. New York also wanted a member of Parliament, I suddenly recalled, to discuss British official reaction to the *Anschluss*. I called two or three M.P. friends. They were all enjoying the English week-end. I called Ellen Wilkinson, Labour M.P. So was she.

" How long will it take you to drive to the BBC? " I asked her.

" About an hour," she said.

I looked at my watch. We had a little more than two hours to go. She agreed to talk.

Gervasi's voice from Rome was on the line. "The Italians can't arrange it on such short notice," he said. "What shall I do?"

I wondered myself. "We'll take you over Geneva," I finally said. "And if that's impossible, phone me back in an hour with your story and I'll read it from here."

Sitting alone in a small studio in Broadcasting House, I had a final check-up with New York three minutes before one a.m. We went over the exact timings of each talk and checked the cues which would be the signals for the speakers in Vienna, Berlin, Paris, and London to begin and end their talks. Rome was out, I told our control room in New York, but Gervasi was on the telephone this minute, dictating his story to a stenographer. We agreed upon a second switchback to London from New York so that I could read it. One a.m. came, and through my earphones I could hear on our transatlantic "feedback" the smooth voice of Bob Trout announcing the broadcast from our New York studio. Our part went off all right, I think. Edgar and Ed were especially good. Ellen Wilkinson, flaunting her red hair, arrived in good time. New York said on the "feedback" afterwards that it was a success. They want another one tonight.

Hitler, say the dispatches, entered Vienna in triumph this afternoon. Nobody fired. Chamberlain has just spoken in the House. He is not going to do anything. "The hard fact is," he says, "that nothing could have arrested what has actually happened — unless this country and other countries had been prepared to use force." There will be no war. Britain and France have retreated one step more before the rising Nazi power.

LATER. — Albion Ross of the New York *Times* staff in Berlin had an interesting line in his talk on our round-up tonight. He said the Berliners had taken the *Anschluss* with " phlegmatic calm."

London, *March* 15

Hitler, speaking in Vienna from the balcony of the Hofburg, palace of the once mighty Habsburgs, today proclaimed the incorporation of Austria in the German Reich. Still another promise broken. He could not even wait for the plebiscite, scheduled for April 10. Talked with Winston Churchill on the phone this morning. He will do a fifteen-minute broadcast, but wants five hundred dollars.

London, *March* 16

Ed telephoned from Vienna. He said Major Emil Fey has committed suicide after putting bullets through his wife and nineteen-year-old son. He was a sinister man. Undoubtedly he feared the Nazis would murder him for having double-crossed them in 1934 when Dollfuss was shot. I return to Vienna day after tomorrow. The crisis is over. I think we've found something, though, for radio with these round-ups.

Vienna, *March* 19

Ed met me at Aspern airport last evening. When we arrived at dusk before my house in the Ploesslgasse, S.S. guards in steel helmets and with fixed bayonets were standing before my door. A glance up the street showed they were guarding all doors, especially that of the Rothschild palace next to us. Ed and I started into our place, but the Nazi guards prodded us back.

"I live here," I said, suddenly angry.

"Makes no difference. You can't go in," one of the guards countered.

"I said I *lived* here!"

"Sorry. Strict orders. No one can enter or leave." He was an Austrian lad, his accent showed, and polite, and my anger subsided.

"Where can I find your commandant?" I asked.

"In the Rothschild palace."

He gave us a towering S.S. man, who escorted us into the gardener's house which adjoined our building and where Rothschild had actually resided the last year. As we entered we almost collided with some S.S. officers who were carting up silver and other loot from the basement. One had a gold-framed picture under his arm. One was the commandant. His arms were loaded with silver knives and forks, but he was not embarrassed. I explained my business and our nationality. He chuckled and told the guard to escort us to my door.

"But you'll have to stay there for a while," he laughed.

We stayed until after dinner. Then wishing to go downtown we crept down the stairs, waited until our guard had paced several steps away from the door, and sneaked out on tiptoe in the darkness. We found a quiet bar off the Kärntnerstrasse for a talk. Ed was a little nervous.

"Let's go to another place," he suggested.

"Why?"

"I was here last night about this time," he said. "A Jewish-looking fellow was standing at that bar. After a while he took an old-fashioned razor from his pocket and slashed his throat."

Tess none too well. The phlebitis still critical. And
her nerves not exactly soothed by the shock of what has
been happening and the noise of Göring's bombers over
the hospital all day long. Ed flies back to London in
the morning.

V I E N N A , *March* 20

Broadcast this morning. Described how Vienna has been completely Nazified in a week — a
terrifying thing. One of the American radio networks
had emphasized all week that *its* correspondent was not
censored in what he said from here. But when he arrived at the studio to go on the air just after me, the
Nazis demanded his script as well as mine and gave it a
going-over.

V I E N N A , *March* 22

Tess's condition still critical. And the atmosphere in the hospital has not helped. First, Tess says,
there was a Jewish lady whose brother-in-law committed
suicide the day Hitler entered town. She screamed all
the first night. Today she left in black mourning clothes
and veil, clutching her baby. There was a second Jewish
lady. No one in her family was murdered, but the S.A.,
after taking over her husband's business, proceeded to
their home and looted it. She fears her husband will be
killed or arrested, and weeps all night long.

On the streets today gangs of Jews, with jeering
storm troopers standing over them and taunting crowds
around them, on their hands and knees scrubbing the
Schuschnigg signs off the sidewalks. Many Jews killing themselves. All sorts of reports of Nazi sadism,
and from the Austrians it surprises me. Jewish men

and women made to clean latrines. Hundreds of them just picked at random off the streets to clean the toilets of the Nazi boys. The lucky ones get off with merely cleaning cars — the thousands of automobiles which have been stolen from the Jews and " enemies " of the regime. The wife of a diplomat, a Jewess, told me to-day she dared not leave her home for fear of being picked up and put to " scrubbing things."

VIENNA, *March 25*

Went with Gillie to see the synagogue in the Seitenstättengasse, which was also the headquarters of the Jewish *Kultusgemeinde*. We had been told that the Jews had been made to scrub out toilets with the sacred praying-bands, the *Tefillin*. But the S.S. guards wouldn't let us in. Inside we could see the guards lolling about smoking pipes. On our way to lunch in a little Italian restaurant back of the Cathedral, Gillie had a run-in with some storm troopers who took him for a Jew though he is the purest of Scots. Very annoying and we drowned our feelings in Chianti. Knick here, and Agnes, though Knick will depart shortly as he is barred from Germany and is not supposed to be here. Huss here trying to get the local INS correspondent, Alfred Tyrnauer, out of jail. His wife most frantic when I talked with her on the phone. The Fodors have gone to Bratislava, taken there on the initiative of John Wiley, who sent them out in a Legation car. Schuschnigg under arrest, and the story is that the Nazis torture him by keeping the radio in his room on night and day.

Vienna, *April* 8

Tess and baby at last home from the hospital. I carried her upstairs from the car this morning and it will be some time before she can walk. But the worst is over.

Vienna, *April* 10 (*Palm Sunday*)

The " plebiscite " passed off today in a weird sort of holiday atmosphere. The Austrians, according to Goebbels's count, have voted ninety-nine per cent *Ja*. Maybe so. It took a brave Austrian to vote *No*, as everyone felt the Nazis had some way of checking up on how they voted. This afternoon I visited a polling station in the Hofburg. The room, I imagine, had once been occupied by the Emperor's guard. I went inside one of the booths. Pasted on the wall in front of you was a sample ballot showing you how to mark yours with a *Yes*. There was also a wide slit in the corner of the booth which gave the election committee sitting a few feet away a pretty good view of how you voted! Broadcast for fifteen minutes at seven thirty p.m., and though the polls had just closed, I said the Austrians were voting ninety-nine per cent *Yes*. A Nazi official told me so just as I went on the air and I assumed he knew. Probably he knew yesterday. And so Austria to-day " votes " away its centuries-old independence and joins the Greater Reich. *Finis Austria!*

Vienna, *April* 12

This crisis has done one thing for us. I think radio talks by Ed and me are now established. Birth of the " radio foreign correspondent," so to speak.

Vienna, *April* 14

Czechoslovakia will certainly be next on Hitler's list. Militarily it is doomed now that Germany has
it flanked on the south as well as the north. All our
broadcasts from Prague now must go by telephone line
through Germany, even if we take them via Geneva.
That will be bad in case of trouble. Must ask the Czechs
about their new short-wave transmitter when I go to
Prague tomorrow.

Prague, *April* 16

Put on President Beneš and Miss Alice
Masaryk in a broadcast to America tonight. Yesterday
I expressed the hope that Dr. Beneš would say something about the German question, though their theme
tonight was ostensibly the Red Cross. Dr. Beneš obliged
me beautifully, though his language was moderate and
reasonable. Strange, then, that when he got to the German question he was badly faded out. Unfortunately
New York booked the show via the German short-wave
station at Zeesen instead of through Geneva as I had
asked. I suspect the Germans faded out Beneš on purpose, though Berlin denied it when I spoke with the
people there on the phone after the broadcast. They
said the fault was here in Prague. The Czechs deny it.
I had a long talk tonight with Svoboda, chief engineer
of the Czech Broadcasting System, urging him to rush
work on his new short-wave transmitter, explaining
that if the Germans got tough, that would be Prague's
only outlet. Promised our co-operation in making
transatlantic tests. A good-natured fellow, he does not
think the Germans will do anything until they've di-
gested Austria, which he thinks will take years. But he
promised to get along with the new *Sender*.

VIENNA, *April* 17 (*Easter*)

Got home this morning. Tess better and we presented the baby with a giant Easter egg I had bought in Prague yesterday. Much fun.

ROME, *May* 2

Some time during the night S.S. Black Guards at the Austro-Italian border got me out of bed in my *wagons-lits* compartment and seized all my money. They argued a long time among themselves about arresting me, but finally desisted. Hitler arriving this evening at sundown. I'm broadcasting from the roof of the royal stables overlooking the entrance to the Quirinale Palace and have it timed for the moment the King and the Führer are due to arrive.

LATER. — Unfortunately for me, the horses pulling Hitler's carriage galloped faster than we all anticipated. When I went on the air this evening, he had arrived, entered the palace, come out and bowed to the populace, disappeared, and as my microphone opened there was nothing left to describe. I had made notes, however, about the background of the visit and had received descriptive reports in German by radio of his dramatic ride up the Triumphal Way, past the splendid ruins of ancient Rome, past the Colosseum, from whose archways columns of red fire flamed, to the palace. But it was pitch-dark when I went on the air, and the electric light attached to the mike suddenly failed. I could not make out a word of my notes. The only thing was to speak ad lib. from memory, but after standing on the wind-swept roof for five hours I discovered that the light in my memory had gone out too.

There was a row of torches burning near by on the roof in honour of Hitler's arrival. I motioned to an Italian engineer to fetch one. It flickered badly, but gave just enough light to enable me to make out a few key points in my scribbled notes. Feel, however, that I talked badly.

ROME, *May* 3

A cable of congratulations from Paul White on last night's talk, which cheers me up. The town full of dicks — fifty thousand of them, they say, German and Italian, to protect the two great men. All the foreign Jews here have been jailed or banished for the duration of the visit. The Italians hardly hide their hostility to the Germans. They watch them walk by, and then spit contemptuously. The Eternal City lovely in this springtime. Wandered down to the Piazza di Spagna, full of superb flowers stacked against the stairways leading up to the baroque church. I shall spend these days wandering about.

FLORENCE, *May* — ?

Followed Hitler up here, but did not have to broadcast. New York wanted me to look up some singing birds — of all things! — for a broadcast, but could not find them. Spent the day at the Uffizi, but somehow the Leonardos, Raphaels, Titians, even the Botticellis, pale a little after the Grecos in Spain. Walked along the Arno. Remembered the magnificent view from Fiesole, an old Etruscan town five miles up in the hills from here, but no time to revisit it. Back to Vienna tomorrow.

VIENNA, *May* 20

While Tess and I were dining tonight with Charles Dimont (of Reuter's) and his dark, beautiful wife in a little Hungarian restaurant near the Opera, he was called away to the phone. He came back greatly excited. London had called. German troops were reported marching on Czechoslovakia. He decided to hire a car and run up towards Bratislava and take a look. I decided to remain in town and get on the phone to Prague, Berlin, and London before jumping one way or the other.

VIENNA, *May* 21

Leaving tonight for Prague. The story is that Hitler has mobilized ten divisions along the Czech frontier. The Czechs have called up one class and have manned their " Maginot Line." Had hoped to remain here a few days since Tess must have another operation day after tomorrow. If there's no war in Czecho we hope to leave here definitely June 10 for our new headquarters in Geneva. Tess's Swiss visa expires then and it will be a long job to get another if we don't get away under the deadline. Have picked Geneva because it's no longer possible to do my job from here, what with the currency restrictions, the Nazi censorship and snooping, and all.

VIENNA, *June* 9

Leaving tomorrow. The Gestapo have been here for two days checking over my books and effects, but they were Austrian fellows and much beer and plenty of sausage made them agreeable and reasonable. Tess in no shape to travel, all bound up in bandages still, but we are going by air.

Geneva, *June* 10

A day! But we're here. Three bad moments.
First, when I went to collect five hundred marks owed
me by the manager of one of the shipping companies.
The Gestapo have been arresting people right and left
for " illegal " exchange transactions. Any passing of
money is suspect. When I walked into the manager's
inner office, X, a Nazi spy who had long posed here as
an anti-Nazi emigrant, stood there grinning at me. I
thought for a second it was a trap. But the manager,
an Englishman, walked down the Ring with me and
gave me the money. Still, X is probably out to get me,
I thought, and I was glad our plane was leaving in two
hours.

At the Aspern airport they behaved very suspiciously.
I explained to the Gestapo chief that Tess was too weak
to stand up and I would go over the luggage with him.
I had laid Tess out on a bench in the waiting-room. He
demanded that she stand up and explain things during
the customs examination. Otherwise we couldn't leave.
I tried to hold her up. Then a police official led me
away. I left the nurse to help as best she could. In a
little room two police officials went through my pocket-
book and my pockets. Everything was in order. They
then led me into a side room. " Wait here," they said.
I said I wanted to go back to help with the baggage inspection, that my wife was in a critical state; but they
shut the door. I heard the lock turn. I was locked in.
Five, ten, fifteen minutes. Pacing the floor. Time for
the airplane to leave. Past time. Then I heard Tess
shout: " Bill, they're taking me away to strip me! " I
had spoken with the Gestapo chief about that, explained
that she was heavily bandaged, the danger of infection
. . . I pounded on the door. No result. Through the

window I could hear and see the Swiss racing the two
motors of their Douglas plane, impatient to get away.
After a half-hour I was led out to a corridor connecting
the waiting-room with the airfield. I tried to get into
the waiting-room, but the door was locked. Finally
Tess came, the nurse supporting her with one arm and
holding the baby in the other.

" Hurry, there," snapped an official. " You've kept
the plane waiting a half-hour." I held my tongue and
grabbed Tess.

She was gritting her teeth, as angry as I've ever seen
her. " They stripped me, the . . ." she kept saying. I
thought she was going to turn and scratch at the official
following us. We hurried across the runway to the
plane. I wondered what could happen in the next seconds before we were in the plane and safe. Maybe X
would come running out and demand my arrest. Then
we were in the plane and it was racing across the field.

Flew blind in storm clouds along the Alps all the way
from Vienna to Zürich, the plane pitching and tossing
and most of the passengers sick and scared. Then there
was Zürich down there, Switzerland, sanity, civilization
again.

LAUSANNE, *June* (*undated*)

We came up the lake on a paddle-steamer,
Tess and Ed Murrow and I, on this glorious June afternoon, the water blue like the Mediterranean, the shores
splashing green, the Jura mountains to the left, a deep,
smoky blue, the Alps to the right, pink and white under
the snow and sun. It was almost overwhelming. Ed and
I here for the semi-annual conference of the International Broadcasting Union. As associate instead of
regular members we refrain from the scraps of the Euro-

pean broadcasters and merely observe, which gives us
time for extra-curricular activities. The Broadcasting
Union, at that, is one of the few examples of real European co-operation. Reason: if the broadcasters don't
co-operate, especially in the matter of wave-lengths,
there won't be any European radio. The Czechs and
some of the English here much exercised about an editorial in the London *Times* on June 3 advising the
Czechs to hold a plebiscite for the Sudeten Germans and
if they want to join the Reich to let them. The *Times*
argues that if this is done, Germany would lose any
claim to interfere in the affairs of Czechoslovakia. The
Old Lady simply won't learn. Ed and Dick Marriot of
BBC, an intelligent and courageous young man, very
pessimistic about the strength and designs of the " appeasement " crowd in London. Major Atkinson of
BBC, whose English translation of Spengler's *Decline
of the West* is even better than the original — one of
the few great translations from the German, an almost
untranslatable language — and who is also a terrific
expert on the American Civil War, came charging up
to me this evening on the terrace where we were having
coffee, a bottle of red Burgundy in one hand and a large
globular glass in the other, and said: " Shirer, what
would have happened at Gettysburg if Lee had . . ."
and he went into some complicated military problem. I
see we shall be fighting the Civil War over here. And
these English military chaps know much more about it
than any American civilian.

ÉVIAN-LES-BAINS, *July* 7

Delegates from thirty-two states here, on
Roosevelt's initiative, to discuss doing something about
refugees from the Third Reich. Myron C. Taylor,

heading the American delegation, elected permanent
president of the committee today. I doubt if much will
be done. The British, French, and Americans seem too
anxious not to do anything to offend Hitler. It's an
absurd situation. They want to appease the man who is
responsible for their problem. The Nazis of course will
welcome the democracies' taking the Jews off their hands
at the democracies' expense. I guess I was a little hasty
thinking the " radio foreign correspondent " had been
born at the time of the *Anschluss*. I've put on Taylor
for a broadcast, but have no invitation from New York
to talk myself on the program of this conference. We
are not really covering it at all. Stumbled into Jimmy
Sheean, whom I have not seen since our Paris days ten
years ago. We had a big reunion at the Casino last
night, Robert Dell of the *Manchester Guardian*, a grand
old man, joining us. Jimmy broke the bank at the
baccarat table while I was winning a couple of thousand
francs more laboriously at roulette, Dell, who is in his
sixties, remaining in the hall to dance. Dinah Sheean
joined us during the evening, she beautiful with large
intelligent eyes. Renewing acquaintance with other old
friends, Bob Pell of the American delegation, John
Elliott, and others. Should mention John Winant,
whom I met a month ago in Geneva and who has been
here, a very likable person, liberal, awkward in manner,
a bit Lincolnesque.

PRAGUE, *August* 4

Lord Runciman arrived today to gum up the
works and sell the Czechs short if he can. He and his
Lady and staff, with piles of baggage, proceeded to the
town's swankiest hotel, the Alcron, where they have al-

most a whole floor. Later Runciman, a taciturn thin-
lipped little man with a bald head so round it looks like
a mis-shapen egg, received us — about three hundred
Czech and foreign reporters — in the reception hall. I
thought he went out of his way to thank the Sudeten
leaders, who, along with Czech Cabinet members, turned
out to meet him at the station, for *their* presence.

Runciman's whole mission smells. He says he has
come here to mediate between the Czech government and
the Sudeten party of Konrad Henlein. But Henlein is
not a free agent. He cannot negotiate. He is completely under the orders of Hitler. The dispute is between Prague and Berlin. The Czechs know that Chamberlain personally wants Czechoslovakia to give in to
Hitler's wishes. These wishes we know : incorporation of
all Germans within the Greater Reich. Someone tonight — Walter Kerr, I think, of the *Herald Tribune*,
produced a clipping from his paper of a dispatch
written by its London correspondent, Joseph Driscoll,
after he had participated in a luncheon with Chamberlain given by Lady Astor. It dates back to last May,
but makes it clear that the Tory government goes so
far as to favour Czecho ceding the Sudetenland outright to Germany. Before the Czechs do this, I'm convinced, they'll fight. For it would mean giving up their
natural defences and their Maginot Line. It would
mean their end. They're willing to give the Sudetens
practical autonomy. But Henlein demands the right to
set up a little Sudeten Nazi state within the state. Once
he has this, of course, he will secede to Germany.

Dined tonight at the Baarandov, overlooking the
lovely Moldau, with Jeff Cox of the *Daily Express* and
Kerr. Prague, with its Gothic and baroque architecture, its winding little streets, its magnificent Charles

Bridge across the Moldau, and the bluffs on one side on which perches the Hradshin castle built by the Habsburgs, has more character than almost any other city in Europe.

Testing daily with Czech radio engineers their new short-wave transmitter. Our engineers in New York, working with RCA, sending a daily report now of reception there. Sunday we will try it out for the first time with a broadcast of some Czech army manœuvres. Svoboda does not think it will carry well to New York.

P r a g u e , *August* 14

A few minutes before we went on the air this afternoon, while the troops on the ground and the air force in the air were rehearsing a grand show, a Skoda fighter diving from ten thousand feet failed to come fully out of its dive. It crashed in front of my microphone and skidded a couple of hundred feet past me. When it came to a stop it was a mass of twisted metal. I was talking at the time, describing the dive. Phoebe Packard of U.P., who was helping in the broadcast, says I kept on shouting into the mike when it crashed, but I do not remember. The pilot and his observer were still alive when we extricated them from the wreckage, but I fear they will not live this day out. Four or five soldiers lying in a skirmish line in front of us were badly hurt when the plane skidded over them. We were all a bit paralysed and I offered to call off the broadcast, but the commanding general said we would go on. Phoebe, large, a bit masculine, and the only woman correspondent to go through both the Ethiopian and the Spanish wars, which have hardened her to such things, remained very calm, though obviously affected.

CBS engineers afterwards said there had been a little

too much gunfire for an ideal broadcast, but they were enthusiastic about the new Czech transmitter. It gives us an independent outlet now if the Germans cut the telephone lines.

PRAGUE, *August 24*

Runciman still fussing about, asking the Czechs to make all the concessions. He has the government busy now working out a plan of cantonal government *à la Suisse*. The situation being momentarily quiet, am going to Berlin tomorrow to take a look at the military parade Hitler is putting on for Horthy, Regent of Hungary.

BERLIN, *August 25*

The military attachés are still a little bit popeyed tonight. Among other things which the Reichs-wehr showed Horthy (and the world) in the big military parade was an enormous field-gun, at least an eleven-inch affair, hauled in four pieces on motor trucks. There were other big guns and new big tanks and the infantry goose-stepped very well. But the big motorized Bertha was the sensation of the day. No one has ever seen a cannon that big outside of a battleship, except for the railroad guns. And how the spectators applauded it! As if it were not inanimate, a cold piece of steel. When I called at the Embassy after the parade, our military experts were busy working out sketches of the gun from memory. No photographing was allowed, except for one or two official shots which did not show much. Ralph [Barnes] as excited as a cat. Some of the American correspondents, more friendly than others to the Nazis, laughed at me at the Taverne tonight when I maintained the Czechs would fight.

Geneva, *September* 9

One last fleeting visit with the family before the war clouds break. In Berlin the best opinion is that Hitler has made up his mind for war if it is necessary to get back his Sudetens. I doubt it for two reasons: first, the German army is not ready; secondly, the people are dead against war. The radio has been saying all day that Great Britain has told Germany she will fight if Czecho is invaded. Perhaps so, but you cannot forget the *Times* leader of three days ago inviting the Czechs to become a more " homogeneous state " by handing the Sudetens over to Hitler.

The atmosphere here in Geneva is delightfully unreal. On Monday the 102nd meeting of the League Council and the 19th meeting of the Assembly open and all the internationalists are convening here to do nothing. The Czech situation is not even on the agenda, and won't be. Who was it put it so well the other day as we were walking along Lake Geneva and the great League Secretariat building came into view? Someone. " A beautiful granite sepulchre! Let us admire its beauty against the green hills and the mountains. There, my friend, are buried the dead hopes of peace for our generation."

Tess, with baby, off to America towards the end of the month to establish residence for her citizenship. I off to Prague tomorrow by plane to cover the peace or the war. Have almost convinced CBS they should let me talk five minutes daily — revolutionary in the broadcasting business!

PRAGUE, *September* 10

All Europe waiting for Hitler's final word to be pronounced at the wind-up of the Nazi Party rally at Nuremberg day after tomorrow. In the meantime we had two speeches today, one by President Beneš here; the other by Göring at Nuremberg, where all week the Nazis have been thundering threats against Czechoslovakia. Beneš, who spoke from the studio of the Czech Broadcasting System, was calm and reasonable — too much so, I thought, though he was obviously trying to please the British. He said: " I firmly believe that nothing other than moral force, goodwill, and mutual trust will be needed. . . . Should we, in peace, solve our nationality affairs . . . our country will be one of the most beautiful, best administered, worthiest, and most equitable countries in the world. . . . I do not speak through fear of the future. I have never been afraid in my life. I have always been an optimist, and my optimism is stronger today than at any other time. . . . Let us all preserve calmness . . . but let us be optimistic . . . and, above all, let us not forget that faith and goodwill move mountains. . . ."

Dr. Beneš delivered it in both Czech and German, so that I understood it, and running into him in the hall of the Broadcasting House when he had finished, I wanted to rush up and say: " But you are dealing with gangsters, with Hitler and Göring! " But I did not have the nerve and merely nodded good-evening and he walked on, a brave little Czech peasant's son who has made many mistakes in the last two decades, but who, when all is said and done, stands for the democratic decencies that Hitler is out to destroy. His face was grave, not nearly so optimistic as his words, and I doubt not he knows the terrible position he is in.

The other speech, Göring's, as given out by Reuter's here: " A petty segment of Europe is harassing human beings. . . . This miserable pygmy race [the Czechs] without culture — no one knows where it came from — is oppressing a cultured people and behind it is Moscow and the eternal mask of the Jew devil. . . ."

PRAGUE, *September* 11

All quiet here, but you can cut the tension with a knife. Reports that the Germans have massed two hundred thousand troops on the Austro-Czech border. In London continuous conferences in Downing Street. In Paris Daladier conferring with Gamelin. But all awaiting Hitler's speech tomorrow. CBS finally okays a five-minute daily report from here, but asks me to cable beforehand when I think the news does not warrant my taking the time.

PRAGUE, *September* 12

The Great Man has spoken. And there's no war, at least not for the moment. That is Czechoslovakia's first reaction to Hitler's speech at Nuremberg tonight. Hitler hurled insults and threats at Prague. But he did not demand that the Sudetens be handed over to him outright. He did not even demand a plebiscite. He insisted, however, on " self-determination " for the Sudetens. I listened to the broadcast of the speech in the apartment of Bill and Mary Morrell overlooking Wilson station. The smoke-filled room was full of correspondents — Kerr, Cox, Maurice Hindus, and so on. I have never heard the Adolf quite so full of hate, his audience quite so on the borders of bedlam. What poison in his voice when at the beginning of his long recital of alleged wrongs to the Sudeteners he paused: " *Ich spreche von der Czechoslovakei!* " His words, his tone, dripping with venom.

Everyone in Czechoslovakia seems to have listened to the speech, the streets being deserted tonight from eight to ten. An extraordinary meeting of the Inner Cabinet Council was convoked immediately afterwards, but Beneš did not attend. Morrell and I put in calls to Karlsbad and Reichenberg to see if the three and a half million Sudeteners had gone berserk after the speech. Fortunately there had been a pouring rain throughout the country. Some six thousand Henlein enthusiasts, wearing Swastika arm bands, paraded the streets of Karlsbad afterwards shouting: " Down with the Czechs and Jews! We want a plebiscite! " But there was no clash. Same story at Reichenberg.

Prague on this day when war and peace have apparently hung in the balance has been dark and dismal, with a cold, biting, soaking rain. I roamed through the old streets most of the day trying to see how a people react with war and invasion staring them in the face and when you know that in twenty-one minutes from the moment of declaration of war, if there is a declaration of war, the bombs may come raining down on you. The Czechs were going about their business as usual, not gloomy, not depressed, not frightened. Either they haven't any nerves at all, or perhaps they're the people with the iron nerves.

The Russians — perhaps aided by the Czechs — did a beautiful job of jamming Hitler's speech tonight. Königsberg, Breslau, Vienna — all the stations in the east — were unintelligible. We had to go way over to Cologne before we could get a decent reception.

PRAGUE, *September* 13–14 (3 *a.m.*)

War very near, and since midnight we've been
waiting for the German bombers, but so far no sign.
Much shooting up in the Sudetenland, at Eger, Elbo-
gen, Falkenau, Habersbirk. A few Sudeteners and
Czechs killed and the Germans have been plundering
Czech and Jewish shops. So the Czechs very rightly
proclaimed martial law this morning in five Sudeten
districts. About seven this evening we learned that Henlein had sent a six-hour ultimatum to the government.
It was delivered at six p.m., expired at midnight. It demanded: repeal of martial law, withdrawal of Czech
police from the Sudetenland, " separation " of military
barracks from the civilian population. Whether it is
backed by Hitler we do not know, though after his
Nuremberg speech there seems little doubt that it is.
Anyway, the Czech government has turned it down. It
could not have done otherwise. It has made its choice.
It will fight. We wait now for Hitler's move.

The tension and confusion this night in the lobby of
the Ambassador Hotel, where the diplomats and correspondents gather, has been indescribable. Fascinating
to watch the reactions of people suddenly seized by
fear. Some can't take it. They let themselves go to a
point of hysteria, then in panic flee to — God knows
where. Most take it, with various degrees of courage
and coolness. In the lobby tonight: the newspapermen
milling around trying to get telephone calls through the
one lone operator. Jews excitedly trying to book on the
last plane or train. The wildest rumours coming in with
every new person that steps through the revolving door
from outside, all of us gathering around to listen, believing or disbelieving according to our feelings. Göring's bombers will come at midnight — unless the

Czechs accept the ultimatum. They will use gas. How can a man get a gas-mask? There are none. What do you do then? Beneš will accept the ultimatum. He must! The newspapermen racing up and down, furious about the telephones, about the Germans, keeping an ear cocked for the first bomb. Packard and Beattie of U.P., Steinkopf of A.P., Red Knickerbocker of INS, Whitaker and Fodor of the Chicago *Daily News*, Alex Small of the Chicago *Tribune*, Walter Kerr of the New York *Herald Tribune*, Gedye and Vadnay of the New York *Times*, and the English correspondents.

An element of comedy helps break the tension. Alex, behind a large beer, Phoebe Packard behind another, frown at a cable Alex has just received. It is from his boss, Colonel McCormick, instructing him with military precision how to cover the war. " Wars always start at dawn. Be there at dawn," cables the colonel, Alex says.

A timid American businessman creeps up to our table, introduces himself. " I'm getting a big kick out of this evening," he says. " You newspaper people certainly lead interesting lives."

" What'll you drink, sir? " someone asks him. We go on with our talk, shout for a telephone.

Midnight nears. Deadline for the ultimatum. An official from the Foreign Office comes in, his face grave. " *Abgelehnt*," he says in German. " Turned down." The ultimatum is turned down. The correspondents fly again to the telephone. Several Jews scurry out. The press agent of the Sudeten party, a big jovial fellow who usually drops in at this time to give us his news, comes in as usual. He is not jovial. " Have they turned it down? " he asks. He hardly waits for the answer. Grabbing a small bag he has left in the corner, he disappears through the door.

Packard or someone finally gets through to the

Sudetenland. They are fighting there with rifles, hand-grenades, machine-guns, tanks. It is war, everyone agrees. Bill Morrell comes through on the phone from Habersbirk. Will I pass his story on to the *Daily Express*? Yes, what is it? He is talking from the police station there, he says. In the corner of the room a few feet away, he says, under a sheet lie the bodies of four Czech gendarmes and one German. The Germans have shot dead all four gendarmes in the town, but Czech reinforcements have arrived and the government is now in control. I call up Mary, his wife, about to become a mother, and tell her Bill is all right. Time for my broadcast. I race up the street to Broadcasting House.

Out in the street, I must say, I felt just a little ashamed. The people in the street were quiet, unexcited. No troops, no police to be seen anywhere. Everybody going home to bed just as they always have. Broadcast, but we could not hear New York and I fear atmospherics. And so to bed.

PRAGUE, *September* 14 (*morning*)

A discouraging cable from Paul White. My broadcast last night failed to get through. Atmospherics or sun spots, he says. Off now for a drive through the Sudetenland to take a look at the fighting, with Hindus, Cox, Morrell.

EVENING. — Drove two hundred miles through Sudetenland. The fighting is all over. The revolt, inspired from Germany with German arms, has been put down. And the Czech police and military, acting with a restraint that is incredible, have suffered more casualties than the Sudeten Germans. Unless Hitler again interferes, the crisis has passed its peak. The

Sudeteners I talked to today very puzzled. They expected the German army to march in Monday night
after Hitler's speech, and when it didn't arrive, but
the Czech army did, their spirits dropped. Only at
Schwaderbach are the Henleinists holding out, and
that's because the Czechs can't fire into the town without their bullets hitting Reich territory. Henlein announces this afternoon from Asch the dissolution of
the committee which had been negotiating here with
the government. Ernst Kundt, his chief delegate, a
swarthy, passionate man and the most decent of the lot,
tells me he's remaining in Prague " if they don't kill
me."

Some time after dinner a newsboy rushed into the
lobby of the Ambassador with extra editions of a German-language paper, the only one I can read since I
do not know Czech. The headlines said: Chamberlain
to fly to Berchtesgaden tomorrow to see Hitler! The
Czechs are dumbfounded. They suspect a sell-out and
I'm afraid they're right. On the way to broadcast tonight, Hindus, who was with me and understands Czech,
stopped to listen to what the newsboys were shouting.
They were yelling, he said: " Extra! Extra! Read all
about how the mighty head of the British Empire
goes begging to Hitler!" I have not heard a better
comment this evening. Broadcast again, but fear we
did not get through. Mighty powerful sun spots at
work against us.

PRAGUE, *September* 15

Feel a little frustrated. New York cables
again that I failed to get through. Tonight I shall
cable my piece to be read. Henlein today issued a
proclamation demanding outright *Anschluss*, after

which he fled to Germany. The government has ordered his arrest as a traitor. Ed Beattie of U.P. telephoned this morning from Eger, and though he is an American to the core, Packard could not understand a word he said. Pack came running to me. " Beattie's gone nuts. Speaks in some strange language. Will you talk to him? " I got on the line. Ed explained in German he was speaking from a Czech police station, that the Czechs understood German and no English and had given him a line on condition he file his story in German so that they could check him. I took it down. Six killed there last night when Czech police stormed Henlein's headquarters in the Hotel Victoria.

Czechs, like everyone else, kept their eyes focused on Berchtesgaden today. Tonight they're asking if the peace which Mr. Chamberlain is trying to extract from Hitler does not call for them to make all the concessions. Government circles very gloomy. Murrow called from London and suggested I get off immediately to Berchtesgaden. Don't know whether I can. Czech trains have stopped running across the border and I can't find a Czech driver who will take his car across the frontier.

LATER. — Ed called to say Chamberlain was returning to London in the morning. My Berchtesgaden trip is off. Relieved. Prefer to cover this war from the Czech side.

Prague, *September* 16

Another cable from New York. For the third successive day they could not hear me, but read my piece which arrived by cable. This *is* bad luck for radio. Berlin reports Hitler has demanded — and Chamberlain more or less accepted — a plebiscite for the Sudeteners.

The government here says it is out of the question. But they are afraid *that* is what happened at Berchtesgaden. In other words that Mr. Chamberlain has sold them down the river. I say in my broadcast tonight: " Will the Czechs consent to breaking up their state and sacrificing their strategic mountain border which has protected Bohemia for a thousand years? . . . I get the impression they will not lie down and trust their fate even to a conference of the four big western powers. . . . The Czechs say: Supposing even that a plebiscite were accepted and the Sudetens turned over to Germany. As compensation Mr. Chamberlain, they think, would give them a guarantee against aggression, solemnly signed by Great Britain, France, Germany, Italy. But what, they ask, would another treaty be worth? "

LATER. — Hoorah! Heard New York perfectly on the feedback tonight and they heard me equally well. After four days of being blotted out, and *these* four days! Runciman has left for London, skipping out very quietly, unloved, unhonoured, unsung.

PRAGUE, *September* 18

The Czechs are stiffening as it becomes evident that Chamberlain is ready to support Hitler's demands for taking over Sudetenland and indeed, in effect, Czechoslovakia. Milo Hodza, the Premier, broadcast to the world today and uttered a definite no to the proposition of a plebiscite. " It is unacceptable. It will solve nothing," he said. Hodza, unlike most Slovaks, struck me as being very high-strung and nervous when I saw him at Broadcasting House after he finished talking. He showed visibly the strain of the last days. Is he talking strong, but weakening, I wonder.

LATER. — I must go to Germany. At midnight Murrow phoned from London with the news. The British and French have decided they will not fight for Czechoslovakia and are asking Prague to surrender unconditionally to Hitler and turn over Sudetenland to Germany. I protested to Ed that the Czechs wouldn't accept it, that they'd fight alone. . . .

" Maybe so. I hope you're right. But in the meantime Mr. Chamberlain is meeting Hitler at Godesberg on Wednesday and we want you to cover that. If there's a war, then you can go back to Prague."

" All right," I said.

I don't care where I go now. I finally collected myself and went over and routed Maurice Hindus out of bed, telling him the news, which he refused to believe. We telephoned to two or three friends in the Foreign Office. By the tone of their voices they had heard the news too, though they said not. They said it was too "fantastic" to believe, which of course it is. Maurice and I took a walk. People were going home from the cafés but they did not seem unduly excited and it was obvious they had not heard the reports from London.

Maurice is to broadcast while I'm away. I take a plane to Berlin in the morning. To bed, four a.m., weary and disgusted.

BERLIN, *September* 19

The Nazis, and quite rightly too, are jubilant over what they consider Hitler's greatest triumph up to date. " And without bloodshed, like all the others," they kept rubbing it in to me today. As for the good people in the street, they're immensely relieved. They do not want war. The Nazi press full of hysterical headlines. All lies. Some examples: WOMEN AND CHIL-

DREN MOWED DOWN BY CZECH ARMOURED CARS, or BLOODY REGIME — NEW CZECH MURDERS OF GERMANS. The *Börsen Zeitung* takes the prize: POISON–GAS ATTACK ON AUSSIG? The *Hamburger Zeitung* is pretty good: EXTORTION, PLUNDERING, SHOOTING — CZECH TERROR IN SUDETEN GERMAN LAND GROWS WORSE FROM DAY TO DAY!

No word from Prague tonight as to whether the Czechs will accept Chamberlain's ultimatum. I still hope against hope they will fight. For if they do, then there's a European war and Hitler can't win it. Ended my broadcast tonight thus: " One thing is certain: Mr. Chamberlain will certainly get a warm welcome at Godesberg. In fact, I got the impression in Berlin today that Mr. Chamberlain is a pretty popular figure around here."

On the train, Berlin–Godesberg, *September* 20

A weird broadcast we've just done. Paul White phoned from New York at six p.m. just as I was packing my bags. I told him he'd have to cancel my regular talk at ten thirty tonight as our train for Godesberg left at ten thirty. He suggested a broadcast from the train, interviewing the correspondents on the chances for peace or war at Godesberg. A phone call to the *Reichs Rundfunk*. Impossible to do it from the train. How about doing it from the Friedrichstrasse station, I asked. Will do, said Dr. Harald Diettrich, youthful, enterprising acting-head of the German short-wave department. A telephone call to New York. White delighted. When I arrived at the station five minutes before ten, when the broadcast was due to begin, the microphone was there and working.

But there were no American correspondents. The platform was empty. At ten I started to chat away ad lib. The only news I had was that the Hungarians and the Poles had been down to Berchtesgaden during the day to demand, like jackals, their share of the Czech spoils. This subject exhausted, I took to reading the headlines from the evening papers. The usual lies, but if I said so, the Nazis would cut me off. Headlines like this: **CZECH SOLDIERS ATTACK GERMAN EMPIRE!** I looked around. Still no correspondents. I hoped they would all miss the train. I talked along about the Czech minorities, I think it was. Finally Huss showed up. I grabbed him by the coat-tails and before he knew it he was on the air. The rest of the newspapermen finally arrived, but they seemed busy sorting out their luggage. Huss began to make frantic signs. God knows how the rest of the show sounded. I put on two or three Englishmen, then Sigrid Schultz, Webb Miller, Ralph Barnes. Philippo Boiano of the *Popolo d'Italia* motioned he wanted to speak. I knew how secretly he hated the Nazis, but I wasn't sure of his English. It was wonderful. No stage accent could have been half so good. Jouve of Havas wanted to talk too. Before I could ask him if he spoke English he was talking — in French. I started to translate what he had said, and then, out of the corner of my eye, I saw the train moving. My finishing sentence was not smooth, but I made the train. Fear the show was a flop at home, but there are more important things to think of now.

Godesberg, *September* 22

      The Swastika and the British Union Jack flying side by side in this lovely Rhine town — very appropriate, I find. Very appropriate, too, to hold your meeting in a Wagnerian town, for it is here, they say, that Wotan, Thor, and the other gods of the early Teutons used to frolic.

This morning I noticed something very interesting. I was having breakfast in the garden of the Dreesen Hotel, where Hitler is stopping, when the great man suddenly appeared, strode past me, and went down to the edge of the Rhine to inspect his river yacht. X, one of Germany's leading editors, who secretly despises the regime, nudged me: " Look at his walk ! " On inspection it was a very curious walk indeed. In the first place, it was very ladylike. Dainty little steps. In the second place, every few steps he cocked his right shoulder nervously, his left leg snapping up as he did so. I watched him closely as he came back past us. The same nervous tic. He had ugly black patches under his eyes. I think the man is on the edge of a nervous breakdown. And now I understand the meaning of an expression the party hacks were using when we sat around drinking in the Dreesen last night. They kept talking about the " *Teppichfresser,*" the " carpet-eater." At first I didn't get it, and then someone explained it in a whisper. They said Hitler has been having some of his nervous crises lately and that in recent days they've taken a strange form. Whenever he goes on a rampage about Beneš or the Czechs he flings himself to the floor and chews the edges of the carpet, hence the *Teppichfresser*. After seeing him this morning, I can believe it.

Chamberlain and Hitler had a three-hour talk this afternoon and will have another tomorrow. Just as I was broadcasting from a little studio we've fixed up in the porter's lodge of the hotel, the two men after their conference stepped out right before my window. Hitler was all graciousness indeed and Chamberlain, looking the image of an owl, was smiling and apparently highly

pleased in his vain way with some manufactured applause by a company of S.S. guards before the door.
Chamberlain, I hear, proposed an international commission to superintend the withdrawal of the Czechs
from Sudetenland and an international guarantee for
what is left of Czechoslovakia. New York cables our
Friedrichstrassebahnhof show last night was a knockout. Strange. New Cabinet in Prague. New Premier:
one-eyed, hard-boiled General Jan Syrovy, Inspector-
General of the army. The Czechs may fight yet.

GODESBERG, *September* 23—4, 4 *a.m.*

War seems very near after this strange day.
All the British and French correspondents and Birchall
of the New York *Times*, who is an English subject,
scurrying off at dawn — in about an hour now — for
the French, Belgian, or Dutch frontier. It seems that
Hitler has given Chamberlain the double-cross. And
the old owl is hurt. All day long he sulked in his rooms
at the Petershof up on the Petersberg on the other side
of the Rhine, refusing to come over and talk with the
dictator. At five p.m. he sent Sir Horace Wilson, his
" confidential " adviser, and Sir Nevile Henderson, the
British Ambassador in Berlin (both of whom, we feel,
would sell out Czecho for five cents), over the river to
see Ribbentrop. Result: Chamberlain and Hitler met
at ten thirty p.m. This meeting, which is the last, broke
up at one thirty a.m. without agreement and now it
looks like war, though from my " studio " in the porter's
lodge twenty-five feet away I could not discern any
strain or particular displeasure in Chamberlain's birdy
face as he said his farewell to Hitler, who also was smiling and gracious. Still the Germans are plunged in deep
gloom tonight, as if they really are afraid of war now

that it's facing them. They are gloomy and yet feverishly excited. Just as I was about to go on the air at
two a.m. with the day's story and the official communiqué, Goebbels and Hadamovsky, the latter Nazi
boss of German radio, came rushing in and forbade Jordan and me to say anything over the air except to read
the official communiqué. Later I grabbed a bit of supper
in the Dreesen lobby. Goebbels, Ribbentrop, Göring,
Keitel, and others walked in and out, all of them looking
as if they had been hit over the head with a sledge-
hammer. This rather surprised me, since it's a war of
their making. The communiqué merely says that Chamberlain has undertaken to deliver to Prague a German
memorandum containing Germany's " final attitude "
concerning the Sudeten question. The point is that
Chamberlain came here all prepared to turn over Sudetenland to Hitler, but in a " British " way — with an
international commission to supervise the business. He
found Hitler's appetite had increased. Hitler wants to
take over *his* way — that is, right away, with no nonsense of an international commission. Actually, it's not
an important point for either, but they seem to have
stuck to their positions.[1]

In meantime, word that the Czechs have *at last*
ordered mobilization.

Five a.m. now. Shall lie down on a table here in the
lobby, as I must be off at six for Cologne to catch the
Berlin plane.

[1] Sir Nevile Henderson in *Failure of a Mission* has told us since
that during the first talk after Chamberlain had outlined his plan of
complete surrender to Hitler, the Führer looked at him and said: " *Es
tut mir furchtbar leid, aber das geht nicht mehr* (I'm awfully sorry,
but that won't do any more)." Chamberlain, says Henderson, expressed his " surprise and indignation."

BERLIN, *September* 24

Today's story is in my broadcast made at midnight tonight. I said: "There was some confusion among us all at Godesberg this morning . . . but tonight, as seen from Berlin, the position is this: Hitler has demanded that Czechoslovakia not later than Saturday, October 1, agree to the handing over of Sudetenland to Germany. Mr. Chamberlain has agreed to convey this demand to the Czechoslovak Government. The very fact that he, with all the authority of a man who is political leader of the British Empire, has taken upon himself this task is accepted here, and I believe elsewhere, as meaning that Mr. Chamberlain backs Hitler up.

"That's why the German people I talked with in the streets of Cologne this morning, and in Berlin this evening, believe there'll be peace. As a matter of fact, what do you think the new slogan in Berlin is tonight? It's in the evening papers. It's this: 'With Hitler and Chamberlain for peace!' And the *Angriff* adds: 'Hitler and Chamberlain are working night and day for peace.'"

So Berlin is optimistic tonight for peace. Unable to telephone or wire Hindus in Prague tonight to give him his time schedule. All communication with Prague cut off. Thank God for that Czech transmitter.[1]

BERLIN, *September* 25

Hitler to make a speech tomorrow evening at the Sportpalast. Seems he is furious at the reports

[1] In the next days it furnished the only means of communication between Prague and the outside world.

from Prague, Paris, and London that his Godesberg
Memorandum goes beyond his original agreement with
Chamberlain at Berchtesgaden. He claims not. No war
fever, not even any anti-Czech feeling, discernible here
on this quiet Sabbath day. In the old days on the eve
of wars, I believe, crowds used to demonstrate angrily
before the embassies of the enemy countries. Today I
walked past the Czech Legation. Not a soul outside, not
even a policeman. Warm and sunny, the last summer
Sunday of the year probably, and half the population
of Berlin seems to have spent it at the near-by lakes or in
the woods of the Grunewald. Hard to believe there will
be war.

BERLIN, *September* 26

Hitler has finally burned his last bridges.
Shouting and shrieking in the worst state of excitement I've ever seen him in, he stated in the Sportpalast
tonight that he would have his Sudetenland by October
1 — next Saturday, today being Monday. If Beneš
doesn't hand it over to him he will go to war, this Saturday. Curious audience, the fifteen thousand party
Bonzen packed into the hall. They applauded his words
with the usual enthusiasm. Yet there was no war fever.
The crowd was *good-natured*, as if it didn't realize what
his words meant. The old man full of more venom than
even he has ever shown, hurling personal insults at
Beneš. Twice Hitler screamed that *this* is absolutely
his last territorial demand in Europe. Speaking of his
assurances to Chamberlain, he said: " I further assured
him that when the Czechs have reconciled themselves
with their other minorities, the Czech state no longer interests me and that, if you please. I would give him an-

other guarantee: We do not want any Czechs." At the
end Hitler had the impudence to place responsibility for
peace or war exclusively on Beneš!

I broadcast the scene from a seat in the balcony just
above Hitler. He's still got that nervous tic. All during his speech he kept cocking his shoulder, and the
opposite leg from the knee down would bounce up.
Audience couldn't see it, but I could. As a matter of
fact, for the first time in all the years I've observed him
he seemed tonight to have completely lost control of
himself. When he sat down after his talk, Goebbels
sprang up and shouted: " One thing is sure: 1918 will
never be repeated! " Hitler looked up to him, a wild,
eager expression in his eyes, as if those were the words
which he had been searching for all evening and hadn't
quite found. He leaped to his feet and with a fanatical
fire in his eyes that I shall never forget brought his right
hand, after a grand sweep, pounding down on the table
and yelled with all the power in his mighty lungs:
" *Ja!* " Then he slumped into his chair exhausted.

BERLIN, *September* 27

A motorized division rolled through the city's
streets just at dusk this evening in the direction of the
Czech frontier. I went out to the corner of the Linden
where the column was turning down the Wilhelmstrasse,
expecting to see a tremendous demonstration. I pic-
tured the scenes I had read of in 1914 when the cheering throngs on this same street tossed flowers at the
marching soldiers, and the girls ran up and kissed them.
The hour was undoubtedly chosen today to catch the
hundreds of thousands of Berliners pouring out of their
offices at the end of the day's work. But they ducked
into the subways, refused to look on, and the handful

that did stood at the curb in utter silence unable to find a word of cheer for the flower of their youth going away to the glorious war. It has been the most striking demonstration against war I've ever seen. Hitler himself reported furious. I had not been standing long at the corner when a policeman came up the Wilhelmstrasse from the direction of the Chancellery and shouted to the few of us standing at the curb that the Führer was on his balcony reviewing the troops. Few moved. I went down to have a look. Hitler stood there, and there weren't two hundred people in the street or the great square of the Wilhelmsplatz. Hitler looked grim, then angry, and soon went inside, leaving his troops to parade by unreviewed. What I've seen tonight almost rekindles a little faith in the German people. They are dead set against war.

Tess, with baby, off today from Cherbourg for America on a voyage she had booked months ago. On the phone last night from Paris she said that France was mobilizing and it was not sure the boat train would go. No word today, so suppose it did.

BERLIN, *September* 28

There is to be no war! Hitler has invited Mussolini, Chamberlain, and Daladier to meet him in Munich tomorrow. The latter three will rescue Hitler from his limb and he will get his Sudetenland without war, if a couple of days later than he boasted. The people in the streets greatly relieved, and if I judge correctly, the people in the Wilhelmstrasse and the Bendlerstrasse (War Department) also. Leaving right after my broadcast tonight for Munich.

MUNICH, *September* 30

It's all over. At twelve thirty this morning
— thirty minutes after midnight — Hitler, Mussolini,
Chamberlain, and Daladier signed a pact turning over
Sudetenland to Germany. The German occupation begins tomorrow, Saturday, October 1, and will be completed by October 10. Thus the two " democracies "
even assent to letting Hitler get by with his Sportpalast
boast that he would get his Sudetenland by October 1.
He gets everything he wanted, except that he has to
wait a few days longer for *all* of it. His waiting ten
short days has saved the peace of Europe — a curious
commentary on this sick, decadent continent.

So far as I've been able to observe during these last,
strangely unreal twenty-four hours, Daladier and
Chamberlain never pressed for a single concession from
Hitler. They never got together alone once and made
no effort to present some kind of common " democratic "
front to the two Cæsars. Hitler met Mussolini early
yesterday morning at Kufstein and they made their
plans. Daladier and Chamberlain arrived by separate
planes and didn't even deem it useful to lunch together
yesterday to map out their strategy, though the two
dictators did.

Czechoslovakia, which is asked to make all the sacrifices so that Europe may have peace, was not consulted
here at any stage of the talks. Their two representatives, Dr. Mastny, the intelligent and honest Czech
Minister in Berlin, and a Dr. Masaryk of the Prague
Foreign Office, were told at one thirty a.m. that Czechoslovakia would *have* to accept, told not by Hitler, but by
Chamberlain and Daladier! Their protests, we hear,
were practically laughed off by the elder statesman.
Chamberlain, looking more like some bird — like the

black vultures I've seen over the Parsi dead in Bombay
— looked particularly pleased with himself when he
returned to the Regina Palace Hotel after the signing
early this morning, though he was a bit sleepy, *pleasantly* sleepy.

Daladier, on the other hand, looked a completely
beaten and broken man. He came over to the Regina to
say good-bye to Chamberlain. A bunch of us were waiting as he came down the stairs. Someone asked, or
started to ask: " *Monsieur le President*, are you satisfied with the agreement? . . ." He turned as if to say
something, but he was too tired and defeated and the
words did not come out and he stumbled out the door
in silence. The French say he fears to return to Paris,
thinks a hostile mob will get him. Can only hope they're
right. For France has sacrificed her whole Continental
position and lost her main prop in eastern Europe. For
France this day has been disastrous.

How different Hitler at two this morning! After being blocked from the Führerhaus all evening, I finally
broke in just as he was leaving. Followed by Göring,
Ribbentrop, Goebbels, Hess, and Keitel, he brushed past
me like the conqueror he is this morning. I noticed his
swagger. The tic was gone! As for Mussolini, he pulled
out early, cocky as a rooster.

Incidentally, I've been badly scooped this night.
Max Jordan of NBC got on the air a full hour ahead of
me with the *text* of the agreement — one of the worst
beatings I've ever taken. Because of his company's
special position in Germany, he was allowed exclusive
use of Hitler's radio studio in the Führerhaus, where
the conference has been taking place. Wiegand, who
also was in the house, tells me Max cornered Sir Horace
Wilson of the British delegation as he stepped out of
the conference room, procured an English text from

him, rushed to the Führer's studio, and in a few moments was on the air. Unable to use this studio on the spot, I stayed close to the only other outlet, the studio of the Munich station, and arranged with several English and American friends to get me the document, if possible immediately after the meeting itself, if not from one of the delegations. Demaree Bess was first to arrive with a copy, but, alas, we were late. New York kindly phoned about two thirty this morning to tell me not to mind — damned decent of them. Actually at eleven thirty p.m. I had gone on the air announcing that an agreement had been reached. I gave them all the essential details of the accord, stating that the occupation would begin Saturday, that it would be completed in ten days, et cetera. But I should have greatly liked to have had the official text first. Fortunately for CBS, Ed Murrow in London was the first to flash the official news to America that the agreement had been signed thirty minutes after midnight. He picked it up from the Munich radio station in the midst of a talk.

LATER. — Chamberlain, apparently realizing his diplomatic annihilation, has pulled a very clever face-saving stunt. He saw Hitler again this morning before leaving and afterwards a joint communiqué was issued. Essential part: "We regard the agreement signed last night and the Anglo-German naval accord as symbolic of the desire of our two peoples never to go to war with one another again." And a final paragraph saying they will consult about further questions which may concern the two countries and are "determined to continue our efforts to remove possible sources of difference and thus to contribute to the assurance of peace in Europe."

LATER. *On Train, Munich–Berlin.* — Most
of the leading German editors on the train and tossing down the champagne and not trying to disguise
any more their elation over Hitler's terrific victory over
Britain and France. On the diner Halfeld of the *Hamburger Fremdenblatt*, Otto Kriegk of the *Nachtausgabe*, Dr. Boehmer, the foreign press chief of the
Propaganda Ministry, gloating over it, buying out all
the champagne in the diner, gloating, boasting, brag-
ging. . . . When a German feels big he feels *big*.
Shall have two hours in Berlin this evening to get my
army passes and a bath and then off by night train to
Passau to go into Sudetenland with the German army
— a sad assignment for me.

[LATER. — And Chamberlain will go back to London
and from the balcony of 10 Downing Street that night
will boast: " My good friends, this is the second time in
our history " (do the crowds shouting: " Good old Nev-
ille " and singing " For he's a jolly good fellow " remember Disraeli, the Congress of Berlin, 1878?) " that
there has come back from Germany to Downing Street
peace with honour. I believe it is peace for our time."
Peace with honour! And Czechoslovakia? And only
Duff Cooper will resign from the Cabinet, saying: " It
was not for Serbia or Belgium we fought in 1914 . . .
but . . . in order that one great power should not be
allowed, in disregard of treaty obligations and the laws
of nations and against all morality, to dominate by
brutal force the continent of Europe. . . . Throughout these days the Prime Minister has believed in addressing Herr Hitler with the language of sweet reasonableness. I have believed he was more open to the
language of the mailed fist. . . ." Only Winston
Churchill, a voice in the wilderness all these years, will

say, addressing the Commons: "We have sustained a total, unmitigated defeat. . . . Do not let us blind ourselves. We must expect that all the countries of central and eastern Europe will make the best terms they can with the triumphant Nazi power. . . . The road down the Danube . . . the road to the Black Sea and Turkey, has been broken. It seems to me that all the countries of Mittel Europa and the Danube Valley, one after the other, will be drawn into the vast system of Nazi politics, not only power military politics, but power economic politics, radiating from Berlin." Churchill — the lone, unheeded prophet in the British land.]

ON TRAIN, REGENSBURG–BERLIN, *October* 2

At Regensburg before dawn yesterday, then by bus to Passau on the Danube, and from there by car with a German General Staff major following the troops picnic-marching into Zone I of the Sudetenland. Back after dark last night in a pouring rain to Passau, where the military censors refused to let me broadcast; a train to Regensburg arriving there at midnight and filing my story by telephone to Press Wireless in Paris to be read in New York, since the RRG in Berlin says the military have put a *Verbot* on all broadcasts, including their own, of the occupation. No plane to Berlin, so this train and will broadcast from there tonight.

BERLIN. LATER. — Military had not yet lifted their *Verbot*, so had to read another piece I had written on train on the political significance of Hitler's great victory at Munich, quoting an editorial by Rudolf Kircher, the only intelligent and courageous editor left in Nazi Germany, in this morning's *Frankfurter Zeitung* wherein he frankly states the advantages of threat-

ening force and war and how Hitler knew all the time
that the democracies were *afraid* of war. When I returned to the hotel, some general in charge of the military censorship at the German radio was on the phone
saying he had just read my piece on the occupation,
that he liked it, that he had had to suppress all the accounts of the German radio reporters so far, but that I
could now broadcast mine. Called Paul White in New
York, but he said the crisis was over and that people at
home wanted to forget it and to take a rest. Which is
all right with me. Can stand some sleep and a change
from these Germans, so truculent and impossible now.

BERLIN, *October* 3

Phoned Ed Murrow in London. He as depressed as am I. We shall drown our sorrows in Paris
day after tomorrow. From my window in the Adlon I
see them dismantling the anti-aircraft gun on the roof
of the I. G. Farben company across the Linden. Thus
ends the crisis. Little things to remember: the characters in the drama: the dignity of Beneš throughout;
Hitler the five times I saw him; the bird, Chamberlain;
the broken little man, Daladier, who seems destined to
fall down (as on February 6, 1934) each time he is in a
hole. To remember too: the mine at a bridge over a
little creek near Krumau which might have blown us to
bits had our German army car gone two feet farther;
the bravery of the Czechs in Prague the night war and
bombs at dawn seemed certain; the look of fear in the
faces of the German burghers in the Wilhelmstrasse the
night the motorized division swept by and war seemed
certain to them, and then the delirious joy of the citizens in Munich — and Berlin — when they learned on
Friday that it was not only peace but victory; the

beaten look of the Sudeten Germans after the Czechs put down their uprising, and the change in their faces a fortnight later when the Reichswehr marched in; and the burgomaster of the Sudeten town of Unterwaldau, Herr Schwarzbauer (Mr. Black Peasant), taking me aside from the German officers and my saying: " What is the worst thing the Czechs did to you, Herr Burgomaster? " and his saying it was frightful, unbelievable, that the Czechs had taken away his radio so he couldn't hear the Führer's words and could any crime be more terrible!

Paris, *October* 8

Paris a frightful place, completely surrendered to defeatism with no inkling of what has happened to *France*. At Fouquet's, at Maxim's, fat bankers and businessmen toasting Peace with rivers of champagne. But even the waiters, taxi-drivers, who used to be sound, gushing about how wonderful it is that war has been avoided, that it would have been a crime, that they fought in one war and that was enough. That would be okay if the Germans, who also fought in one war, felt the same way, but they don't. The guts of France.— France of the Marne and Verdun — where are they? Outside of Pierre Comer, no one at the Quai d'Orsay with any idea at all of the real Germany. The French Socialists, shot through with pacifism; the French Right, with the exception of a few like Henri de Kerillis, either fascists or defeatists. France makes no sense to me any more.

Ed Murrow as gloomy as I am. We try to get it out of our systems by talking all night and popping champagne bottles and tramping the streets, but it will take more time, I guess. We agree on these things: that war

is now more probable than ever, that it is likely to come
after the next harvest, that Poland is obviously next on
Hitler's list (the blind stupidity of the Poles in this
crisis, helping to carve up Czechoslovakia!), that we
must get Warsaw to rig up a more powerful short-wave
transmitter if they want the world to hear their side,
and that we ought to build up a staff of American radio
reporters. But honestly we have little head for business.
Ed says American radio has done a superb job in reporting this crisis, but we don't much care — about
anything — and soon even the champagne becomes
sickening. We depart.

Run into Gallico. He is off on a tour of the capitals
for material for his stories. I give him letters to the
correspondents in each place, we dine at Maxim's, but I
cannot stand it any longer. Off in the morning for
Geneva. Almost the first chance in a year to get reac-
quainted with Tess and Eileen. But they are off in
America.

GENEVA, *November* 6

Lovely Indian summer here for a month, but
now the snow is creeping down on the Alps and this
morning the Juras across the lake were also coated
white. Soon we can ski. A month of the worst mental
and spiritual depression of my life. I'm still in such a
state that I've done two crazy things: started a play;
and taken up — at my age, thirty-four! — golf. Perhaps they'll restore sanity. There is a beautiful course
at Divonne in the foot-hills of the Juras from which
you can look over the lake and see Mont Blanc in all its
snowy pink splendour about the time the sun is setting.
Arthur Burrows, English, fifty-two, secretary of the
International Broadcasting Union, and I fool around

over the links, tearing up the turf, soon losing count
of the scores, if any, knocking off after the first nine
holes to go down to Divonne village, which is on the
French side of the frontier, for a magnificent nine-
course lunch washed down by two bottles of Burgundy,
and return, feeling mellow and good, for the last nine
holes. The play is called: " Foreign Correspondent."
It is affording me much relief.

WARSAW, *November* 11

Broadcast a half-hour program for the twentieth anniversary of the Polish Republic. The show got
hopelessly tangled up for some reason. Sitting in the
Palace I began by saying: " Ladies and gentlemen, the
Polish anthem . . ." which was to be played by a band
in a studio in the other part of town. Instead of the
band, President Mosieski started to speak. He had
promised to speak in English, but through the earphones I could make out only Polish. I dashed down
the Palace corridors to his room to inquire. A tall adjutant stopped me at the door. " The President promised
to speak English," I said. He looked at me curiously,
opening the door slightly. " He *is* speaking English,
sir," he protested. Dashed back to my room to intro-
duce Ambassador Tony Biddle, who was to say a few
well-chosen words. He started blabbing and, thinking
he had suddenly become a victim of " mike fright," I
moved to cut him off. Then he motioned to his script.
It was a mass of hieroglyphics. " Polish ! " he whispered. " Phonetic. . . ." He was giving a little message in Polish. When he had finished we laughed so
hard the Poles in the Palace became a little uneasy.

Afterwards met Duranty, and it was one of his " Russian nights," he insisting on talking Russian to the

droshky-driver and insisting we be taken to a Russian café. The wind from Duranty's Russian steppes was whipping the snow in our faces, and after what seemed an age the driver finally pulled his dying nag up before a decrepit old building.

" Café Rusky? " Walter shouted. We could not see the driver through the curtain of snow. No, it was not a Russian café. It was a Polish institution, a disorderly house. Then in the blizzard a long argument in Russian between the Moscow correspondent of the New York *Times* and the Polish driver of a dilapidated horse and buggy. The snow piled up on us. Long after midnight we found a Russian café. It was full of rather plump girls who spoke Russian and who Walter said were *echt Russisch* and there was much vodka and balalaika-playing and singing and the girls would warm their backs against a great porcelain stove, getting a little more tired and sleepy each time, a little sadder, I thought.

The Poles a delightful, utterly romantic people, and I have had much good food and drink and music with them. But they are horribly unrealistic. In their trust of Hitler, for instance. *Polskie Radio* promises to get along with their new short-wave transmitter. I explained to them our experience with the Czechs.

BRUSSELS, *November* 20

Here as observer for an international radio conference to draw up new wave-lengths. As there is nothing for me to do, have shut myself in my room for a week and finished the play.

BELGRADE, *November* 26

Here for another " anniversary " broadcast like the one at Warsaw.

LATER. *On train to Rome.* — Miss Campbell from our London office phoned at six p.m. to tell me the Pope was dying. I caught young Sulzberger of the New York *Times* at a cocktail party, induced him to do my broadcast Sunday, explained how, and caught this train at nine p.m. for Rome.

ROME, *November* 29

The Pope has once again fought off death after a severe heart attack on Tuesday. Arranged with Father Delaney, a brilliant and extremely pleasant young Jesuit from New York attached to Vatican Radio, to help us in the elaborate coverage I've arranged for the Pope's death. Conferences yesterday and today with the Vatican authorities on the matter, which of course is extremely delicate since he is still alive. But we all agreed we must make our preparations. The Italians are putting in extra lines for us from St. Peter's to their studios. Much good talk and spaghetti and Chianti and to Paris by plane tomorrow though an Italian friend of mine who is also a close friend of Ciano's tipped me off I ought to stay for tomorrow's meeting of the Fascist Chamber. But an urgent matter of ours with the French government needs straightening out.

PARIS, *December* 1

My friend was trying to do me a favour. The Fascists in the Chamber yesterday staged a big demon-

stration against France yelling: " Tunis! Savoy!
Nice! Jibouti! " But the Quai d'Orsay here claims
Daladier will say no. Munich was enough for the moment. A German refugee and his wife, he a former
trades-union official, she a novelist of sorts, came to my
hotel an hour after I arrived last evening (my Italian
plane had a narrow escape when a strut broke between
Rome and Genoa, and I was still a little nervous) and
told me they were going to jump off a bridge over the
Seine and end their lives. I took them around the corner
for a good meal at Le Petit Riche and they calmed
down. I hope I've persuaded them not to jump into the
Seine. They had received an order of expulsion from
France effective next week, though he has been doing
some work for the French government. Shall try to
intervene at the Quai d'Orsay for them.

PARIS, *December* 6

Bonnet, one of the chief architects of Munich
and a sinister figure in French politics, today signed a
" good neighbour " declaration with Ribbentrop, another sinister one, at the Quai d'Orsay. Paris, I find,
has somewhat recovered from its defeatist panic of the
Munich days. When Ribbentrop drove through the
streets from the Gare d'Orsay, they were completely
deserted. Several Cabinet members and many leading
figures here have refused to attend the social functions
being accorded him. On the other hand Ribbentrop's
French admirers run high up in political, business, and
social circles. Today's agreement states that the two
countries solemnly declare that no territorial or border
question now exists and that they will consult in case
of future disagreement. What a farce!

P A R I S , *December* 15

Tess and baby back today on the *Queen Mary*. Off to Geneva for the Christmas holidays.

G S T A A D , S W I T Z E R L A N D , *December* 26

One of the most beautiful mountain spots I've ever seen and the snow so grand I've taken up skiing again for the first time since my accident six years ago. The wealthy English and French here in force and inanely oblivious of Europe's state. Last night at the big Christmas ball I found the merry-makers so nauseating that we left early. This has been a year — the baby, the *Anschluss*, the Czech crisis, and Munich. As usual Tess and I wonder where we'll be a year from now, and what the year will bring.

R O M E , *January* 11, 1939

Chamberlain and Halifax arrived today to appease the Duce. At the station Chamberlain, looking more birdlike and vain than when I last saw him at Munich, walked, umbrella in hand, up and down the platform nodding to a motley crowd of British local residents whom Mussolini had slyly invited to greet him. Mussolini and Ciano, in black Fascist uniforms, sauntered along behind the two ridiculous-looking Englishmen, Musso displaying a fine smirk on his face the whole time. When he passed me he was joking under his breath with his son-in-law, passing wise-cracks. He looks much older, much more vulgar than he used to, his face having grown fat. My local spies tell me he is much taken with a blonde young lady of nineteen whom he's installed in a villa across from his residence and that

the old vigour and concentration on business is beginning to weaken. Chamberlain, we're told, much affected
by the warmth of the greeting he got at the stations
along the way to Rome. Can it be he doesn't know how
they're *arranged?*

Geneva, *January* 19

The League in its last death-throes has been a
sorry sight the last four days. Bonnet and Halifax
here to see that there is no nonsense to delay Franco's
victory. Del Vayo yesterday made a dignified speech
before the Council. Halifax, to show his colours, got up
in the middle of it and ostentatiously strode out. Had a
long talk with Del Vayo tonight. He was depressed, discouraged, and though he did not say so, I gathered it
is all up with the Republic. Franco, with his Germans
and Italians, is at the gates of Barcelona. Lunch with
Edgar [Mowrer], Knick, Harry Masdyck, and Mme.
Tabouis. Much talk, but our side has lost.

Rome, *February* 12

Friday morning about six fifteen Cortesi
phoned me at Geneva from Rome to say the Pope had
died. There was a train for Milan at seven two a.m. I
aroused Tess and she helped me catch it. Today, Sunday, broadcast from the piazza in front of St. Peter's,
stopping people who were filing out of the church after
viewing Pius XI's remains as they lay in state, and interviewing them. As I am not a Catholic and there is
much about the church and the Vatican that I do not
know — though I've been studying countless books for
a year — I am getting churchmen to do most of the
broadcasts.

ROME, *February (undated)*

Pius XI was buried today, the service beautiful, but St. Peter's very cold, and there was a long hitch, due, it seems, to the fact that the mechanics who were to seal the casket before it was lowered to the vault below ran out of solder. An S O S call was sent out for some, but as most of the workshops in Rome had closed for the day, it was some time before a sufficient quantity could be found. Father Delaney, broadcasting the service for us from atop one of the pillars, did a magnificent job, filling in beautifully the hour or so that elapsed while they were hunting the solder.

ROME, *March* 3

Eugenio Cardinal Pacelli is the new Pope, elected yesterday, and a very popular choice all around except perhaps in Germany. We had great luck with broadcasting the news a few moments after the election, though earlier in the day it looked disastrous for us. Suffering from the flu when I left Lausanne the day before, I had such a violent attack of it by the time I reached Milan that I had to go to a hotel there and take to bed. I managed to get to the train somehow, but was completely out when I arrived in Rome yesterday morning. Tom Grandin, our Paris correspondent, intelligent, but green at radio, having just been hired, arrived from Paris about noon, but he tells me I was completely out of my head and that in my delirium my instructions on what to do made no sense. He did gather that I had arranged a broadcast from the balustrade around St. Peter's during the afternoon. He got there, found Father Delaney, who was talking for us, and just as they were signing off, they got a message through their earphones from inside the Vatican to stand by, passed it on to New York, who understood. In a moment they were announcing the name of the new pontiff.

ROME, *March* 9

A storm brewing in what is left of poor Czechoslovakia. Dr. Hacha, the weak little President — successor to the great Masaryk and the able Beneš — has proclaimed martial law in Slovakia and dismissed Father Tiso and the Slovak Cabinet. But Tiso, I know, is Berlin's man. Strange — maybe not? — that Germany and Italy have never given rump Czecho the guarantee they promised at Munich. The Italian Foreign Office people admit London and Paris have been pressing Hitler for the guarantee, but they say Hitler considers Prague still too " Jewish and Bolshevik and democratic." I don't recall any reservations about that at Munich.

Still in bed with flu and must wait here for the Pope's coronation Sunday.

GENEVA, *March* 14

The radio reports Slovakia has declared its " independence." There goes the remains of Czechoslovakia. Should go to Prague, but I haven't the heart. Am I growing too soft-hearted, too sentimental to be a good reporter? I don't mind so much the killings, bloodshed — I've seen and got over quite a little of that in the last fourteen years — but Prague now — I can't face it. The radio says [Czech President] Hacha and [Foreign Minister] Chvalkovsky arrived in Berlin tonight. To save the pieces?

PARIS, *March* 15

The German army has occupied Bohemia and
Moravia on this blizzardy day of spring, and Hitler in
a cheap theatrical gesture from the Hradshin castle
above the Moldau in Prague has proclaimed their an-
nexation to the Third Reich. It is almost banal to record his breaking another solemn treaty. But since I
was personally present at Munich, I cannot help recall-
ing how Chamberlain said it not only had saved the peace
but had really saved Czechoslovakia.

Complete apathy in Paris tonight about Hitler's
latest coup. France will not move a finger. Indeed,
Bonnet told the Chamber's Foreign Affairs Committee
today that the Munich guarantee had " not yet become
effective " and therefore France had no obligation to do
anything. Ed Murrow telephones that the reaction in
London is the same — that Chamberlain in Commons
this afternoon even went so far as to say that he refused
to associate himself with any charges of a breach of faith
by Hitler. Good God!

Should have gone to Prague or Berlin today, I suppose, but talked it over with Murrow from Geneva early
this morning and we decided the Nazi censorship in both
places would be complete and that, with what inside stuff
I could pick up here and knowing the background, I
could tell a better story from Paris. I was relieved. My
Paris plane, after getting iced up and lost in a snowstorm near the Bellegarde Pass shortly after we left
Geneva, turned round and finally got us back to the airport. I took the noon train. Bonnet has laid down a
radio censorship and I fought with his hirelings until
long after midnight tonight over my script.

PARIS, *March* 22

Someone — I think it was Pertinax, who is
just back from London — told me yesterday a weird
tale of how Chamberlain suddenly reversed his whole
position last Friday in his Birmingham speech. Two
days before, he had told Commons that he would not
charge Hitler with bad faith. In Birmingham he severely denounced Hitler for " treaty-breaking." Pertinax says that Sir Horace Wilson, the dark little man
behind the scenes at Godesberg and Munich had actually drafted the Birmingham speech for the Prime Minister along the appeasement lines of his remarks in the
House, but that half the Cabinet and most of the leading
London newspaper editors were so up in arms when they
heard of it that Chamberlain suddenly felt forced to reverse his whole policy and actually wrote most of his new
speech on the train en route to Birmingham.

How shoddy Paris has become in the last ten years!
Some Frenchmen point to the neon signs, the gaudy
movie palaces, the automobile sales windows, the cheap
bars which now dominate the once beautiful Champs-
Elysées, and say: " That is what America has done to
us." Perhaps so, but I think it is what France has done
to herself. France has lost something she had when I arrived here fourteen years ago: her taste, part of her soul,
the sense of her historical mission. Corruption everywhere, class selfishness *partout* and political confusion
complete. My decent friends have about given up.
They say: " *Je m'en fous* (To hell with it)." This leads
to the sort of defeatist, anarchistic *je m'en fousism* which
a writer like *Céline* is spreading.

GENEVA, *March* 29

Madrid surrendered yesterday, the rest of republican Spain today. There are no words to express
what I feel tonight. Franco's butchery will be terrible.

BERLIN, *April* 1

Just as Hitler began his broadcast at Wilhelmshaven this afternoon, an order came through to the
RRG control room where I was standing by, to stop the
broadcast from getting abroad. For a moment there was
great confusion in the control room. I protested ve-
hemently to the Germans about cutting us off, once
Hitler had started to speak. But orders from Wilhelmshaven were explicit. They came from Hitler himself,
just before he started speaking. The speech was also
not being broadcast directly in Germany, but only from
recordings later. This and our being cut off meant Hitler wanted to reflect on what he said in the heat of the
moment before giving his words wider circulation. You
can always edit recordings. I suggested to Dr. Ratke,
head of the short-wave department, he should announce
to our network in America that the speech of Hitler had
been shut off owing to a misunderstanding and that the
Führer was actually talking at this moment. A very ex-
citable man, he refused. Instead he ordered some silly
music records played. Just what I expected happened.
Within fifteen minutes, Paul White was urgently on the
line from New York. Why was Hitler cut off? Reports
in New York he has been assassinated. He hasn't been
killed? How do you know? Because I can hear him this
moment on the telephone circuit to Wilhelmshaven. The
Germans are recording the speech.

I could not go on the air afterwards until the Germans

had received the approved version of Hitler's speech, which, as a matter of fact, differed not at all from the original. Hitler very bellicose today, obviously in a rage against Chamberlain, who in the House yesterday enunciated at last a complete change in British foreign policy and announced that Britain would go to the aid of Poland if Polish independence were threatened. Off to Warsaw tomorrow to see when the German attack is expected.

WARSAW, *April 2*

Attended a pitiful air-show this Sunday afternoon, my Polish friends apologizing for the cumbersome slow bombers and the double-decker fighters — all obsolete. They showed a half-dozen modern fighters that looked fast enough, but that was all. How can Poland fight Germany with such an air force?

WARSAW, *April 6*

Beck [the Polish Foreign Minister], who committed this country to a pro-Nazi, anti-French policy for so many years, has been in London and tonight we have an Anglo-Polish communiqué announcing that the two countries will sign a permanent agreement providing for mutual assistance in case of an attack on either of them by a third power. I think this will halt Hitler for the time being, since force is something he understands and respects and there is no doubt in my mind after a week here that the Poles will fight and that if Britain and France fight too, he is in a hole. I feel uneasy about three things only: Poland's terrible strategic position since Germany (with Poland's help and encouragement!) moved her army into the Protectorate and Slovakia, thus flanking this country on the south (it is already flanked on the north by East Prussia) ; the West Wall, which, when completed next winter, will discourage France and Britain from attacking Germany in the west and thereby aiding Poland; and, finally, Russia. I have dined and drunk with a dozen Poles this week — from the Foreign Office, the army, and the old Pilsudski legionnaires who run *Polskie Radio* — and they will not bring themselves to realize that they cannot afford the luxury of being enemies of both Russia and Germany and that they must choose and that if they bring in Russia along with France and Britain they are saved. They reach for another piece of this wonderful smoked Vistula salmon they have here and wash it down with one of the fifty-seven varieties of vodka and point out the dangers of Russian help. To be sure, there is danger. There is the danger that the Red army, once on Polish soil, will not leave, that it will Bolshevize the country with its propaganda (this country has been so misruled by the colonels that no doubt it does offer fertile ground for the Bolsheviks), and so on. True. Then make your peace with the Nazis. Give them Danzig and the Corridor. Never! they say.

Still, on this spring day after the British guarantee we all feel better. Fodor, who leaves by boat tonight for Easter holidays in England (he's barred from crossing Germany), optimistic. The Embassy people, Biddle and the military, happy. Only Second Secretary Landreth Harrison is sceptical. He keeps pointing out the weaknesses of the Poles to the point of exasperation. He is a man of prejudices, though intelligent.

Rumours today of German troop movements, but the Poles discount them. *Polskie Radio* still stalling on their new short-wave transmitter. Bad. Off to Paris tomorrow morning for an Easter broadcast, then to Geneva for Easter Monday.

BERLIN, *April* 7

When the Orient Express pulled into the Schlesischer Bahnhof here this evening, the first thing I saw was Huss's face on the platform and I knew there was bad news. He said London had phoned to get me off the train as the British had reports of German troop movements on the Polish frontier. I had watched for these as we came across the border, but saw nothing. London was nervous about Albania, he said. "What's happened there?" I asked. The Italians went in there this morning, he said. Today. Good Friday. Have satisfied myself the Germans are not contemplating anything against Poland this Easter, so will take the plane to Paris tomorrow morning.

LONDON, *April* 23

Broadcast with Lord Strabolgi, my main point being that the whole life of Germany was now geared to war, but that there were signs of economic cracking. Iron was so short they were tearing down the iron fences of the Reich. And the nerves of the German people were becoming frayed and they were against going to war. Strabolgi so cheered by my news he asked me to come down and address a committee meeting at the House of Lords, but I declined. Flying back to Berlin for the Reichstag, April 28.

BERLIN, *April* 28

Hitler in the Reichstag today denounced a couple more treaties (I could hardly repress a chuckle at this part of his speech) and answered Roosevelt's plea that he give assurance that he will not attack the rest of the independent nations of Europe. His answer to the President rather shrewd, I think, in that it was designed to play on the sympathies of the appeasers and anti-New-Dealers at home and the former in Britain and France. He claimed he had asked the nations which Roosevelt thought threatened whether they so considered themselves and " in all cases the reply was negative." States like Syria, he said, he could not ask because " they are at present not in possession of their freedom, but are occupied and consequently deprived of their rights by the military agents of democratic countries." And " the fact has obviously escaped Mr. Roosevelt's notice that Palestine is at present occupied not by German troops but by the English." And so on in this sarcastic manner, from which, with a masterly touch — Hitler was a superb actor today — he drew every last drop of irony. America champions the conference method of settling disputes? he asked. But was it not the first nation to shrink from participation in the League? " It was not until many years later that I resolved to follow the example of America and likewise leave the largest conference in the world."

In the end, however, Hitler agreed to give each of the states listed by the President " an assurance of the kind desired by Mr. Roosevelt." But of course this was just a little Nazi hokum. The sausage-necked deputies below us rocked with raucous laughter throughout the session, which was just what Hitler desired. It was a superb example of his technique of laughing off embarrassing questions, for Roosevelt's proposal was a reasonable one after all.

The breaking of two more treaties was loudly applauded by the rubber-stamp " parliamentarians." Hitler denounces the naval accord with Britain on the grounds that London's " encirclement policy " has put it out of force — a flimsy excuse; of course no excuse at all. The second treaty denounced, the 1934 pact with Poland, is more serious, the excuse, incidentally, being the same. Hitler in his speech reveals the content of his " offer " to Poland: Danzig to be returned to Germany, and the Reich given an extra-territorial road through the corridor to East Prussia. To scare the Poles he says the offer was made " only once." That is, his terms are higher today. Still much doubt here among the informed whether Hitler has made up his mind to begin a world war for the sake of Danzig. My guess is he hopes to get it by the Munich method.

London, *June* (*undated*)

Leaving tomorrow on the maiden voyage of the new *Mauretania* for home. Tess cables she has just been granted her citizenship by a Virginia court.

Aboard *Mauretania* (*undated*)

A dull voyage. Sir Percy Bate, chairman of Cunard, assures me there will be no war.

Washington, *July 3*

Hope I can stay a little while in my native land. It takes some getting used to again after being almost continuously away since the age of twenty-one. Little awareness here or in New York of the European crisis, and Tess says I'm making myself most unpopular by taking such a pessimistic view. The trouble is everyone here knows all the answers. They *know* there will be no war. I wish I *knew* it. But I think there will be war unless Germany backs down, and I'm not certain at all

she will, though of course it's a possibility. Congress
here in a hopeless muddle. Dominated by the Ham
Fishes, Borahs, Hiram Johnsons, who stand for no foreign policy at all, it insists on maintaining the embargo
on arms as if it were immaterial to this Republic who
wins a war between the western democracies and the
Axis. Roosevelt's hands absolutely tied by Congress —
a situation like that which confronted Lincoln at the beginning of his first term, except that he did something
about it, and Roosevelt, they say here, is discouraged
and won't. He sees the European situation correctly,
but because he does, because he sees the danger, the
Borahs and Fishes call him a war-monger.

Oh well, it's pleasant to be here with the family and
loaf and relax for a few fleeting days.

New York, *July* 4

A pleasant afternoon at the Fair with the Bill
Lewises. We must start back to Europe tomorrow.
Alarming news from Danzig, and the office worried I
won't get back in time. Hans Kaltenborn so sure there
will be no war, he is sending his son off on his honey-
moon to the Mediterranean, he tells me tonight.

Aboard *Queen Mary, July* 9

Much good company aboard. Paul Robeson,
whom I have not seen since he stormed London in *Show
Boat* ten years or so ago. In the evening we sit and
argue, Robeson, Constantine Oumansky, Soviet Ambassador in Washington, Tess, and I. Oumansky tells me
he has been down to third class to lecture to some American students on " Soviet Democracy." But he takes my

kidding good-naturedly. Soviet democracy! I do not
envy him his job. His predecessor in Washington is now
in the dog-house. I have known many Soviet diplomats,
but they have all been liquidated sooner or later. Oumansky thinks the Soviets will line up with Britain and
France in a democratic front against fascist aggression
if Paris and London show they mean business and are
not merely trying to manœuvre Russia into a war alone
(or alone with Poland) against Germany. So far, he
says, the British and French have done nothing but stall
in their negotiations with the Kremlin.

Much wild ping-pong with Tess on this voyage.

Lᴏɴᴅᴏɴ, *July* 14

Paul White from New York and our " European staff," consisting of Murrow, Tom Grandin from
Paris, and myself here conferring on war coverage. We
worked out technical matters such as transmission lines
and short-wave transmitters and arranged to build up a
staff of Americans (the New York *Times*, for example,
has several Englishmen on its foreign staff) as regular
staff correspondents, figuring that the American press
associations and newspapers will not allow their men to
broadcast, once the war starts. We hear our rival network plans to engage a number of big-name foreigners
such as Churchill here, Flandin in France, Gayda in
Italy, et cetera, but we think our plan is better. American listeners will want news, not foreign propaganda, if
war comes. We distressed at the failure of the Poles to
rush their new short-wave transmitter to completion, as
this may leave us in a hole. A wild game of golf with
Ed and it was good — after listening to my Labour
friends in Parliament curse conscription and the Con-

servatives express hopes for further appeasement — to hear my caddy say in a thick cockney: " Seems as 'ow we'll have to give that bloke Hitler a damned good beatin' one o' these days. . . ."

PARIS *(undated)*

John Elliott, formerly Berlin, now Paris correspondent of the *Herald Tribune*, tells me that in all the years he has been writing the day-to-day history of Europe for his paper he has received but a dozen or so letters from readers who were interested enough in what he had written to write him. But after two or three broadcasts from Paris during the March 15 Prague occupation he received scores of letters, praising, protesting, inquiring.

GENEVA, *July* 28

Fodor and Gunther dropped in tonight and we argued and talked most of the night through. John fairly optimistic about peace. Fodor, a trained engineer himself, had a lot of material about Germany's lack of iron. You can't store much iron ore, Fodor says. John's latest, *Inside Asia*, going blazes. We argued a little about India, on which subject, I fear, I'm a crank. John not so impressed by Gandhi as I was.

GENEVA, *August* 3

Much golf, including a comical game with Joe Phillips, and tramps in the near-by mountains, and swims in the lake with my family, with whom I'm beginning to get acquainted again. From a personal viewpoint it will be nice if there's no war. But must get off to Danzig next week to see.

BERLIN, *August* 9

The people in the train coming up from Basel last night looked clean and decent, the kind that made us like the Germans, as people, before the Nazis. For breakfast in the Adlon this morning I asked for a glass of orange juice, if they had any.

" Certainly we have oranges," the waiter said, haughtily. But when he brought the breakfast there was no orange juice. " Not a one in the hotel," he admitted sheepishly.

A discussion this day with Captain D. A World War officer of proved patriotism, he was against war during the Munich crisis, but changed, I noticed, after April 28, when Hitler denounced the Polish and British treaties. He became violent today at the very mention of the Poles and British. He thundered: " Why do the English butt in on Danzig and threaten war over the return of a German city? Why do the Poles [*sic*] provoke us? Haven't we the right to a German city like Danzig? "

" Have you a right to a Czech city like Prague? " I asked. Silence. No answer. That vacant stare you get on Germans.

" Why didn't the Poles accept the generous offer of the Führer? " he began again.

" Because they feared another Sudetenland, Captain."

" You mean they don't trust the Führer? "

" Not much since March 15," I said, looking carefully around before I spoke such blasphemy to see I was not being overheard. Again the vacant German stare.

Lunch with Major Eliot and his wife. He has just come from London and Paris and thinks highly of the French army and the British air-force, which was good

news to me. Met Joe Barnes (*Herald Tribune*) at the
Taverne at midnight. He just back from Danzig and
Poland. His theory is that if Hitler waits nine months
he'll have Danzig and perhaps more without much
trouble and certainly without war. He thinks Polish resistance to Hitler's demands would collapse, that Poland
simply couldn't afford to stay mobilized any longer
than that. I argued that Britain and France could afford to foot the bill for the Poles. Joe didn't think they
would. I won't say he's dead wrong, but think he under-
estimates the change in France and Britain. Joe's description of the backwardness of the Poles very impressive. He and Maurice Hindus visited the villages. Only
two million people in Poland read any kind of newspaper, he reports, and many villages are without a single
radio.

BERLIN, *August* 10

How completely isolated a world the German
people live in. A glance at the newspapers yesterday
and today reminds you of it. Whereas all the rest of the
world considers that the peace is about to be broken by
Germany, that it is Germany that is threatening to attack Poland over Danzig, here in Germany, in the world
the local newspapers create, the very reverse is being
maintained. (Not that it surprises me, but when you
are away for a while, you forget.) What the Nazi
papers are proclaiming is this: that it is Poland which is
disturbing the peace of Europe; Poland which is threatening Germany with armed invasion, and so forth. This
is the Germany of last September when the steam was
turned on Czechoslovakia.

"POLAND? LOOK OUT!" warns the *B.Z.* headline,
adding: "ANSWER TO POLAND, THE RUNNER –

AMOK (AMOKLÄUFER) AGAINST PEACE AND RIGHT IN EUROPE!"

Or the headline in *Der Führer*, daily paper of Karlsruhe, which I bought on the train: "WARSAW THREATENS BOMBARDMENT OF DANZIG — UNBELIEVABLE AGITATION OF THE POLISH ARCHMADNESS (POLNISCHEN GRÖSSENWAHNS)!"

For perverse perversion of the truth, this is good. You ask: But the German people can't possibly believe these lies? Then you talk to them. So many do.

But so far the press limits itself to Danzig. Will the Germans keep their real designs under cover until later? Any fool knows they don't give a damn about Danzig. It's just a pretext. The Nazi position, freely admitted in party circles, is that Germany cannot afford to have a strong military power on her eastern frontier, that therefore Poland as it is today must be liquidated, not only Danzig, which is Poland's life-line, taken, but also the Corridor, Posen, and Upper Silesia. And Poland left a rump state, a vassal of Germany. Then when Hungary and Rumania and Yugoslavia have been similarly reduced (Hungary practically is already), Germany will be economically and agriculturally independent, and the great fear of Anglo-French blockade, which won the last war and at the moment probably could win the next, will be done away with. Germany can then turn on the West and probably beat her.

Struck by the ugliness of the German women on the streets and in restaurants and cafés. As a race they are certainly the least attractive in Europe. They have no ankles. They walk badly. They dress worse than English women used to. Off to Danzig tonight.

DANZIG, *August* 11

For a place where the war is supposed to be
about to break out, Danzig does not quite live up to its
part. Like the people in Berlin, the local inhabitants
don't think it will come to war. They have a blind faith
in Hitler that he will effect their return to the Reich
without war. The Free City is being rapidly milita-
rized, German military cars and trucks — with Danzig
licence plates! — dash through the streets. My hotel,
the Danzigerhof, full of German army officers. The
roads leading in from Poland are blocked with tank-
traps and log-barriers. They remind me of Sudetenland just a year ago. The two strategic hills of Bi-
schofsberg and Hagelberg have been fortified. And a
lot of arms are being run under cover of night across
the Nogat River from East Prussia. They are mostly
machine-guns, anti-tank and air-guns and light artillery. Apparently they have not been able to bring in
any heavy artillery. Most of the arms are of Czech
manufacture.

The town completely Nazified. Supreme boss is Albert Forster, the Nazi *Gauleiter*, who is not even a
Danziger, but a Bavarian. Herr Greiser, the President
of the Senate, is a more moderate man, but takes his
orders from Forster. Among the population, much less
tension than I'd expected. The people want to be joined
to Germany. But not at the cost of war or the loss of
their position as an outlet for Polish trade. Without
the latter, reduced though it is since the building of the
purely Polish port of Gdynia, twelve miles west of here,
they starve, unless Germany conquers Poland. Like all
Germans they want it both ways.

Danzig is a pleasing town to look at. I like the heavy
Baltic-German towers, the Gothic Hanseatic steep-

gabled houses with the heavily ornamented façades. Reminds me of the other Hanseatic towns — Bremen, Lübeck, Bruges. Walked around the port. Very dead-looking. Few ships. More drunkenness here in Danzig than I've seen outside of America. The *Schnapps* — they call it " Danzig goldwater " because of the little golden particles floating in it — is right good and strong.

Lunch with our consul, Mr. Kuykendahl, who is helpful and aware of his key position. John Gunther turns up from nowhere for lunch. Afterwards John and I taxi over to Zoppot, the Baltic's leading summer resort, whiling away the afternoon and evening on the pier, the beach, in the gaming rooms of the Casino (where we both lose at roulette), talking a blue streak, settling the world's problems. Towards midnight he dashes off for Gdynia to catch the night express for Warsaw.

DANZIG, *August* 12

I have more and more the feeling that Danzig is not the issue and I'm wasting my time here. The issue is the independence of Poland or German domination of it. I must push on to Warsaw. Have been on the phone to Berlin several times today. The Berlin radio people are stalling on facilities for my broadcast from here tomorrow. Will phone *Polskie Radio* in Warsaw to see if they have a microphone at Gdynia. I could do my talk from there. I don't like the idea of the Germans keeping me from talking altogether since I've come all this way and have something to say. The local Nazis very cool to me.

In a wagonlit, Gdynia–Warsaw, *August* 13,
   midnight

   I did my broadcast to New York from Gdynia
instead of Danzig. The Germans in Berlin wouldn't
say yes or no. The Poles in Warsaw pitched in gallantly. Pleased at defeating Nazi efforts to silence me.
I had planned to drive the twelve miles from Danzig
to Gdynia, but my German chauffeur got cold feet, said
we'd be shot at by the Poles in a Danzig car. I dashed
down to the station and caught a train. A devil of a
time finding the radio studio in Gdynia. No one knew
where it was. It was not in the phone book. The telephone central didn't know. The army — the navy —
the police — none knew. Finally, after I'd given up
hope of broadcasting at all, we discovered it in the Post
Office building. The radio telephone circuit with London, from where the talk was short-waved to New York,
was completed only at the last minute. But reception,
London said, was good. Chatted with two Polish radio
engineers who had driven over from Thurn to do the
broadcast. They were calm, confident. They said:
" We're ready. We will fight. We were born under
German rule in this neighbourhood and we'd rather be
dead than go through it again."
   After dinner, waiting for the Warsaw Express, I had
time to look at this port town. The Poles, with French
backing, have done a magnificent job. Fifteen years
ago, Gdynia was a sleepy fishing village of 400 souls.
Today it's the largest port in the Baltic, with a population of over 100,000. Lacking natural facilities, the
Poles have simply pushed piers out into the sea. The
city itself looks like a mushroom growth, much like some
of our Western towns thirty-five years ago. It is one
of the promises of Poland.

LATER. — A point about the Danzig situation: Hitler is not yet ready for a showdown. Otherwise the Danzig Senate would not have backed down a week ago when, after informing Poland that the Polish customs officials in Danzig must cease their functions, it gave in to a Polish ultimatum and withdrew the order. But this may be only a temporary German setback.

WARSAW, *August* 16

Much excitement in official Polish circles to-day. Conferences between Smigly-Rydz, Beck, and the generals. A Polish soldier has been shot on the Danzig frontier. Result: an order tonight instructing Polish troops to shoot anyone crossing the Danzig border on sight and without challenge. Lunch at Ambassador Biddle's. He is full of enthusiasm for his job and chockfull of good information, though I do not always agree with his conclusions. He is very pro-Polish, which is natural, and all right with me. Biddle is afraid the French and British are going to try appeasement again and suggests that Professor Burkhardt, the League High Commissioner in Danzig, and a Swiss, who saw Hitler at Berchtesgaden last week-end, may turn out to be another Runciman.

WARSAW, *August* 20

Broadcast to America at four a.m. today. Walking home to the hotel at dawn, the air was soft and fresh and the quiet soothing. Getting off to Berlin tonight on orders from New York — my fate always to get caught, I fear, on the wrong side. All in all, the Poles are calm and confident and Berlin's gibes and Goebbels's terrific press campaign of lies and invented incidents leave them cold. But they are too romantic, too confident. You ask them, as I've asked a score of officials in the Foreign Office and the army this past week, about Russia and they shrug their shoulders. Russia does not count for them. But it ought to. I think the Poles will fight. I know I said that, wrongly, about the Czechs a year ago. But I say it again about the Poles. Our Embassy is divided. Most think Poland will give a good account of itself. Our military attaché thinks the Poles can hold out alone against Germany for six months. Harrison, on the other hand, thinks the country will crack up. Major Eliot here. Thinks the Polish army is pretty good, but not sufficiently armed nor fully aware of its awful strategic position. To record: a riotous dinner John [Gunther] gave — much vodka, smoked salmon, and talk; lunch today with young Richard Mowrer, the very image of his father, Paul Scott Mowrer, and with his bride, who is most attractive. And last night before my broadcast a tramp through Warsaw with Maurice Hindus. *Polskie Radio* new short-wave transmitter not yet ready, which worries me.

BERLIN, *August 23*

Hans Kaltenborn, our star foreign-news commentator, was turned back by the secret police when he arrived at Tempelhof from London this afternoon. We have been nicely double-crossed by the Nazis. On orders from New York, I had inquired in official circles about his coming and had been told that there was no objection to his visiting here though he could not broadcast from Germany nor see any officials. I became suspicious when the passport officials continued to hold him after all the other passengers had been cleared. His wife, several German relatives of hers, and I waited patiently beyond the brass railing which separated us from him. It was sultry and hot, and as it became evident what was up, we all perspired profusely. The German relatives, who were exposing themselves to possible arrest by merely being there, remained bravely at the rail. I finally complained to a Gestapo man about keeping us standing so long, and after much heated argument he allowed Hans to accompany us all to the terrace of the airport café, where we ordered beer. Hans had arrived at three forty-five p.m. At quarter to six a Gestapo officer came up and announced that Hans would be taking the six o'clock plane back to London.

"Why, he's just come from there," I spoke up.

"And he's returning there now," the officer said.

"May I ask why?" Hans said, boiling inside but cool outside, though beads of sweat bubbled out on his forehead.

The officer had a ready answer. Looking in his notebook, he said with tremendous seriousness: "Herr Kaltenborn, on such and such a date in Oklahoma City you made a speech insulting the Führer."

"Let me see the text of that, please," Hans spoke up. But you do not argue with the Gestapo. There was no answer. Hans rushed out to get in the plane, but there was no room after all, and he came back and joined our table. I asked the Gestapo if he couldn't take the night train to Poland. By now I was afraid he might have to spend the night in jail. I said I would get the American Embassy to guarantee that he wouldn't jump off the train in Germany. Finally, reluctantly, they consented. I called Consul Geist. He would play the game. We adjourned again to our beers. Then the Gestapo man came running up out of breath. There was *doch* a place on the plane for the culprit. They had thrown someone off. And Hans was hustled out. As he got

beyond the railing he remembered his pockets stuffed
with American tobacco for me. He started to toss some
of it to me, but a Gestapo agent stopped him. *Verboten.*
Then he disappeared.

LATER (*Four hours after midnight*).—
Great excitement at the Taverne tonight. About
two a.m. we get the terms of the Russian-German pact.
It goes much further than anyone dreamed. It's a
virtual alliance and Stalin, the supposed arch-enemy
of Nazism and aggression, by its terms invites Germany
to go in and clean up Poland. The friends of the Bolos
are consternated. Several German editors — Halfeld,
Kriegk, Silex — who only day before yesterday were
writing hysterically about the Bolo peril, now come in,
order champagne, and reveal themselves as old friends
of the Soviets! That Stalin would play such crude
power politics and also play into the hands of the Nazis
overwhelms the rest of us. The correspondents, especially the British, take to champagne or cognac to drown
their feelings. Stalin's step should kill world Communism. Will a French Communist, say, who has been
taught for six years to hate Nazism above all else, swallow Moscow's embracing of Hitler? Maybe, though,
Stalin is smart. His aim: to bring on a war between
Germany and the West which will result in chaos, after
which the Bolsheviks step in and Communism comes to
these countries or what is left of them. Maybe, too, he's
not smart. Hitler has broken every international agreement he ever made. When he has used Russia, as he
once used Poland, with whom in 1934 he made a similar
agreement, then good-bye Russia. Joe [Barnes], who
is shaken by the news though he is the only one here
who really knows Russia, and I argue the points. We
sit down with the German editors. They are gloating,

boasting, sputtering that Britain won't dare to fight now, denying everything they have been told to say these last six years by their Nazi lords. We throw it into their faces, Joe and I. The argument gets nasty. Joe is nervous, depressed. So am I. Pretty soon we get nauseated. Something will happen if we don't get out. . . . Mrs. Kaltenborn comes in. I had made a date with her here for three a.m. I apologize. I have to go. Joe has to go. Sorry. We wander through the Tiergarten until we cool off and the night starts to fade.

BERLIN, *August* 24, *seven p.m.*

It looks like war tonight. Across the street from my room they're installing an anti-aircraft gun on the roof of I. G. Farben. I suppose it's the same one I saw there last September. German bombers have been flying over the city all day. It may well be that Hitler will go into Poland tonight. Many think so. But I think that depends upon Britain and France. If they emphasize they will honour their word with Poland, Hitler may wait. And get what he wants without war. Went over to INS to get the text of Chamberlain's statement to the house. It sounds firm. Ed telephoned from London an hour ago and said he was in Commons and it was firm. Hitler certainly seems to be standing firm. Yesterday the British Ambassador, Henderson, flew down to Berchtesgaden to see him. He told him the British would honour their pledge to help Poland if Germany attacked, regardless of the Russo-German treaty. Hitler replied no British guarantee could make Germany " forsake her *Lebensrecht.*"

With Russia in his bag, Hitler is not compromising, apparently. Russia in his bag! What a *turn* events have taken in the last forty-eight hours. Bolshevik Russia and Nazi Germany, the arch-enemies of this earth, suddenly turning the other cheek and becoming friends and concluding what, to one's consternation, looks like an alliance.

It all broke Monday night (August 21) at eleven p.m. The German radio suddenly stopped in the middle of a musical program and a voice announced that Germany and Russia had decided to conclude a non-aggression pact. I missed it. I was at the *Herald Tribune* office chewing the rag with Joe [Barnes] until five minutes to eleven. No inkling of it then, except — I remembered later — a vague hint from the Wilhelmstrasse that there might be a story later that evening. Fatty, a German newspaperman, I think, mentioned it. Actually I got the news from London when Ed Murrow called at midnight. The RRG would not let me broadcast that night. Apparently they were waiting for " editorial " orders. The day before, on Sunday, there had been a hint of something with the announcement of a new trade agreement between Russia and Germany. The friendly words about this in the local press, which until then had been violent in its denunciation of Russia and Bolshevism, should have warned me, but didn't. The announcement was as much of a bomb-shell for most of the big Nazis as for the rest of the world. Not more than a dozen persons were in on Hitler's secret.

The German press the next day (Tuesday, August 22) was wonderful to behold. Dr. Goebbels's *Angriff*, the most ferocious Red-baiter of them all, wrote: " The world stands before a towering fact: two peoples have placed themselves on the basis of a common foreign policy which during a long and traditional friendship produced a foundation for a common understanding "! (Exclamation point mine, not *Angriff's*.) And Dr. Karl Silex, once an honest foreign correspondent and now cringing editor of the *Deutsche Allgemeine Zeitung*, in a front-page editorial called the new agreement a " natural partnership." For years — since he became a Nazi slave — he has been violently attacking Bolshevism and Soviet Russia.

There's no doubt that Hitler's amazing move is popular among the masses. On Tuesday I made a point of riding around on the subway, elevated, street-cars, and buses. Everyone was reading the story in his newspaper. From their faces, from their talk, you could see they liked the news. Why? Because it means to them that the dreaded nightmare of encirclement — war on two fronts — apparently has been destroyed. Yesterday it was there. Today it is gone. There will be no long front against Russia to hold this time.

The last of the English correspondents left tonight for the nearest frontier — the Danish — on orders from their Embassy. Selkirk Panton of the *Daily Express* rushed in to ask me if I would take over his car until the scare was over and he came back.[1] He thought he would be back in ten days, he said. Another Munich, you know. The Adlon bar very lonely tonight with the English gone. Much talk that Hitler has ordered the Germans to march into Poland at dawn. I doubt it. The German people haven't yet been sufficiently worked up for war. No " cause " yet. No slogan. The papers haven't yet written a word that war is imminent. The people in the streets are still confident Hitler will pull it off again without war. I cannot see war being popular among the masses as in 1914.

[1] Panton was arrested in Copenhagen in April 1940, when the Germans marched in, and interned on a Danish island. The French Minister in Copenhagen insisted on taking out all French and Polish correspondents caught there by the Germans. The British Minister made no effort to and the four English journalists there were all arrested and interned.

Berlin, *August* 25

Someone in New York insisting we go ahead with a program planned several weeks ago to be called "Europe Dances"—pick-ups from night-clubs in London, Paris, Berlin. I'm arranging one from St. Pauli's, a so-called "*Hamburger Lokal*," but wired Murrow today suggesting we call it off. War's too imminent for that sort of thing. Much uneasiness tonight because all afternoon and evening telephones and telegraph communications with the outside world were cut. When I arrived at the *Rundfunk* to do my broadcast tonight at one a.m., I had little hope of getting through, but the officials said nothing and I went ahead. Apparently it was the first word America had had from Berlin all day, and judging from what we heard on the feedback, there was some relief in New York when I reported all calm here and no war yet. Radio has a role to play, I think. Henderson saw Hitler twice today, and early this morning is flying to London. As long as they find something to negotiate about, there will be no war.

Berlin, *August* 26

With Henderson off to London this morning and not expected back before tomorrow (Sunday) night. I think we're in for a breathing-spell over the week-end. There is certainly no sign that Hitler is weakening. But the Wilhelmstrasse still hopes that Chamberlain will weaken. Our Embassy today issued a formal circular to all Americans here asking those whose presence was not absolutely necessary to leave. Most of the correspondents and businessmen have already sent out their wives and children. The big Nazi rally at Tannenberg scheduled for tomorrow, at which Hitler was to have spoken, has been cancelled because of the "gravity of the situation," so I shall not have to go there. Talked with Murrow on phone and he readily agreed we should cancel our "Europe Dances" program. Some choice headlines in the German press today: The *B.Z.*: "COMPLETE CHAOS IN POLAND —GERMAN FAMILIES FLEE—POLISH SOLDIERS PUSH TO EDGE OF GERMAN BORDER!" The *12-Uhr Blatt:* "THIS PLAYING WITH FIRE GOING TOO FAR—THREE GERMAN PASSENGER PLANES SHOT AT BY POLES—IN CORRIDOR MANY GERMAN FARMHOUSES IN FLAMES!"

Another hot day and most of the Berliners betook themselves to the lakes around the city, oblivious of the threat of war.

LATER. *One thirty a.m.*—Broadcast shortly after midnight. Have been trying not to be a prophet, but did say this: "I don't know whether we're going to have war or not. But I can tell you that in Berlin tonight the feeling is that it will be war unless Germany's demands against Poland are fulfilled." Tomorrow morning's (Sunday's) papers reveal for the first time that Hitler is demanding now not only Danzig and the Corridor but everything Germany lost in 1918, which means Posen and Silesia. Just before I went on the air DNB informed me that rationing will be instituted beginning Monday. There will be ration cards for food, soap, shoes, textiles, and coal. This will wake up the German people to their situation! It is just possible, however, that Hitler is doing this to impress London and Paris. The Nazi Party rally at Nuremberg was called off tonight. This will also arouse the people from their apathy. Tomorrow morning's papers will steep up the tension. Headline in *Völkische Beobachter*, Hitler's own newspaper: "WHOLE OF POLAND IN WAR FEVER! 1,500,000 MEN MOBILIZED! UNINTER-RUPTED TROOP TRANSPORT TOWARD THE FRONTIER! CHAOS IN UPPER SILESIA!"

No mention of any German mobilization, of course, though the Germans have been mobilized for a fort-night.

Berlin, *August* 27 (*Sunday*)

Hot and sultry today, which makes for an in-crease in tension. Henderson failed to return today as expected, causing the Wilhelmstrasse to accuse the British of stalling. (In another fortnight the rains start in Poland, making the roads impassable.) Some Nazis, however, think Henderson's delay in London means the British are giving in. Tomorrow's *Völkische Beobachter* will ask the people to be patient: "The Führer is still demanding patience from you because he wants to exhaust even the last possibilities for a peaceful solution of the crisis. That means a bloodless fulfilment of the irreducible German demands." This is a nice build-up to convince the people that if war does come, the Führer did everything possible to avoid it. The *V.B.* ends by saying that Germany, however, will not renounce her demands. "The individual, as well as the nation, can renounce only those things which are not vital." There you have German character stripped to the bone. A German cannot renounce vital things, but he expects the other fellow to. Hitler this afternoon addressed the members of the Reichstag in the Chancellery, though it was not a regular session. No report of his speech available. A DNB communiqué merely says the Führer "outlined the gravity of the

situation." This is the first time the German people
have been told by Hitler that the " situation is grave."

Food rations were fixed today and I heard many Germans grumbling at their size. Some: meat, 700 grams
per week; sugar, 280 grams; marmalade, 110 grams;
coffee or substitute, one eighth of a pound per week. As
to soap, 125 grams are allotted to each person for the
next four weeks. News of rationing has come as a heavy
blow to the people.

Representative Ham Fish, who seems to have been
taken in completely by Ribbentrop, who gave him an
airplane to rush him to the inter-parliamentary meeting in Scandinavia the other day to tell the assembled
democrats how serious was the situation, arrived today
and struck us as very anxious to continue on his way.
Joe [Barnes] and I observed him talking very seriously
at lunch in the Adlon courtyard with Dr. Zallatt, a
minor and unimportant official of the Foreign Office
who is supposed to be in charge of American press matters there, but whom no American correspondent both-
ers with because he knows nothing. Later, after keeping
the press corps waiting an hour, Fish emerged from
lunch and in a grave tone said: " Excuse me, gentlemen,
for being late, but I have just been having a talk with
an important official of the German government." The
boys suppressed their laughter only with difficulty.
Fish left this afternoon on the first train. Geoffrey
Parsons, chief editorial writer of the *Herald Tribune*,
calm, intelligent, tolerant, profound, left last night for
Paris. He had seen Churchill last week and believes it
will be war.

Despite everything the odds in the Wilhelmstrasse
today are still for peace.

Bᴇʀʟɪɴ, *August* 28

They're all putting themselves way out on
a limb. Difficult for any of Europe's leaders to retreat
now. At two this morning we get the text of letters exchanged Saturday and Sunday between Daladier and
Hitler. Daladier in a noble tone asks that Hitler hold
back from war, says that there is no question which
cannot be solved peacefully, reminds Hitler that Poland
after all is a sovereign nation, and claims that France
will honour its obligations to Poland. Hitler regrets
that France intends to fight to " maintain a wrong."
And then for the first time he reveals his demands. Danzig and the Corridor must be returned to Germany,
he says. He realizes full well the consequences of war,
he claims, but concludes that Poland will fare worse than
anyone else.

There was a fine line in Daladier's letter, the last sentence: " If French and German blood is now to be
spilled, as it was twenty-five years ago . . . then each
of the two peoples will fight confident of its own victory.
But surely Destruction and Barbarism will be the real
victors."

Ed [Murrow] phones from London at one thirty p.m.
He is tired, but in good spirits. We are both broadcasting four or five times a day — from noon until
four a.m. Ed disagrees with what Bill Stoneman told
me on the phone last night from London: namely, that
the British were selling out. Ed says they can't now.
He thinks Henderson, who is returning to Berlin from
London this afternoon, will bring an answer to Hitler
" that will shock him." Announcement of food cards
and the publication of the text of the letters of Hitler
and Daladier seem to have made the people in the street
at last realize the seriousness of the situation, judging

by their looks. An old German reading the letters said
to me: " *Ja*, they forget what war is like. But I don't.
I remember."

Troops, east-bound, pouring through the streets today. No crack units these. They were being transported in moving-vans, grocery trucks, et cetera. Germany has assured Belgium, Holland, Luxemburg, and
Switzerland that it will respect their neutrality in case
of war.

LATER. — Henderson arrived back by plane
at eight thirty p.m., went to the Chancellery at ten
thirty p.m., and stayed until eleven forty. No reliable
news about this crucial meeting, though the official line
at the Wilhelmstrasse at midnight was by no means
pessimistic.

BERLIN, *August* 29

The average German today looks dejected.
He can't get over the blow of the ration cards, which to
him spells war. Last night when Henderson flew back
with London's answer to Hitler's demands — on a night
when everyone knew the issue of war or peace might be
decided — I was amazed to see that less than 500 people out of a population of 5,000,000 turned out in
front of the Chancellery. These few stood there grim
and silent. Almost a defeatism discernible in the people.
One man remarked to me last night: " The Corridor?
Hell, we haven't heard about *that* for twenty years.
Why bring it up now? "

LATER. *Three a.m.* — At seven fifteen tonight Hitler gave Henderson his reply to the British

proposals.[1] To the surprise of the Wilhelmstrasse, the British Ambassador did not fly off to London with it, though the Germans had a plane ready for him at Tempelhof. He merely filed it in the regular diplomatic way. It looks as though the British were getting tough at last. Some of the correspondents, including myself, at the Taverne tonight had the feeling that the British had the corporal on the run. The German editors were not so boastful tonight at the Taverne. The truth is, Hitler is hesitating. Many ardent Nazis think he should have moved last Friday. If it's true that the British have him on the run, will the English conservatives still make a deal to save him? I dropped into the British Embassy this evening to see an old friend. The halls were full of luggage. " We're all packed," he laughed.

BERLIN, *August* 30

The British reply to Hitler's latest came bouncing back to Berlin tonight. With what result, we don't know. Henderson has seen Ribbentrop again, but no news of it. Tonight may well be decisive. DNB [the German news agency] has announced it will be issuing news all night tonight. This sounds ominous. The Wilhelmstrasse took pains this evening to point out to us that the non-aggression pact with Russia is also a consultative pact and that this part of it had been put into operation the last few days. This puzzles me, but I said in my broadcast tonight: " That would seem to

[1] Only on the night of August 31, nine hours before the war started, did we learn that the reply contained a demand that Poland send a representative invested with plenipotentiary powers on Wednesday, August 30 — that is, within twenty-four hours. Henderson remarked to Hitler: " That sounds like an ultimatum," but the Great Man denied it. Throughout this period the correspondents were kept largely in the dark about the negotiations, with the Wilhelmstrasse tipping us (falsely) to take " an optimistic line."

mean — and, indeed, informed circles in the Wilhelmstrasse leave no doubt about it — that the Germans and
Soviets also have been doing some talking the last few
days, and, as one writer says tonight, ' talking about
Poland.' In this connection the German press tonight
does not omit to mention a dispatch from Moscow to the
effect that not only has Russia not withdrawn her three
hundred thousand men from its western frontier, as reported, but on the contrary has strengthened her forces
there — that is, on the Polish border. I don't know the
significance of that. I only know that it's given some
prominence here."

LATER. — Poles ordered general mobilization
at two thirty p.m. today. It isn't terribly important,
because Poland has already mobilized about as many
men as it has guns and shoes for. But the story gives
the German press an excuse to hail Poland as the aggressor. (Germany has mobilized too, though not formally.) Since Hitler now has publicly demanded the return of Danzig and the Corridor, the German people
ought to know who the aggressor is liable to be. But
they are swallowing Dr. Goebbels's pills, I fear.

At midnight Hitler announces formation of a War
Cabinet — to be called a Ministerial Council for the
Defence of the Reich. Göring to preside; other mem-
bers are Frick, Funk, Lammers, and General Keitel.

The sands are running fast tonight.

BERLIN, *August* 31 (*morning*)

Everybody against the war. People talking
openly. How can a country go into a major war with
a population so dead against it? People also kicking
about being kept in the dark. A German said to me
last night: " We know nothing. Why don't they tell us

what's up? " Optimism in official circles melting away
this morning, I thought. Huss thinks Hitler may have
one great card left, an agreement with Stalin to attack
the Poles in the back. I highly doubt it, but after the
Russo-German pact anything is possible. Some think
the Big Boy is trying to get off the limb now — but
how?

LATER. — Broadcast at seven forty-five p.m.
Said: " The situation tonight is very critical. Hitler
has not yet answered the British note of last night. . . .
An answer may not be necessary. . . . The new Defence Council sat all day. The Wilhelmstrasse has been
seething with activity. . . . There has been no contact
between the German and British governments. Instead
. . . between Russia and Germany. Berlin expects the
Soviets to ratify the Russo-German pact this evening.
. . . The British Ambassador did not visit the Wilhelmstrasse. He had a talk with his French colleague,
M. Coulondre. Then he saw the Polish Ambassador,
M. Lipski. Bags at these three embassies are all
packed. . . ."

LATER. *Three thirty a.m.* — A typical Hitler swindle was sprung this evening. At nine p.m. the
German radio stopped its ordinary program and broadcast the terms of German " proposals " to Poland. I
was taken aback by their reasonableness, and having to
translate them for our American listeners immediately,
as we were on the air, I missed the catch. This is that
Hitler demanded that a Polish plenipotentiary be sent
to Berlin to " discuss " them by last night, though they
were only given to Henderson the night before.[1] An

[1] Even this was not true. Henderson revealed later that Ribbentrop — in a most insolent mood — read the sixteen points to him so
rapidly that he could not grasp them. When he asked for a copy of
them, the German Foreign Minister refused!

official German statement (very neat) complains that
the Poles would not even come to Berlin to discuss them.
Obviously, they didn't have time. And why should Hitler set a time limit to a sovereign power? The " proposals " — obviously never meant seriously — read like
sweet reason, almost. They contain sixteen points, but
the essential ones are four: (1) Return of Danzig to
Germany. (2) A plebiscite to determine who shall have
the Corridor. (3) An exchange of minority populations. (4) Gdynia to remain Polish even if the Corridor
votes to return to Germany.

Tonight the great armies, navies, and air forces are
all mobilized. Each country is shut off from the other.
We have not been able today to get through to Paris
or London, or of course to Warsaw, though I did talk
to Tess in Geneva. At that, no precipitate action is
expected tonight. Berlin is quite normal in appearance
this evening. There has been no evacuation of the
women and children, not even any sandbagging of the
windows. We'll have to wait through still another night,
it appears, before we know. And so to bed, almost at
dawn.

BERLIN, *September* 1

At six a.m. Sigrid Schultz — bless her heart
— phoned. She said: " It's happened." I was very
sleepy — my body and mind numbed, paralysed. I
mumbled: " Thanks, Sigrid," and tumbled out of bed.
The war is on!

PART II

The War

WLS

BERLIN, *September* 1, *later*

It's a " counter-attack "! At dawn this morning Hitler moved against Poland. It's a flagrant, inexcusable, unprovoked act of aggression. But Hitler and the High Command call it a " counter-attack." A grey morning with overhanging clouds. The people in the street were apathetic when I drove to the *Rundfunk* for my first broadcast at eight fifteen a.m. Across from the Adlon the morning shift of workers was busy on the new I. G. Farben building just as if nothing had happened. None of the men bought the Extras which the newsboys were shouting. Along the east-west axis the Luftwaffe were mounting five big anti-aircraft guns to protect Hitler when he addresses the Reichstag at ten a.m. Jordan and I had to remain at the radio to handle Hitler's speech for America. Throughout the speech, I thought as I listened, ran a curious strain, as though Hitler himself were dazed at the fix he had got himself into and felt a little desperate about it. Somehow he did not carry conviction and there was much less cheering in the Reichstag than on previous, less important occasions. Jordan must have reacted the same way. As we waited to translate the speech for America, he whispered: " Sounds like his swan song." It really did. He sounded discouraged when he told the Reichstag that

Italy would not be coming into the war because "we are unwilling to call in outside help for this struggle. We will fulfil this task by ourselves." And yet Paragraph 3 of the Axis military alliance calls for immediate, automatic Italian support with "all its military resources on land, at sea, and in the air." What about that? He sounded desperate when, referring to Molotov's speech of yesterday at the Russian ratification of the Nazi-Soviet accord, he said: "I can only underline every word of Foreign Commissar Molotov's speech."

Tomorrow Britain and France probably will come in and you have your second World War. The British and French tonight sent an ultimatum to Hitler to withdraw his troops from Poland or their ambassadors will ask for their passports. Presumably they will get their passports.

LATER. *Two thirty a.m.* — Almost through our first black-out. The city is completely darkened. It takes a little getting used to. You grope around the pitch-black streets and pretty soon your eyes get used to it. You can make out the whitewashed curbstones. We had our first air-raid alarm at seven p.m. I was at the radio just beginning my script for a broadcast at eight fifteen. The lights went out, and all the German employees grabbed their gas-masks and, not a little frightened, rushed for the shelter. No one offered me a mask, but the wardens insisted that I go to the cellar. In the darkness and confusion I escaped outside and went down to the studios, where I found a small room in which a candle was burning on a table. There I scribbled out my notes. No planes came over. But with the English and French in, it may be different tomorrow. I shall then be in the by no means pleasant predicament of hoping they bomb the hell out of this town without getting me. The ugly shrill of the sirens, the rushing to a cellar with your gas-mask (if you have one), the utter darkness of the night — how will human nerves stand that for long?

One curious thing about Berlin on this first night of the war: the cafés, restaurants, and beer-halls were packed. The people just a bit apprehensive after the air-raid, I felt. Finished broadcasting at one thirty a.m., stumbled a half-mile down the Kaiserdamm in the dark, and finally found a taxi. But another pedestrian appeared out of the dark and jumped in first. We finally shared it, he very drunk and the driver drunker, and both cursing the darkness and the war.

The isolation from the outside world that you feel on a night like this is increased by a new decree issued tonight prohibiting the listening to foreign broadcasts. Who's afraid of the truth? And no wonder. Curious that not a single Polish bomber got through tonight. But will it be the same with the British and French?

BERLIN, *September 2*

The German attack on Poland has now been going on for two days and Britain and France haven't yet honoured their promises. Can it be that Chamberlain and Bonnet are going to try to sneak out of them? Hitler has cabled Roosevelt he will not bomb open towns if the others don't. No air-raid tonight. Where are the Poles?

BERLIN, *September 3*

Hitler's " counter-attack " on Poland has on this Sabbath day become a world war! To record the date: September 3, 1939. The time: eleven a.m. At

nine o'clock this morning Sir Nevile Henderson called
on the German Foreign Minister and handed him a note
giving Germany until eleven o'clock to accept the British demand that Germany withdraw her troops from
Poland. He returned to the Wilhelmstrasse shortly
after eleven and was handed the German reply in the
form of a memorandum. The extras are out on the
streets now. The newsboys are giving them away. The
D.A.Z. here. Its headlines:

BRITISH ULTIMATUM TURNED DOWN
ENGLAND DECLARES A STATE OF WAR WITH GERMANY
BRITISH NOTE DEMANDS WITHDRAWAL OF OUR TROOPS IN THE EAST
THE FÜHRER LEAVING TODAY FOR THE FRONT

A typical headline over the official account:

GERMAN MEMORANDUM PROVES ENGLAND'S GUILT.

I was standing in the Wilhelmplatz about noon when
the loud-speakers suddenly announced that England
had declared herself at war with Germany. Some 250
people were standing there in the sun. They listened
attentively to the announcement. When it was finished,
there was not a murmur. They just stood there as they
were before. Stunned. The people cannot realize yet
that Hitler has led them into a world war. No issue has
been created for them yet, though as this day wears on,
it is plain that " Albion's perfidy " will become the issue
as it did in 1914. In *Mein Kampf* Hitler says the greatest mistake the Kaiser made was to fight England, and
Germany must never repeat that mistake.

It has been a lovely September day, the sun shining,
the air balmy, the sort of day the Berliner loves to spend

in the woods or on the lakes near by. I walked in the
streets. On the faces of the people astonishment, depression. Until today they have been going about their
business pretty much as usual. There were food cards
and soap cards and you couldn't get any gasoline and
at night it was difficult stumbling around in the black-
out. But the war in the east has seemed a bit far away
to them — two moonlight nights and not a single Polish
plane over Berlin to bring destruction — and the papers saying that German troops have been advancing
all along the line, that the Polish air force has been
destroyed. Last night I heard Germans talking of the
" Polish thing " lasting but a few weeks, or months at
the most. Few believed that Britain and France would
move. Ribbentrop was sure they wouldn't and had told
the Führer, who believed him. The British and French
had been accommodating before. Another Munich, why
not? Yesterday, when it seemed that London and Paris
were hesitating, everyone, including those in the Wilhelmstrasse, was optimistic. Why not?

In 1914, I believe, the excitement in Berlin on the
first day of the World War was tremendous. Today,
no excitement, no hurrahs, no cheering, no throwing of
flowers, no war fever, no war hysteria. There is not even
any hate for the French and British — despite Hitler's
various proclamations to the people, the party, the East
Army, the West Army, accusing the " English warmongers and capitalistic Jews " of starting this war.
When I passed the French and British embassies this
afternoon, the sidewalk in front of each of them was
deserted. A lone *Schupo* paced up and down before
each.

At lunch-time we gathered in the courtyard of the
Adlon for drinks with a dozen members of the British
Embassy staff. They seemed completely unmoved by

events. They talked about *dogs* and such stuff. Some mystery about the French not acting in concert with the British today, Coulondre's ultimatum not running out until five p.m., six hours after Britain was at war. But the French tell us this was due to faulty communications with Paris.[1]

The High Command lets it be known that on the western front the Germans won't fire *first* against the French.

LATER. — Broadcast all afternoon and evening. Third night of the black-out. No bombs, though we rather expected the British and French. The newspapers continue to praise the decree against listening in to foreign broadcasts! What are they afraid of?

BERLIN, *September* 4

After midnight and no air-raid, even with the British and French in the war. Can it be that in this new World War they're not going to bomb the big cities, the capitals, the civilians, the women and children at home, after all? The people here breathing easier already. They didn't sleep much the first couple of nights.

On the feedback from New York tonight I heard the story of the sinking of the *Athenia* with 1,400 passengers, including 240 Americans, aboard. The English said it was a German U-boat. The Germans promptly denied it, though the German press and radio have been forbidden to mention the matter until tomorrow. I felt lousy talking from here at all tonight after that story and went out of my way to explain my

[1] Actually Bonnet boasted after the Franco-German armistice that he had refused the plea of Halifax for a simultaneous declaration of war. He played for peace at any price until the very end.

personal position as an American broadcaster — that I had been assigned to give the news from Germany, that official statements such as the denial that a German submarine had torpedoed the *Athenia* were part of that news, and that my orders from home were to refrain from expressing my personal opinions. The High Command has installed military censorship of everything I say, but fortunately the chief censor is a naval officer, an honourable and decent man. I have had some warm words with him the last couple of days, but within the limits of his job he has been reasonable.

The war is starting to hurt the average man. Tonight a decree providing for a surtax on the income tax of a straight fifty per cent and a big increase in the tax on beer and tobacco. Also a decree fixing prices and wages.

The staffs of the French and British embassies got away today in two big Pullman trains. I was a little struck by the weird fact that while the killing goes on, all the diplomatic niceties were strictly observed by both sides to the very last.

The faces of the Germans when word came in late tonight that the British had bombed Cuxhaven and Wilhelmshaven for the first time! This was bringing the war home, and nobody seemed to like it.

BERLIN, *September 5*

Very strange about that western front. The Wilhelmstrasse assured us today that not a single shot has been fired there yet. Indeed, one official told me — though I doubt his word — that the German forces on the French border were broadcasting in French to the poilus: " We won't shoot if you don't." Same informant claimed the French had hoisted a streamer from a bal-

loon saying the same thing. Today the RRG[1] gave
its first broadcast from the front, and it sounded plenty
realistic. It was of course a recording. The Germans
say they will let me do radio recordings at the front,
but American networks won't permit the broadcasting
of recordings—a pity, because it is the only way radio
can really cover the war from the front. I think we're
throwing away a tremendous opportunity, though God
knows I have no burning desire to die a hero's death at
the front. The fortress of Graudenz fell today and the
Germans have smashed through the Corridor. After a
slow start they seem to be going awfully fast. In the
south Cracow is surrounded.

BERLIN, *September* 6

Cracow, second town of Poland, was captured
this afternoon. The High Command also states that
Kielce has fallen. Looking for it on my map, I was
amazed to find that it lies way to the east of both Lodz
and Cracow, almost due south of Warsaw. Nobody had
any idea the German army had got that far. In one
week the Germans have pushed far beyond their 1914
frontiers. It begins to look like a rout for the Poles.

I learned tonight that the liner *Bremen* has succeeded
in evading the British blockade and today put in at
Murmansk on the northern coast of Russia after a dash
from New York. I'm pretty sure I'm the only one in
town who knows it and I led off my broadcast with the
yarn. At the last minute the military censor rushed in
and cut it out; said I couldn't mention it.

LATER.—Joe [Barnes] and I met in my
room at one a.m. to talk things over. We have an idea

[1] *Reichs Rundfunk Gesellschaft* — the German State Broadcasting
Company.

that Britain and France will not shed much blood on
the western front, but will maintain an iron blockade
and wait for Germany to collapse. In the meantime
Poland will of course be overrun.

BERLIN, *September* 7

Have heard much talk today about peace!
Idea is that after Germany's victory over Poland Hitler
will offer the West peace. I wrote this rather carefully
for my broadcast this evening, but the censor wouldn't
allow a word of it.

It's just a week since the "counter-attack" began
and tonight I learn from an army friend that the Germans are within twenty miles of Warsaw. A new decree
today providing the death penalty for anyone "en-
dangering the defensive power of the German people"
— a term which will give Gestapo chief Himmler plenty
of leeway. Another decree forces workers to accept new
jobs even if they pay lower wages than jobs previously
held.

BERLIN, *September* 8

The German High Command announces that
at five fifteen p.m. today German troops reached Warsaw. The radio broadcast the news at seven fifteen p.m.
Immediately afterwards a band played *Deutschland
über Alles* and the *Horst Wessel* song. Even our military attachés were stunned by the news. There was no
wild rejoicing in the streets of Berlin tonight. In the
subway going out to the radio studio I noted the strange
indifference of the people to the big news. And while
Poland is being overrun, not a shot yet—so the Germans say — on the western front! The first person to
be executed under yesterday's decree—Himmler has

lost no time — is one Johann Heinen of Dessau. He was shot, it's announced, " for refusing to take part in defensive work."

NBC and Mutual have stopped their European broadcasts. Ed Klauber cables we shall continue alone. Smart we were to build up a staff of American radio reporters. Home early tonight at one a.m. for the first time since the war started and shall get a night's sleep for once. Heard Ed broadcasting from London tonight. He sounded dead tired, as am I after being on the air night and day with practically no sleep for a month.

Bᴇʀʟɪɴ, *September* 9

The second air-raid alarm of the war at four a.m. today, but I did not hear it, being engulfed in my first good night's sleep in ages. No more news of the German army's entry into Warsaw and I begin to suspect yesterday's announcement was premature. O. W., back from the front, told me this noon that he'd seen some of the horribly mutilated bodies of Germans killed by Poles. He described also how he'd seen the Germans rounding up Polish civilians — men, women, boys — and marching them into a building for a summary court-martial and then out into the back yard against a wall, where they were disposed of by German firing squads. Our military attaché says you can do that, that that's the way cricket is played with franc-tireurs, but I don't like it, even if they are snipers, and I doubt from what O. W. says that the court-martial makes any great effort to distinguish actual franc-tireurs from those whose only guilt is being Poles.

Göring broadcast today — from a local munitions factory. He warned the people it might be a long war.

He threatened terrible revenge if the British and French
bombed Germany. He said seventy German divisions
now in Poland would be released within a week for service "elsewhere." Apparently the war in Poland is all
but over. Most of the correspondents a bit depressed.
Britain and France have done nothing on the western
front to relieve the tremendous pressure on Poland. It
begins to look as though in Hitler we have a new Napoleon who may sweep Europe and conquer it.

BERLIN, *September* 10

One week after the Anglo-French declaration
of a state of war the average German is beginning to
wonder if it's a world war after all. He sees it this way.
England and France, it is true, are formally fulfilling
their obligations to Poland. For a week they have been
formally at war with Germany. But has it been war?
they ask. The British, it is true, sent over twenty-five
planes to bomb Wilhelmshaven. But if it is war, why
only twenty-five? And if it is war, why only a few leaflets over the Rhineland? The industrial heart of Germany lies along the Rhine close to France. From there
come most of the munitions that are blowing up Poland
with such deadly effect. Yet not a bomb has fallen on
a Rhineland factory. Is that war? they ask. The long
faces I saw a week ago today are not so long this Sunday.

Life here is still quite normal. The operas, the theatres, the movies, all open and jammed. *Tannhäuser* and
Madame Butterfly playing at the Opera. Goethe's
Iphigenie at the State Theatre. The Metropol, Hitler's
favourite show-house, announces a new revue Wednesday. The papers tonight say two hundred football
matches were played in Germany today.

BERLIN, *September* 11

The High Command says a gigantic battle in Poland, with the prospect of the annihilation of the Polish army, is nearing its end. They are fighting now along the San River, south-*east* of Warsaw. For the first time today the war communiqué mentions French artillery-fire on the western front. The Protectorate government in Prague announced today that any Czechs captured fighting with the enemy would be shot as traitors.

LATER (*midnight*).— In the subway, going out to broadcast tonight, I heard considerable grumbling about the war. The women, especially, seemed depressed. And yet when I came back after the broadcast, a big crowd, mostly women, got on at the station under the Deutsches Opernhaus. They had been to the Opera and seemed oblivious of the fact that a war was on, that German bombs and shells were falling on the women and children in Warsaw. I doubt if anything short of an awful bombing or years of semi-starvation will bring home the war to the people here.

Classic headline in the *D.A.Z.* tonight: "**POLES BOMBARD WARSAW!**" The press full of the most fantastic lies. Latest is that two British secret-service agents organized the slaying of Germans at Bromberg. When I kidded my military censor, a decent fellow, about it, he blushed.

But one thing — is it possible that if the British and French decide upon a long war of attrition, the mass of the German people will forget their feelings towards the regime and regard it as their duty to defend the Fatherland? Some things I've heard today from Germans make me think so.

BERLIN, *September* 14

Yesterday from Führer Headquarters came an official announcement signed by the *Oberkommando* (but obviously dictated by Hitler) saying that as long as Polish civilians insisted on resisting the German army in the towns, Germany would use every means at its disposal, especially air bombing and heavy artillery, to show the civilians the "pointlessness of their resistance." D. and H. and W., who were at the front for three days this week, say that almost every other town and village in Poland they saw was either half or totally destroyed by bombs or artillery.

All of us here still baffled by the inaction of Britain and France. It is obvious from the broadcasts of Ed and Tom from London and Paris that the Allies are exaggerating their action on the western front. The Germans maintain that there have been only skirmishes there so far and point out that the French are not even using airplanes in their "attacks." Y. of our Embassy took issue today with Ambassador Biddle's telegrams from Poland telling of the terrible bombings of the Polish towns. Y. holds Hitler is justified in bombing and bombarding towns where the civilian population offers resistance. Guess I'm losing my balance, but I disagree.

The maid came in tonight to say how terrible war was.

"Why do the French make war on us?" she asked.

"Why do you make war on the Poles?" I said.

"Hum," she said, a blank over her face. "But the French, they're human beings," she said finally.

"But the Poles, maybe they're human beings," I said.

"Hum," she said, blank again.

Berlin, *September* 15

I heard today on very good authority that Russia may attack Poland.

A few words on a dry subject. How does the Allied blockade affect Germany? It cuts her off from about 50 per cent of her normal imports. Chief products of which Germany is deprived are: cotton, tin, nickel, oil, and rubber. Russia might supply some cotton, but her total exports last year were only 2.5 per cent of Germany's annual needs. On the other hand Russia could probably supply Germany all the manganese and timber she needs, and — with Rumania — enough oil for military purposes at least. Iron? Last year Germany got about 45 per cent of her iron ore from France, Morocco, or other places from which she is now cut off. But Sweden, Norway, and Luxemburg provided her with eleven million tons. These supplies are still open. All in all, Germany is certainly hard hit by losing the sources of 50 per cent of her imports. But with the possibilities open to her in Scandinavia, the Balkans, and Russia she is not hit nearly so badly as she was in 1914.

Just two weeks ago today the great " counter-attack " against Poland began. In fourteen days the mechanized German military machine has rolled back the Polish army more than two hundred miles, captured a hundred thousand prisoners, and practically liquidated Poland. Today one German army stands before the citadel in Brest-Litovsk, where Germany dictated a harsh treaty to Bolshevik Russia in 1918. Another German army is nearing the Rumanian border, thus bringing Germany to the front door of vast oil sources and stocks of wheat. To be sure, a gallant Polish army, completely surrounded at Kutno, seventy-five miles west of Warsaw, holds out. But for how long? Warsaw too holds out.

But for how long? The war in Poland is over. German divisions are already being rushed to the west. My censor did not object when I suggested tonight that Russia will now step in and occupy the parts of Poland inhabited by Russians. More talk about peace today.

Example of how our isolationists are appreciated in Naziland: Headline in the *Börsen Zeitung:* "SENATOR BORAH WARNS AGAINST THE WAR AGITATORS IN U.S.A."

BERLIN, *September* 16

Every German I've met today liked Colonel Lindbergh's broadcast. The story gets a good play in the Berlin newspapers, which is more than Roosevelt's speeches get. The headlines are friendly. The *Börsen Zeitung:* "COLONEL LINDBERGH WARNS AGAINST THE AGITATION OF THE WESTERN POWERS."

An American woman I know bought a tin of sardines today. The grocer insisted on opening the can in the shop. Reason: you can't hoard tinned food if your grocer opens it first.

LATER (*midnight*). — The Germans have just announced that if Warsaw does not surrender within twelve hours, the German army will use all military methods to subdue it. That means bomb it and bombard it. There are more than half a million civilians in the city, the majority women and children.

BERLIN, *September* 17

At six o'clock this morning, Moscow time, the Red army began an invasion of Poland. Russia of course had a non-aggression pact with Poland. What ages ago it seems now — though it really wasn't ages ago — that I sat in Geneva and other capitals and heard the Soviet statesmen talk about common fronts against the aggressor. Now Soviet Russia stabs Poland in the back, and the Red army joins the Nazi army in over-running Poland. All this of course is heartily welcomed in Berlin this morning.

My military censor was really quite decent today. He let me broadcast this: "If Warsaw does not sur-render, it means that one of Europe's largest cities will be blown up by the German army and a good share of the human beings living there with it. Certainly his-tory knows no parallel. . . . The Germans say it is the Poles in Warsaw who are violating international law by making their civilians help defend the capital. But, as I say, I just can't follow the things that are hap-pening in this war."

Off to the " front " tomorrow, if we can find one.

Zoppot, near Danzig, *September* 18

Drove all day long from Berlin through Pom-erania and the Corridor to here. The roads full of motorized columns of German troops *returning* from Poland. In the woods in the Corridor the sickening sweet smell of dead horses and the sweeter smell of dead men. Here, the Germans say, a whole division of Polish cavalry charged against hundreds of German tanks and was annihilated. On the pier of this summer resort where just five weeks ago John [Gunther] and I sat far into the peaceful night arguing whether the guns would go off or not in Europe, we watched tonight the battle raging around Gdynia. Far off across the sea you could see the sky light up when the big guns went off.

Dr. Boehmer, press chief of the Propaganda Ministry in charge of this trip, insisted that I share a double room in the hotel here with Phillip Johnson, an American fascist who says he represents Father Coughlin's *Social Justice*. None of us can stand the fellow and suspect he is spying on us for the Nazis. For the last hour in our room here he has been posing as anti-Nazi and trying to pump me for my attitude. I have given him no more than a few bored grunts.

Dᴀɴᴢɪɢ, *September* 19–20, *two thirty a.m.*

Sit here in the local radio station shivering and waiting to broadcast at four a.m. I talked at midnight, but Berlin on the phone said they did not think CBS picked me up. We shall try once again at four.

Today I have had a glimpse of an actual battle, one of the last of the Polish war, which is as good as over. It was going on two miles north of Gdynia on a ridge that stretched for seven miles inland from the sea. There was something about it that was very tragic and at the same time grotesque.

We stood on a hill called the Sternberg in the midst of the city of Gdynia under a huge — irony! — cross. It was a German observation post. Officers stood about, peering through field-glasses. Across the city over the roofs of the modern buildings of this model new town that was the hope of Poland we watched the battle going on two miles to the north. We had been awakened this morning in our beds in a hotel at Zoppot by it. At six a.m. the windows in my room shook. The German battleship *Schleswig-Holstein*, anchored in Danzig, was firing shells from its eleven-inch guns over our heads. And now, we could see, the Germans had the Poles surrounded on three sides, and the sea, from which German destroyers were peppering them, cut them off on the fourth. The Germans were using everything in the way of weapons, big guns, small guns, tanks, and airplanes. The Poles had nothing but machine-guns, rifles, and two anti-aircraft pieces which they were trying desperately to use as artillery against German machine-gun posts and German tanks. You could hear the deep roar of the German artillery and the rat-tat-tat of the machine-guns on both sides. The Poles — we gathered from the sound of their fire, because you could see very little, even through glasses — not only were defending themselves from trenches and behind clumps of bushes but were using every building they held as machine-gun nests. They had turned two large buildings, one an officers' school, the other the Gdynia radio station, into fortresses and were firing machine-guns from several of the windows. After a half-hour a German shell struck the roof of the school and set it on fire. Then German infantry, supported — or through the glasses it looked as though they were *led* — by tanks, charged up the hill and surrounded the building. But they did not take it. The Poles kept machine-gunning them from the basement windows of the burning building. Desperate and brave the Poles were. A German seaplane hovered over the ridge, spotting for the artillery. Later a bombing plane joined it and they dived low, machine-gunning the Polish lines. Finally a squadron of Nazi bombers appeared.

It was a hopeless position for the Poles. And yet they fought on. The German officers with us kept praising their courage. Directly below us in Gdynia's streets, women and children stood about, sullen and silent, watching the unequal battle. Before some of the buildings long lines of Poles stood waiting for food. Before

mounting the hill I had noted the terrible bitterness in
their faces, especially in those of the women.

We watched the battle until noon. In that time the
Germans must have advanced about a quarter of a mile.
Their infantry, their tanks, their artillery, their signal
corps, all seen.ed to work as a precise machine. There
was not the slightest sign of strain or excitement in the
German officers at our observation post. Very business-
like they were, reminding me of the coaches of a cham-
pionship football team who sit on the sidelines and
calmly and confidently watch the machine they've
created perform as they knew all the time it would.

As we prepared to go, Joe [Barnes] turned to me.
"Tragic and grotesque," he said. It was, all right.
The unequal battle, the dazed civilians in the streets
below — tragic indeed. And grotesque the spectacle of
us, with little danger to ourselves, standing there watching the killing as though it were a football game and
we nicely placed in the grand-stand. Grotesque, too, to
have a grand-stand seat from which to watch the women
in the streets below, for whom all the thunder of the
guns that we were hearing was a bitter personal tragedy.

As we left I asked an officer about the Polish artillery.

"They haven't any," he said. "If they had just one
'75,' they could have blown us all to bits. It's only two
miles over there, and this would have been a natural
target."

We drove to the Westerplatte, a small island between
Danzig and the sea which had been used by the Poles
as a supply depot. For five days a small Polish garrison
had held out on the island against the eleven-inch guns
of the *Schleswig-Holstein* firing at point-blank range
and Stukas dropping five-hundred-pound bombs. Even
the Germans recognized its bravery, and when the Poles

finally surrendered, their commander was allowed to keep his sword. Today the Westerplatte looked like the wasteland around Verdun. Interesting: the bombs tossed by the Stukas were more deadly and more accurate than the shells from the old battleship. A round Polish bunker not over forty feet in diameter had received two direct hits from five-hundred-pound bombs. The ten-foot thickness of concrete and steel had been torn to pieces like tissue paper. Near by we saw the graves of what was left of the Poles who had been inside.

In the afternoon we drove to the Danzig Guild Hall, a Gothic building of great beauty, to hear Hitler make his first speech since his Reichstag address of September 1 started off the war. I had a seat on the aisle, and as he strode past me to the rostrum I thought he looked more imperious than I had ever seen him. Also he was about as angry during his speech as I've ever seen him. When he spoke of Britain his face flamed up in hysterical rage. Afterwards a Nazi acquaintance confided to me that the " old man " was in a terrible rage because he had counted on making today's speech in Warsaw, that he had waited three or four days outside the Polish capital, burning to enter it like a conquering Cæsar and make his speech of victory, and that when the Poles inside refused to surrender and each day continued their stubborn resistance, his patience had cracked and he rushed to Danzig to make his speech. He had to talk! We had expected Hitler to offer peace to the West and announce what the future of Poland would be. He did neither, merely remarking that Poland would never be re-created on the Versailles model and that he had no war aims against Britain and France, but would fight them if they continued the war. When Hitler brushed past me going down the aisle, he was followed by

Himmler, Brückner, Keitel, and several others, all in dusty field-grey. Most of them were unshaven and I must say they looked like a pack of Chicago gangsters. Himmler, who is responsible for Hitler's protection, kept shoving people back in the aisle, muttering at them. The army, I hear, would like to get rid of him, but fear to do so. The black-out was called off here tonight. It was good to see the lights again.

BERLIN, *September* 20

Hitler lent us one of his thirty-two-passenger planes to bring us back from Danzig. Tonight the press talks openly of peace. Says the *Frankfurter Zeitung:* "Why should England and France waste their blood against our Westwall? Since the Polish state has ceased to exist, the treaties of alliance with it have no more sense." All the Germans I've talked to today are dead sure we shall have peace within a month. They are in high spirits. When I said to some of them today that the best time to have wanted peace was three weeks ago, before Hitler attacked Poland, and that maybe the British and French wouldn't make peace now, they looked at me as if I were crazy. Peace now, I feel, would only be an armistice during which Hitler would further undermine the spirit of resistance in the democracies and strengthen his own armed forces until the day when he felt sure he could overrun the west of Europe.

The battle which is nearly over west of Warsaw and which will probably go down in history as the Battle of Kutno is a second Tannenberg. I asked a General Staff officer about that today. He gave me some figures. At Tannenberg the Russians lost 92,000 prisoners and 28,000 dead. Yesterday at Kutno alone the Germans took 105,000 Polish prisoners; the day before, 50,000. The High Command, usually sparse with its adjectives, calls Kutno " one of the most destructive battles of all time." After my brief look at the front it is plain, though, what has happened to the Poles. They have had no defence against the devastating attacks of the German bombers and the German tanks. They pitted a fairly good army by World War standards against a 1939 mechanized and motorized force which simply *drove* around them and through them. The German air force in the meantime destroyed their communications. The Polish High Command, it is true, seems to have had no idea of what it was up against. Why it kept its best army around Posen even to begin with, not to mention *after* the Germans had got *behind* Warsaw, mystifies even us amateur strategists. Had the Poles withdrawn behind the Vistula the first week of the war, they might have held out until winter, when the mud and the snow would have stopped the Germans.

Two bomb explosions in Berlin last Sunday night, one in front of the Air Ministry, the other in the entry-way of secret-police headquarters in the Alexander-platz. No mention of them, of course, in the press or on the radio. The perpetrators got away in the black-out.

If the war goes on, it is still a question in my mind whether the mass of the people won't swing behind the regime. The people, who are very patriotic, and are being fed a terrific barrage of propaganda about England alone being responsible for the war, may get the general idea that they have to " defend the Fatherland." I have still to find a German, even among those who don't like the regime, who sees anything wrong in the German destruction of Poland. All the moral attitudes of the outside world regarding the aggression against Poland find little echo among the people here. People

of all classes, women as well as men, have gathered in
front of the windows in Berlin for a fortnight and approvingly gazed at the maps in which little red pins
showed the victorious advance of the German troops in
Poland. As long as the Germans are successful and do
not have to pull in their belts too much, this will not
be an unpopular war.

In the Saar village of Ottweiler yesterday the Germans buried with full military honours Lieutenant Louis
Paul Dechanel of the French army. His father had
been President of France. He was killed leading a detachment against the Westwall. At his burial a German military band played the *Marseillaise*. The Germans took a news-reel of the ceremony and will use it
in their propaganda to show the French they haven't
anything against France. The hell with radio. Just
learned my Danzig broadcast did not get through.

BERLIN, *September* 21

In an order of the day to his troops last night
General von Brauchitsch, the commander-in-chief of
the army, announced that the operations against Poland were concluded. Thus ends the " counter-attack."
In eighteen days this amazing fighting machine which
is the German army has overrun Poland, annihilated
its armies, chased its government from Polish soil. But
Warsaw still holds out gallantly.

Heard President Roosevelt ask the special session of
Congress to repeal the neutrality law and allow cash-
and-carry goods to be sold to those who could buy —
France and Britain. Hardly had the President stopped
talking before the Wilhelmstrasse issued a statement to
the foreign press charging the President with being
unneutral. Last summer I tried to find out whether

America came into the calculations of the Nazis at all.
I couldn't find any evidence that they gave a damn
about us. 1914–17 all over again. But now they're beginning to think about us.

Great hopes here that Russia will help Germany to
survive the blockade. First, I can't understand Hitler's
putting himself in a position where his very existence
depends upon the good graces of Stalin. Second, I
can't understand the Soviets pulling Nazi Germany's
chestnuts out of the fire.

The war, maybe, is just beginning, even though the
Germans, after annihilating Poland, would like to see
it ended. Wonder why Hitler said at Danzig two nights
ago — and the press echoed it — " We will never capitulate." Why bring up the subject when your position looks so strong? Talked to Tess. She is better and
is running the Geneva office in my absence.

Berlin, *September* 22

The *D.A.Z.*, commenting on Roosevelt's message asking for the repeal of the neutrality law, says
tonight: " America is not Roosevelt, and Roosevelt must
reckon with the American people." Yesterday the *B.Z.*
saw some hope in what it called the " Front of Reason "
in America. In that front it put Senators Borah and
Clark, Colonel Lindbergh, and Father Coughlin!

Berlin, *September* 23

General von Fritsch, the man who built up the
modern German army and then retired just before the
Anschluss because of a fight with Hitler over attacking

Austria, which he opposed, has been killed in action before Warsaw. A little strange. He had no command but was with the regiment of which he is honorary colonel.

Starting day after tomorrow, new ration cards for food. The German people will now get per week: one pound of meat, five pounds of bread, three quarters of a pound of fats, three quarters of a pound of sugar, and a pound of *ersatz* coffee made of roasted barley seeds. Heavy labourers are to get double rations, and Dr. Goebbels — clever man! — has decided to classify us foreign correspondents as heavy labourers.

BERLIN, *September 24*

The High Command, reviewing the Polish campaign, says the fate of Poland was really decided in eight days. By that time the German army had already obtained its main strategical object, the trapping of the main part of the Polish forces within the great elbow of the Vistula River. Some other things: 450,000 Polish troops captured, 1,200 guns taken, and 800 airplanes either destroyed or captured; and at the end of eighteen days of fighting not a single Polish division, not even a brigade, was left intact.

Dr. Goebbels convoked a special press conference this morning. We piled over to the Propaganda Ministry thinking maybe peace had come, or something. The little *Doktor* stalked in, snorting like a bull, and proceeded to devote his entire time to an attack on Knickerbocker, whom he called " an international liar and counterfeiter." The Doc said that he himself, as a journalist, had never defamed anyone in his life! Seems Knick published a story saying the top Nazis had de-

posited gold abroad to guard against a rainy day in
case they lost the war. This made Doktor G. furious.
He revealed he had broadcast from the German short-
wave stations Thursday night (September 21) a call to
Knick offering him ten per cent of any sum he could
prove the Nazis had salted abroad. A curious offer. He
said he gave him until Saturday night (last night) to
prove it. Apparently Knick was at sea, bound for New
York. The story around here is that Knick radioed
back that as with all German ultimatums the time limit
had expired before he received it.

BERLIN, *September* 26

They buried General von Fritsch here this
morning. It rained, it was cold and dark — one of the
dreariest days I can remember in Berlin. Hitler did
not show up, nor Ribbentrop, nor Himmler, though
they all returned to Berlin from the front this afternoon. The official death notices in the papers omitted
the usual " Died for Führer " and said only: " Died
for the Fatherland." Yesterday after Goebbels had
finished fuming, some of us correspondents gathered in
the street outside and concluded that Fritsch was either
shot by order of Himmler, his mortal enemy, or was so
disgusted with life and the state to which Hitler had
led Germany (disgusted perhaps too at the senseless
slaughter by German bombs and shells of the women
and children in Warsaw?) that he deliberately sought
to be killed; that is, committed suicide. What, we asked,
was a general of his rank doing in the front line outside of Warsaw, where the snipers have been picking
off German troops at an alarming rate? Actually, I
hear, he was killed while advancing with a small detachment of scouts up a street in a suburb across the Vistula

from the capital. A curious thing for Germany's greatest modern military figure to be doing.[1]

Hitler showed a typical smallness in declining to attend the funeral. He cannot forgive a man who has crossed him, even in death. He could not forgive von Kahr, who suppressed his beer-house *Putsch* in 1923, and so had him shot in the 1934 purge.

The war comes home to more and more families that you know. Fräulein T. lost her brother yesterday in Poland. In the World War she had lost her father and another brother. The papers full of the little advertisements that are the official death notices inserted by families in Germany. About half omit the "Died for Führer" expression, retaining only the "Died for the Fatherland." It is one of the few ways of showing your feelings towards Hitler.

Germany, now that it has destroyed Poland, would like peace with the West. Big peace offensive started today. Newspapers, radio full of it. The line: Why do France and Britain want to fight now? Nothing to fight about. Germany wants nothing in the West.

LATER. — Seven members of the American consulate staff in Warsaw arrived here tonight and we had drinks in the Adlon bar. They told a terrible tale of the bombardment of the city and the slaughter of the civilian population. Some of them seemed still shell-shocked. They got out during a temporary truce between the Germans and the Poles. One German shell scored a direct hit on the consulate, but fortunately the

---

[1] Many months later I learned from an unimpeachable source that Fritsch did seek death and that three letters he wrote shortly before the action proved it. It is said in German army circles that his wound, though serious, would in all probability not have caused his death had he not refused the pleas of his adjutant to let himself be carried to the rear. He would not listen to it. He bled to death.

staff had taken refuge in the cellars of the Embassy.

New restrictions today on clothing. If I order a new suit, my tailor must make it out of a piece of cloth exactly 3.1 metres by 144 centimetres.[1] Also the papers inform us we can no longer get our shoes half-soled. No more leather. We must wait for a new substitute material not yet out.

Also, how to shave? A decree says you can have only one piece of shaving soap or one tube of shaving cream during the next four months. I shall start a beard.

BERLIN, *September* 27

Warsaw capitulated today after a heroic but hopeless stand. The High Command says the Polish commander offered to surrender this morning after he had been " impressed by the German attack."

In the first battle between a naval fleet and airplanes (for years the admirals and air commanders have fought out on paper the question whether a fleet is vulnerable to air attack) the Germans today claim to have destroyed a British aircraft-carrier and damaged a battleship without losing a single plane.

I went to the State Opera tonight before my broadcast, George Kidd of U.P. suggesting it would be good for our nerves. It was the opening night of the season and the piece an old favourite, Weber's *Freischütz*. I was a little surprised at the state of my nerves. I could not sit through it. I could not stand the sight of all the satisfied burghers, men and women, many of them in evening dress, and even the music didn't sound right. Amusing only was a special sheet of paper in the program instructing what to do in case of an air-raid alarm. Since there is no cellar in the Opera, a map

[1] About 3.3 by 1.5 yards.

showed me how to get to *my* cellar, which was Number
One *Keller*. The alarm, the instructions said, would be
announced from the stage. I was then to keep calm, call
for my hat and coat at the *Garderobe*, and proceed to
the cellar. At the all-clear I was to return to the Opera,
check my hat and coat, and the opera would go on from
where it left off. There was no alarm.

Ribbentrop is in Moscow and we wonder what he's
up to.

Berlin, *September* 28

At midnight tonight I did a microphone interview with Germany's ace submarine skipper, Captain
Herbert Schultze. It turned out much better than I
expected. During the afternoon and evening I had had
many doubts and a big headache. With the help of
some naval officer friends, I cornered Schultze in the
Admiralty this afternoon. He was just back from his
first " killing." He turned out to be a clean-cut fellow
of thirty, hard as nails and full of that bluff self-con-
fidence which you get, I suppose, when you gamble daily
with your own life and the lives of others.

He was a little afraid of his English, he said, and
after listening to a specimen, I was too. In fact, I
couldn't understand a word he said and we had to converse in German. Someone suggested that his English
would improve during the afternoon, that he was merely
a little rusty. This offered hope, and I cabled New York
that the interview was on for tonight. I put my questions to him and the captain sat down to write out
answers in German. When he had finished a page, I
dictated an English translation to an Admiralty secretary who for some reason wrote English faultlessly but
had great difficulty in understanding it when spoken.

We sweated away all afternoon — four hours — and finally achieved a fifteen-minute script.

There were two points in the script, the very ones which made it most interesting, which added to my own perspiration. The captain told a story of how he had torpedoed the British ship *Royal Sceptre*, but, at the risk of his own skin, had arranged rescue of those aboard by another British vessel, the *Browning*. Now, a few days before, I remembered, London had reported that the *Royal Sceptre* had been torpedoed without warning and that the crew and passengers, numbering sixty, had presumably perished. I wondered who was right.

Captain Schultze, as we worked out our interview, also mentioned that he was the U-boat commander who had sent a saucy radio message to Mr. Winston Churchill advising him of the location of a British ship which he had just sunk so that the First Lord might save the crew. But only a day or two before, Mr. Churchill had told the House of Commons that the German submarine commander who had sent him that message had been captured and was now a prisoner of His Majesty's government.

I reminded the captain of that, and asked him if he could give me the text of his message. His logbook was at Kiel, but we telephoned there and had the message read back to us. That made me feel a little better. Shortly before the broadcast this evening something else happened which made me feel better still. As we were leaving the Admiralty, an officer brought us a Reuter dispatch saying that the *Browning* had just landed at Bahia, Brazil, with the crew and passengers of the *Royal Sceptre* all safe.

One good break followed another. To my surprise, as our broadcast got under way, the captain's English did indeed improve, just as predicted. His accent was terrific, but in some way his words poured out very distinctly. You could understand every syllable. Most men of his type, I've found, when put before a microphone, read their lines mechanically. But to my delight he proved to be a natural speaker, talking as though we had never written a line.[1]

BERLIN, *September* 29

Germany's peace offensive is now to be backed by Russia.

In Moscow last night Ribbentrop and Molotov signed a treaty and a declaration of purpose. The text of the latter tells the whole story:

" After the German government and the government of the U.S.S.R., through a treaty signed today, definitely solved questions resulting from the disintegration of the Polish state and thereby established a secure foundation for permanent peace in eastern Europe, they jointly voice their opinion that it would be in the interest of all nations to bring to an end the state of war presently existing between Germany and Britain and France. Both governments therefore will concentrate their efforts, if necessary, in co-operation with other friendly powers, towards reaching this goal.

" Should, however, the effort of both governments remain unsuccessful, the fact would thereby be established that Britain and France are responsible for a continuation of the war, in which case the governments of Germany and Russia will consult each other as to necessary measures."

[1] Later the British Admiralty confirmed his version of both the *Royal Sceptre* episode and the saucy message to Mr. Churchill, including the fact that Schultze had not been captured.

This is ludicrous, but may mean that Russia comes into the war on the side of Germany. The same Nazi circles which last August said that Britain and France wouldn't fight after the first Nazi-Soviet accord, to-night were sure that the two democracies would agree to stop the war now. They may be wrong again, though I'm not quite sure.

BERLIN, *September* 30

The talk of peace dominates all else here to-day. The Germans are sure of it, and one of the secretaries of the Soviet Embassy told me today Moscow was too. He said London and Paris would jump at the chance for peace now. The *Völkische Beobachter* observes today: " All Europe awaits the word of peace from London. Woe to them who refuse it. They will some day be stoned by their own people."

Did a four-way broadcast with London, Paris, and New York tonight, but seeing the show was running late, I slashed my part so much it didn't make much sense.

Ciano to see Hitler here tomorrow. Talk of the Germans using him to pressure London and Paris to make peace.

BERLIN, *October* 2

Just heard the BBC announce that English planes had flown over Berlin last night. A surprise to us here. No air-raid alarm. No sound of planes. But they're all lying these days. The Germans say they've sunk the *Ark Royal,* for instance.

The family of Eleanor K., a naturalized American girl of German parentage who has been very helpful

to me here for years, has been after me since yesterday
to do something about locating her. She left Amsterdam for Berlin a few days ago, but failed to arrive. I
went over to the consulate today and got G. to put
through a blitz call to the German secret police at the
Dutch border. Answer: Eleanor is under arrest there.
How shall I explain that to her family?

The local enthusiasm for peace a little dampened today by Churchill's broadcast last night. I have been
wondering about that one tube of shaving cream my
ration gives me for the next four months. My beard
will be pink.

A. blew in Saturday (September 30) accompanied
by an American girl he had met in Warsaw. They had
been wandering in the wilds of eastern Poland for three
weeks — between the German and Russian armies. He
said they had lived for days on stale bread, wandering
from village to village. Stale bread was all the peasants
would sell them, though they had butter and eggs and
meat. Most villages had already set up local soviets.
A., who never loved the Poles and rather liked the Nazis,
says whole villages in eastern Poland far off the beaten
track, off the railroads and main roads, villages with no
military importance whatsoever, have been destroyed
by the German Luftwaffe for no reason he could think
of. He says the German planes would often dive on
lone peasant women in lonely fields and toss a bomb on
them or machine-gun them. He saw the bodies. A. and
his lady friend finally made their way to the German
lines, rode for several days in open box-cars with German refugees, and eventually got to Germany.

Whitey, back from Poland, says he flew over Warsaw
Saturday (September 30) and it was in flames. What
few buildings he could see in the heart of town that
weren't burning were in ruins. He thinks tens of thou-

sands of civilians in the city have perished. He spent
three days with the Soviet army, but was not greatly
impressed. He was struck by the number of women in
the Red army. Whitey took part in a peculiar mission.
Göring had a report that several German airmen captured by the Poles had been murdered in a concentration camp near the Russian border. Four German
planes, one with Whitey and some German officers, the
other three loaded with coffins, set off to find the bodies.
They dug up graves all over eastern Poland, but never
the right ones. Finally in a field they thought they
had at last discovered what they were after. There was
a big mound, freshly covered over. They dug furiously.
They found — fifty dead horses.

BERLIN, *October* 4

Two choice press bits today: The *12-Uhr
Blatt* headline in red ink all over page 1: "ENG-
LAND'S RESPONSIBILITY — FOR THE OUT-
RAGEOUS PROVOKING OF WARSAW TO
DEFEND ITSELF." The *Nachtausgabe's* editorial, ar-
guing that America is not nearly so anxious to join the
war " as are Herr Roosevelt and his Jewish camarilla."

BERLIN, *October* 5

Reichstag tomorrow. Hitler is expected to
offer peace terms. No one expects them to be very generous. He himself flew to Warsaw today to hold a triumphant review of his troops. He made a speech to his
soldiers, the speech of a conquering Cæsar.

The people here certainly want peace. The government may want it for the moment. Will Britain and
France make it now, and then maybe next year have
to mobilize again? Hitler has won the war in Poland

and lost the peace there — to Russia. The Soviets, without a fight, get nearly half of Poland and a stranglehold on the Baltic states and now block Germany from its two main goals in the east, Ukrainian wheat and Rumanian oil. Hitler is hastily withdrawing all Germans from the Baltic states, where most of them have been settled for centuries. Estonia has capitulated to Moscow and agreed to the Soviets' building an air and naval base on its soil. The foreign ministers of Latvia and Lithuania are shuttling back and forth between their capitals and Moscow trying to save the pieces. And once the Soviets get a wedge in these Baltic states, how soon will they go Bolshevik? Soon. Soon.

BERLIN, *October* 6

Hitler delivered his much advertised " peace proposals " in the Reichstag at noon today. I went over and watched the show, my nth. He delivered his " peace proposals," and they were almost identical with those I've heard him offer from the same rostrum after every conquest he has made since the march into the Rhineland in 1936. These must have been about the fifth. And though they were the fifth at least, and just like the others, and just as sincerely spoken, most Germans I've talked to since seem aghast if you suggest that perhaps the outside world will put no more trust in them than they have learned by bitter experience to put in the others.

Hitler offered peace in the west if Britain and France stay out of Germany's *Lebensraum* in eastern Europe. The future of Poland he left in doubt, though he said Poland would never again endanger (!) German interests. In other words, a slave Poland, similar to the present slave Bohemia.

I doubt very much if England and France will listen
to these " proposals " for five minutes, though some of
my colleagues think so on the ground that, now that
Russia has come up against Germany on a long front
and this past week has been busy establishing herself
in the Baltic states, it would be smart of London and
Paris to conclude peace and sit back until Germany and
Russia clash in eastern Europe. Pertinax wrote a few
months ago that the German problem would never be
settled until Germany had a barrier on the East that
it *knew* it could not break. Then it would stop being
expansive, stop disturbing the rest of Europe, and turn
its undoubted talents and energy to more peaceful pur-
suits. Russia might provide that barrier. At any rate
Russia is the winner in this war so far and Hitler is
entirely dependent upon the good graces of Stalin, who
undoubtedly has no good graces for anyone but himself and Russia.

Hitler was calmer today than usual. There was much
joviality but little enthusiasm among the rubber-stamp
Reichstag deputies except when he boasted of German
strength. Such a boast sets any German on fire. The
members of the Cabinet — up on the stage where the
opera singers used to perform — stood about before
the session chatting easily, Ribbentrop with Admiral
Raeder, Dr. Goebbels with von Neurath, etc. Most of
the deputies I talked to afterwards took for granted
that peace was assured. It was a lovely fall day, cold
and sunny, which seemed to contribute to everybody's
good feelings. As I walked over to the Reichstag (held
as usual in the Kroll Opera) through the Tiergarten
I noticed batteries of anti-aircraft everywhere.

The early edition of tomorrow morning's *Völkische
Beobachter*, Hitler's own sabre-rattler among the jour-
nals, seems transformed into a dove of peace. Its flam-

ing headlines: "GERMANY'S WILL FOR PEACE —
NO WAR AIMS AGAINST FRANCE AND ENG-
LAND — NO MORE REVISION CLAIMS EXCEPT
COLONIES — REDUCTION OF ARMAMENTS —
CO-OPERATION WITH ALL NATIONS OF
EUROPE — PROPOSAL FOR A CONFERENCE."

If the Nazis were sincere they might have spoken
this sweet language before the " counter-attack " was
launched.

BERLIN, *October* 8

A whole page of paid death notices in the
Völkische Beobachter today. How many only sons lost!
Two typical notices: " In a hero's death for Führer,
Volk and *Vaterland,* there died on September 18, in the
fighting in Poland, my beloved only son, aged 22." And
" For his beloved Fatherland, there fell on Septem-
ber 20 in the battle around Kutno my only son, aged
25." Both notices signed by the mother.

I leave tomorrow for Geneva to recover my senses
and fetch some winter clothing, as the weather has
turned cold. I did not bring any winter things when I
left Geneva exactly two months ago. I did not know.
Two months! What an age it seems. How dim in memory the time when there was peace. That world ended,
and for me, on the whole, despite its faults, its injustices,
its inequalities, it was a good one. I came of age in that
one, and the life it gave was free, civilized, deepening,
full of minor tragedy and joy and work and leisure,
new lands, new faces — and rarely commonplace and
never without hope.

And now darkness. A new world. Black-out, bombs,
slaughter, Nazism. Now the night and the shrieks and
barbarism.

GENEVA, *October* 10

Home at last for two or three days. The sensation indescribable. The baby asleep when I arrived tonight; her face on the pillow, sleeping. Tess at the station, pretty and . . . She drove us home — Demaree Bess, who had come down from Berlin with me, and Dorothy. It was strange driving through Geneva town to see the blinding street-lights, the blazing store-windows, the full headlights on the cars — after six weeks in blacked-out Berlin. Strange and beautiful.

In Basel this noon Demaree and I stuffed ourselves shamefully with food. We ordered a huge dish of butter just to look at it, and Russian eggs and an enormous steak and cheese and dessert and several litres of wine and then cognac and coffee — a feast! And no food cards to give in. All the way down in the train from Basel we felt good. The mountains, the chalets on the hillsides, even the sturdy Swiss looked like something out of paradise.

Coming up the Rhine from Karlsruhe to Basel this morning, we skirted the French frontier for a hundred miles. No sign of war and the train crew told me not a shot had been fired on this front since the war began. Where the train ran along the Rhine, we could see the French bunkers and at many places great mats behind which the French were building fortifications. Identical picture on the German side. The troops seemed to be observing an armistice. They went about their business in full sight and range of each other. For that matter, one blast from a French " 75 " could have liquidated our train. The Germans were hauling up guns and supplies on the railroad line, but the French did not disturb them.

Queer kind of war.

GENEVA, *October* 11

A curious sensation to see the Swiss papers reporting *both* sides of the war. If you had that in the dictatorships, maybe the Cæsars couldn't go to war so easily. Much fun romping around with Eileen and Tess. Coming down with a cold. No heat in the houses here yet.

BERLIN, *October* 15

Back again, depressed, the week in Switzerland over in no time. Of my three and a half days in Geneva, two spent down with a cold and fever and one preparing a broadcast which never got through because of atmospherics. But it was grand just the same. Tess came along as far as Neuchâtel in the train and it was sad parting in the little station above the lake there. Swiss train full of soldiers. The country has one tenth of its population under arms; more than any other country in the world. It's not their war. But they're ready to fight to defend their way of life. I asked a fat businessman in my compartment whether he wouldn't prefer peace at any price (business is ruined in a Switzerland completely surrounded by belligerents and with every able-bodied man in the army) so that he could make money again.

" Not the kind of peace that Hitler offers," he said. " Or the kind of peace we've been having the last five years."

In the early evening, coming down the Rhine, the same unreal front. Soldiers on both sides looking but not shooting. Frankfurt station in the black-out was a bit of a nightmare. Hundreds of people, many of them soldiers, milling around on the almost pitch-dark platform trying to get on the train, stumbling over baggage and into one another. I had a sleeping-car reservation but could not find the car in the darkness and went back to my coach, sitting through the night until Berlin. The corridor of the blacked-out train packed with people who stood up all night in the darkness.

At Anhalter station I bought the morning papers. Big news. "GERMAN SUB SINKS BRITISH BATTLESHIP 'ROYAL OAK'!" British Admiralty admits it. That's a blow. Wonder how it was done. And where?

LATER. — Russell Hill, a very intelligent youth of twenty-one who divides his time between broadcasting for us and being assistant correspondent of the *Herald Tribune*, tells me that Wednesday (October 11) a false report of an armistice caused scenes of great rejoicing all over Berlin. Early in the morning, he says, a broadcast on the Berlin wave-length announced that the British government had fallen and that there would be an immediate armistice. The fat old women in the vegetable markets, Russell reports, tossed their cabbages into the air, wrecked their own stands in sheer joy, and made for the nearest pub to toast the peace with *Schnaps*. The awakening that afternoon when the Berlin radio denied the report was something terrific, it seems.

My room waiter tells me there was much loud anti-aircraft fire heard in Berlin last night, the first since the war began. Propaganda Ministry explains tonight a German plane got lost over the city and was shot down.

BERLIN, *October* 18

The place where the German U-boat sank the British battleship *Royal Oak* was none other than the middle of Scapa Flow, Britain's greatest naval base! It sounds incredible. A World War submarine commander told me tonight that the Germans tried twice to get a U-boat into Scapa Flow during the last war, but both attemps failed and the submarines were lost.

Captain Prien, commander of the submarine, came tripping into our afternoon press conference at the Propaganda Ministry this afternoon, followed by his crew — boys of eighteen, nineteen, twenty. Prien is thirty, clean-cut, cocky, a fanatical Nazi, and obviously capable. Introduced by Hitler's press chief, Dr. Dietrich, who kept cursing the English and calling Churchill a liar, Prien told us little of how he did it. He said he had no trouble getting past the boom protecting the bay. I got the impression, though he said nothing to justify it, that he must have followed a British craft, perhaps a mine-sweeper, into the base. British negligence must have been something terrific.

BERLIN, *October* 19

Germans shut both NBC and us off the air this noon. I saw Hill's script beforehand and approved it. The Nazi censor maintained it would create a bad impression abroad. In the afternoon I called on Dr. Boehmer and told him we would stop broadcasting altogether if today's action meant we could only talk about matters which created a nice impression. He assured me it was all a mistake. Tonight for my broadcast the censor let me say what I wanted. The High Command tonight issues a detailed report of what has been happening on that mysterious western front. Nothing much at all has happened, it says, and I'm inclined to believe it, though Paris has swamped America for weeks with wild tales of a great French offensive against the Westwall. High Command says German losses up to October 17 in the west have been 196 killed, 114 missing, 356 wounded. Which tends to prove how local the action there has been. I'm almost convinced that the German army tells the truth in regard to its actions. The navy exaggerates, the air force simply lies.

Berlin, *October* 21

The Wilhelmstrasse furious at the Turks for signing a mutual-assistance pact with the British day before yesterday. Papen jerked back here hurriedly and was called before the master, my spies tell me, for a dressing-down. It's the first diplomatic blow the Germans have taken in a long time. They don't like blows.

Berlin, *October* 22

Eintopf — one-pot — day — this Sunday. Which means all you can get for lunch is a cheap stew. But you pay the price of a big meal for it, the difference going to the Winter Relief, or so they say. Actually it goes into the war chest. Suddenly and without warning at eight fifteen tonight Goebbels went on the air and blasted away at Churchill, accusing him of having sunk the *Athenia*. He called Churchill a liar a dozen times and kept shouting: " Your impudent lies, Herr Churchill! Your infernal lies! " From Goebbels!

BERLIN, *October* 24

The German people who have been hoping
for peace until the bitter end were finally told tonight
by Ribbentrop in a speech at Danzig that the war will
now have to be fought to a finish. I suppose every government that has ever gone to war has tried to convince
its people of three things: (1) that right is on its side;
(2) that it is fighting purely in defence of the nation;
(3) that it is sure to win. The Nazis are certainly trying to pound these three points into the skins of the
people. Modern propaganda technique, especially the
radio, certainly helps them.

Three youths in Hanover who snatched a lady's
handbag in the black-out have been sentenced to death.

BERLIN, *October* 28

I hear in business circles that severe rationing of clothing will begin next month. The truth
is that, having no cotton and almost no wool, the German people must get along with what clothing they
have until the end of the war.

BERLIN, *October* 29

I've been looking into what Germans are reading these dark days. Among novels the three best-sellers
are: (1) *Gone with the Wind*, translated as *Vom Winde
Verweht* — literally " From the Wind Blown About ";
(2) Cronin's *Citadel*; (3) *Beyond Sing the Woods*, by
Trygve Gulbranssen, a young Norwegian author. Note
that all three novels are by foreign authors, one by an
Englishman.

Most sought-after non-fiction books are: (1) *The*

Coloured Front, an anonymous study of the white-versus-Negro problem; (2) *Look Up the Subject of England*, a propaganda book about England; (3) *Der totale Krieg*, Ludendorff's famous book about the Total War — very timely now; (4) *Fifty Years of Germany*, by Sven Hedin, the Swedish explorer and friend of Hitler; (5) *So This is Poland*, by von Oertzen, data on Poland, first published in 1928.

Three anti-Soviet books, I'm told, are still selling well despite official orders to soft-pedal any anti-Soviet or anti-Bolshevik talk since the August pact with Moscow. Most popular of these books is *Socialism Betrayed*, by a former German Communist named Albrecht. Detective stories still hold their own in wartime Germany, and hastily written volumes about submarine and aerial warfare are also doing well. A German told me today that the only American magazine he could find at his news-stand this afternoon was one called *True Love Stories*, or something like that, October issue.

Theatres here doing a land-office business, playing mostly the classics, Goethe, Schiller, Shakespeare. Shaw is the most popular living playwright here now. Only successful German modern play on is Gerhart Hauptmann's new one, *The Daughter of the Cathedral*. Poor old Hauptmann, once an ardent Socialist and a great playwright, has now become a Nazi and a very senile man.

In the movie world the big hit at the moment is Clark Gable in *Adventure in China*, as it's called here. It's packing them in for the fourth week at the Marmorhaus. A German film is lucky if it holds out a week.

The power of radio! My remarks about the scarcity of shaving soap and the probability of my having to

grow a beard have brought a great response from home.
I gave up my beard after ten days. It was pink and
straggly and everyone laughed.

BERLIN, *October* 30

Bad news for the people today. Now that it
has become cold and rainy, with snow due soon, the government has decreed that only five per cent of the population is entitled to buy new rubbers or overshoes this
winter. Available stocks will be rationed first to post-
men, newsboys, and street-sweepers.

BERLIN, *October* 31

Consider the words of Comrade Molotov,
spoken before the Supreme Soviet Council in Moscow
today, as reported here: " We stand for the scrupulous
and punctilious observance of pacts . . . and we declare that all nonsense about Sovietizing the Baltic
countries is only to the interest of our common enemy
and of all anti-Soviet provocateurs."
The secret police announced that two men were shot
for " resisting arrest " yesterday. One of them, it is
stated, was trying to induce some German workers to
lay down their tools in an important armament factory.
Himmler now has power to shoot anyone he likes without trial.

BERLIN, *November* 2

General Hugh Johnson, one of the few Americans — Lindbergh is another — often quoted in the
Nazi press, makes the front pages here today. John-

son's views on the American ship *City of Flint*, which was captured by the Nazis the other day are headlined in the *12-Uhr Blatt*: "UNCALLED-FOR INDIGNATION OVER THE 'CITY OF FLINT' — GENERAL JOHNSON AGAINST OBVIOUS AGITATION."

The anti-Comintern is dead. I learn the Nazi anti-Comintern museum, which used to show us the horrors of Bolshevism here, has quietly closed down. This week the Nazi editor of the *Contra-Komintern* wrote his subscribers apologizing for the non-appearance of the magazine in September and explaining that it would be coming out under a new name. He intimated that the editors had ascertained that Germany's real enemies after all were not Bolsheviks, but Jews. "Behind all the enemies of Germany's ascendancy," he writes, "stand those who demand our encirclement — the oldest enemies of the German people and of all healthy, rising nations — the Jews."

BERLIN, *November* 4

The radio people here in great secrecy had kindly offered to take me up to a Baltic port and let me broadcast the arrival of the *City of Flint*, which was scheduled for tomorrow. But the Norwegians seized it day before yesterday and saved me the assignment. The Wilhelmstrasse furious and threatening the Norwegians with dire consequences if they don't turn the American ship over to Germany.

BERLIN, *November* 5

CBS wants me to broadcast a picture of Hitler at work during war-time. I've been inquiring around among my spies. They say: He rises early, eats

his first breakfast at seven a.m. This consists usually
of either a glass of milk or fruit-juice and two or three
rolls, on which he spreads marmalade liberally. Like
most Germans, he eats a second breakfast, this one at
nine a.m. It's like the first except that he also eats a
little fruit. He begins his working day by wading into
state papers (a job he detests, since he hates detail
work) and discussing the day's program with his adjutants, chiefly S.A. Leader Wilhelm Brückner, and
especially with his deputy, Rudolf Hess, who was once
his private secretary and is one of the few men he trusts
with his innermost thoughts. During the forenoon he
usually receives the chiefs of the three armed services,
listens to their reports and dictates decisions. With
Göring he talks about not only air-force matters but
general economic problems, or rather results, since he's
not interested in details or even theories on this subject.

Hitler eats a simple lunch, usually a vegetable stew
or a vegetable omelet. He is of course a vegetarian, teetotaller, and non-smoker. He usually invites a small
circle to lunch, three or four adjutants, Hess, Dr. Diettrich, his press chief, and sometimes Göring. A one-per-
cent beer, brewed specially for him, is served at this
meal, or sometimes a drink made out of kraut called
" Herve," flavoured with a little Mosel wine.

After lunch he returns to his study and work. More
state papers, more conferences, often with his Foreign
Minister, occasionally with a returned German ambassador, invariably with some party chieftain such as Dr.
Ley or Max Amann, his old top sergeant of the World
War and now head of the lucrative Nazi publishing
house Eher Verlag, which gets out the *Völkische Beobachter* and in which Hitler is a stockholder. Late in the
afternoon Hitler takes a stroll in the gardens back of the
Chancellery, continuing his talk during the walk with

whoever had an appointment at the time. Hitler is a
fiend for films, and on evenings when no important conferences are on or he is not overrunning a country, he
spends a couple of hours seeing the latest movies in his
private cinema room at the Chancellery. News-reels are
a great favourite with him, and in the last weeks he has
seen all those taken in the Polish war, including hundreds of thousands of feet which were filmed for the
army archives and will never be seen by the public. He
likes American films and many never publicly exhibited
in Germany are shown him. A few years ago he insisted
on having *It Happened One Night* run several times.
Though he is supposed to have a passion for Wagnerian
opera, he almost never attends the Opera here in Berlin.
He likes the Metropol, which puts on tolerable musical
comedies with emphasis on pretty dancing girls. Recently he had one of the girls who struck his fancy to
tea. But only to tea. In the evening, too, he likes to
have in Dr. Todt, an imaginative engineer who built the
great Autobahn network of two-lane motor roads and
later the fortifications of the Westwall. Hitler, rushing
to compensate what he thinks is an artistic side that was
frustrated by non-recognition in his youthful days in
Vienna, has a passion for architects' models and will
spend hours fingering them with Dr. Todt. Lately,
they say, he has even taken to designing new uniforms.
Hitler stays up late, and sleeps badly, which I fear is
the world's misfortune.

BERLIN, *November* 7

The Queen of the Netherlands and the King
of the Belgians have offered to mediate peace. Small
hope. The offer coolly received here. The Dutch and
Belgians still decline to have staff talks together. But

their historic neutrality, their refusal to ally themselves with one side or the other, may land them in the soup unless they junk it. Much talk here about the Germans pushing through Holland. This would not only turn the Maginot Line, but give the Germans air bases a hundred miles from the English coast.

LATER. — Four or five of us American correspondents had a talk with Göring tonight at — of all places — the Soviet Embassy, to which we had repaired for the annual reception on the anniversary of the Bolshevik Revolution. Amid the glittering decorations and furnishings left over from Czarist Russia, but with the portrait of Lenin smiling down upon us, Göring stood against the buffet table sipping a beer and smoking a long stogey. He was in an expansive mood, and when a frightened adjutant reminded him he was speaking to the " American press," he said he didn't mind. We thought — naïvely, I suppose — that he might be resentful of the repeal a few days ago of our neutrality bill and of the boast at home that we would soon be selling thousands of planes to the Allies to help beat Nazi Germany. He wasn't. Instead, he kidded us about our capacity to build planes.

" If we could only make planes at your rate of production," he said, " we should be very weak. I mean that seriously. Your planes are good, but you don't make enough of them fast enough."

" Well, will Germany deliver a mass attack in the air before these thousands of American planes are delivered to the Allies? " we asked.

He laughed. " You build your planes, and our enemies theirs, and we'll build ours, and one day you'll see who has been building the best and the most planes."

The talk continued:

"What do you think of the general situation?"

"Very favourable to Germany."

"So far your air force has only attacked British warships. Why?"

"Warships are very important objects. And they give us good practice."

"Are you going to begin bombing enemy ports?"

"We're humane."

We couldn't suppress our laughter at this, whereupon Göring retorted: "You shouldn't laugh. I'm serious. I *am* humane."

BERLIN, *November* 8

Without previous notice, Hitler made an unexpected speech in the Bürgerbräu Keller in Munich tonight on the anniversary of his 1923 beer-house *Putsch*. Neither the radio nor the press hinted that he would be speaking tonight, and officials in the Wilhelmstrasse learned about it only an hour before it took place. Speech broadcast by all German stations, but for some reason was not offered to us for transmission to America. Hitler told the people to make up their minds to a long war and disclosed that on the Sunday two months ago when Britain and France came into the war, he ordered Göring to prepare for five years of conflict.

BERLIN, *November* 9

Twelve minutes after Hitler and *all* the big party leaders left the Bürgerbräu Keller in Munich last night, at nine minutes after nine o'clock, a bomb explosion wrecked the hall, killed seven, wounded sixty-three. The bomb had been placed in a pillar directly behind the rostrum from which Hitler had been speaking. Had he remained twelve minutes and one second longer he surely would have been killed. The spot on which he stood was covered with six feet of debris.

No one yet knows who did it. The Nazi press screams that it was the English, the British secret service! It even blames Chamberlain for the deed. Most of us think it smells of another Reichstag fire. In other years Hitler and all the other bigwigs have remained after the speech to talk over old times with the comrades of the *Putsch* and guzzle beer. Last night they fairly scampered out of the building leaving the rank and file of the comrades to guzzle among themselves. The attempted " assassination " undoubtedly will buck up public opinion behind Hitler and stir up hatred of England. Curious that the official Nazi paper, the *Völkische Beobachter*, was the only morning paper today to carry the story. A friend called me with the news just as I had finished broadcasting at midnight last night, but all the German radio officials and the censors denied it. They said it was a silly rumour.

BERLIN, *November* 11

Armistice Day. An irony! Listened to the broadcast from Munich of the state funeral for the beer-house victims. Hitler present, did not speak. Hess spoke. He said: " This *attentat* has taught us how to hate." I think they knew before.

Informed today that someone last night threw a brick into the window where the court photographer, Heinrich Hoffmann, exhibits his flattering portraits of Hitler. A policeman fired, but the culprit got away in the black-out. Police protection of big shots being increased.

Something's in the wind. Learned today that Hitler's headquarters train has steam up. Party gossip about a mass air attack on England. A drive through Holland and Belgium. Or one through Switzerland.

BERLIN, *November* 12

The Germans announce they've shot " by sentence of court-martial " the Polish mayor of Bromberg. They say an investigation showed he was " implicated in the murder of Germans and the theft of city funds." That, I suppose, is a German peace. I cannot recall that the Allies shot the mayors of German towns after the Rhineland occupation.

BERLIN, *November* 12

The ration cards for clothing out today, and many long German faces to be seen. There are separate cards for men, women, boys, girls, and babies. Except for the babies, everyone gets a hundred points on his card. Socks or stockings take five points, but you can buy only five pair per year. A pair of pyjamas costs thirty points, almost a third of your card, but you can save five points if you buy a nightgown instead. A new overcoat or suit takes sixty points. I figured out tonight that with my card, which limits your purchases by the seasons, I could buy from December 1 to April 1: two pairs of socks, two handkerchiefs, one muffler, and a pair of gloves. From April 1 to September 1: one shirt, two collars, and a suit of underwear. For the rest of the year: two neckties and one undershirt.

BERLIN, *November* 18

Yesterday nine young Czech students at the University of Prague were lined up before a German firing squad and executed. At the press conference this noon we asked the authorities why and they replied that the students had staged anti-German demonstrations in Prague on October 23 and November 15. " There can be no joking in war-time," said our spokesman, a little bored by our question. Later in the day the Germans admitted that three more Czechs, two of them policemen, were shot for " attacking a German." I would bet my shirt that in the twenty years that three million Sudeten Germans lived under Czech rule not a single one of them was ever executed for taking part in any kind of demonstration.

Here in Germany three youths were executed yesterday for " treason." And two youngsters aged nineteen were sentenced to death in Augsburg today for having committed a theft in the home of a soldier.

Beach Conger of the *Herald Tribune*, who arrived here only a month ago, left today by request. The Nazis didn't like a story he had written. They demanded a retraction. He declined. At the last minute, Beach says, a high Nazi official called him in and " offered " to get him the job as Berlin correspondent of a big American radio network, which rather surprised him, as it did me. Most of the American correspondents were at the station to see him off, and there were flowers for Mrs. Conger.

Though the Nazis don't like me, I suppose I shall never get kicked out of here. The trouble is my radio scripts are censored in advance, so that whatever I say over the air cannot be held against me. The newspaper correspondents can telephone out what they please, subject to the risk of getting what Conger got. This is almost a worse form of censorship than we have, since the New York offices of the press associations and New York newspapers do not like their correspondents to be kicked out.

BERLIN, *November* 19

For almost two months now there has been no military action on land, sea, or in the air. From talks with German military people, however, I'm convinced it would be a mistake to think that Germany will accept the Allied challenge to fight this war largely on the economic front. That is just the kind of war in which the Reich would be at a disadvantage. And that's one of the reasons why most people here expect military action very soon now.

Frank, the Governor-General of occupied Poland, to-day decreed that the Jewish ghetto in Warsaw henceforth must be shut off from the rest of the capital by barricades and placed under sharp police control. He says the Jews are " carriers of diseases and germs." An American friend back from Warsaw tonight tells me the Nazi policy is simply to exterminate the Polish Jews. They are being herded into eastern Poland and forced to live in unheated shacks and robbed of any opportunity of earning bread and butter. Several thousand Jews from the Reich have also been sent to eastern Poland to die, he says.

BERLIN, *November* 20

The Nazis forced poor Prince August Wilhelm, fourth son of the Kaiser, to appear before our press conference at the Propaganda Ministry this evening and deny that Hitler had done anything to any

member of the Hohenzollern family, as rumour had had
it of late. " Auwi," as he's popularly called, is the only
Hohenzollern who was once an active Nazi. He was in
fact a storm trooper in the S.A. and was introduced to
us today by Dr. Boehmer as " *Obergruppenführer*
Prince August Wilhelm." Nervous and a bit ashamed
of his role, he told us what he had been told to say, ending his remarks with a resounding " *Heil Hitler!* " A
curious end, I mused, for the Hohenzollerns, that resourceful Prussian family which produced Frederick
the Great and Frederick's father and Wilhelm II and
raised first Prussia and then Germany to a world power.

BERLIN, *November* 21

Gestapo chief Himmler claimed today that
he has found the man who planted the bomb that so
narrowly missed blowing Hitler to bits at Munich a
fortnight ago. His name is given as Georg Elser,
thirty-six, and behind him, says Himmler, was the British Intelligence Service and Otto Strasser, a former
Nazi leader and now a bitter enemy of Hitler, who lives
in France. Himmler's account of how Elser did it
sounds fishy indeed. As one German put it to me today
after reading the account: " Now I'm sure Himmler
planted that bomb." [1]

[1] For months we were to ask at nearly every Nazi press conference when the trial of Elser would take place. At first we were told
he would be tried before the Supreme Court at Leipzig as were the
"perpetrators" of the Reichstag fire, which seemed appropriate
enough, since both events cast suspicion on the Nazis themselves.
After a few weeks our daily question: " When will Elser be tried? "
provoked scarcely restrained laughter from the correspondents and
increasing embarrassment for Dr. Boehmer, foreign press chief of
the Propaganda Ministry, Dr. Schmidt, press chief of the Foreign
Office, and the latter's deputy, Baron von Stumm. Finally we were
given to understand that the question wasn't funny any more, and
after some months, having squeezed all we could out of our joke,
we dropped it. So far as is known, Elser was never tried. Whether
he was executed also is not known.

Himmler also announced today, as if to confuse the public, that the alleged leader of the British Intelligence Service for Western Europe, a certain Mr. Best, and his accomplice, a certain Captain Stevens, had been nabbed by the Gestapo on November 9 at the German-Dutch frontier. This clears up the kidnapping case we heard about from Amsterdam. The Dutch say it took place on Dutch soil.

A writer in the *Völkische Beobachter* will say tomorrow that after seeing Elser " you almost forget you are in the presence of a satanic monster. His eyes are intelligent and the face rather soft."

What Himmler and his gang are up to, obviously, is to convince the gullible German people that the British government tried to win the war by murdering Hitler and his chief aides. The censor today cut out all reference in my script to the Reichstag fire.

Berlin, *November* 23

Thanksgiving today. At the home of Chargé d'Affaires Alexander Kirk a hundred or so hungry Americans charged into several turkeys assembled on the buffet table. At dinner I had another turkey at the Oechsners', dragging Dorothy [Oechsner] over to the studio at midnight with me for a little interview on the air as to how she did it in war-time rationed Germany. She explained nicely how she got the whipped cream for the pumpkin pie by use of a new-fangled machine which extracts cream from butter.

After December 1, horses, cows, and pigs not residing on regular farms are to get food cards too.

BERLIN, *November* 26

Bill White, son of William Allen, has been
here and this week helped me make a study of night life
in war-time which CBS wants me to air tonight. We
found it booming. Off to Geneva tomorrow for a few
days.

GENEVA, *December* 1

The Soviet Union has invaded Finland! Yesterday Red air-force bombers attacked Helsinki, killing
seventy-five civilians, wounding several hundred. The
great champion of the working class, the mighty
preacher against " Fascist aggression," the righteous
stander-up for the " scrupulous and punctilious observance of treaties " (to quote Molotov as of a month ago),
has fallen upon the most decent and workable little democracy in Europe in violation of half a dozen " solemn " treaties. The whole moral foundation which the
Soviets have built up for themselves in international relations in the last ten years has collapsed like a house
of cards, which the skeptics and anti-Communists always claimed it was. Stalin reveals himself of the same
stamp as Hitler, Mussolini, and the Japs. Soviet foreign policy turns out to be as " imperialist " as that of
the czars. The Kremlin has betrayed the revolution.

I have raged for thirty hours; could not sleep last
night, though I got little chance to. Since yesterday
noon I have been continually on the telephone to Helsinki, Stockholm, Berlin, Bern, Amsterdam, and London, organizing communications from Finland for our
broadcasts, determined to get them through not only
for our own sakes, but so the Finnish case may get a
hearing at home. It has been hard sledding, one defeat

after another, but we're getting our broadcasts through.
To begin with, Maxie tied up the Geneva transmitter,
our only neutral outlet, for NBC. He also got to the
Finns and Swedes first and somehow put over the idea
that the talks of the Finnish President, Kallio, and the
Foreign Minister, Erkko, were to be exclusive for NBC.
A telephone call to the authorities in Helsinki cleared
that up so far as the Finns were concerned, but I had
great trouble convincing the Swedes in Stockholm, on
whom I must depend for relaying everything from Finland, that the talks were not exclusive for NBC but were
for us too. Searched all yesterday afternoon for a transmitter. The RRG in Berlin would give me neither a
transmitter nor transit telephone lines through Germany. They have orders not to offend Russia. Called
Amsterdam and tried to get the Dutch to lend me a
transmitter but they were too frightened for their neutrality, which of course neither Russia nor Germany will
respect one day if it is profitable not to. Finally Ed
[Murrow] solved all our difficulties, though we will not
tell the Germans nor the Swedes nor even the Finns. He
got the BBC to pick up the Swedish medium-wave transmitter, which in turn was taking the Helsinki broadcast
by telephone line from Finland, and rebroadcasting it.
The BBC then piped their pick-up to Rugby, where it
was short-waved to our studios in New York. The ordinary way to have done a broadcast from Helsinki would
have been to bring it by telephone line from Helsinki
through Sweden and Germany to Switzerland and then
short-wave it to New York through the Geneva transmitter. But Germany's refusal to give us transit telephone facilities and Maxie's tying up the local transmitter balked that. New York says our transmission
from Helsinki was infinitely better than the opposi-

tion's; theirs apparently was done by having Geneva
pick up the Stockholm medium-waver, but since London
has better facilities for receiving than has Geneva, our
hook-up was bound to be superior.

This afternoon I arranged with the Helsinki correspondent of the *Christian Science Monitor* to do the
first eyewitness account of the Helsinki bombing — a
scoop. And Harald Diettrich, head of Germany's short-
wave organization and a cool and fine technician (he
has almost an artist's appreciation of the technical job
American broadcasters are doing to get their European
pick-ups, and though a fanatical Nazi who bears watching, he is the one man in Germany I work smoothly and
successfully with), told me on the phone he would do
his best to get Goebbels to allow us transit telephone facilities if I guarantee my speakers are all Americans.

Running a temperature from the flu, but shall keep
going on these Finnish broadcasts. Tess pitched in
wonderfully, spending several hours shouting into the
phone in several languages, including the Scandinavian, which (Danish) she speaks perfectly, dispatch-
ing and receiving telegrams, which must be done exclusively over the phone, and generally helping. My
telephone bill yesterday and today, including numerous urgent calls to Helsinki, Stockholm, Berlin, Amsterdam, London, and New York, has run over a thousand dollars and my cable and telegraph bill must come
to almost half that. But Paul White and Klauber say:
" Get the broadcasts."

BERLIN, *December* 7

Caught Bill White by telephone in Stockholm
and got him off to Helsinki to cover the Finnish war for

us.[1] Amusing note: Some of our people in New York thought one of his broadcasts from here the other night was very unneutral and cabled that while they personally agreed with Bill's personal anti-Nazi bias, he should strive to be more objective. When I got to the Rundfunk House on my return day before yesterday, Diettrich approached me with Bill's manuscript in his hand. I thought he was going to make an angry scene.

" Read this," he said.

" What's the matter with it? " I said, determined to defend it, though it had gone rather far in its biting irony against the Nazis.

"Why, it's wonderful! We here thought it was a wonderful broadcast, witty but fair — the kind you might do some time if you could forget your personal antipathy to Nazism," he said.

If I live in Germany a hundred years I shall never understand these people.

BERLIN, *December* 10

Ed [Murrow] and I on this Sabbath evening have just had the first telephone conversation to take place between Berlin and London since the telephone lines were cut at the beginning of the war. It was broadcast. Paul White's idea, I believe, he being a fiend for " features." Our voices actually travelled a long way. I heard Ed's after it had gone by short-wave from London to New York, from where it was short-waved back to Berlin. Mine travelled the same route in the opposite direction. So that we would not give information of benefit to the enemy, we worked out our conversation in advance, I submitting my questions and Ed's answers as

---

[1] His moving Christmas broadcast from the Finnish front was to inspire Robert Sherwood's play *There Shall Be No Night*.

well as his questions and my answers beforehand to the
Germans and he doing the same with the British. Both
sides proved very decent about the whole script. It was
good to hear Ed's voice. Once or twice he faded out and
I couldn't hear the cue to cut in, but on the whole it
was great fun.

It seems that Eleanor K. was arrested by the Gestapo
at Bentheim near the Dutch border on her way from
Amsterdam to Berlin and jumped out of the top storey
of the local hotel where she had been confined. By a
miracle she was not killed, though she broke her back,
both legs, and an arm. She has now been released and
has left for New York, I hear. Must get to the bottom
of this. I am positive the secret police had nothing on
her.

BERLIN, *December* 13

The liner *Bremen* has successfully run the
British blockade and made its way back from Murmansk along the Norwegian coast to a German port.
The British navy hasn't looked very good on this one.
Jordan and I scrapping as to who shall have the radio
interview with Commodore Ahrens, the *Bremen's* skipper. I do not like this kind of competition. By scrapping we play right into Nazi hands. The Propaganda
Ministry is now insisting that Lothrop Stoddard, the
American author who once skyrocketed himself to fame
with the book *The Rising Tide of Color* and whose
writings on racial subjects, I'm told, are featured in
Nazi school textbooks, do the interview for both of us.
I can't have the Propaganda Ministry name my speakers, and have rejected the proposal even if CBS loses the
broadcast.

Ribbentrop's White Book entitled *Documents on the*

Origins of the War, published by the Foreign Office,
is out today in several languages. From a first hasty
perusal, I conclude it is about as dishonest as the man
himself and the master he serves. Somewhere in *Mein
Kampf* Hitler criticizes the old Imperial government
for its lukewarm propaganda between 1914 and 1918 as
to the origins of the war. Berlin at that time, it seems,
took the stand that Germany in 1914 was no more to
blame for the war than any other nation. Hitler thought
that was bad propaganda. He says the Imperial government should have dinned it into the ears of all Germans that the Allies were exclusively responsible for the
war. He's doing that now.

In an introduction Ribbentrop repeats an old lie
which Hitler has assiduously built up as a gospel truth
in this country: namely, that after Versailles Great
Britain opposed every attempt by Germany to free herself from the chains of the peace treaty by peaceful
means. Did Britain oppose German conscription in
1935? The occupation of the Rhineland in 1936? The
Anschluss in 1938? The ceding to Germany of the Sudetenland, which had never belonged to it, in 1938?

The Christmas trees are in and being snapped up.
No matter how tough or rough or pagan a German may
be, he has a childish passion for Christmas trees. People
everywhere bravely trying to make this Christmas seem
like the old ones in the time of peace. I did a little Christmas shopping today, and it was a bit sad. There were
so many nice things in the windows which you couldn't
buy because they were only there for show, on the
orders of the authorities. Germans usually give wearing apparel and soaps and perfumes and candy to one
another for Christmas, but this year, with these articles
rationed, they must find something else. In the shops,
which were crowded, they were buying today mostly

books, radios, gramophones, records, and jewelry. I tried to buy some gramophone records for the four girl secretaries at the *Rundfunk* who have been most friendly and helpful to me, but found you could only buy new records if you turned in your old ones. Having none, I was out of luck. The government is loosening up a little on rations over Christmas. Everyone will get a quarter of a pound of butter and a hundred grams of meat extra, and four eggs Christmas week instead of one.

New title for Churchill in the Nazi press these days: *Lügenlord* — " lying lord." Most common reference to Churchill in the Nazi press is simply by his initials W.C., the letters painted on every water-closet in Germany, which is why the Nazis use them.

BERLIN, *December* 14

The German papers tonight celebrate a great sea victory of the pocket-battleship *Graf Spee* over three British cruisers off Montevideo. On the radio I heard London hailing it as a British victory, which reminds one of Jutland, it, too, having been celebrated as a triumph by both Britain and Germany. The German papers claim the British cruisers used mustard-gas shells, though in German naval circles this charge is not taken seriously. Dr. Goebbels is certainly going to town on this story.

BERLIN, *December* 18

The populace is still a little bit puzzled about how the big victory of the *Graf Spee* suddenly ended by the pocket-battleship scuttling itself off Montevideo yesterday afternoon. But Goebbels and Göring have pulled a neat one to make them forget it as soon as possible. The attention of the German people tomorrow morning will be concentrated by the press and radio on something else, an alleged victory — this time in the air — off Helgoland. An official statement which the papers and radio have been told to bang for all it's worth says that thirty-four out of forty-four British bombers were shot down this afternoon north of Helgoland. A very *timely* victory. We had just left the evening press conference after firing embarrassing questions about the *Graf Spee* and were putting on our overcoats downstairs when Dr. Boehmer rushed in breathlessly and said he had some big news and would we please return upstairs to the conference room. Then he read us in breathless tones the communiqué about the thirty-four British planes being shot down. Suspect it is eyewash.

Hear that the navy is fuming to Hitler about the way Goebbels bungled the propaganda on the *Graf Spee*. The admirals are especially sore because the day before it sank itself, Goebbels had the press play up a dispatch (and radioed photographs) from Montevideo saying the pocket-battleship had suffered only superficial damage and that British reports that it had been badly damaged were pure lies.

More astute propaganda is that which tries to whip up the support of the people for this war by telling them of the dire consequences should the Allies win. Tomorrow the *Völkische Beobachter* will publish a map showing how Germany will look in case of a Franco-British victory. Newspapers in the Allied lands have already published it, the *V.B.* claims, though I doubt not that the Nazi editors have done some neat touching-up. According to this map, France has the Rhineland, Poland has eastern Germany, Denmark has Schleswig-Holstein, Czechoslovakia has Saxony, and to the south there is a huge Habsburg Empire which includes most

of southern Germany. What is left of Germany is la-
belled " Occupied Territory." Clever propaganda, and
the German people will fall for it.

LATER. — When I mentioned the above story
in my broadcast I commented: " I have seen no map of
how Europe will look if Germany wins the war." My
censors held this was unfair and cut it out.

BERLIN, *December* 21

A curious communiqué from the German navy
today: " The High Command of the Navy announces:
The commander of the *Graf Spee*, Captain Hans
Langsdorff, did not want to survive the sinking of his
ship. True to old traditions and in the spirit of the
training of the Officers Corps of which he was a member
for thirty years, he made this decision. Having brought
his crew to safety he considered his duty fulfilled, and
followed his ship. The navy understands and praises
this step. Captain Langsdorff has in this way fulfilled
like a fighter and a hero the expectations of his Führer,
the German people, and the navy."

The wretched German people, deprived of all truth
from outside, will not be told that Captain Langsdorff
did *not* follow his ship to the bottom, but committed
suicide by putting a revolver-shot through his head in
a lonely hotel room in Buenos Aires. They will not be
told — though the navy did its best to hint at it in this
communiqué — that Hitler, in a burst of fury over the
defeat, ordered the Captain to end his life.

Hitler and Ribbentrop have wired their Christmas
greetings to Comrade Josef Stalin. How ludicrous.
Wires Hitler: " Best wishes for your personal well-
being as well as for the prosperous future of the peoples

of the friendly Soviet Union." [1] The Russians are not going so fast in Finland after a month of fighting. I recall what the counsellor of the Soviet Embassy told me here a few days before the fighting began. " It will be all over in three days," he boasted.

Eleven admitted executions here in the last two days. About half for espionage and the rest for " damaging the interests of the people in war-time " — the sentences in all but one case being passed by the " People's Court " whose proceedings are never published. One of the eleven was sentenced by the court to fifteen years' imprisonment for " damaging the people's interests," but Himmler wasn't satisfied with the sentence, so he simply had the poor fellow shot. " Shot while offering resistance to state authority," Himmler says. And Heinrich Himmler is such a mild little fellow when you talk to him, reminding you of a country school-teacher, which he once was — pince-nez and all. Freud, I believe, has told us why the mild little fellows or those with a trace of effeminacy in them, like Hitler, can be so cruel at times. I guess I would prefer my cruelty from great thundering hulks like Göring.

Many long prison sentences being meted out to Germans who listen to foreign radio stations, and yet many continue to listen to them. So many, in fact, that an official warning was issued today. It concluded: " No mercy will be shown the idiotic criminals who listen to the lies of the enemy." I passed an afternoon with a German family the other day, mother, two daughters, one son. They were a little apprehensive when they turned on the six p.m. BBC news. The mother said that besides the porter, who is the official Nazi spy for the

[1] To which Stalin replied: " The friendship of the peoples of Germany and the Soviet Union, cemented by blood, has every reason to be lasting and firm "!

apartment house, they had just learned that a Jewish tenant in return for receiving clothing ration cards (Jews get food cards, but no clothing cards) had turned informer for the house, and they had to be very careful. They played the radio so low I could hardly catch the news, and one of the daughters kept watch by the front door.

BERLIN, *December 24–5, three a.m.*

Christmas Eve. Raining out, but it will turn to snow. The first war Christmas somehow has brought the war home to the people more than anything else. It was always the high point of the year for Germans but this year it's a bleak Christmas, with few presents, Spartan food, the men folk away, the streets blacked out, the shutters and curtains drawn tight in accordance with police regulations. On many a beautiful night I have walked through the streets of Berlin on Christmas Eve. There was not a home in the poorest quarter that did not have its candlelit Christmas tree sparkling cheerfully through the uncurtained, unshaded window. The Germans feel the difference tonight. They are glum, depressed, sad. Hitler has gone to the western front, though we have not been allowed to say so. He pulled out on the 21st in a huff, skipping his traditional Christmas party for the Chancellery staff and his old party cronies, though it had been all planned. Myself, I went to the Oechsners' for Christmas dinner this evening, and a right good one it was. There a good portion of what remains of the shrinking American colony gathered and I'm afraid we all were just a little too desperate in our effort to forget the war and the Germans and enjoy for the fleeting moment Christmas in " the good old American way." Dead, they are, for us all — the " good old ways." But there was turkey and trimmin's and Dorothy had done an artist's job with pumpkin pie and whipped cream and real coffee, and there was much good red wine, which has been very scarce here of late, alas, and champagne and a giant Christmas tree and a lovely creature with straw-blond hair and innocent blue eyes who danced like a swish of the wind and who tomorrow is setting off with her husband for the Finnish front to work amidst the blood of men's wounds.

I had to leave at midnight for my broadcast. At the *Rundfunk* they had set up a big Christmas tree in one of the offices and when I arrived the people were dancing and making merry with champagne. My broadcast, I fear, was inexcusably sentimental. I kept thinking of the way Schumann-Heink used to sing *Stille Nacht* in my childhood days in Chicago before the World War. Lord Haw-Haw, the British traitor who goes here by the name of Froehlich, but whose real name is William Joyce and whose voice millions of English listen to on the radio every night, and his English wife were at the party, but I avoided them. Later Jack Trevor, an English actor, who has also turned traitor and broadcasts German propaganda to England, came in, much in his cups. I cannot stomach him either.

In two hours — at five a.m. — must start out by car for Hamburg and Kiel, where I will do a Christmas broadcast tomorrow night from the German fleet. Since I cannot be in Geneva for Christmas, I'm glad to have a distraction like this. No foreigner has yet seen the German fleet since the war began. The Nazis had promised me a broadcast from the Westwall to balance a broadcast our Paris staff arranged from the Maginot Line, but someone double-crossed me and gave it to the opposition. I stopped our evening broadcasts for a week as protest.

BERLIN, *December* 27

   This has been quite a Christmas holiday. Two days with the German fleet, the first foreigner given the opportunity.

Up hours before dawn on Christmas morning, but my army chauffeur got lost in the black-out and heavy fog over Berlin and it took us two hours to find my guide, Oberleutnant X from the High Command. A typical World War type of officer, monocle and all, he was so angry he could hardly speak. He fumed that he had been standing on a darkened corner for two hours in the pouring rain and that we had passed him several times.

At Hamburg the rain was still coming down in sheets when we arrived. The city reminded me very much of Liverpool. We finally found the docks and waded through foot-deep puddles to where the warships were. I spent an hour going through the new 10,000-ton cruiser *Admiral Hipper*, which was tied up at a dock. Much debris on its decks and beneath its decks, but the officers explained it was merely undergoing the usual overhaul which every new vessel needs. They swore the ship had not been damaged by enemy action. For some reason I get along all right with German naval people, and when over our port wine and sandwiches I reminded them that the British Admiralty had recently reported the torpedoing of a cruiser by a British U-boat the commander winked and beckoned me to follow him. We climbed and climbed up a narrow ladder-way until I was sweating and out of breath, my overcoat torn in five places. Finally we emerged on the battle tower.

" Look over there," he said slyly. A hundred yards away a somewhat smaller cruiser was propped up in dry-dock, a huge hole that must have been fifty feet in diameter torn in its side exactly amidships, or whatever

the sailors call the middle. It was the cruiser *Leipzig*
and the officer said they had been lucky to get it back
into port afloat after a British torpedo had hit it
squarely. The BBC, he said, had claimed the ship had
been sunk. But there it was, and though it was Christmas Day, a swarm of workers were labouring on it. A
little way down the river, returning to our car, I noticed the 35,000-ton battleship *Bismarck*. It looked
very near completion. Great secrecy surrounded this
and its sister ship — the only two 35,000-ton battleships laid down by the German navy.

As we sped towards Kiel in the late afternoon, it grew
colder, the rain turned to snow, and the car had difficulty getting over the hills because of the ice. At Kiel
some official representing, I suppose, the Propaganda
Ministry welcomed me with a little speech.

" I have just heard," he said, " that you have stopped
at Hamburg and seen all our warships there. Did you
see the cruiser *Leipzig*, Herr Shirer? "

" Yes, sir, and . . ."

" Those British liars, they say they have sunk the
Leipzig, Herr Shirer."

" It didn't look sunk to me, I must admit, and I'll be
glad to broadcast that I've seen it, that it wasn't sunk,
but that . . ."

He cut me off with a mighty roar. " Herr Shirer,
that is fine. You will answer this dastardly English lie,
isn't it? You will tell the truth to the great American
people. Tell them that you have seen the *Leipzig* with
your own eyes, isn't it? — and that the ship has not
been scratched."

Before I could interrupt he was pushing me down a
gangplank towards a naval launch. I turned to my
Oberleutnant to protest. His monocle dropped out of
his eye and a look of such distress came over him that I

desisted. After all, what could he say in this company, which now included several naval officers who were waiting in the launch?

Out in Kiel harbour I was surprised to see that almost the entire German fleet was concentrated here for Christmas. I noticed the pocket-battleship *Deutschland*, two cruisers of the *Cologne* class (for days in Berlin I had boned up on types of German naval vessels so that I could recognize them and felt proud when an officer confirmed that they *were* of the *Cologne* class), both 26,000-ton battleships, and about fifteen submarines, not including three in dry-dock. If the British only knew, I could not help thinking, they could come over this night, which will see almost a full moon, and wipe out the whole German fleet. Just one real big bombing attack. Kiel harbour looked beautiful in the greying light of the late Christmas afternoon. The hills around the bay were white with snow.

Our launch finally stopped next to an immense dry-dock. One of the 26,000-ton battleships was in it, the *Gneisenau*. My hosts decided to show me over it. They were quick to explain that it, too, was in for a general overhauling, and I must admit that on the one side of the hull that I could see, there were no holes. We spent an hour going through the immense craft. I was surprised at the spirit of camaraderie between officers and men on the ship and so was — I soon noticed — my monocled *Oberleutnant* from the World War. Four or five senior officers accompanied me through the ship, and when we entered one of the crew's quarters there was no jumping up, no snapping to attention as I had expected. The captain must have noticed our surprise.

" That's the new spirit in our navy," he said proudly. He also explained that in this war the men on all German men-of-war get exactly the same kind and the same amount of food as the officers. This had not been true in the last war and he quoted some naval proverb to the effect that the same food for officers and men puts an end to discontent and helps win the war. I remembered — as no doubt did he — that the German revolution in 1918 started here in Kiel among the discontented sailors.

When we returned to shore in the launch, a magnificent full moon was rising behind the snow-banked hills, spreading a silvery light over the water and making the ships stand out in outline. Back at the hotel we discussed our broadcast which was to take place from a submarine tender, where the crew of a U-boat just returned would be celebrating Christmas. The naval officers agreed to meet me at nine p.m. We would drive to the ship. The broadcast was scheduled for ten fifteen. Nine o'clock came. No officers. Nine fifteen. Nine thirty. I had not the slightest idea where our ship was docked. Even if I had had, I doubted whether a taxi-driver could find it in the black-out. At five minutes to ten my naval officers finally arrived. We reached the ship just in time to begin the broadcast, though I had planned a rehearsal or two and certainly needed at least one. Wolf Mittler, a big, genial chap from the RRG who had come up to help me, snapped in and got the crew, who were seated around a table in the bowels of the ship, to sing Christmas songs. The moon over the harbour was now well up and it was so superb I decided to start the broadcast on the top deck, describing the scene even though the head naval officer warned me that I must not — for God's sake — tell the British that the whole German fleet was there, which was reasonable enough under the circumstances. I would start up on deck under the moonlight and then slide down a hatch with my microphone to the crew's quarters below for

the main part of the show. The first part went off all
right, and after exhausting my adjectives I started to
slide down the hatch, grasping my portable microphone.
Alas, I am not a sailor. Before I had reached bottom, or
whatever the sailors call it, I had ripped a sleeve and
smashed the face of the stopwatch strapped to my wrist.
Only I didn't notice it at once. I barged into the crew's
quarters, got the boys to singing, described how the men
just back from the U-boat killings celebrate Christmas,
called for volunteers to say a few words in English, and
the show was going all right. I glanced at my watch to
see how our timing was. No face left to it. I made
motions to the captain for his watch, but he didn't get
my sign language. Finally I closed the show. Later
Berlin told us we were only ten seconds off. In the rush
we had forgotten the censor. And I had ad-libbed a line
about the *Leipzig* being badly damaged but not sunk.
Apparently none of the officers understood English, for
nothing was said.

Surprising with what ingenuity these tough little
sailors had fixed up their dark hole — for that it was —
for Christmas. In one corner a large Christmas tree
shone with electric candles, and along one side of the
room the sailors had rigged up a number of fantastic
Christmas exhibits. One was a miniature ice-skating
rink in the midst of a snowy mountain resort on which
couples did fancy figure-skating. A magnetic contrap-
tion set the fancy skaters in motion. Another showed
the coastline of England and another electrical con-
traption set a very realistic naval battle in action.
After the broadcast we sat around a long table, officers
and men intermingled in a manner that shocked my
Oberleutnant, singing and talking. The commandant
served rum and tea, and then case after case of Munich
beer was brought out. The *Oberleutnant* and I had a

bit of trouble downing the beer from the bottle, there being no glasses. Towards midnight everyone became a bit sentimental.

" The English, why do they fight us? " the men kept putting it to me, but it was obviously not the time nor place for me to speak out my own sentiments. Impressive, though, the splendid morale of these submarine crews, and more impressive still the absolute lack of Prussian caste discipline. Around our table the officers and men seemed to be on an equal footing and to like it.

We walked back to the hotel through the moonlight, and after a final round of drinks to bed at three.

BERLIN, *December* 28

I must record Dr. Ley's Christmas proclamation. " The Führer is always right. Obey the Führer. The mother is the highest expression of womanhood. The soldier is the highest expression of manhood. God is not punishing us by this war, he is giving us the opportunity to prove whether we are worthy of our freedom."

Himmler has suddenly decided to revoke the permission for cafés and bars to stay open all night on New Year's Eve and warns the public against excessive drinking on that night. Is he afraid the people of this land may go out on a binge, get drunk (which Germans rarely do, normally), and express their feelings about this war? At any rate, everyone must shut up shop at one a.m. on New Year's.

BERLIN, *December* 31

A flood of New Year's proclamations from all and sundry — Hitler, Göring, Himmler, etc. Hitler holds out hope of victory to the people in 1940. Says

he: " United within the country, economically prepared
and militarily armed to the highest degree, we enter this
most decisive year in German history. . . . May the
year 1940 bring the decision. It will be, whatever happens, our victory." He goes to extreme lengths to justify *his* war, and if the German people were not so
poisoned by propaganda and suppression of the slightest factual news from abroad, they would laugh. He
says the " Jewish reactionary warmongers in the capitalistic democracies " started the war! Words have no
more meaning for the man nor, I fear, for his people.
He says: " The German people did not want this war."
(True.) " I tried up to the last minute to keep peace
with England." (False.) " But the Jewish and reactionary warmongers waited for this minute to carry out
their plans to destroy Germany." (False.)

Curious how the Germans, who should know better by
this time, try to *scare* the English by blustering threats.
Göring has a piece in tomorrow's *V.B.:* " Until now
German airplanes have been content to keep a sharp eye
on England's war measures. But it needs only the word
of the Führer to carry over there, instead of the present
light load of cameras, the destructive load of bombs. No
country in the world is so open to air attack as the British Isles. . . . When the German air force really gets
started, it will make an attack such as world history has
never seen."

Cold, and a coal shortage. The office boy said tonight
we were out of coal at the office and that there was no
more coal to be had.

BERLIN, *January* 1, 1940

What will this year bring? The decision, as
Hitler boasted yesterday? I haven't met a German yet

who isn't absolutely certain. Certain it is that this
phony kind of war cannot continue long. Hitler has
got to go forward to new victories or his kind of system
cracks.

More drunkenness on the Kurfürstendamm last night
than I've ever seen in Berlin. Himmler had thousands
of police scattered over town to see that no one used his
car and that the cafés shut up promptly at one a.m.
Saw the old year out at Sigrid Schultz's, then an hour
or so with the Germans at the *Rundfunk*, then with Russell Hill over to Virginia's. About two a.m. in the Kurfürstendamm we jumped into a taxi. A German, his
wife and daughter, aged about twelve, sprang in
through the other door and we agreed to share it, there
being practically no taxis out. A soldier and his girl
then climbed in next to the driver. We had not gone far
when a policeman stopped us and ordered us all out, on
the ground that we could not ride in a taxi unless we
were on state business. I admitted I had no state business at two a.m. on New Year's Eve, but pointed out
that we had a child with us and that she was ill. He
finally allowed us to pile in again. We rode a few blocks
and then the soldier began to throw a fit — whether
from drink or shell-shock I couldn't tell. At any rate,
he clamoured for the driver to stop and let him out, and
his girl screamed first at him and then at the driver to
do something. The driver, whether from drink or nature I don't know, was inclined to do nothing. We kept
on going. Then the alarming psychological atmosphere
of the front seat began to spread to the rear one, where
we five were jammed in. The little girl suddenly started
to scream, whether from claustrophobia or fear of the
screaming soldier, or both, Russell and I were not sure.
She too cried to get out. Her mother joined her. Then
her father. Finally the driver, apparently awakened

by the bedlam, decided to stop. Out on the curb the
father and the soldier began to engage in a fierce argument as to who had spoiled whose New Year's Eve.
Russell and I and the taxi-driver stole away, leaving
them to fight it out. The frayed nerves of the war, we
decided.

BERLIN, *January 3*

I learned today what the Russians have promised to deliver to Germany this year:

1,000,000 tons of fodder and grain;

500,000 tons of oil seeds;

500,000 tons of soya beans;

900,000 tons of petroleum;

150,000 tons of cotton (this is more cotton than Russia had to export to the whole world last year);

Three million gold marks' worth of leather and hides.

This looks good on paper, but I would bet a lot the
Russians deliver no more than a fraction of what they
have promised.

An official statement announces that Göring is to become absolute dictator of Germany's war economy — a
job he has had in effect for a long time. The press is
beginning to harp about "Britain's aggressive designs
in Scandinavia." Hitler, we hear, has told the army,
navy, and air force to rush plans for heading off the
Allies in Scandinavia should they go in there to help
Finland against Russia. The army and navy are very
pro-Finnish, but realize they must protect their trade
routes to the Swedish iron-ore fields. If Germany loses
these, she is sunk.

BERLIN, *January* 8

Did a mike interview with General Ernst Udet tonight, but Göring, his boss, censored our script so badly that it wasn't very interesting. I spent most of the day coaching the general on his English, which is none too good. Udet, a likable fellow whom I used to see occasionally at the Dodds', is something of a phenomenon. A professional pilot, who only a few years ago was so broke he toured America as a stunt flyer, performing often in a full-dress suit and a top hat, he is now responsible for the designing and production of Germany's war planes. Though he never had any business experience, he has proved a genius at his job. Next to Göring and General Milch, he is given credit in inner circles here for building up the German air force to what it is today. I could not help thinking tonight that a man like Udet would never be entrusted with such a job in America. He would be considered " lacking in business experience." Also, businessmen, if they knew of his somewhat Bohemian life, would hesitate to trust him with responsibility. And yet in this crazy Nazi system he has done a phenomenal job. Amusing: last night Udet put on a little party in his home, with three generals, napkins slung over their shoulders, presiding over his very considerable bar. There were pretty girls and a great deal of cutting up. Yet these are the men who have made the Luftwaffe the most terrible instrument of its kind in the world.

BERLIN, *January* 9

Harry C., probably the best-informed man we have in the Moscow Embassy, passed through today with his wife, who is going to have her baby in America.

Harry, no Bolo-baiter, had some weird tales. He says the one and only thought of a Russian nowadays is to toe the Stalin line so that he can save his job or at least his life. The Russians, he says, have hopelessly bungled the attack on Finland. A hundred thousand casualties already, the hospitals in Leningrad and the north jammed with wounded. But they are the lucky ones because thousands of lightly wounded died of cold and exposure. Harry says everyone in Moscow, from Stalin down, thought the Red army would be in Helsinki a week after the attack started. They were so sure that they timed an attack on Bessarabia for December 6, and only called it off at the last minute.

This has been one of the coldest days I've experienced in fourteen years in Europe. Tens of thousands of homes and many offices are without coal. Real suffering among many. With the rivers and canals, which transport most of the coal, frozen over, the Germans can't bring in adequate supplies. Learn that eighteen Poles were killed and thirty wounded recently in a Polish prison camp. The S.S. here claim there was a " revolt." The army is protesting to Hitler about the senseless brutality of the Gestapo in Poland, but I doubt if that will change matters.

Must note a new propaganda campaign to convince the German people that this is not only a war against the " plutocratic " British and French, but a holy struggle against the Jews. Says Dr. Ley in the *Angriff* tonight: " We know that this war is an ideological struggle against world Jewry. England is allied with the Jews against Germany. . . . England is spiritually, politically, and economically at one with the Jews. . . . For us England and the Jews remain the common foe. . . ."

BERLIN, *January* 11

Cold. Fifteen degrees below zero centigrade outside my window. Half the population freezing in their homes and offices and workshops because there's no coal. Pitiful to see in the streets yesterday people carrying a sack of coal home in a baby-carriage or on their shoulders. I'm surprised the Nazis are letting the situation become so serious. Everyone is grumbling. Nothing like continual cold to lower your morale.

Hitler is back in town and last night at the Chancellery, I hear, he and Göring lambasted the big industrialists, who had been hurriedly convoked from the Rhineland, for being slack. These great tycoons, who made it possible with their money for Hitler to climb to power, sat there, I'm told, with red faces and never dared utter a peep. Hitler also saw the military yesterday and to-day and there is talk about a big push in the spring. The army, according to my spies, is still against an offensive on the Maginot Line despite party pressure for it. Will the Germans try to go through Holland, as many think? They want air bases on the Dutch coast for the take-off against Britain. Also fantastic talk here of an invasion of England; of the Germans going into Sweden to sew up their Swedish iron-ore supplies, the justification to be that the Swedes are plotting to let in Allied armies to fight in Finland.

Learned today from a traveller back from Prague that producers of butter, flour, and other things in Slovakia and Bohemia are marking their goods destined for Germany as " Made in Russia." This on orders from Berlin, the idea being to show the German people how much " help " is already coming from the Soviets.

A Wilhelmstrasse official admitted to me today that

the Germans had imposed forced labour on all Jews in Poland. He said the term of forced labour was " only two years." [1] A German school-teacher tells me this one: the instructors begin the day with this greeting to their pupils: " *Gott strafe England!* " — whereupon the children are supposed to answer: " He will."

AMSTERDAM, *January* 18

Ed [Murrow] and I here for a few days to discuss our European coverage, or at least that's our excuse. Actually, intoxicated by the lights at night and the fine food and the change in atmosphere, we have been cutting up like a couple of youngsters suddenly escaped from a stern old aunt or a reform school. Last night in sheer joy, as we were coming home from an enormous dinner with a fresh snow drifting down like confetti, we stopped under a bright street-light and fought a mighty snow-ball battle. I lost my glasses and my hat and we limped back to the hotel exhausted but happy. This morning we have been ice-skating on the canals with Mary Marvin Breckinridge, who has forsaken the soft and dull life of American society to represent us here. The Dutch still lead the good life. The food they consume as to both quantity and quality (oysters, fowl, meats, vegetables, oranges, bananas, coffee — the things the warring peoples never see) is fantastic. They dine and dance and go to church and skate on canals and tend their businesses. And they are

[1] The official German decree read: " All Jews from fourteen to sixty years of age are subject to forced labour. The length of forced labour is two years, but it will be prolonged if its educational purpose is not considered fulfilled. Jews called up for forced labour must report promptly, and must bring food for two days and their bedding. Skilled Jewish workers must report with their tools. Those who don't are subject to sentences running to ten years in the penitentiary."

blind — oh, so blind — to the dangers that confront
them. Ed and I have tried to do a little missionary
work, but to no avail, I fear. The Dutch, like everyone else, want it both ways. They want peace and the
comfortable life, but they won't make the sacrifices or
even the hard decisions which might ensure their way of
life in the long run. The Queen, they say, stubbornly
refuses to allow staff talks with the Allies or even with
the Belgians. In the meantime, as I could observe when
I crossed the border, the Germans pile up their forces
and supplies on the Dutch frontier. If and when they
move, there will be no time for staff talks with the Allies.
The Dutch tell you that if they even whisper to the
Allies about joint defence plans, Hitler will consider
that an excuse to walk in. As though Hitler will ever
want for an excuse if he really decides to walk in.

Ed a little alarming with his tales of British mud-
dling and the comfortable belief in Britain that the
Allies will win the war without losing many men or
doing much fighting by merely maintaining the blockade and waiting until Germany cracks. We broadcast
together tonight to America from Hilversum.

AMSTERDAM, *January* 20

Ed off today to Paris and I, alas, must head
back tonight to Berlin. I've invited Marvin to come up
next month and do the " women's angle." Ran into
Tom R., an American businessman, in the bar of the
Carlton this afternoon. He gave me the story at last
of what happened to Eleanor K.[1] He himself was involved. He had given her a couple of business letters
to certain parties in Germany which he says he did not

1 See pages 228–9 and 257.

think were compromising, but which obviously were.
These were the letters which in the end almost led to
her death. Eleanor did not look at them, merely tuck-
ing them into her bag. At Bentheim, on the Dutch-
German border, the Gestapo discovered them. They arrested her, but allowed her to be confined in the local
hotel, there being no suitable jail. Each day there were
long hours of questioning, with the Gestapo inquisition-
ers trying to break her down and make her admit what
she in truth refused to: that she knew the contents of
her letters and was really a courier in the service of
shady business interests inside and outside Germany
which were engaging in unlawful financial practices.
To make matters worse, one of the letters was to a Jew
in Berlin. One night in the hotel Eleanor fell into a
mood of deep depression. The Gestapo had questioned
and threatened her all day. She saw herself receiving a
long prison sentence. She had intended to return to
America for good in a few weeks. Now she would spend
years in a Nazi concentration camp or a damp prison
cell. She decided to make sure she wouldn't. She decided to kill herself. The resolve made, she prepared for
it coolly. She procured a rope, tied one end to the radiator, the other around her neck, opened the window, sat
down on the window-ledge, and began to swallow strong
sleeping-pills. She would soon be unconscious, she knew,
would topple out of the window, and the rope would do
the rest. Why it didn't, she will never know, Tom says.
Probably the rope slipped off the radiator. All she
knows is that some days later they told her in the hospital that the snow in the street below had broken her
fall, that she had lain there for five hours until someone had stumbled across her half-frozen form in the
first light of dawn, and that she had broken almost

every bone in her body, but probably would recover. Eventually she was removed to a prison hospital in Berlin, where the American consulate, in great secrecy, procured her release and quietly got her out of the country. She is now in America, Tom says.

BERLIN, *January* 22

I got an idea yesterday of how German transportation, at least of railroad passengers, has been paralysed by the severe winter and the demands of the army. At the German border we were told that the usual express train to Berlin had stopped running. With fifty other passengers I took refuge from the blizzard in the station at Bentheim and waited several hours until the railroad officials organized a local train which they said would take us some twenty-five miles of the two hundred and fifty miles to Berlin. The train, which was unheated, soon stopped; we piled out in the snow with our luggage as best we could, there being no porters in Germany nowadays. By the time it was dark, we had progressed on various local trains about seventy-five miles when in one little station word came that an express train from Cologne would be coming along soon and would pick us up for Berlin. But when it came in, it was jammed and there were at least five hundred people on the platform who wanted to get aboard. There was a free-for-all fight. I used college football tactics and charged in behind my baggage, just managing to squeeze into the outer platform of a third-class coach, the rest of the crammed passengers shouting and cursing at me. For the next eight hours I stood in that unheated spot until we got almost to Berlin. Several hundred irritable passengers stood in the corridors most of the night, and there were thousands on the station platforms we stopped at who never got on the train at all. Such grumbling I have not heard from Germans since the war started.

BERLIN, *January* 24

I think Percival W., a retired American businessman of German parentage who has spent most of his life in this country, sees something I've been trying to get straight. I had never met him before, but he dropped up to my room this morning for a chat. We discussed the German conception of ethics, honour, conduct. Said he: " For Germans a thing is right, ethical, honourable, if it squares with the tradition of what a German thinks a German should do; or if it advances the interests of Germanism or Germany. But the Germans have no abstract idea of ethics, or honour, or right conduct." He gave a pretty illustration. A German friend said to him: " Isn't it terrible what the Finns are doing, taking on Russia? It's utterly wrong." When Mr. W. remonstrated that, after all, the Finns were only doing what you would expect all decent Germans to do if they got in the same fix — namely, defending their liberty and independence against wanton aggression — his friend retorted: " But Russia is Germany's friend."

In other words, for a German to defend his country's liberty and independence is right. For a Finn to do the same is wrong, because it disturbs Germany's relations with Russia. The abstract idea there is missing in the German mentality.

That probably explains the Germans' complete lack of regard or sympathy for the plight of the Poles or

Czechs. What the Germans are doing to these people — murdering them, for one thing — is right because the Germans are doing it, and the victims, in the German view, are an inferior race who must think right whatever the Germans please to do to them. As Dr. Ley puts it: " Right is what the Führer does." All this confirms an idea I got years ago: that the German conception of " honour," about which Germans never cease to talk, is nonsense.

Mr. W. tells me he was in Germany until shortly before we entered the war in 1917 and that until the winter of 1916–17 there was no suffering among the civilian population at all. He says the present rations and shortages are about the same as Germany experienced in the third year of the World War. He is sure things cannot go on as at present, with the front quiet and nothing but hardship, especially the suffering from the cold we've had for more than a month now. " What the Germans must have," he said in departing, " are a lot of quick victories."

Joe [Harsch] dropped in yesterday. He said it was so cold in his flat when he was trying to type his dispatch that he had to keep a pan of water warming on the kitchen stove and dip his fingers into it every five minutes in order to hit the keys of his typewriter. To-day the burgomaster warns the populace that they must not use gas for heating rooms or water. Hot water, even if you have coal, is restricted now to Saturdays. I've started another beard therefore.

BERLIN, *January* 25 (*midnight*)

Dined alone at Habel's. A 1923 half-bottle of Bordeaux rouge, but despite the waiter's assurances, it was not a good enough wine to withstand that age;

1934 is the best year now for ordinary wines. I was about to leave when a white-haired old duffer sat down at my table. As he had no fat card for a meat dish he had ordered, I offered him one of mine. We started talking.

" Who will v.in the war? " he asked.

" I don't know," I said.

" Why, *selbstverständlich*, Germany," he laughed. He argued that in 1914 Germany had the whole world against her, now only Great Britain and France, and Russia was friendly.

" Each side thinks it will win," I said. " In all the wars."

He looked at me with pity in his old eyes. " Germany will win," he said. " It is certain. The Führer has said so."

But as we talked I was conscious that my remarks were jarring him. He became aggressive, irritated. He said Britain and France started the war.

" But you attacked Poland, and some people feel *that* started the war," I put in. He drew himself up in astonishment.

" I beg your pardon," he gasped, and then proceeded for ten minutes to repeat every lie about the origins of the war that Hitler has told. (The German people *do* believe Hitler then, I mused.) " The documents issued by our Foreign Office have proved beyond the shadow of doubt," he went on, " that Britain and France started the war and indeed planned it for more than a year."

" They don't prove it to me," I said.

This caused him to lose his breath. When he had re-covered he said: " As I was saying, the documents prove it. . . ."

I noticed my sour remarks were attracting the at-tention of the rest of the room and that two hatchet-

faced men with party buttons at the next table seemed
to be on the point of intervening with some heroics of
their own. I upped and left, bidding the old gentleman
good-night.

At six p.m. Fräulein X called for some provisions I
had brought her from relatives abroad. She turned out
to be the most intelligent German female I have met in
ages. We talked about the German theatre and films,
about which she knew a great deal. She had some interesting ideas about German character, history, direction. The trouble with the Germans, she said, was
that they were " *geborene Untertanen* " — born subjects, though " *Untertan* " conveys also a connotation of
submissive subjects. Authority and direction from a
master above was about all a German wanted in life.

" A German," she said, " will think he has died a good
German if he waits at a curb at a red light, and then
crosses on a green one though he knows perfectly well
that a truck, against the law though it may be, is bearing down upon him to crush him to death."

What embittered her — and she was brilliantly bitter — was that this Germany was staking all in a war
which might end the very Western civilization which
certain elements in Germany had not only contributed
to but had tried to make one with Germany's culture.
She thought the present regime cared not a whit about
Western civilization and represented the barbarian element which had always lurked below the surface in German history and for whom life only had meaning when
it meant glorified war, force, conquest, brutality, and
grinding down a weaker foe, especially if he were a
Slav. She blasted away about the German's utter lack
of political sense, his slavishness towards authority, his
cowardly refusal to think or act for himself.

The non-European, anti-Western civilization ele-

ment, as she put it, now has the upper hand in Germany
and she thought the only way the west-European nature
of the German could be saved would be by another defeat, even another Peace of Westphalia (which split up
Germany in 1648 into three hundred separate states).
I'm rather inclined to agree.

BERLIN, *January* 27

Some miscellany. With the publication of a
pocket-sized edition of *Mein Kampf* for the troops at
the front, total sales of Hitler's Bible, I learn today,
have now reached the fantastic total of 5,950,000 copies.
. . . The greatest organized mass migration since the
exchange of populations between Greece and Turkey
after the last war is now coming to an end in Poland.
Some 135,000 Germans from Russian-occupied eastern
Poland and 100,000 Germans from the Baltic states are
now being settled in the part of Poland which Germany
has annexed outright. To make room for them an equal
number of Poles are being turned out of house, home,
and farm and sent to occupied Poland. . . . Dr.
Frank, German Governor-General of Poland, has decreed the death sentence for Poles who hold back goods
from sale or refuse to sell their wares when offered a
" decent " price. This will enable the Germans to complete their pillage of Poland. If a Pole objects, off with
his head. . . . A German court in Posen has sentenced
eight Poles, including three women, to death for allegedly *mistreating* German flyers — probably parachutists. Even the Germans admit that not one of the flyers
was killed.

A phony war. Today's dispatches from the front deal
exclusively with an account of how German machine-
guns fought French *loud-speakers!* It seems that along

the Rhine front the French broadcast some recordings which the Germans say constituted a personal insult to the Führer.

"The French did not realize," says the DNB with that complete lack of humour which makes the Germans so funny, "that an attack on the Führer would be immediately rejected by the German troops." So the Germans opened fire on the French loud-speakers at Altenheim and Breisach. Actually the army people tell me that the French broadcast recordings of Hitler's former speeches denouncing Bolshevism and the Soviets.

BERLIN, *January* 28

It was difficult to believe in Berlin on this Sabbath day that a great war was on. The streets and parks are covered deep with snow and in the Tiergarten this afternoon thousands were skating on the ponds and lagoons. Hundreds of children were tobogganing. Do children think about war? I don't know. This afternoon in the Tiergarten they seemed to be thinking only of their sleds and skates and the snow and ice.

BERLIN, *January* 30

Marvin Breckinridge here and tomorrow I shall get off on a jaunt which Hitler's press chief and confidant, Dr. Diettrich, is organizing (to keep us in a friendly temper) to Garmisch. From there I hope to steal away to the Swiss mountains for a fortnight with Tess and Eileen. Hitler made an unexpected speech at the Sportpalast tonight on the occasion of the seventh anniversary of the Nazis taking over power. I had no burning desire to attend, so Marvin went off to cover it. She got a great kick out of watching the man.

Garmisch-Partenkirchen, *February* 3

A little ludicrous, broadcasting from here. Winter sport competitions are on, with all the German satellite nations participating, but they have no interest for us and I'm supposed to confine my daily broadcasts to the more serious subject of the terrible war. The trouble with that is that the only microphone in town is in the ice stadium. Yesterday on my two ten p.m. broadcast I had just launched into a deep discussion of the possibilities that lie before these unhappy people at war when someone scored a goal on the rink just below me, bedlam broke loose in the stadium, and it proved difficult to keep my mind on Hitler's next move. Tonight broadcasting at fifty minutes past midnight, the hockey games were over and in fact the stadium was so deserted that I had to wait a long time in the snow before I could arouse the night watchman to let me in. In the little studio atop the stadium it was so cold my teeth chattered with loud clicks and I had to blow on my fingers to keep them nimble enough to turn the pages of my script. I fear CBS listeners may not have appreciated the strange noises.

I feel sorry for Bob X, a young American correspondent who came down with us. He just couldn't take the strain of association with the Nazis since the war began, which is understandable. Arriving here, he let himself go — a plain case of nerves — drank more than he should have, expressed his honest thoughts, which alcohol sometimes releases, but unfortunately also made a general nuisance of himself. I gather the Nazis, on his return to Berlin, will ask him to leave. Two of our leading American correspondents today refused to sit at the same table in the dining-room with him, which I

thought was a little uncalled for. They are the two
who court the Nazis the most.

Hitler decreed today that henceforth babies must
have ration cards for clothing. A country is hard up
when it has to save on diapers.

On the Train Munich–Lausanne, *February* 4

Three stories I must put down:

1. In Germany it is a serious penal offence to listen
to a foreign radio station. The other day the mother
of a German airman received word from the Luftwaffe
that her son was missing and must be presumed dead. A
couple of days later the BBC in London, which broadcasts weekly a list of German prisoners, announced that
her son had been captured. Next day she received *eight*
letters from friends and acquaintances telling her they
had heard her son was safe as a prisoner in England.
Then the story takes a nasty turn. The mother denounced all eight to the police for listening to an English broadcast, and they were arrested.

(When I tried to recount this story on the radio, the
Nazi censor cut it out on the ground that American listeners would not understand the heroism of the woman
in denouncing her eight friends!)

2. The parents of a U-boat officer were officially informed of their son's death. The boat was overdue and
had been given up by the German Admiralty as lost.
The parents arranged a church funeral. On the morning of the service the butcher called and wanted a few
words with the head of the house in private. Next came
the grocer. Finally friends started swarming in. They
had all heard the BBC announce that the son was among
those taken prisoner from a U-boat. But how to call

off the funeral without letting the authorities know that someone in the confidence of the family had listened to a foreign station? If the parents wouldn't tell, perhaps they themselves would be arrested. A family council was held. It was decided to go through with the funeral. After it was over, the mourners gathered in the parents' home, were told the truth if they already didn't know it, and everyone celebrated with champagne.

3. A big German film company completed last summer at the cost of several million marks a movie based on the exploits of the German Condor Legion in Spain. It was a super-film showing how German blood had been shed in the holy war in Spain against Bolshevism. Hitler, Göring, Goebbels, Himmler, saw it, praised it. Then came the Nazi-Soviet pact last August. The film is now in storage. It was never shown to the public.

Villars-sur-Ollon, Switzerland, *February* 20

Across the valley from the window, the great sweep of the Dents du Midi Alpine peaks. Towards evening in the setting sun these snowy mountain-sides take on a magnificent pink. Down in bed with my annual flu for ten days. Must start back to Berlin tomorrow. Spring will soon be here. Action. The offensive. The war. Far away it has seemed here. Tess coming in at dusk with flushed cheeks after a four-mile ski run down the mountain behind the hotel, Eileen coming in with redder cheeks after playing around all day in the snow. In the evening — before I got sick — an excellent, unrationed dinner and then talk and dancing in the bar with people who still retain their senses. At first, and the last three days after I got out of bed, skating on the rink below with Wellington Koo, Chinese

Ambassador in Paris, himself recovering from the grippe and just learning to skate. Koo, who looks thirty and is probably over fifty, trying to impart to me the long view which the Chinese have learned to take, and I never patient nor wise enough to take. He sees the China war and this war as just chapters in a long story, places where men stop and pause on a long hard road, and he speaks softly and trudges along on his faltering skates.

BERLIN, *February 23*

My birthday. Thought of being thirty-six now, and nothing accomplished, and how fast the middle years fleet by.

Disagreeable experience at the Swiss border yesterday: the Swiss relieved me of all my provisions — chocolate, soap, canned food, coffee, and a bottle of whisky which Winant had given me. I see their point. They are cut off from the outside world and want to keep what they have and not let it get into the hands of the Germans. But I was sore. On the German side the Gestapo stripped two thirds of the passengers, including all the women. For some reason, possibly because I was the last to get my passport okayed and the train was late, they let me off.

Arrived here this morning (Friday) to find it a meatless day. The food *is* abominable. Because of the cold spell, no fish. Even at the Adlon I could get only potatoes and some canned vegetables, and my friends said I was lucky because for several days there had not been even potatoes, the city's supply having been spoiled by freezing. The newspapers seem inane after the Swiss. But the Germans swallow the fare, the lies. After this terrible winter their morale is lower, but they seem to

be in the same cow-like mood. It's hard to see the limit
of what they will take.

Much talk here of the spring offensive. But where?

BERLIN, *February 25*

X told me a fantastic story today. He claims
a plan is afoot to hide S.S. shock troops in the bottom of
a lot of freighters, have them put in at ports in Scandinavia, Belgium, and Africa, and seize the places. I don't
get the point. Even if they got into the ports, which is
doubtful, how could they hold them? I suspect this
story is a plant and that the Nazis would like us to put
it out as part of their nerve war. I shan't.

BERLIN, *February 27*

Marvin has been digging out some interesting
side-lights on life in war-time Germany. She visited
one of the nine Nazi Brides' Schools where the wives or
prospective wives of S.S. men are taught to be good
Hausfrauen and fruitful producers of cannon-fodder
for the next war.[1] They are also taught how to read
Nazi newspapers and listen to the radio. Marvin noticed only two books in the girls' dormitories, *The Belief
in the Nordic State* and *Men. . . .* Because of the

[1] Within or without wedlock. On October 28, 1939 Heinrich Himmler, chief of the German police and leader of the S.S., decreed: " Beyond the borders of perhaps necessary bourgeois laws, customs, and
views, it will now be the great task, *even outside the marriage bond,*
for German women and girls of good blood, not in frivolity but in
deep moral earnestness, to become mothers of the children of soldiers
going off to war. . . . On the men and women whose place remains at
home by order of the state, these times likewise impose more than
ever the sacred obligation to become again fathers and mothers of
children." (Italics mine.) Himmler promised that the S.S. would
take over the guardianship of all legitimate and illegitimate children
of Aryan blood whose fathers met death at the front.

shortage of soap, which curtails laundering, Marvin found that German clergymen had taken to wearing clerical collars made of paper. They cost eight cents, can be worn inside out the second day, and are then thrown away. . . . Marvin says many public buildings have been quietly closed for lack of coal, including the Engineering College of the University, the State Library, and most of the schools. Churches are not allowed to burn coal until further notice. She relates that when she called on an elderly German woman the other day, the old lady met her wearing two sweaters, a fur coat, and overshoes. The temperature in her drawing-room was 46 degrees Fahrenheit. . . . Though the quota of Germans allowed entrance into America annually is 27,000, Marvin found a waiting-list of 248,000 names at the American consulate. Ninety-eight per cent were Jews — or about half the Jewish population left in Germany.

BERLIN, *March* 1

Sumner Welles arrived this morning. He's supposedly over here on a special mission from the President to sound out the European leaders on their respective standpoints. He saw Ribbentrop and State Secretary Weizäcker today and will see Hitler tomorrow. Much talk around town that the Nazis will pull a fast one on him and suggest a peace that *sounds* good. Possible; not probable.

Because the offensive seems imminent. Troop trains pouring through Berlin every day west-bound. Many men called up for active service in the last few days. All air-wardens have been warned to be ready for duty after March 15. One hears — you never *know* here — of big troop concentrations against Holland.

From what I saw in the Netherlands, the Dutch will be
easy pickings for the Germans. Their army is miserable. Their famous defensive water-line is of doubtful
worth. Switzerland will be tougher to crack, and I
doubt if the Germans will try.

Welles received us in the Embassy after lunch. A
taciturn fellow, he said he could say nothing. I gathered from what little he did say that he was interested in
seeing Göring. Is it because in the end he thinks Göring
may lead a conservative government?

BERLIN, *March* 3

Welles left tonight, his lips sealed to the last.
Those of the Wilhelmstrasse were not, however. They
gave the American correspondents front-page copy.
They told us Hitler had made it plain to Welles:

1. That there is no chance for an immediate, negotiated peace. The war must be fought out to the bitter
end. Germany is confident of winning it.

2. That Germany must be given a free hand in what
she considers her *Lebensraum* in eastern Europe. She
will never consent to restore Czechoslovakia, Poland,
or Austria.

3. A condition of any peace must be the breaking of
Britain's control of the seas, including not only her
naval disarmament but the abandonment of her great
naval bases at Gibraltar, Malta, and Singapore.

I doubt if this tall talk impressed Welles, who struck
me as sufficiently cynical. At any rate, the Germans
did not, as some expected, offer a nice-sounding but
meaningless peace proposal. My spies report Hitler is
in a confident mood these days and thinks he can win
the war outright and quickly.

Touching how the German people have had a naïve

hope that Welles's visit might pave the way to peace. Several Germans dropped in today to inquire whether "Welles had any luck."

BERLIN, *March* 4

Last night, by request, I broadcast a piece about the actual routine of broadcasting from here in war-time. Had never stopped to think of it before. Some extracts, for the record: The daily broadcast at six forty-five p.m., New York time, means our talking from here at a quarter to one on the following morning. If I could get gasoline for my car I could drive to the studio in twelve minutes. As it is, I have a ten-minute walk down the completely blacked-out Wilhelmstrasse to the subway. It is a rare night that I do not collide with a lamp-post, a fire-hydrant, or a projecting stairway, or flop headlong into a pile of snow. Safely in the subway, I have a half-hour's ride to the Rundfunk House. As half of the route is above ground, the train is plunged in darkness for fifteen minutes. My pockets are stuffed full of passes. If I cannot find the right one I must wait in the vestibule on arriving at the station and fill out a paper permitting me to enter. Finally arrived, I go to an office and write my script. Two offices down I can hear Lord Haw-Haw attacking his typewriter with gusto or shouting in his nasal voice against "that plutocrat Chamberlain." A half-hour before my broadcast I must have my script in the hands of the censors. Follows a half-hour battle with them. If they leave enough to make it worth while to do the broadcast, as they usually do, I must then, in order to reach the studio and microphone, dash through winding corridors in the Broadcasting House, down many stairs, and out into a pitch-dark vacant lot in the middle

of which are hidden steps — the lot being terraced —
being careful not to bump into several sheds lurking in
the way or to fall into a snow-drift. In the course of
this journey through the lot, I must get past at least
three steel-helmeted S.S. guards whom I cannot see in
the darkness, but who I know are armed with sawed-off
automatic rifles and have orders to shoot anyone not
halting at their challenge. They must see my pass. I
search for it with my frozen fingers, and if I'm lucky
and find it, I arrive at the studio in time and not too
much out of breath, though not always in the sweetest
of tempers. If the censors keep me, or the guards keep
me, I arrive late, out of breath, sore and sour. I suppose listeners wonder why we pant so often through
our talks.

BERLIN, *March* 8

Diplomatic circles buzzing with talk of a
secret peace parley in Stockholm to end the Russo-
Finnish war. A decree today orders all persons and
firms who possess old metal or scrap iron to deliver it
to the state. Lack of iron may lose Germany the war.

BERLIN, *March* 10

Today is Memorial Day in Germany, a day
to remember the dead who've been slain in all the wars.
In former years the Germans remembered the two million men slaughtered between 1914 and 1918. Today
the Nazis ask the people not to think too much of the
World War dead, but to concentrate their thoughts on
those who have been done to death or will die in this
war. How perverse human beings can be! A front-page
editorial in the *Lokal Anzeiger* says: " This is no time

for being sentimental. Men are dying for Germany day and night. One's personal fate now is unimportant. There is no asking why if one falls or is broken."

That's the trouble. If the Germans asked why, the flower of their youth might not always be condemned to be butchered on the battlefield. General von Rundstedt, one of the leading military figures in the conquest of Poland, writes in the *Völkische Beobachter:* " Memorial Day — 1940: Certainly we think earnestly of the dead, but we do not mourn." And this paper bannerlines in red ink across Page one: "OVER THE GRAVES FORWARD!"

Hitler spoke today in a courtyard in the Zeughaus, the War Museum. There amidst the museum pieces — the arms and weapons Europeans have used to kill one another in all the wars of the past, he orated. His voice was full of hatred, which he might have been expected to avoid on Memorial Day. Has the man no other emotion? He promised his people that the end of this war would give Germany the most glorious military triumph in history. He thinks only of arms. Does he understand the economic role in this war?

Ribbentrop off to Rome to make sure what Mussolini will do when the German offensive starts and also to see the Pope. Talk of a new concordat. Monsignor Cesare Orsenigo, the Papal Nuncio, has been quietly paying visits to the Wilhelmstrasse for weeks. Germany didn't observe the last concordat, persecuting the church whenever it pleased. But they will probably sign a new one. It will mean prestige for Hitler at home and abroad.

All Germans I talk to afraid hell will break loose this month.

BERLIN, *March* 11

A talk today with General von Schell, a wizard who is responsible for oil and automobiles. He claimed he would have enough oil for a ten-year war. He said his factories were now producing only 20 types of trucks as compared with 120 last year.

Beginning April 20, all German youths between ten and eighteen will be compelled to join the Hitler Youth. Conscription of youth was laid down in a law dated 1936, but only goes into effect now. Boys between seventeen and eighteen will receive preliminary military training.

BERLIN, *March* 13

In Moscow last night peace was made between Russia and Finland. It is a very hard peace for Finland and in Helsinki today, according to the BBC, the flags are at half-mast. Berlin, however, is delighted. For two reasons: (1) It releases Russia from the strain of war, so that she now may be able to furnish some badly needed raw materials to the Reich. (2) It removes the danger of Germany having to fight a war on a long northern front, which she would have had to supply by sea and which would have dispersed her military forces now concentrating in the west for the decisive blow, which may begin any day now.

I think in the end Norway and Sweden will pay for their refusal to allow Allied troops across their territories to help Finland. To be sure, they were not in a pleasant spot. Baron von Stumm of the F.O. confirmed to me today that Hitler had informed both Oslo and Stockholm that had Allied troops set foot in Scandinavia, Germany immediately would have invaded the

north to cut them off. The trouble with the Scandinavians is that a hundred years of peace have made them
soft, peace-at-any-pricers. And they have not had the
courage to look into the future. By the time they make
up their minds to take sides, it will be too late, as it
was with Poland. Sandler, Sweden's Foreign Minister,
alone seems to have seen the situation correctly, and he
has been forced to resign.

Finland now is at the mercy of Russia. On any fake
pretext the Soviets can henceforth overrun the country,
since the Finns must now give up their fortifications,
as the Czechs had to do after Munich. (Czecho lasted
five and a half months after that.) Have we not reached
a stage in history where no small nation is safe any
longer, where they all must live on sufferance from the
dictators? Gone are those pleasant nineteenth-century
days when a country could remain neutral and at peace
just by saying it wanted to.

With peace in Finland, the talk here is once more of
the German offensive. X, a German, keeps telling me
it will be frightful; poison gas, bacteria, etc. Like all
Germans, though he should know better, he thinks it
will be so terrible that it will bring a quick victory for
Germany. It never occurs to him that the enemy too
has poison gas and bacteria.

A record: A letter from Carl Brandt posted in New
York October 7 last year arrived day before yesterday,
March 11. It had been opened by both the British and
German censors.

BERLIN, *March* 14

In London last night, one Mohamed Singh
Azad shot and killed Sir Michael O'Dwyer. Not
Gandhi, but most of the other Indians I know, will feel

this is divine retribution. O'Dwyer was once Lieuten-
ant-Governor of the Punjab and bore a share of responsibility in the 1919 Amritsar massacre, in which
General Dyer shot fifteen hundred Indians in cold blood.
When I was at Amritsar eleven years after, in 1930,
the bitterness still stuck in the people there. Goebbels
makes the most of the assassination. *Nachtausgabe*
headline tonight: "THE DEED OF AN INDIAN
FIGHTER FOR FREEDOM — SHOTS AGAINST THE
OPPRESSOR." This from Germans who are carrying
out mass murders in Bohemia and Poland.

ITEMS: Two more Germans beheaded today
for "damaging the people's interests." A third sentenced to death; same charge. . . . The Germans boast
that prices here have not risen. Today in the Adlon I
paid a dollar for a dish of boiled carrots. . . . Göring
today decrees that the people must give up their copper,
bronze, brass, tin, lead, and nickel. How can Germany
fight a long war lacking these? In 1938 Germany imported from abroad nearly a million tons of copper,
200,000 tons of lead, 18,000 tons of tin, and 4,000 tons
of nickel.

BERLIN, *March 15*

A year ago last night Hitler got Hacha, then
President of what was left of Czechoslovakia after
Munich and the Nazi-engineered " secession " of Slovakia, into his Chancellery and after threatening until
four a.m. that he would destroy Prague and its million
people with the Luftwaffe, forced the poor old man to
" ask " for German " protection." (Strange how few
Germans know *yet* of what took place that night.) Today Hitler forces Hacha to send him a " congratula-

tory" telegram, praising him for having destroyed Czechoslovakia and wishing him victory in this war. Hitler's cynicism is of rich quality, but millions of Germans believe that today's exchange of telegrams is perfectly sincere. Hitler replies that he is " deeply moved " by Hacha's wire and adds: " Germany has no intention of threatening the national existence of the Czechs." When he has already destroyed it! Neurath, a typical example of the German aristocrats who sacrificed their souls (they had no minds) to Hitler, sends him a slavish telegram thanking him for his " historic deed " and pledging the " unbreakable loyalty of Bohemia and Moravia." In an interview with the German press Neurath says the Czechs are content with their lot, all except " a few intellectuals and those elements of disturbance which were put down in a manner the sharpness of which was not misunderstood." He refers to the mass shooting of Czech students last fall.

My good friend Z, a captain in the navy on duty with the High Command, has not appeared in uniform all week. Today he told me why. " I have no more white shirts. I have not been able to have my laundry done for eight weeks. I have no soap to wash my shirts myself, being in the same position as the laundry. I have only colored shirts left. So I wear civilian clothes." A nice state for the navy to be in.

BERLIN, *March* 17

Much excitement on this Palm Sunday in official quarters over a war communiqué claiming that the Luftwaffe hit and damaged three British battleships in Scapa Flow last night. More important to me was that for the first time the Germans admitted that during the raid their planes also bombed British air bases at Stromness and Kirkwall. In this half-hearted war this is the first time that one side has purposely dropped bombs on the *land* of the other. It heralds, I suppose, the spring opening of the war in earnest. Editor Kircher of the *Frankfurter Zeitung* attempts to answer a question this morning that has bothered neutral military minds for a long time. Why haven't the Germans used their acknowledged air superiority over the Allies? Why are they waiting while the Allies, with American help, catch up? Kircher's answer is that the Allies have not been catching up, that Germany's relative superiority has been greatly increased in the last seven months.

Spring at last threatens to arrive. Millions of Germans are beginning to thaw out after the worst winter they can remember. For some reason there was no hot water in most apartments today, though it was Sunday. Several friends lined up in my room for a bath.

BERLIN, *March* 18

For two and a half hours this morning while a snowstorm raged, Hitler and Mussolini conferred at the Brenner. We opine Hitler wanted to make sure of the Duce before embarking on his spring plans, whatever they are. The Wilhelmstrasse plant tonight was that Hitler had won over Musso to the idea of joining a tripartite bloc with Germany and Soviet Russia which will establish a new order in Europe. Maybe so.

BERLIN, *March* 19

John Chapman, whom I have not seen since high-school days in Cedar Rapids, Iowa, called. He is foreign editor of *Business Week*, and has just come up

from the Balkans and Italy. He had some good dope.
He doubts that Italy will go into the war. So do I.
Italy *can* be blockaded. John said he noticed a lessen-
ing of the drive in Fascism. People are more relaxed.
Il Duce does not push them so hard. He's aging, growing fat, and spends much time with his youthful blonde
mistress, by whom — John was told in Rome — he has
just had a child. John said he saw Pétain in Madrid.
The old man said: " I pray that the Germans try to
break through the Maginot Line. It can be broken
through — at a cost. But let them infiltrate through.
I'd like to be in command of the Allied army then."

I called on Major X of the X Embassy this afternoon. He sees three possibilities open to Germany
now:

1. Germany can make peace. He thinks Hitler wants
peace. And that he could afford to offer a peace which
would sound pretty fair and might be acceptable to all
but the English, and which would still consolidate most
of his gains. Such a peace, he argued, would be equiva-
lent to a great German victory.

2. Germany can continue as at present, keeping
Scandinavia and Italy neutral and co-operative economically, and developing southeastern Europe and
especially Russia. This would take time, at least three
years, but once developed, it would make the Allied
blockade comparatively ineffective. The major pointed
out that no nation which lost control of the seas had
ever in all history won a major war. But he thinks it
might be accomplished this time if Germany keeps her
northern, southern, and southeastern doors open and
develops Russia sufficiently. He regards the Russian
tie-up as Hitler's master stroke, but says it was forced
upon him by the German General Staff, which simply
told him that war with the West was impossible if Rus-

sia joined the Allies, or even remained strictly neutral,
but unfriendly to Germany.

3. Germany can try to force the issue on the western
front. This he regards as improbable. The German
General Staff, he says, has a great respect for the
Maginot Line and the French army. He admits the
Maginot Line might be pierced — at great cost — but
that this would not necessarily win the war.

BERLIN, *March* 20

Last night the British answered for the bombing of Scapa Flow by strafing the German seaplane
bases on the island of Sylt for nearly seven hours. As
usual, the High Command claims no damage was done.
The British, according to the BBC, did a lot. At noon
the government offered to fly us up to see for ourselves,
then called it off. I had written of the offer in good
faith in my script; word came of the cancellation while
I was speaking, and so I announced it at the end of my
talk. Tonight while waiting to go on the air, I turned on
the BBC. To my surprise (and embarrassment, because
a RRG official was sitting at my side) the British announcer broadcast my entire noon script. He imitated
my voice so exactly, especially my closing announcement about the cancellation of our trip to Sylt, that he
could only have got it from a recording which the BBC
must have made of my talk. I probably will hear more
of this.

All Berlin papers on orders from Goebbels headline
the attack on the German base at Sylt: "BRITISH
BOMB DENMARK!" It seems that a couple of bombs
did fall on Danish territory. But it's a typical falsifica-
tion.

Headline in the *12-Uhr Blatt* today over its report

of Chamberlain's speech in the House last night: "HOLI-
DAY OF LIES IN LOWER HOUSE. — THE PIRATES
CONFESS THEIR CRIME AGAINST THE NEU-
TRALS!"

BERLIN, *March* 21

They took the American correspondents up
to Sylt after all today, but I was not invited. They telephoned Berlin tonight that they had not seen much
damage at the chief seaplane base at Hoernum, which
was the only one they were shown — a fact I pointed
out in my broadcast tonight. The Nazi press has been
ordered to make a terrific play tomorrow morning of
the reports of these American correspondents.

Three more Poles sentenced to death at Posen today
for allegedly slaying a German during the war. I hear
sixteen Polish women are in a Berlin jail waiting to have
their heads lopped off, all of them having been sentenced
to death.

BERLIN, *March* 22

Induced Irwin, of NBC, also to point out that
the American correspondents were not shown all of Sylt.
This afternoon the High Command was very angry
with me for having mentioned this.

Good Friday today. The sidewalks thronged. No
special Easter joy noticeable in the faces. Long lines
the last few days before the candy shops. How patiently Germans will stand for hours in the rain for a
tiny ration of holiday candy! Last week's ration of one
egg was increased by two eggs; this week's by one.

LATER. — Radio people called up. They will
fly Irwin and me to Sylt tomorrow to inspect the *northern* part of the island.

BERLIN, *March* 23

　　　At midnight last night the RRG phoned to
say our trip to Sylt could not be arranged after all.
What did the British do on the northern end of the
island that the Luftwaffe does not want Irwin and me
to see?

Great goings-on at the radio this noon. An officer of
the High Command accused Irwin and me of having
sabotaged our newspaper colleagues. He said that after
we spoke yesterday no American newspaper would publish the stuff the agencies were putting out about Sylt
from their Berlin correspondents. However, the Germans certainly publish what the American newsmen
wrote. It makes wonderful propaganda.

It is announced today that all church bells made of
bronze are to come down and be melted up for cannon.
Next week begins a nation-wide house-to-house collec-
tion of every available scrap of tin, nickel, copper,
bronze, and similar metals of which the Germans are so
short. Today the army ordered all car-owners whose
automobiles are laid up by the war-time ban — which
means ninety per cent of them — to surrender their batteries.

Easter tomorrow. The government tells the people
they must remain at home and not try to travel as in
other years because there won't be any extra trains. No
private cars will be permitted to circulate tomorrow. It
would be pleasant to be home. Last year, too, I was
away, speeding through this town from Warsaw to
Paris, and Europe jittery about Mussolini's invasion
of Albania and rumours that Hitler would walk into
Poland. Long ago, it seems.

Berlin, *March* 24

Easter Sunday, grey and cold, but the rain has held off. I cancelled my engagements with some German friends for lunch and tea. Couldn't face a German today, though they are no friends of Hitler. Wanted to be alone. Got up about noon and listened to a broadcast from Vienna. The Philharmonic, and a nice little thing from Haydn.

In the afternoon, a stroll. Unter den Linden thronged with people. Surely the Germans must be the ugliest-looking people in Europe, individually. Not a decent-looking woman in the whole Linden. Their awful clothes probably contribute to one's impression. Comparatively few soldiers in the street. Few leaves granted? Meaning? Offensive soon?

I was surprised to notice how shabby the Kaiser's Palace at the end of the Linden is. The plaster falling off all over the place. Very dilapidated. The stone railing of the balcony on which Wilhelm II made his famous appearance in 1914 to announce to the delirious mob at his feet the coming of war appeared to be falling to pieces. Well, they were not delirious before Hitler's balcony when this war started.

I tried to read in the faces of the thousands what was in their minds this Easter day. But their faces looked blank. Obviously they do not like the war, but they will do what they're told. Die, for instance.

Berlin, *March* 25

The DNB today: " At some places along the Upper Rhine front Easter Sunday, there were on the French side demonstrations against the English war, which clearly showed how foolish the French troops consider it to be that Germany and France have become enemies as a result of British connivance."

BERLIN, *March* 28

Germany cannot stay in the war unless she continues to receive Swedish iron, most of which is shipped from the Norwegian port of Narvik on German vessels which evade the blockade by feeling their way down the Norwegian coast and keeping within the three-mile limit, where they are safe from the British navy. Some of us have wondered why Churchill has never done anything about this. Now it begins to look as if he may. The Wilhelmstrasse says it will watch him. For Germany this is a life-and-death matter. X assures me that if British destroyers go into Norwegian territorial waters Germany will act. But how is not clear. The German navy is no match for the British.

I hope I didn't put myself out on a limb, but from what I've heard this week I wrote tonight in my broadcast: " Some people here believe the war may spread to Scandinavia yet. It was reported in Berlin today that last week a squadron of at least nine British destroyers was concentrated off the Norwegian coast and that in several instances German freighters carrying iron received warning shots. . . . From here it looks as if the neutrals, especially the Scandinavians, may be drawn into the conflict after all."

I often write a paragraph like that to see how the military censor will react. He made no objection, which is interesting.

BERLIN, *March* 30

The Nazis launched last night what they thought would be a bomb-shell in America. Today it looks more like a boomerang. And a fine example of clumsy German diplomatic blundering.

The Foreign Office released a new White Book containing what is purported to be sixteen documents discovered by the Germans in the Warsaw Foreign Office. Ribbentrop says they are secret reports of various Polish envoys. The most important are from the Polish ambassadors in London, Paris, and Washington. They "implicate" American ambassadors Kennedy, Bullitt, and Biddle, and the point of them is that these diplomats, backed by Roosevelt, were leading conspirators in forcing this war on Germany!

Though it seems incredible that even the Germans could be so stupid, my friends in the Foreign Office say that Ribbentrop actually thought these "revelations" would make Roosevelt's position so untenable that his defeat in the next election — or the defeat of his candidate, should he not run — would be assured. Having got wind of the strong sentiment in America to stay out of war, Ribbentrop thought these "documents" would greatly strengthen the hand of the American isolationists by convincing the American people that Roosevelt and his personally appointed ambassadors had not only had a hand in starting the war but had done everything to get us in. Happily, first American reactions are good and the New York press is suggesting the documents are fakes. They may not be faked; probably only doctored.

LATER. — One of the most amusing Nazi fakes I've seen in a long time appears in the evening press. It tells the German people that the publication of the Polish " documents " has hit America like a bomb-shell. The implication is that Roosevelt has been dealt a staggering blow. Secretary Hull issues an official denial of the allegations in the " documents." The DNB twists it around and heads it: "HULL DISAVOWS USA AMBASSADORS!" A crude piece of faking!

The only trouble is that men like Ham Fish and Senator Rush Holt may snatch at Nazi propaganda such as this to help fight Roosevelt. The DNB cables flatly that Senator Holt " agrees with the German White Book."

BERLIN, *April* 2

I broadcast tonight: " Germany is now waiting to see what the Allies intend to do in stopping shipments of Swedish iron ore down the Norwegian coast to the Reich. It's accepted here as a foregone conclusion that the British will go into Scandinavian territorial waters in order to halt this traffic. It's also accepted as a foregone conclusion here that the Germans will react. . . . Germany imports ten million tons of Swedish iron a year. Germany cannot afford to see these shipments of iron stopped without fighting to prevent it."

But how? S. whispers about Nazi troops being concentrated at the Baltic ports. But what can Germany do against the British navy?

BERLIN, *April* 7

The *V.B.* today: " Germany is ready. Eighty million pairs of eyes are turned upon the Führer. . . ."

BERLIN, *April* 8

The British announce they have mined Norwegian territorial waters in order to stop the German
iron ships coming down from Narvik. The Wilhelmstrasse says: " Germany will know how to react." But
how? There are two rumours afloat tonight, but we can
confirm nothing. One, that the German fleet has sailed
into the Kattegat, north of Denmark, west of Sweden
and south of Norway, and is heading for the Skagerrak. Two, that a German expeditionary force is forming at the Baltic ports and that dozens of passenger
ships have been hurriedly collected to transport it to
Scandinavia.

BERLIN, *April* 9

Hitler this spring day has occupied a couple
more countries. At dawn Nazi forces invaded the two
neutral states of Denmark and Norway in order, as an
official statement piously puts it, " to protect their freedom and independence." After twelve swift hours it
seems all but over. Denmark, with whom Hitler signed
a ten-year non-aggression pact only a year ago, has
been completely overrun, and all important military
points in Norway, including the capital, are now in
Nazi hands. The news is stupefying. Copenhagen occupied this morning, Oslo this afternoon, Kristiansand
this evening. All the great Norwegian ports, Narvik,
Trondheim, Bergen, Stavanger, captured. How the
Nazis got there — under the teeth of the British navy
— is a complete mystery. Obviously the action was long
prepared and longer planned and certainly put into operation *before* the British mined Norwegian territorial
waters day before yesterday. To get to Narvik from

German bases would have taken at least three days.

At ten twenty this morning we were urgently convoked to a special press conference at the Foreign Office to begin at ten thirty. We waited a half-hour. At
eleven a.m. Ribbentrop strutted in, dressed in his flashy
field-grey Foreign Office uniform and looking as if he
owned the earth. Schmidt, his press chief, announced
the news and read the text of the memorandum addressed
in the early hours of this morning to Norway and Denmark, calling on them to be " protected " and warning
that " all resistance would be broken by every available
means by the German armed forces and would therefore
only lead to utterly useless bloodshed."

" The Reich government," Schmidt, a fat, lumpy
young man, droned on, " therefore expects the Norwegian government and the Norwegian people to have
full understanding for Germany's procedure and not
to resist in any way. . . . In the spirit of the good
German-Norwegian relations which have existed so
long, the Reich government declares to the Royal Norwegian government that Germany has no intention now
or in the future of touching upon the territorial integrity and political independence of the Kingdom of
Norway."

Ribbentrop sprang up, snake-like, and said: " Gentlemen, yesterday's Allied invasion of Norwegian territorial waters represents the most flagrant violation of
the rights of a neutral country. It compares with the
British bombardment of Copenhagen in 1807. However " — showing his teeth in a smug grin — " it did not
take Germany by surprise. . . . It was the British intention to create a base in Scandinavia from which Germany's flank could be attacked. We are in possession,
gentlemen, of incontestable proof. The plan included
the occupation of all Scandinavia — Denmark, Nor-

way, Sweden. The German government has the proofs
that French and British General Staff officers were already on Scandinavian soil, preparing the way for an
Allied landing.

" The whole world can now see," he went on, somehow reminding you of a worm, " the cynicism and brutality with which the Allies tried to create a new theatre
of war. A new international law has now been proclaimed which gives one belligerent the right to take unlawful action in answer to the unlawful action of the
other belligerent. Germany has availed itself of that
right. The Führer has given his answer. . . . Germany has occupied Danish and Norwegian soil in order
to protect those countries from the Allies, and will defend their true neutrality until the end of the war. Thus
an honoured part of Europe has been saved from certain downfall."

The little man, the once successful champagne sales-
man who had married the boss's daughter, who had cur-
ried Hitler's favour in the most abject fashion, who had
stolen a castle near Salzburg by having the rightful
owner sent to a concentration camp, stopped. Glancing
over the room, he essayed another grin — inane, vapid.

" Gentlemen," he shouted, " I thank you again and
wish you a good-morning." Followed by his uniformed
lackeys, he strode out.

I was stunned. I shouldn't have been — after so
many years in Hitlerland — but I was. I walked up the
Wilhelmstrasse and then through the Tiergarten to
cool off. At noon I drove out to the *Rundfunk* to do my
regular broadcast. The people in the streets, I noticed,
were taking the news calmly. Few even bothered to buy
the extras which the newsboys were beginning to shout.
From a score of rooms at the RRG, Goebbels's unpleasant voice came roaring out over the loud-speakers. He

was reading the various memorandums, proclamations, news bulletins — all the lies — with customary vehemence. I noticed for the first time a swarm of censors. They warned me to " be careful." I glanced over the late German dispatches. A special communiqué of the High Command said Copenhagen had been completely occupied by eight a.m. The German forces, it said, had been transported in ships from Baltic ports during the night, landed at Copenhagen at dawn, and had first occupied the citadel and the radio station.[1] It was clear that the Danes had offered no resistance whatsoever. The Norwegians, it appeared, had, though the Germans were confident it would cease by nightfall. I phoned a couple of friends. The Danish Minister here had protested in the Wilhelmstrasse early this morning, but had added quickly that Denmark was not in a position to fight Germany. The Norwegian Minister — a man notorious in Berlin for his pro-Nazi sympathies, I recalled — had also protested, but had added that Norway would fight. I wrote my sad little piece, and spoke it.

LATER. — Apparently something has gone wrong with the Norwegian part of the affair. The Norwegians were not supposed to fight, but apparently did — at least at one or two places. There are reports of German naval losses, but the Admiralty keeps mum. All the Danish and Norwegian correspondents were fished out of their beds at dawn this morning and locked up at the Kaiserhof. It was the first they knew that their countries had been protected.

The Nazi press has some rare bits tonight: The *Angriff:* " The young German army has hoisted new glory to its banners. . . . It is one of the most brilliant

[1] This was a lie, as later entries will show.

feats of all time." A feat it is, of course. The *Börsen Zeitung:* " England goes coldbloodedly over the dead bodies of the small peoples. Germany protects the weak states from the English highway robbers. . . . Norway ought to see the righteousness of Germany's action, which was taken to ensure the freedom of the Norwegian people."

Tomorrow the *Völkische Beobachter,* Hitler's own pride (and money-maker) will bannerline in red ink: "GERMANY SAVES SCANDINAVIA!" The exclamation point is not mine.

Broadcast for a third time at two a.m., and now, sick in the stomach from nothing I've eaten, to bed.

BERLIN, *April* 10

It is plain from what I have heard today that Hitler and the High Command expected Norway to give up without a scrap. Now that it hasn't, the complete confidence of yesterday is evaporating. An inspired statement today warned the populace that " yesterday was only the beginning of a daring enterprise. Allied counter-action is still to be reckoned with." As a matter of fact, I get an impression in army and navy circles that if the British go in with their navy and back it up with strong landing-forces, Germany will have a much bigger fight on her hands than she bargained for. The German weak spot is its lack of a navy. The garrisons in the western Norwegian ports can only be supplied by sea. Also there are no suitable airfields north of Stavanger.

Following a brief account of the naval battle between German and British destroyers at Narvik today, the High Command mentions something that has us a bit baffled. It remarks that on April 8 — that is, the day

before the Germans seized the Norwegian harbours —
" a British destroyer was sunk in another affair." Several of us have a hunch that if we could find out what
that " other affair " was, we might penetrate the mystery of how the German navy managed to get warships
and landing-parties into so many Norwegian ports so
quickly without the British navy doing anything about
it.[1] As it is, it is incomprehensible.

BERLIN, *April* 11

London reports that Bergen and Trondheim
have been recaptured by the Allies. The German High
Command flatly denies it. It also categorically denies
London reports that there has been a great naval battle
in the Skagerrak — scene of the World War Battle of
Jutland, incidentally. Only naval losses admitted up
to date are the 10,000-ton cruiser *Blücher* in Oslo
Fjord and the 6,000-cruiser *Karlsruhe* off Kristiansand, both sunk by Norwegian coastal batteries the
morning of the 9th.

Learn that Hitler has warned Sweden of the dire
consequences of acting unneutral at this present juncture. As far as I can learn the Swedes are scared stiff,
will not come to the aid of their Norwegian brethren,
and will take their medicine later. Strange how these
little nations prefer to be swallowed by Hitler one at
a time.

[1] The destroyer, we would learn later, was the *Glow-worm*, the
only craft in the whole British navy to encounter any of the scores
of German war vessels and transports which stole up the Norwegian
coast *before* April 9. It sighted the German 10,000-ton cruiser *Admiral Hipper* off the Norwegian coast on April 8, but was blown to
bits before it could get away. Had just a small British naval force,
such as later went into Narvik, been within striking distance of the
Norwegian coast on April 8, Hitler's Norwegian venture would have
failed. One can only conclude that the British navy was caught nap-
ping.

A Foreign Office spokesman told us today that Mr.
Hambro, President of the Norwegian parliament, was
an " unclean gentleman and a Jew." The Nazi man in
Norway turns out to be a former War Minister, one
Vidkun Quisling, and he seems to have had a fairly
strong fifth-column organization. One man in the Wilhelmstrasse told me he would be the Norwegian premier.
The *Börsen Zeitung* complains of King Haakon's " unintelligible attitude. . . . By his inflexible attitude he
has shown himself to be badly advised and not the true
protector of the interests of his people."

The BBC tonight quotes Churchill as having said in
the House of Commons today that " Hitler has committed a grave strategical error " and that the British
navy will now take the Norwegian coast and sink all
ships in the Skagerrak and the Kattegat. God, I hope
he's right.

BERLIN, *April* 14

I've at last found out how the Germans, without an adequate navy, occupied the chief Norwegian
ports along a thousand-mile coastline under the very
nose of the British fleet. German troops with guns and
supplies were transported to their destinations in cargo
boats which ostensibly were on their way to Narvik to
fetch Swedish iron. These freighters, as they've been
doing since the beginning of the war, sailed within the
Norwegian three-mile limit and thus escaped discovery
by the British navy. Ironically! — they were even escorted to their goals by Norwegian warships which had
orders to protect them from the British!

But that does not explain how the British let half the
striking power of the German fleet — seven destroyers,

one heavy cruiser, and one battleship — get all the way
up the Norwegian coast unobserved.

German naval circles admit that their seven destroyers were wiped out by a superior British attacking force
at Narvik yesterday, but say they hold the town. Tomorrow's papers however will say: "GREAT BRITISH
ATTACK ON NARVIK REPULSED." When I showed
an early edition of one of the papers to a naval captain
tonight, he blushed and cursed Goebbels.

Learn General von Falkenhorst has posted the following proclamation in Oslo: " The Norwegian government has turned down several offers of co-operation.
The Norwegian people must now decide the future of
their Fatherland. If the proclamation is obeyed, as it
was with great understanding in Denmark, Norway
will be spared the horrors of war. However, if any
more resistance is offered and the hand which was held
out with friendly intentions rejected, then the German
High Command will feel itself forced to act with the
sharpest means to break the resistance."

Hitler is sowing something in Europe that one day
will destroy not only him but his nation.

BERLIN, *April* 17

Hitler has sent greetings today to the royal
family of Denmark on the occasion of the birth of a
daughter to the Crown Princess!

The German press and radio turned its big guns on
Holland today. Said an inspired statement from the
Foreign Office: " In contrast to Germany, the Allies do
not wish to prevent the little states from being drawn
into the war "!

BERLIN, *April* 18

       Joe [Harsch] back from Copenhagen with
a nice tale. He reports that on the evening of April 8
the Danish King, somewhat disturbed over that day's
reports, summoned the German Minister and asked him
for assurances. The Minister swore to His Majesty
that Hitler had no intention of marching into Denmark
and that the day's silly rumours were merely " Allied
lies." Actually at that moment, as the German Minister
knew, several German coal ships were tied up in Copenhagen harbour, where they had arrived two days previously. Under the hatches, as he also knew, were German
troops.

     At dawn up came the hatches and the German soldiers
piled out. The Royal Palace is but a short distance
from the docks. Up the streets towards the palace
marched the Nazi troops. The amazed Danes, going to
work on their bicycles, could not believe their eyes.
Many said afterwards they thought it was some film
being shot. As the Germans approached the palace, the
King's guards, however, opened fire. The Germans returned it. When the King heard the firing, Joe says,
he sent his adjutant out to tell his guards for goodness'
sake to stop shooting. The adjutant, waving wildly a
white handkerchief, dashed out and gave the order to
cease fire. The Germans, thankful for this co-operation, surrounded the palace. Meanwhile Danish workmen, riding to work on their bicycles, were ordered by
the Germans to take a side street and avoid the palace.
Some of them did not understand German quickly
enough. The Germans fired, killing a dozen or so. X,
a Yankee businessman who happened to be in Copenhagen, thinks the Germans are minimizing their naval
losses. For one thing, he says he saw the masts of a

sunken pocket-battleship not sixty miles from Copenhagen.

Today, it is true, the German Admiralty called on
the populace to show more patience and discipline and
stop besieging the Admiralty for news of relatives. It
promised that the relatives of the dead would be duly
notified. Meanwhile I learn that the Gestapo has forbidden relatives who do know that one of their kin has
been killed to publish death notices in the papers. Only
two or three families of the top naval men who were
killed have been permitted to publish the fact.

Wounded sailors and soldiers who escaped with their
lives from the *Blücher* are arriving with horrible burns
on their faces and necks. It seems that when the cruiser
went down, it set loose on the water a lot of burning oil.
Many men swimming about were burned to death. I
suppose some of them died half from drowning, half
from burning — a nice combination.

Not a word about these things in the press. The German people are spoon-fed only the more pleasant and
victorious aspects of the war. I doubt that in their present mood they could stand much bad news.

Note that the Danes have been ruined by the German occupation. Denmark's three million cows, three
million pigs and twenty-five million laying hens live on
imported fodder, mostly from North and South America and Manchukuo. Those supplies are now cut off.
Denmark must slaughter most of its livestock, one of its
main sources of existence.

BERLIN, *April* 19

An official communiqué today: " In view of
the hostile attitude of the Norwegian King and the
former Norwegian government, the Norwegian Minister

and the staff of the Norwegian Legation have been asked to leave German territory by today." They have.

Hitler's fifty-first birthday tomorrow, and the people have been asked to fly their flags. Said Dr. Goebbels in a broadcast tonight: " The German people have found in the Führer the incarnation of their strength and the most brilliant exponent of their national aims." When I passed the Chancellery tonight, I noticed some seventy-five people waiting outside for a glimpse of the leader. In other years on the eve of his birthday there were ten thousand.

BERLIN, *April* 21

The secrecy of the Allies about *where* their troops have landed in Norway was lifted by the High Command today. They have landed at Namsos and Aandalsnes, the two railheads north and south respectively of Trondheim, the key port half-way up the Norwegian coast occupied by the Germans. A friend of mine on the High Command tells me that the whole issue in Norway now hangs on the outcome of the battle for Trondheim. If the Allies take it, they have saved Norway, or at least the northern half. If the Germans, pushing northward up the two railway lines from Oslo, get there first, then the British must evacuate. The Germans today occupied Lillehammer, eighty miles north of Oslo, but they still have a hundred and fifty miles to go. What the Germans fear most, I gather, is that the British navy will go into Trondheim Fjord and wipe out the German garrison in the city before the Nazi forces from Oslo can possibly get there. If it does, the German gamble is lost.

I feel better tonight, after working this out, than at any other time since the war began.

BERLIN, *April* 22

Opposition to the German forces driving northward on Trondheim is stiffening. For the first time tonight the German High Command speaks of stubborn resistance in this sector. But the Luftwaffe is giving the British bases at Namsos, Aandalsnes, and Dombas a terrible pounding. General Milch, Göring's right-hand man, has been dispatched to Norway to direct the air force. It's Germany's biggest hope there now.

BERLIN, *April* 23

Joseph Terboven, the tough young Nazi *Gauleiter* of Cologne, who was more than a match for Fritz Thyssen there, has been named Reich's commissar for Norway. In other words, if Hitler wins, Norway will be just another Nazi province.

Off to Lausanne to a meeting of the International Broadcasting Union. Spring along the lake under the Alps will be good.

BERLIN, *April* 29

Returned this morning from Switzerland. The crucial battle for Trondheim will probably be fought this week. The Germans, I find, are much more confident than a week ago when I left. Apparently the British expeditionary force is not so strong as they had expected. It seems evident from what I heard in Switzerland and here today that the first British troops thrown into the fighting around Lillehammer a week ago were few in numbers and miserably equipped — no tanks, no artillery, few anti-tank guns.

Fred N., the best-informed man we have on this cam-

paign at the Embassy, shocked me today by saying he
still doubted whether the British were really taking the
Norwegian campaign seriously. To cheer myself up I
recalled to him that in the last war it took the British
two years to get within striking distance of Bagdad,
and then their main army and their commander-in-chief
were captured by the Turks. A year or two later, however, the British took Bagdad and drove the Turks and
Germans out of Mesopotamia. What the British army
and navy need is a reverse or two. Then perhaps they
will become serious.

I heard just now that the original British force embarked in central Norway has been decimated.

BERLIN, *May* 1

Two days ago, for the fourth or fifth time
since the war began, I travelled down the Rhine from
Basel towards Frankfurt. The first twenty miles or so
out of Basel, you skirt the Rhine where it divides France
and Germany. Actually you ride through a sort of no-
man's land, as the main German lines are behind the
railroad tracks on the slopes that form the high ground
of the Black Forest. Two great armies stand divided
by the river. Yet, all was quiet. In one village playground — it was Sunday — German children were
playing in full sight of some French soldiers loitering
on the other side of the river. In an open meadow, not
two hundred yards from the Rhine and in full sight of a
French block-house, some German soldiers were frolicking about, kicking an old football. Trains on both sides
of the Rhine, some loaded with those very articles which
are working such deadly havoc in Norway, chugged
along undisturbed. Not a shot was fired. Not a single
airplane could be seen in the skies.

Last night I said in my broadcast: "What kind of war, what kind of game, is this? Why do airplanes bomb communications behind the lines in Norway, as they did in Poland, as they did everywhere in the World War, and yet here on the western front, where the two greatest armies in the world stand face to face, refrain completely from killing?"

Is gas getting short? In Berlin 300 out of 1,600 taxis stopped running today and some twenty-five per cent of the private cars and trucks still allowed to circulate have been suddenly ordered to cease circulating.

It's clear that the Germans, with all the air bases in the north, have complete superiority in the air in Norway. Will this in itself be enough to allow them to advance victoriously to Trondheim? I'm afraid it will. It is this threat of the Luftwaffe that is making the British navy hold back. How otherwise explain the failure of the British to attack Trondheim from the sea, as they attacked Narvik, which is out of the reach of most German planes? But unless the British do go in from the sea, they'll probably never get it. It's a race, and the Germans are moving fast.

LATER. — Today, which is German Labour Day and a holiday for all but munition workers, has seen Hitler issuing a grandiose order of the day to his troops in Norway. Last night the High Command announced that German troops coming north from Oslo and a German detachment coming south from Trondheim had made contact just south of the latter town. The battle for Trondheim has been won by Hitler. Where the Allies are, and what they're doing, are not clear. But it doesn't make much difference. They had a wonderful opportunity to stop Hitler and they've muffed it. One's worst suspicions seem to be confirmed — namely, that the British never went into the fight for Trondheim (read Norway) seriously.

"The intention of the Allies," cries Hitler triumphantly, "to force us to our knees by a tardy occupation of Norway has failed." Hitler addresses his order to the "Soldiers of the Norwegian Theatre of War." Three weeks ago Ribbentrop told us that the Führer had prevented Norway from becoming a "theatre of war."

So this May Day turns out to be a day of victory for the Germans. Hitler, for the first time since he came to power, did not speak or make a public appearance. His deputy, Rudolf Hess, spoke in his place — from the Krupp munition works at Essen. He kept referring to Mr. Hambro as "that Jew, Mr. Hamburger."

Judging from the looks of the good burghers who thronged the Tiergarten today, the one wish in their hearts is for peace, and to hell with the victories. Still, I suppose this triumph in Norway will buck up morale, after the terrible winter. S., a veteran correspondent here, thinks every man, woman, and child in this country is a natural-born killer. Perhaps so. But today I noticed in the Tiergarten many of them feeding the squirrels and ducks — with their rationed bread.

BERLIN, *May* 2

A blue day for the Allies. In Joe's room we listened to the six p.m. BBC broadcast for the bad news. Chamberlain had just announced in Commons the awful reverse. The British force which had been landed south of Trondheim, and which for the past ten days had been resisting the Germans moving towards Trondheim from

Oslo, has been evacuated from Aandalsnes, their coastal base. Thus the British abandon southern and central Norway — the most important parts. The Norwegians in that considerable area, who have been putting up an epic fight, are left to their fate. Chamberlain admitted that it was the German air force that had prevented the British from landing tanks and artillery at Aandalsnes. But what about Churchill's boast of April 11? What about the British navy?

The feat of the German army in advancing more than two hundred miles north up the Osterdal and Gudbrandsdal valleys from Oslo to Trondheim, and at the same time easily holding Trondheim with a small force against Allied attacks from both the north and the south, is certainly a formidable one. The whole seizure of Norway, though aided by the basest treachery, has undoubtedly been a brilliant military performance. After three weeks the British, with all their sea power, have not even been able to take Narvik.

Chamberlain boasted that as a result of the partial destruction of the German fleet the Allies had been able to strengthen their naval forces in the Mediterranean. Mussolini's bluff that he might hop into the war behind Hitler thus was taken seriously by the old man. It certainly wasn't here. It seems incredible to us here that Britain would withdraw the naval forces which would have enabled it to take Trondheim and thus defeat Hitler in Norway in order to strengthen its position against the tin-pot strength of Italy in the Mediterranean.

BERLIN, *May 4*

The British have pulled pell-mell out of Namsos to the north of Trondheim, thus completing the debacle of Allied aid to the Norwegians in central Norway.

Where was the British navy which Churchill only a
fortnight ago boasted would drive the Germans out of
the Norwegian waters? I saw a German news-reel today. It showed the Germans landing tanks and heavy
guns at Oslo. Except for the use of submarines, and
apparently not many of these, the Allies made no serious effort to stop German supplies from reaching Norway through Oslo. They didn't even risk destroyers in
the Skagerrak and Kattegat, not to mention cruisers
and battleships.

Is it that air power has shown in this short Norwegian campaign that it has superseded naval power?
At least, within flying distance of your land bases? In
1914–18 such a German thrust as has now taken place
would have been unthinkable. But with the Luftwaffe
holding the flying fields in Denmark and Norway, the
Allied fleet not only did not venture into the Kattegat
to stop the German shipment of arms and men to Oslo,
but has not even attempted action at Trondheim, Bergen, or Stavanger, with the exception of one eighty-
minute shelling of the Stavanger airfield the first week
of the war. The Germans now boast that air power has
demonstrated its superiority over naval power.

To sum up: Göring's planes accomplished four vital
tasks in Norway: (1) They kept the sea route through
the Kattegat to Oslo free of British warships and thus
enabled the main German land force to be liberally
supplied with men, artillery, tanks. (2) They prevented (or successfully discouraged) the British navy
from attacking the vital German-held ports of Stavanger, Bergen, and Trondheim. (3) By continually
bombing the Allied ports of debarkation, they made it
almost impossible for the British to land heavy artillery
and tanks, as Mr. Chamberlain admitted. (4) By

bombing and machine-gunning enemy positions, they
made it fairly easy for the German land troops to advance through difficult country.

In other words, they revolutionized war in and around
the North Sea.

I talked to my policeman friend today. He thinks the
war will develop in a few weeks into bombing the big
towns, and even gas. I agree. Hitler wants to finish the
war this summer if he can. If he can't, despite all the
German victories, he's probably lost.

A decree today explains that while there are plenty
of oil supplies, consumption must be further reduced.
Many cars and trucks still operating are to be taken out
of circulation. Two questions pop up: (1) Supplies
are not so big? (2) Available oil will be needed for
further military action on a big scale now that the British have pulled out of Namsos and the Germans have
won the war in Norway?

The German papers today are full of accusations that
Britain now intends to " spread the war." In the Mediterranean or Balkans or *somewhere else,* by which I take
it they mean Holland.

As an escape, I suppose, I read some Goethe letters
this afternoon. It was reassuring to be reminded of the
devastation of Germany that Napoleon wrought. Apparently Jena, near Goethe's Weimar, was pretty
roughly handled by the French troops. But through
it all the great poet never loses hope. He keeps saying
that the Human Spirit will triumph, the European
spirit. But today, where is the European spirit in Germany? Dead. . . . Dead . . .

Goethe harps on the theory that a writer can only
get things done by retiring from the world when he has
work to do. He complains that the world takes, but does

not give. Some of his letters on local administrative
problems in Weimar are amusing. He had his small,
bickering side. And — surprising — he is very subservient to his Prince Ruler!

BERLIN, *May* 6

Bernhard Rust, Nazi Minister of Education,
in a broadcast to schoolchildren today, sums up pretty
well the German mentality in this year of 1940. He
says: "God created the world as a place for work and
battle. Whoever doesn't understand the laws of life's
battles will be counted out, as in the boxing ring. All
the good things on this earth are trophy cups. The
strong win them. The weak lose them. . . . The German people under Hitler did not take to arms to break
into foreign lands and make other people serve them.
They were forced to take arms by states which blocked
their way to bread and union."

The crying problem of Europe, I am beginning to
think, is not Communism or Fascism — is not therefore
social. It is the problem of Germanism, of the mentality so clearly expressed by Rust. Until it's solved, there
will be no peace in Europe.

German schoolgirls today were asked to bring the
combings from their hair to school. The combings will
be collected to make felt.

BERLIN, *May* 7

For three or four days now the German newspapers have been carrying on a terrific campaign to
convince somebody that the Allies, having failed in Norway, are about to become " aggressors " in some other
part of Europe. Six weeks ago we had a similar cam-

paign to convince somebody that the Allies were about
to become the " aggressors " in Scandinavia. Then Germany, using the alleged Allied intention of aggression
as an excuse, went in herself.

Where is Germany going in next? I'm suspicious of
Holland, partly because it's the one place not specifi-
cally mentioned in this propaganda campaign. Or are
the Allies, having sucked the German army far from
home bases into Norway, going to draw it far into the
Balkans?

Amusing to read the headlines today: "CHAMBER-
LAIN, THE AGGRESSOR. ALLIED PLANS FOR
NEW AGGRESSION!" If the German people were
not so intellectually drunk themselves, or so stupid,
they might see the humour in it.

My guess: the war in the next few weeks will be on
all over Europe. And, finally, with all the weapons:
bombing of open towns, gas, and all.

BERLIN, *May* 8

Could not help noticing a feeling of tension
in the Wilhelmstrasse today. Something is up, but we
don't know what. Ralph Barnes, just in from Amsterdam, says the guards on his train pulled down the
window-blinds for the first twenty-five miles of the journey from the Dutch-German frontier towards Berlin.
I hear the Dutch and Belgians are nervous. I hope they
are. They ought to be. I cabled New York today to
keep Edwin Hartrich in Amsterdam for the time being.
They wanted to send him off to Scandinavia, where the
war is over.

Just before I went on the air today, Fred Oechsner
telephoned to say that Webb Miller had been found
dead on a railroad track at Clapham Junction, near

London. The news shocked me greatly. I have known him for twelve years, liked him, admired him. In my first years over here as a green newspaperman, he befriended and helped me. In the last decade our paths often crossed, in India, the Near East, the Balkans, Germany, Geneva, Italy, and of course in London, where he was U.P.'s star correspondent and European chief. Webb was an inordinately modest man, despite as distinguished a journalistic career as any American has had in our time. His success never went to his head. I remember him on many a big story being as excited and nervous, and if it were an interview, as shy, as the youngest and most inexperienced of us. His shyness was terrific and he never lost it. I wonder what killed him? Tired? Sleepy? I know it wasn't suicide.

I went out to a suburb last night to see the film of havoc wrought by the German air force in Poland. It is called *Feuertaufe* — or *Baptism of Fire*. The wanton destruction of Polish towns and villages, but especially of Warsaw, is shown nakedly. The German audience took the film in dead silence.

Later. — My censors were quite decent today. They let me hint very broadly that the next German blow would fall in the west, — Holland, Belgium, the Maginot Line, Switzerland. Tonight the town is full of rumours. The Wilhelmstrasse is especially angry at an A.P. report that two German armies, one from Bremen, the other from Düsseldorf, are moving towards the Dutch frontier.

Berlin, *May* 9

What an irony that Webb Miller, who had spent most of the last twenty-four years covering wars,

and was often under fire, should have escaped them all
only to die by falling out of a railroad coach far from
a field of battle! The German press full of absurd
stories today that Webb was murdered by the British secret service. This is worse than nonsense. Contempti-
ble. (What happens to the inner fabric of a people
when they are fed lies like this daily?)

Hitler, in ordering the release of some Norwegian
prisoners, proclaims today: " Against the will of the
German people and its government, King Haakon of
Norway and his army staff brought about war against
Germany "!

LATER. — The shouting headlines increased
in size tonight, all thundering the accusation that *England* plans a big act of aggression, somewhere. "BRIT-
AIN PLOTS TO SPREAD THE WAR," they roar.

All of which moved me to say in my broadcast tonight. " Regardless of who spreads it, there seems little
doubt that it will spread. And it may well be, as many
people over here think, that the war will be fought and
decided before the summer is over. People somehow
seem to feel that the Whitsuntide holidays this week-
end will be the last holidays Europe will observe for
some time."

My censors didn't like the paragraph, but after some
argument they let it pass. Their line was that there
was no question of Germany spreading the war.

BERLIN, *May* 10

The blow in the west has fallen. At dawn today the Germans marched into Holland, Belgium, Luxemburg. It is Hitler's bid for victory now or never.
Apparently it was true that Germany could not outlast

the economic war. So he struck while his army still had
supplies and his air force a lead over the Allies'. He
seems to realize he is risking all. In an order of the day
to the troops he begins: " The hour of the decisive battle for the future of the German nation has come." And
he concludes: " The battle beginning today will decide
the future of the German nation for the next thousand
years." If he loses, it certainly will.

As I see it, Hitler had three choices: to wait and fight
the war out on the economic front, as was done all winter; to meet the Allies in some easy spot, say the Balkans; to seek a decision in the west by striking through
neutral Holland and Belgium. He has chosen the third,
and the biggest risk.

I can't boast that I was prepared for it. In fact,
after broadcasting as usual last night at twelve forty-
five a.m., I was sound asleep when the phone rang at
seven this morning. It was one of the girls at the *Rundfunk*. She broke the news.

" When do you want to broadcast? " she asked.

" As soon as I can get there," I said.

" Ribbentrop has a press conference at the Foreign
Office at eight," she offered.

" I'll skip it," I said. " Tell New York — send them
an urgent — to monitor DJL — and that I'll be on the
air in an hour."

Actually it was two hours or so before I could get
on the air. Time dressing, time getting out to the *Rundfunk*, time getting the whole story. There was considerable excitement at the *Rundfunk*, and it was some time
before I could wrest the various communiqués from the
hands of the German announcers. Fortunately, the
censors, who must have been tipped during the night,
were on the job and did not hold me up long. Except
I could not call in my lead what the Germans were do-

ing in Holland and Belgium " an invasion." They denied it was. I flamed up, but finally decided that since
the censors had overlooked the word " invasion " three
times in the script, it might be worth while to substitute
" march in " in the lead in order to give radio listeners
in America a story from Berlin. I didn't like the com-
promise. It was a question of sacrificing the whole important story for one word. And anyway, America
knew an invasion when it happened.

LATER. — The people in Berlin, I must say,
have taken the news of the battle which Hitler says is
going to decide the future of their nation for the next
thousand years with their usual calm. None of them
gathered before the Chancellery as usually happens
when big events occur. Few bothered to buy the noon
papers which carried the news. For some reason Goebbels forbade extras.

The German memorandum " justifying " this latest
aggression of Hitler's was handed to the ministers of
Holland and Belgium at six a.m., about an hour and a
half after German troops had violated their neutral
soil. It sets up a new record, I think, for cynicism and
downright impudence — even for Hitler. It requests
the two governments to issue orders that no resistance
be made to German troops. " Should the German forces
encounter resistance in Belgium or Holland," it goes
on, " it will be crushed with every means. The Belgian
and Dutch governments alone would bear the responsibility for the consequences and for the bloodshed which
would then become unavoidable."

The memorandum, which Ribbentrop also read to the
correspondents at the eight a.m. press conference, argues that Britain and France were about to attack Germany through the two Low Countries and that the

Reich therefore deemed it necessary to send in its own troops to " safeguard the neutrality of Belgium and Holland." This nonsensical hypocrisy is " backed up " by a spurious " document " from the High Command claiming that it has proofs that the Allied troops were about to march into Belgium and Holland in an effort to seize the Ruhr.

It's evident that the German army has struck with everything it has. The air force has gone all out and is obviously going to take full advantage of its superiority over the Allies. The High Command says that at dawn the Luftwaffe bombed scores of airfields in Holland, Belgium, and France as far south as Lyon. And then this is news: a communiqué speaks of German troops having been landed *by air* at many airports in Belgium and the Netherlands. The Germans claim they seized the airfields and occupied surrounding territory. Apparently, though the High Command censor would not let me say it in my talks today, they've been dropping thousands of parachutists. A report that the German parachutists have already occupied part of Rotterdam is not confirmed. It sounds inconceivable, but after Norway anything can happen.

First German reports claim they've crossed the river Maas (Meuse) and captured Maastricht, and have also driven through Luxemburg and into Belgium. Tonight the German army lies before Liége, which held it up for several days in 1914, and where Ludendorff first attracted attention.

War on civilians started too. The other side reported German planes had killed many. Tonight the Germans claimed three Allied planes dropped bombs in the middle of Freiburg, killing twenty-four civilians. As a taste of what this phase of the war is going to be like, a German communiqué tonight says that " from now on, every enemy bombing of German civilians will be answered by five times as many German planes bombing English and French cities." (Note Nazi technique there. (1) The statement is part of the nerve war on the enemy. (2) It is designed to make German civilians stand up to bombings by assuring them the English and French are getting five times worse.)

That's one taste. Here's another: When the Belgian and Dutch ministers called for their passports at the Wilhelmstrasse today and at the same time lodged strong protests at the ruthless violation of their neutrality, an official statement was promptly published here saying that " an official on duty [at the Foreign Office] after reading the contents, which were arrogant and stupid, refused to accept them, and asked the two ministers to request for their passports in the usual manner "! The Germans are out of their minds.

Tired, after broadcasting all this day, and sick in the pit of the stomach.

BERLIN, *May* 11

The German steamroller sweeps on through Holland and Belgium. Tonight the Germans claim to have captured what the High Command claims is Liége's most important fort, Eben-Emael, which commands the junction of the Meuse (Maas) River and the Albert Canal. The High Command, which under Hitler's leadership is missing no opportunities for propaganda, makes it look mysterious by saying that the fort was taken by a " new method of attack." Is history repeating itself? In 1914, when Liége held up the Germans for twelve days, the German army also had a surprise — the new 42-centimetre howitzer, which smashed the Belgian forts as if they were made of wood.

The Germans are keeping mum about their troops landed behind the Dutch lines at The Hague and Rotterdam by parachute and by plane. But the High Command, stung by Allied reports, did deny today that the Dutch had recaptured the airfields at The Hague or Rotterdam. The parachutists, then, carry portable radio transmitters too!

Strange, the apathy of the people in the face of this decisive turn in the war. Most Germans I've seen, outside of the officials, are sunk deep in depression at the news. The question is: How many Germans support this final, desperate gamble that Hitler has taken? Discussing it at the Adlon today, most of the correspondents agreed: many, many. And yet I can't find any Germans who actually believe Hitler's excuse that he went into the neutral countries, whose integrity he had guaranteed, to counter a similar move which the Allies were about to begin. Even for a German, it's an obvious lie.

Goebbels's propaganda machine, shifting into high gear, discovers today, twenty-four hours after the official announcement that twenty-four persons had been killed by the bombing at Freiburg, that thirteen of the twenty-four were children who were peacefully frolicking on the municipal playground. What were a lot of children doing on a playground in the midst of an air-raid? This particular Goebbels fake is probably produced to justify German killings of civilians on the other side.

The Berlin papers have great headlines today about the "shameful" protests of the two Low Countries against being invaded.

The Nazis locked up in the Kaiserhof yesterday all the Dutch journalists who were not Nazis, including Harry Masdyck. who did not quite believe it would

come when it did. A Dutch woman reporter for the
Nazi Dutch paper has been sitting at the *Rundfunk*
since dawn yesterday broadcasting false news to the
Dutch people in their own language. A sort of Lady
Haw-Haw.

Have one more broadcast at four thirty a.m., which
is only ten thirty p.m. last night in New York. On the
job since eight a.m.

BERLIN, *May* 12

Sunday, and got a little sleep. Hill took the
noon broadcast.

After a mere two days of fighting the High Command claims to have occupied all of northeastern Holland east of the Zuider Zee, broken through the first and
second defence lines in the heart of the Netherlands,
and pierced the eastern end of the Belgian line of defence along the Albert Canal. A year or so ago I had
a look at that canal, which the Belgians had fortified
with bunkers. It looked like a very formidable tank-
trap with its deep and very steep, paved sides. Can it
be that the Belgians didn't blow up the bridges?

A typical Sunday in Berlin today, with no evidence
that the Berliners, at least, are greatly exercised at the
battle for their thousand-year existence. Cafés have
been ordered to close at eleven p.m. instead of one a.m.
That will get the folk home before the night air-raids
start, though we've had none yet. Also, dancing has
been *verboten* for the time being.

The radio warned tonight that if Germans were mistreated in Holland, there is " ample opportunity of re-
taliating on the numerous Dutch nationals living in
Germany."

BERLIN, *May* 13

Astounding news. The headlines at five p.m.: "LIÉGE FALLEN! GERMAN LAND FORCES BREAK THROUGH AND ESTABLISH CONTACT WITH AIR-FORCE TROOPS NEAR ROTTERDAM!"

No wonder a German officer told me today that even the *Oberkommando* was a little taken aback by the *pace*.

The air-force troops were the parachutists and those landed by plane on the beach near The Hague beginning with the first day of the campaign. It was these men who took part of Rotterdam (!) including the airport, though they had no artillery and the Dutch should have had plenty, being a wealthy people. How a German land force has travelled clear across the southern part of Holland to the sea is a mystery to all of us here. It would have to be a motorized force, and in Holland there are scores of canals and rivers in their path. One supposes the Dutch would have blown up the bridges.

"SWASTIKA FLIES FROM THE CITADEL OF LIEGE," say the headlines tonight. Apparently the German army which had forced the Albert Canal circled down to Liége from the northwest, where it was most weakly held, the Belgians having expected the main attack from the opposite direction. Liége held out for twelve days in 1914. If it has fallen now in four, that looks bad for the Allies.

The foreign radio stations continue to tell of German parachutists dropping all over Belgium and Holland and seizing airports and towns. (Here we can get no information on the subject whatsoever.) It's a new form of warfare and it will be interesting to see what effect it has, if any, on a long, hard campaign, if this is to be one and not another German walkover.

Last night Premier Reynaud of France announced
that German parachutists found behind the lines in anything but a German uniform would be shot on sight.
Tonight the Wilhelmstrasse told us it was informing the
Allied governments that for every German parachutist
shot, the Germans would execute ten French prisoners!
Nice pleasant people, the Germans. That takes us back
a thousand or two years. But keep in mind that this is
merely a part of Hitler's new technique of terror.

I passed some time at the Embassy today. Everyone depressed at the news and most think — on the
fourth day of the offensive! — that it is all over with
the Allies. I tried to recall how black August 1914 must
have seemed to Paris and London as the Germans swept
on the capital and the French government fled to Bordeaux. Tess said on the telephone last night that the
Swiss were calling up every available male. When will
it be Switzerland's turn? I asked her to try to book on
the first ship home and take the baby. She won't. Her
arguments: she has my Geneva office to run, she doesn't
like the family to get too far apart, and now that the
war is becoming a war, she wants to see it.

BERLIN, *May* 14

We're all a little dazed tonight by the news.
The Dutch army has capitulated — after only five
days of fighting. What happened to its great water
lines, which were supposed to be impassable? To its
army of over half a million men?

An hour before we learned this from a special communiqué, we were told of Rotterdam's fall. " Under the
tremendous impression of the attacks of German dive-
bombers and the imminent attack of German tanks, the
city of Rotterdam has capitulated and thus saved itself

from destruction," read the German announcement. It was the first news we had that Rotterdam was being bombed and was at the point of being destroyed. How many civilians were killed there, I wonder, in this war which Adolf Hitler " promised " would not be carried out against civilians? Was the whole city, the half million or so people in it, a military objective so that it had to be destroyed?

Having broken through at Liége, the Germans claimed tonight to have pierced the second line of Belgian defences northwest of Namur. They must be very close to Brussels. Tanks and airplanes, especially airplanes, are doing the job for the Germans. How criminal of the British and French to have neglected their air forces!

A little tired of the way the German radio announces each new victory. The program is halted, there are fanfares, then the communiqué is read, then a chorus sings the current hit: "We March on England." For the big victories the two national hymns are added.

Berlin, *May* 15

Very long, stunned faces among the foreign correspondents and diplomats today. The High Command claims to have broken through the Maginot Line near Sedan and that German forces have crossed the Meuse River both at Sedan and between Namur and Givet, farther north. To anyone who has seen that deep, heavily wooded Meuse Valley, it seems almost incredible that the Germans could get across it so quickly, provided there is any army at all defending the western bank. But both sides speak of big tank battles *west* of the Meuse.

Almost all of my friends have given up hope; not I,

yet. It must have looked even darker in Paris in August 1914, when nothing appeared to stand in the way of the German army and the capital. Our military people remind us that the main battle has not yet started, that the Germans have not yet run up against the bulk of the French and British armies. And the Belgians still have a half-million men in the fight. The line today held by the Allies is roughly: Antwerp, Louvain, Namur, then down the Meuse to Sedan, with the Germans across the river at several points.

There was increasing talk from Rome today that Italy, now that the Germans appear to be winning, may jump into the war this week-end. Tess phoned this morning from Geneva to give me this news. Again I urged her to leave with the child, and at last she seems willing. She and Mrs. V., with her two youngsters, will strike out across France for Spain. From Lisbon they can get the Clipper to New York. Worried all day about this. If Italy attacks France, going across to Spain from Geneva will be unpleasant, if not impossible.

It seems the reason the Dutch gave up yesterday was that the Germans bombed the hell out of Rotterdam, and threatened to do the same to Utrecht and Amsterdam. Hitler's technique of helping his armies by threatening terror or meting it out is as masterful as it is diabolical.

His High Command, for instance, tonight threatened to bomb Brussels unless all troop movements, which the Germans claim their reconnaissance planes have observed there, cease immediately. " If the Belgian government," says the communiqué, " wishes to save Brussels from the horrors of war, it must immediately put a stop to troop movements in the city and the work on fortifications."

A nice war.

Berlin, *May* 16

Worried about Tess and the baby. If Italy
goes into the war in the next day or two, as some think,
escape for them in that direction is out. Today there
are reports of more German activity along the Swiss
border. The Nazis may break into Switzerland any moment now. The trouble is the French won't let the Americans out through France. They are not issuing transit
visas at the moment. Yet the American government has
advised Americans in Switzerland to leave immediately
for Bordeaux, where they'll be picked up by American
ships. Most of our consulate people at Geneva have
sent out their own women and children with their diplomatic passports through France. I believe Hitler will
bomb Geneva to destruction just out of personal hate
for the League and what Geneva stands for.

Will Brussels be bombed, after last night's German
threat? P., always well informed on German intentions,
thinks Hitler will bomb Paris and London to daylights
within the next forty-eight hours.

I just saw two uncensored news-reels at our press
conference in the Propaganda Ministry. Pictures of
the German army smashing through Belgium and Holland. Some of the more destructive work of German
bombs and shells was shown. Towns laid waste, dead
soldiers and horses lying around, and the earth and
mortar flying when a shell or bomb hit. Yelled the German announcer: "And thus do we deal death and destruction on our enemies!" The film, in a way, summed
up the German people to me.

Towards sundown Joe [Harsch] and I took a walk
in the Tiergarten and agreed: The savage destruction
by high explosives and steel of the other fellow is a
beautiful thing and the fulfilment of a high aim in Ger-

manic life; blow up his home and his wife and his children. But let him do the same to you — then he is a
barbarian destroying the innocent. The film, we recalled, switched back to Freiburg, where the Germans
now claim some thirty-five people, including thirteen
children (though Goebbels forgot to mention the children until twenty-four hours after he had announced
the bombing and the number of victims), were killed
by Allied bombs. Said the announcer angrily: " Thus
do our brutal and unscrupulous enemies bomb and kill
and murder innocent German children."

" It's the old story," I said to Joe. " The German
always wants it both ways."

How would I get through the war without the Tiergarten, one of God's great parks? We remarked on
what a deep green the grass had today and argued
about the respective merits of mowing grass, as at
home, and letting it grow long, for hay, as here. Curious that the lawn-mower is almost unknown on the Continent. The foliage around the little stream in the
middle of the park was so luxuriant today, it reminded
me of the Barbizon paintings. Or of a Normandy lily
pond by Monet. Missing was only a stately lady clad
in *fin de siècle* garb sitting very upright in a rustic boat
in the middle of the pond.

Picked up on the shortwave Roosevelt reading a
special message to Congress. He came through very
clearly. In great form, I thought. He proposed we
build 50,000 (!) planes a year and deliver Allied orders
immediately. He said Germany now had 20,000 planes
to the Allies' 10,000 and was still building them faster.
This is a truth obvious to all of us here, but when we
used to report it we were accused of making Nazi propaganda. Roosevelt received the greatest ovation I've
ever heard in a broadcast from Congress. It makes you

feel good that they're waking up at home at last.

How long before we're in this war, as at least a mighty supplier to the Allies — if there's still time? The Germans say we're too late. The *Herald Tribune* came out today, according to the BBC, for a declaration of war on Germany. This led some of the American correspondents at dinner tonight to speculate as to what chances we who are stationed here would have of getting out, were diplomatic relations to be severed. The majority thought we would be interned. No one liked the prospect.

We're on the eve tonight of a great battle, perhaps the decisive battle of the war, on a front stretching for 125 miles from Antwerp through Namur to a point south of Sedan. It looks as though the Germans were going to throw in everything they have, which is plenty. Their drive through Belgium appears to have been halted yesterday on the Meuse River and the Dyle Line farther north. But it is only a pause before the great final attack. Hitler must win it, and all the battles in the next weeks or months, or he's finished. His chances look very good. But great decisive battles in history have not always been won by the favourites.

Berlin, *May* 17

What a day! What news! At three p.m. the High Command came out with its daily communiqué. I would not have believed it except that the German land army has seldom misled us since the first days of the Polish war on what it has accomplished. Often its claims have sounded incredible, only to turn out in the end to have been correct.

Today the High Command states its armies have broken through the Belgian Dyle defence line south of

Wavre and have taken the "northeast front" of the
fortress of Namur. More important still — it claims its
forces have broken through the Maginot Line on a one-
hundred-kilometre front (!) stretching from Maubeuge
to Carignan, southeast of Sedan. This indeed looks bad
for the Allies. And it begins to look too as if the help
— especially in badly needed planes (for the Germans
are winning this campaign largely through effective
use of a superior airforce), which Roosevelt offered
to the Allies yesterday — will come too late. Unless
the Germans are immediately slowed down, and then
stopped. That they haven't been yet, the BBC admitted this evening. It spoke of fighting going on at
Rethel, which is half-way to Reims from Sedan. We
here had no idea the Germans had broken through that
far. At the *Rundfunk* tonight I noticed the military
people for the first time spoke of a "French rout."

I went on the air as soon as I could translate the communiqué — at three thirty p.m. — with an extra broadcast of the news. I returned to the Embassy, where I
found everyone dazed at events. A few seemed cheered
by an editorial in the *D.A.Z.* which declared that the
big decision had not yet fallen and that a hard road still
lay ahead for the Germans. But hell, this offensive is
only eight days old. And the Germans have overrun
Holland and half of Belgium and are now half-way
from the French border to Reims!

Worried about Tess. Phoned her this noon and urged
her to get off today over France towards Spain with the
baby. Now, tonight, I hope she hasn't done it, especially as the French are making them go way north to
Paris first, in order to get to Bordeaux. Paris is no
place to get into now, after today's news. The Germans may beat her there. Annoyed because I couldn't
get through to her again on the phone tonight, which

makes me think she already has left for France. Think best thing for her to do is to take refuge in a Swiss mountain village. Perhaps Hitler won't bomb a small Swiss mountain village.

Today turned warm and sunny, and you couldn't tell from the apathetic, almost lazy attitude of Berliners taking the sun in the Tiergarten that a decisive, perhaps *the* decisive battle of the war was on. Not a single air-raid alarm here yet since the new offensive started, though we hear that the Ruhr and the Rhine towns are catching it at night.

LATER. — The High Command late tonight announced that German troops entered Brussels at sundown. During the day they had pierced the Allied lines north and south of Louvain. Things seem to be moving fast. In 1914 it took sixteen days for the Germans to reach Brussels. This time, eight days.

BERLIN, *May* 18

Going to the front tomorrow. At last will get a chance — maybe — to see how this German army colossus has been doing it, walking through Belgium, Holland, and now northern France, so fast.

I hesitated about going for fear the decision might come in France while I was away and that the story in that case would really be here and I'd miss it. Also they've given us so many dud trips since this war started last September that it's highly possible we shan't see anything of real interest.

I finally decided to take the chance. We leave at ten a.m. tomorrow, and will first drive to Aachen. Nine in the party: four Americanos, three Italians, a Spaniard, and a Jap.

Antwerp fell today. And while the German army is rolling back the Allied forces in Belgium towards the sea, the southern army, which broke through the Maginot Line between Maubeuge and Sedan, is driving rapidly towards Paris. A piece in the well-informed (on military matters) *Börsen Zeitung* tonight hints that the German armies now converging on Paris from the northeast may not try to take Paris immediately, as they did in 1914, but strike northwest for the Channel ports in an effort to cut off England from France. A second force, it hints, may strike in the opposite direction and try to take the Maginot Line in the east from behind.

German reports admit the Allies are putting up fierce resistance in Belgium and France, but say that they are being " outclassed " by the sheer mass of German metal, especially tanks and airplanes. Perhaps in the next few days I'll be able to see for myself.

AACHEN, HOTEL INTERNATIONAL, *May* 19 (*midnight*)

Most amazing thing about this Ruhr district, the industrial heart of Germany, which Allied planes were to have (and could have, we thought) knocked out in a few days, is that, so far as I can see, the night bombings of the British have done very little damage.

I thought the night bombings of western Germany, the deadly effects of which the BBC has been boasting since the big offensive began, would have affected the morale of the people. But all afternoon, driving through the Ruhr, we saw them — especially the womenfolk — standing on the bridges over the main roads cheering the troops setting off for Belgium and France.

We drove through many of the Ruhr centres which the Allies were supposed to have bombed so heavily the last few nights. We naturally couldn't see all the factories and bridges and railroad junctions in the Ruhr, but we saw several, and nothing had happened to them. The great networks of railroad tracks and bridges around Essen and Duisburg, where British night bombings had been reported from London, were intact. The Rhine bridges at Cologne were up. The factories throughout the Ruhr were smoking away as usual.

Just east of Hannover there had been a night raid by the British a few hours before we arrived. Local inhabitants told us twenty civilians, all in one house, had been killed. Fifteen miles east of Hannover we spotted a big Handley-Page bomber lying smashed in a field two hundred yards off the *Autobahn*. Gendarmes told us it had been brought down by anti-aircraft fire. The crew of five escaped in parachutes. Four had given themselves up to the village burgomaster in the town near by; one was still at large and the peasants and the gendarmes were scouring the countryside for him. We inspected the machine. Gunner's rear cockpit very small, and he had no protection. Front engines and pilot's cabin badly smashed and burned. Funny: the glass in the rear cockpit had not been broken. German air-force mechanics were busy removing the instruments and valuable metal. The Germans need all they can find. Hundreds of peasants stood by, looking at the debris. They didn't seem at all unnerved.

We kept getting lost all day. Very dumb chauffeur leading our column of four cars. Our driver remarked: "In peace-time he was a taxi chauffeur. He's always getting lost and always taking the longest way round." We missed Cologne completely after we'd spotted the towers of the Cathedral across the green fields, and only turned back after we were half-way to Frankfurt and it began to get dark. Almost a full moon towards the end, and it was very beautiful driving into Aachen along a road arched with trees. Along the road, endless columns of troops, in trucks and on foot, were moving up to the front, singing and in good spirits.

(An example of the German army's terrific attention to detail: For three hundred miles along the *Autobahn* from Berlin to Cologne, broken-down farm implements made to look like anti-aircraft guns from any altitude at all were placed every two hundred yards. Ploughs with the shaft pointed to the sky to look like a gun; rakes, harrows, wheelbarrows, sewing-machines — every conceivable old implement had been carefully arranged to look like a piece of *flak*,[1] so that an Allied pilot flying along the road would get the idea that it was suicide to swoop down on that road. Noticed on the map found in the British plane near Hannover that strong concentrations of German anti-aircraft were marked in red ink. Another purpose of the farm machines of course was to impede the landing of Allied planes on the highway. Telephone posts driven into the narrow strip of ground between the double lanes also served this purpose.)

Except for a few German bombers starting out from near Hannover, we saw not a single plane in the sky all day, even when we drew close to the Belgian frontier. We passed the Cologne airdrome. It was packed with planes, but the hangars had not been touched. Beautifully camouflaged with netting they were. Obviously these night attacks of the British have failed not only to put the Ruhr out of commission, but even to damage the German flying fields. A phony sort of war the Allies still seem to be fighting.

[1] German for anti-aircraft gun.

My room here in the Hotel International is on the very top floor, or rather in the attic. Unpleasant room to be in if the British bombers come over tonight. But it has been dark for two hours now (one a.m.) and no sign of them yet.

LATER. *Three thirty a.m.* — They came over at two fifty a.m. I awoke to the crashing of anti-aircraft cannon and the rat-tat-tat of a machine-gun on the roof across the street. The British, judging by the sound of their motors, and by the way a gun on the station a hundred yards from my window kept firing away, were hitting for the Aachen railroad yards. No air-raid alarm. We got our first warning from the sudden thunder of the *flak* guns. I went out into the hall to see what people do on such occasions, how they react. A half-dozen frightened women were frantically rushing downstairs in their nightgowns, fear frozen on their faces. A few men, whom I took to be officers, sauntered down. But none of our party of nine journalists. False bravery? Because the army officers were not frightened, just taking no unnecessary chances. The raid lasted twenty-five minutes, and then all was quiet. I feel very sleepy, but we must be up at five.

AACHEN, *May* 20 (*midnight*)

This has been a day in my life. To have seen the destruction of war, what guns and bombs do to houses and people in them, to towns, cities, bridges, railroad stations and tracks and trains, to universities and ancient noble buildings, to enemy soldiers, trucks, tanks, and horses caught along the way.

It is not pretty. No, it is not beautiful. Take Louvain, that lovely old university town, burned in **1914** by the Germans in their fury and rebuilt — partly by American aid. A good part of it is a shambles. The great library of the university, rebuilt by the donations of hundreds of American schools and colleges, is completely gutted. I asked a German officer what happened to the books.

" Burned," he said.

I must have looked a little shocked as I watched the desolation and contemplated this one little blow to learning and culture and much that is decent in European life.

The officer added: " Too bad. A pity. But, my friend, that's war. Look at it."

I did. But it hurt.

My broadcast, which I'm to make from Cologne at four thirty a.m., if I get there, gives a résumé of what we saw today. Here is a more or less chronological account:

We were off shortly after dawn from Aachen (Aix-la-Chapelle) across the Dutch province of Limburg to Maastricht. Little evidence that the Dutch did much fighting here. The houses whole, the windows unshattered. An occasional Dutch pillbox showed signs of having been hit by machine-gun fire, but nothing heavier. Apparently the Dutch made no attempt to slow up the Germans by blowing up the road to Maastricht. One bridge over a creek had been damaged. That was all.

We crossed over the Maas (Meuse) at Maastricht. The river is broad here and was a natural line of defence, though the Dutch did not take much advantage of it. They had done a half-hearted job of blowing up the bridges. Blown up one out of seven or eight spans on the two bridges I saw. The Germans evidently had substitute spans, made of steel frames, waiting in the rear, and within a few hours of bringing them up had the bridges good as new. German supply columns were thundering over both bridges when we arrived.

7.30 a.m. — Arrived at the Albert Canal. With its steep banks, thirty feet high, which the Belgians had cemented to make it impossible to climb them, it was a good defence line, especially against tanks. Only the Belgians had not blown up the bridge. I asked a German officer why.

" We were too quick for them," he said. Apparently what happened here, and at most of the other important bridges over the Albert Canal, all leading to Liége, was that German parachutists rushed the bridges from behind, wiped out the defending machine-gun crews, even overpowered the pillboxes also defending the bridges, and cut the wires leading to the explosive charges in the bridges before the Belgians could set them off. This particular bridge over the canal was protected by a bunker at the Belgian end of the bridge itself, and by two other bunkers lying a hundred yards to the right and left of the bridge. The bunker at the bridgehead must have been taken in the same mysterious way that Fort Eben-Emael was taken at Liége — by parachutists with some newfangled weapon.

The German officer warned us not to go inside the bunker, as mines were still lying about, but a couple of us ventured in. I saw at once that there had been a *fire* inside the bunker. From that I concluded — though with several reservations — that the parachutists who took the pillbox from behind must have had a fire-pistol of some kind and shot their flames inside the pillbox. Near by I noticed freshly dug graves over which Belgian steel helmets were posed on sticks. Probably the crew of the pillbox.

Speed played a role too, with its resultant surprise.
The motorized Germans had crossed the Dutch border
twenty miles away at five a.m. and were over this canal
into Belgium (past Maastricht, which should have been
strongly defended but wasn't) at ten a.m. — five hours.

You were immediately struck by the difference between Holland and Belgium. As soon as we crossed into
Belgium, we started running into blocks of pulverized
houses along the road. Obviously the Belgians were of
a different metal from the Dutch. At the outset they
fought like lions. From house to house.

7.45. Tongres. — Here for the first time we
suddenly came across real devastation. A good part of
the town through which we drove was smashed to pieces.
Stuka dive-bombers and artillery, an officer explained.
The railroad station was a shambles; obviously hit by
Stukas. The railroad tracks all around torn and
twisted; cars and locomotives derailed. One could — or
could one? — imagine the consternation of the inhabitants. When they had gone to bed that Thursday night
(May 9), Belgium had been at peace with the world, including Germany. At dawn on Friday the German
bombers were levelling the station and town — the
houses in which they had gone to bed so peacefully —
to a charred mass of ruins. The town itself was absolutely deserted. Two or three hungry dogs nosed sadly
about the ruins, apparently searching for water, food,
and their masters.

8.10. St. Trond. — This town is some twelve
miles to the west of Tongres. As we felt our way slowly
through the debris in the streets, I scrawled a few rough
notes: "houses smashed . . . shambles . . . bitter
faces Belgian civilians . . . they just starting to re-

turn . . . women sobbing . . . their menfolk? . . .
where? . . . here houses destroyed at random . . .
Stukas careless? . . . on purpose? . . . war of roads
. . . the German army on wheels . . . Germans
simply went up the roads . . . with tanks, planes, artillery, anti-tank stuff, everything . . . all morning,
roads massed with supplies, troops going up . . . curious, not a single Allied plane yet . . . and these endless columns of troops, guns, supplies, stretching all the
way from the German border . . . what a target! . . .
Refugees streaming back along the roads in the dust
and heat . . . tears your heart out. . . ."

The refugees trudged up the road, old women lug-
ging a baby or two in their old arms, the mothers lug-
ging the family belongings. The lucky ones had theirs
balanced on bicycles. The really lucky few on carts.
Their faces — dazed, horrified, the lines frozen in sor-
row and suffering, but dignified. What a human being
can't take! And survive and go on! — In a few hours
they would go picking through the charred heaps of
what the day before yesterday or so had been their
homes.

8.30. Tirlemont. — A German officer remarks here: " It took us five days to get to Tirlemont."
We have come about a hundred kilometres from Aachen
— twenty kilometres a day. Not bad. I notice that in
all that distance I have not seen one bomb crater in the
road. I deduce that while German Stukas put the Belgian railroad out of action, they were careful not to
blow up the roads or *their* bridges. Apparently the
German command decided in advance not to try to use
the Belgian railways; only the roads. Their army was
built to go on gasoline-motored vehicles.

We came to a terrific hole in the road, just as it

crossed a creek at the entrance to the town. A pit thirty
yards in diameter and twenty-five feet deep. The officer explained the French blew this one up.

"French dynamite experts," he said. "At places
they have done a beautiful job. But they did not stop
our tanks. The tanks went round through the factory
you see at the left, piercing the factory walls as if they
were made of tissue paper, crossed the creek a couple of
hundred yards upstream, and pursued the enemy. We
lost little time," he added, "even though you have to
admit the French did a good job of it here." His admiration for the French dynamiters was terrific.

Much evidence of street fighting here in Tirlemont.
Houses pockmarked with machine-gun bullets; many
levelled to the ground by Stukas and artillery.

9.15. Louvain. — This ancient university
city, burnt by the Germans in a burst of fury in 1914,
is now again — to a considerable extent — destroyed.
That's the first impression and somehow it hits me between the eyes. Block upon block upon block of houses
an utter shambles. Still smouldering. For the town was
only taken two or three days ago.

We drive through the ruins to the university, to the
university library. It too was burned by the Germans
in 1914, and rebuilt (rebooked too?) by donations from
hundreds of American institutions of learning.

"What happened to the library?" I ask the local
commandant, an elderly, pouch-faced colonel who is
certainly not an *unsympathisch* fellow.

"We shall be there in a minute. You will see," he
says. He is silent for a moment. Maybe he notices
my impatience. He adds: "There was a sharp battle
here in the town itself. Heavy street fighting. Town
changed hands several times. We would come in and

they would drive us out. There was bound to be damage, *mein Herr*."

It has been destroyed then, I conclude. In a minute we are there, driving up the square in front of the library, which is broken by rows of trenches. We climb out of our cars and look. . . .

The great library building is completely gutted. The ruins still smoulder. Some of the girders that held the roof remain. The Tudor-like façade, blackened by smoke, holds out proudly, though a German soldier runs up to me as I approach and warns not to get too close, as the walls may cave in at any moment. We go in close, anyway.

I'm fascinated by the inscriptions on the stones. I note a few down on a scrap of paper: THE FINCH SCHOOL; UNIVERSITY OF ROCHESTER; PHILLIPS ACADEMY, ANDOVER; UNIVERSITY OF ILLINOIS; AMERICAN ASSOCIATION OF UNIVERSITY WO-MEN; PUBLIC SCHOOLS OF THE CITY OF PHILADELPHIA IN PENNSYLVANIA. And so on. They and many others of the kind donated the money to rebuild this library. I look for the famous inscription about which there was so much silly controversy (it doesn't sound quite so silly today) between some of the American donors and the Belgian authorities about the time I first arrived in Europe in 1925 when the building was being completed. I can't find it. I try to remember its exact wording and can't. But I think it ran something like this: " Destroyed by German fury; rebuilt by American generosity."

" And the books? " I ask my commandant, who strikes me more and more like a decent fellow. " Burnt," he says, " all of them, probably."

A Nazi worker with a gnarled, dishonest face, whose yellow arm-band proclaims his belonging to the *Or-*

ganisation Todt, which goes in after the German army
and clears up the debris, comes up to me, and offers:
" The British did it. Set it afire before they left. Typical, ain't it? "

I do not say anything, but later when I have the
colonel alone, I put it to him. He eyes me and shrugs
his shoulders and says: " *Mein Herr,* there was a battle
in this town, as I told you. Heavy fighting in the streets.
Artillery and bombs. You see how much has been destroyed. I do not know myself that one building was
destroyed differently from the next. Whether the library went like the others or in another way."

Before we left Berlin a certain officer in the German
army had come down to the Wilhelmplatz to tell us:
" Gentlemen, we have just had word. From Louvain.
The British have plundered that fine old town. Plundered it in the most shameful manner."

We spend the morning in Louvain, looking over the
ruins, snooping into some of the buildings that still
stand, talking with the first returning inhabitants and
with priests and nuns, some of whom have lived out the
three-day battle huddling in the cellar of a near-by
convent and monastery. We do not see or hear one
shred of evidence that the British plundered the town.
Nor — it is only fair to say — do any of the regular
army officers suggest it.

When we enter the town at nine fifteen a.m., the battered streets are deserted. Not a civilian about; only
a few troops and *Arbeitsdienst* men in Czech uniforms
(are there not enough German uniforms to go around?)
or *Organisation Todt* men in nondescript working
clothes and yellow arm-bands.

Forty-one thousand people lived in Louvain until the
morning Hitler moved west. A week later, when the
Nazi army poured into the town, not a one of them was

there. How many civilians were killed we could not find out. Probably very few. Perhaps none. What happened was that the population, gripped by fear of the Nazi hordes and remembering no doubt how the last time the Germans came, in 1914, two hundred of the leading citizens, held as hostages, had been shot in reprisal for alleged sniping, fled the city before the Germans arrived.

When we leave, about noon, we see the first ones straggling back. Look at their faces. Dazed. So . . . horror-stricken. So . . . bitter and resentful. And yet — so dignified! I see it — dignity masking suffering is, in a way, on the human face at such moments, a noble and even a beautiful thing. Our super-sophisticates like Aldous Huxley need to see more of this — in the flesh, amongst the ruins.

Our commandant takes us to the Cathedral and the City Hall. Except for a broken window or two, they are untouched. They must have escaped the burning of the town in 1914, for they are not new edifices. A German officer remarks to me: " The Stukas have one advantage over ordinary bombers."

" What's that? " I ask.

" They're more accurate. See how the *Rathaus* and Cathedral here have been spared. Ordinary bombers attacking the town probably would have hit them, too. Not our Stukas. They hit their targets."

We file into the City Hall. In a long mediæval hall, probably the reception room, for it's in the front, we see immediately that this has been a British headquarters. On a large table made of unpainted wood: maps, note pads, whisky bottles, beer bottles, cans of biscuits with their quaint English labels. They bear evidence that the British were but lately here.

A corridor leads off to smaller, inner rooms where various British officers seem to have installed themselves. On their desks, more maps, French-English dictionaries. On one I notice an artillery manual. The floor in one room is bloodstained. The commandant ventures the information that two wounded Belgians bled to death there. In each room under the sweeping Renaissance paintings on the walls, dishevelled mattresses on which the British slept. Most of them bloodstained, as if in the last days they were used not to sleep on, but to die on.

When we leave the City Hall, filing out through the large reception room I notice that a great bronze plaque standing against the back wall has been tampered with, and one half ripped away and removed.

" How about *it?* " I ask an officer.

He puffs out something about the honour of the German armed forces, and that this plaque commemorated the martyrs of Louvain — the two hundred civilians who were shot as hostages by the German army in 1914, and that, as the whole world knew, those two hundred leading citizens had only been shot as a result of the Belgians' sniping at German soldiers,[1] and that the plaque said something about the barbarity of the German soldiers, and that there was the honour of the German army to uphold, and that as a consequence the half of the plaque which told of the " heroic martyrs and the barbaric Germans " had been removed, but that the other half, commemorating the heroic deeds of the Belgian army in 1914 in defence of the land, had been left because the Germans had nothing against that — just the opposite.

In the shambles of the square by the railroad station

[1] There was no sniping in 1940.

a massive monument in stone around which Germans
and British fought this time for three days still stands.
It also commemorates the good burghers who were shot
in 1914. It even lists their names. So far the Germans
have not dynamited it.

We pause on the square for breath. Refugees, fear
on their faces still, and shock, begin to trickle in, picking their way over the ruins. They are silent, bitter,
proud. Though it breaks your heart to do it, we stop
a few and try to question them. Some of our number
want to get to the bottom of the German charge that
the British set fire to the Louvain library in the belief
that the Germans would be blamed and American opinion thus further inflamed against the Nazis. But eyeing the German officers with us, they grow sly, act shy,
and tell us nothing. They saw nothing, they all insist.
They were not in the town during the fighting. They
had fled to the hills.

" How could I see anything? " one old man protests,
glaring bitterly at the Germans. A Belgian priest is
just as cagey. " I was in the cellar of the monastery,"
he says. " I prayed for my flock." A German nun tells
how she and fifty-six children huddled in the cellar of
the convent for three days. She does remember that the
bombs started falling Friday morning, the 10th. That
there was no warning. The bombs were not expected.
Belgium was not in the war. Belgium had done nothing
to anybody. . . . She pauses and notices the German
officers eyeing her.

" You're German, aren't you? " one of them says.

" *Ja*." Then she puts in hurriedly, in a frightened
voice: " Of course, as a German, I was glad when it was
all over and the German troops arrived."

The commandant, encouraged, wants to take us out
to the convent to speak to more German nuns, but we

figure it is only for propaganda, and urge the officers
of our party to push on. We set out for Brussels.

About noon we are speeding along a dusty road towards Brussels when someone sights Steenockerzeel and
the mediæval-like old castle where Otto von Habsburg
and his mother, Zita, former Empress of Austria-
Hungary, have been living. We stop to take a look. It
has been bombed.

Otto's castle is an ancient edifice, ugly with its numerous towers and conglomerate outline. Around it is
a muddy moat. As we approach we see that a part of
the roof has been blown off, and one wall looks shaky.
Windows broken. Evidently there has been concussion
from a high explosive. Coming closer we see two huge
bomb craters, actually forming a part of the moat and
enlarging it. The house obviously still stands only because both bombs, and they must have been five-hun-
dred-pounders at least, fell in the moat, and the water
and mud deadened the explosive force. The moat being
but sixty feet from the castle, the bombs were certainly
well aimed. Evidently the work of Stukas.

But why bomb Otto von Habsburg's castle? I ask
an officer. He can't figure it out. Finally he suggests:
"It was undoubtedly used by the British as headquarters. It would therefore be a fair military target."
Later when we have gone through the castle from bottom to top, we find no evidence that the British have
been there.

The castle, we soon notice, once we are inside, has
been plundered, though not very well. There is evidence that the occupants left in great haste. In the upstairs bedrooms women's clothes are lying on the floor,
on chairs, on beds, as if those who were there could not
make up their minds what dress to take, and did not

have the time nor the luggage space to take very much.
All the closets are filled with dresses and robes, hanging
neatly from hangers. In one room, occupied by a man,
books, sweaters, suits, golf-sticks, victrola records, and
notebooks are scattered about. In the salon downstairs,
a large room furnished in horrible bourgeois taste, books
and notebooks and china lie in disorder on a large table.
An enormous book on bugs had evidently been well
thumbed through by someone, perhaps Otto. In what
I take to be his study upstairs, I notice a book in French
entitled: *The Coming War.* I look over his books.
There are some very good ones in French, German,
English. Obviously he had an excellent taste in books.
Many, of course, are his university textbooks, on politics, economics, etc.

We rummage for a half-hour through the rooms.
They are poorly furnished for the most part. The
bathrooms very primitive. I remember the splendour
I've seen in the Hofburg in Vienna, where the Habsburgs ruled so long. A far cry to this. Some of our
party are loading up with souvenirs, swords, ancient
pistols, various knick-knacks. I pick up a page of English composition which Otto evidently did when he was
boning up on his English prior to his recent visit to
America. Feel like a robber. A German officer hands
me Otto's student cap. Sheepishly I take it. Someone
discovers some of Zita's personal calling cards and
hands me one. It says: " *L'Impératrice d'Autriche et
Reine de Hongrie.*" I pocket it, plunderer that I
am. A sad, hungry, bewildered dog wanders around
the litter in the rooms and follows us out to our
car. We leave the castle to him. No human being is
about.

From Steenockerzeel to Brussels the roads are
jammed with German army trucks and motorized guns

speeding westward, on the right side; on the left side
an unbroken column of tired refugees returning in the
heat and the dust to their destroyed towns. An appetite
for a good hearty lunch in Brussels had been growing in
me. This sight takes it away.

   2 p.m., Brussels. — Brussels has been spared
— the one lone city in Belgium that has not been in
whole or in part laid waste. Hitler threatened to bomb
or destroy it on the ground that the Belgians were
moving troops through it and that it was no longer an
open city. Perhaps its rapid fall saved it.

   Here and there, as you drive through the town, you
see a demolished house where a stray German bomb
fell (just to terrorize the people?). And all the bridges
over the canal in the middle of the city — and there
must have been a dozen of them — were blown up by
the British. . . .

   It's a warm late-spring day, and the streets are
thronged with the local inhabitants. The same bitter,
but proud faces we have seen in the other towns. The
German officer in charge of our four cars stops to ask
a passer-by the way to a restaurant where we are booked
to eat. The gentleman, a professorial-looking fellow
with a beard and a wide-brimmed black hat, gives directions. He is coolly polite. The officer thanks him
with a salute. The professor tips his hat stiffly.

   Soon we are in the centre of town, in front of the
East Station, and speeding, the claxon shrieking ruthlessly and needlessly, down the street to the square in
front of the Hotel Metropole. How many days and
nights I've walked this street in the time of peace . . .
observed the good burghers of Brussels, the painted
whores, the streets full of good things you never saw in
Germany, oranges, bananas, butter, coffee, meat; the

movie fronts with posters of the latest from Hollywood and Paris, the café terraces, always jammed on the square.

We eat at the Taverne Royale, which I often frequented when in Brussels. I'm a little embarrassed showing up there with German officers. Fortunately the head waiter and his staff do not recognize me — or act as if they didn't. The restaurant, like the Hotel Metropole, has been taken over by the army, though during the meal two or three civilians stray in and are served — as exceptions, I suppose. We eat well. The Germans from the Foreign Office and the Propaganda Ministry and the officers, especially. Food like this has not been available in Berlin for years.

Some of our party buy out the restaurant's stock of American tobacco in a few minutes. I take three packages of Luckies myself. I cannot resist after a year of smoking " rope " in Germany. I will save them for breakfast; one a day, after. Most buy by the carton, which relieves my conscience. We pay in marks at the absurd rate of ten francs to one mark. After lunch most of the party go out to plunder with their paper marks, now worth a great deal. They buy shoes, shirts, raincoats, women's stockings, everything. One Italian buys coffee, tea, two gallons of cooking oil, besides shoes and clothes.

F. and I go off to find a shop I used to patronize here; not to buy, but to talk. The wife of the *patron* is tending it. She half remembers me. She is dazed, frightened — but brave. She does not yet realize what has happened. She says: " It came so suddenly. I can't get it straight yet. First the German attack. Then the government fled. We didn't know what was happening. Then Friday [today is the following Monday], about eight in the evening, the Germans marched in." She admits the German soldiers are behaving " correctly."

" Where's your husband? " I ask.

" I don't know. He was mobilized. He went to the front. I've heard nothing. I only keep hoping he is alive."

A couple of German soldiers sauntered in and bought half a dozen packages of American cigarettes each. In Germany the most they would have been allowed to buy would have been ten bad German cigarettes. When they had gone, she said :

" I keep the store open. But for how long? Our stocks came from England and America. And my child. Where the milk? I've got canned milk for about two months. But after that — "

She paused. Finally she got it out:

" In the end, how will it be? I mean, do you think Belgium will ever be like before — independent, and with our King? "

" Well, of course, if the Allies win, it will be like the last time. . . ." We gave the obvious reply.

" If? . . . But why do they retreat so fast? With the British and the French, we had more than a million men in Belgium. And they didn't hold out as long as the few Belgians in 1914. I don't understand it."

We didn't either, and we left. Back at the restaurant where our cars were waiting, some of our party were returning, their arms laden with booty. Many were not back yet, so F. and I wandered over to the Rathausplatz. Above the City Hall the Swastika floated in the afternoon sun. Otherwise, except for the German troops clustered about, the square looked the same. We spotted the offices of an American bank. We went inside and asked for the manager. Previously at luncheon we had asked the Germans to take us to the American Embassy, but they had refused. The American Embassy

staff fled with the Belgian government, they told us. I
protested that at least a secretary of Embassy would
have been left in charge. No, they claimed, only a porter was left. This was manifestly an untruth, but F.
and I gave it up. It was too far to walk in the short
time we had.

The two managers of the bank — one had arrived
from New York two days before Belgium was invaded
— seemed glad to see us. Our Ambassador Cudahy and
his entire staff had remained in Brussels, they told us.
But they had been unable to communicate with the outside world. So far as they knew, all Americans were
safe. Some, along with a party of Jewish refugees, had
tried to get out a couple of nights before the Germans
entered. But twenty miles outside the capital the Germans had bombed the railroad bridge, and the train
had had to stop. There was some panic, especially
among the Jews, which is understandable. The Jews
and five or six Americans had decided to go on towards
the coast on foot. The rest, including one of the managers, had returned to Brussels. No one knew what had
happened to those who pushed on to the coast.

Stray items about Brussels: Street-cars running, but
no private motor traffic permitted. Germans had seized
most of the private cars. No telephone service permitted. Movies closed; their posters still advertising
French and American films. The army had forbidden
the population to listen to foreign broadcasts. Signs
were up everywhere, with an appeal of the burgomaster,
written in French and Flemish, asking the population
to remain calm and dignified in regard to the German
troops. American offices had a notice written on the
stationery of the American Embassy, stating: " This is
American property under the protection of the U. S.
Government."

Left Brussels in the late afternoon, our cars filled
with the loot almost everyone had bought. We returned
to Aachen about nine thirty p.m. I had some luck. I've
arranged with RRG in Berlin to broadcast from Cologne at four thirty a.m. this night.

I've just finished the piece. Had to get the censors
from the Propaganda Ministry and the High Command out of bed to read it. Though I've had little sleep
for some time, I do not feel sleepy or tired. I hired a
car and a chauffeur to drive me to Cologne — about
forty miles. He insists on starting now — one a.m.
Says the troops on the road will slow us up, maybe too
the British bombers. So far they've not been over tonight, though it's almost full moon.

May 21, 6.15 a.m. — Broadcast went off all
right. No English bombers. Had difficulty in finding
the broadcasting studio in the black-out. Finally a fat
blonde, standing on a doorstep with a soldier, gave us
directions in Cologne that worked. Snatched a half-
hour's sleep at the studio, and dozed for the hour and
a half that it took us to drive back to Aachen. Dozed
almost all the way, that is. It was a beautiful dawn
and I finally woke up to feel it. Down to breakfast now
and we're off to the front at six thirty a.m. No time to
take my clothes off, but did snatch a shave.

Footnote to May 20. — Returning from
Brussels to Aachen, we ran across a batch of British
prisoners. It was somewhere in the Dutch province of
Limburg, a suburb, I think, of Maastricht. They were
herded together in the brick-paved yard of a disused
factory. We stopped and went over and talked to them.
They were a sad sight. Prisoners always are, especially
right after a battle. Some obviously shell-shocked, some

wounded, all dead tired. But what impressed me most
about them was their physique. They were hollow-
chested and skinny and round-shouldered. About a
third of them had bad eyes and wore glasses. Typical, I
concluded, of the youth that England neglected so crim-
inally in the twenty-two post-war years when Germany,
despite its defeat and the inflation and six million un-
employed, was raising *its* youth in the open air and the
sun. I asked the boys where they were from and what
they did at home. About half of them were from offices
in Liverpool; the rest from London offices. Their military training had begun nine months before, they said,
when the war started. But it had not, as you could see,
made up for the bad diet, the lack of fresh air and sun
and physical training, of the post-war years. Thirty
yards away German infantry were marching up the
road towards the front. I could not help comparing
them with these British lads. The Germans, bronzed,
clean-cut physically, healthy-looking as lions, chests developed and all. It was part of the unequal fight.

The English youngsters, I knew, had fought as
bravely as men can. But bravery is not all; it is not
enough in this machine-age war. You have to have a
body that will stand terrific wear and tear. And then,
especially in this war, you must have all the machines of
warfare. I asked the English about that. There were
six of them, standing a little apart — all that were left,
they told me, from a company that had gone into battle
near Louvain.

" We didn't have a chance," one of them said. " We
were simply overwhelmed. Especially by those dive-
bombers and tanks."

" What about your own bombers and tanks? " I
asked.

" Didn't see any." This answer was chorused.

Three of the men had dirty, bloody bandages over one eye. One of the three looked particularly depressed, and stood there gritting his teeth in pain.

"A shame," his comrade whispered to me. "He's lost the eye. Feels pretty rotten about it."

"Tell him it isn't so bad," I said, trying in my awkward way to be comforting. "I lost the sight of one eye myself," I said, "and you never notice it." But I don't think he believed me.

On the whole, though, despite the shell-shock, despite the black future as prisoners, they were a cheery lot. One little fellow from Liverpool grinned through his thick glasses.

"You know, you're the first Americans I've ever seen in the flesh. Funny place to meet one for the first time, ain't it?" This started the others to make the same observation, and we had a good laugh. But inside I was feeling not so good. F. and I gave them what cigarettes we had and went away.

AACHEN, *May* 21

Finally got to the actual front today and saw my first battle — along the Scheldt River in western Belgium. It was the first actual fighting I had seen since the battle for Gdynia in Poland last September.

Driving to the front we again went through Louvain. Surprising how many people had returned. The peasants had brought in food. To our amazement, a small vegetable market was functioning in a ruined street.

Heading southwest from Brussels, we drove along the road to *Tournai*, still in Allied hands. At *Tubize*, a few miles southwest of Waterloo, the familiar signs of recent fighting — the houses along the streets demolished, half-burnt debris everywhere. So far, I thought, this war has been fought along the roads — by two armies operating on wheels. Almost every town wholly or partially destroyed. But the near-by fields untouched. Returning peasants already tilling them.

About noon we reached *Enghien* and drove to the headquarters of General von Reichenau, commander of the 6th Army. Headquarters were in a château not far from the town. In the park leading to the *Schloss* anti-aircraft guns were mounted everywhere. It was one of those pleasant Renaissance châteaux that dot the countryside in Belgium and France, and the park and lawn leading up to it were cool and green.

Reichenau, whom I had seen occasionally in Berlin before the war, greeted us on the porch. He was tanned and springy as ever, his invariable monocle squeezed over one eye. With typical German thoroughness and with an apparent frankness that surprised me, he went over the operations thus far, stopping to answer questions now and then. In a brief cable to CBS scribbled out later from my notes taken during the interview, I wrote:

" Despite the German successes up to date, Reichenau emphasized to us that the fighting so far had been only an enveloping movement, and that the decisive battle had yet to take place.

" ' When and where? ' I asked him.

" ' Where,' he laughed, ' depends partly on what the enemy does. When, and how long it will last, I leave to the future. It can be short or long. Remember, the preliminary fighting at Waterloo lasted several days. The decisive battle at Waterloo was decided in eight hours.'

" Reichenau admitted that ' possibly our progress will now be slowed up if Weygand decides to make a grand stand. We started this battle absolutely confi-

dent. But we have no illusions. We know we still have
a big battle ahead of us.'

"Reichenau said the German losses were comparatively small, so far, averaging about one tenth of the
number of prisoners taken. Last official counting of
prisoners was 110,000, not counting the half-million
Dutch who surrendered.

"Someone asked how the German infantry got across
the rivers and canals so fast, seeing that the Allies destroyed the bridges pretty well.

"'Mostly in rubber boats,' he said."

Some further quotations from Reichenau I noted
down roughly:

"Hitler is actually directing the German army from
his headquarters. Most of the blowing up of bridges
and roads in Belgium carried out by French special-
ists. . . . I ride 150 miles a day along the front and I
haven't seen an air-fight yet. We've certainly been surprised that the Allies didn't try at least to bomb our
bridges over the Maas River and the Albert Canal.
The British tried it only once in the day-time. We shot
down eighteen of them. But there seems to be no doubt
that the English are holding back with their air force.
At least that's the impression I get."

And I got the impression that this rather bothered
him!

Further notes of talk with Reichenau:

"English have two army corps in Belgium, largely
motorized. Belgians hold the north sector; British the
centre and southern flanks. . . . We encountered one
Moroccan division. It fought well, but lacked staying
power and didn't hold out long. . . . The hardest
fighting the first days was along the Albert Canal.
Then, later, along the Dyle Line, especially around
Gembloux, northwest of Namur."

A few more questions and answers. The general is in an almost jovial mood. He is not tense. He is not worried. He is not rushed. You wonder: " Have these German generals no nerves? " Because, after all, he is directing a large army in an important battle. A few miles down the road two million men are trying to slaughter one another. He bosses almost a million of them. The general smiles and, jauntily, says good-bye.

" I've just given permission for you to go to the front," he says. His eyes light up. " You may be under fire. But you'll have to take your chances. We all do."

He turns us over to his adjutant, who wines us with an excellent Bordeaux, no doubt from the cellar below. Then off to the front.

Soon we hear the distant rumble of artillery. We are on the road to Ath, which, I note on my map, is as near to Lille, still held by the French, as it is to Brussels. More evidences now that the battle is just ahead. The Red Cross ambulances pass by more frequently. The stench of dead horses in the village streets. In the pastures off the roads, cattle lying motionless on the grass, felled by a bomb or a shell.

Near Ath we make a little detour and hit down a pleasant country lane. A first lieutenant, recently an official in a Wilhelmstrasse ministry, who is one of our guides, stands up, Napoleon-like, in the front seat of his car and goes through great gesticulations to give us signals, now to turn, now to stop, etc. Our drivers, all soldiers, say his excited signals mean nothing; the boys at the wheels of our cars laugh. . . . But the lieutenant apparently smells the blood of battle, though we are still some distance from it.

We come, all of a sudden, on a very pungent smell. All that is left of a small, miscellaneous French column

after a German air attack. Along the narrow road are
a dozen dead horses stinking to heaven in the hot sun,
two French tanks, their armour pierced like tissue paper, an abandoned six-inch gun and a 75; and a few
trucks, abandoned in great haste, for scattered about
them are utensils, coats, shirts, overcoats, helmets, tins
of food, and — letters to the wives and girls and mothers
back home.

I note the freshly dug graves just off the road,
marked by a stick on which hangs a French helmet. I
pick up some of the letters, thinking perhaps one day
I can mail them or take them to their destination and
explain, maybe, what the last place, where the end came,
was like. But there are no envelopes, no addresses, no
last names. Just the scrawled letters: " *Ma chère Jac-
queline*," " *Chère Maman*," etc. I glance through one
or two. They must have been written before the push began. They tell of the boredom of army life and how you
are waiting for your next leave in Paris, " *ma chèrie*."

The stench of the dead horses in the late spring sun-
shine is hard to endure, though someone has sprinkled
lime on them. So we push on. We pass a tiny village.
Five or six farmhouses at the crossing of a path with
the road. Cattle graze in the pastures. Pigs squeal
about the barnyards. All are thirsty, for the farmhouses are deserted. The cows have not been milked
for some days and their udders are painfully swollen.

We can hear the guns pounding very clearly now.
We speed down the dusty road past endless German columns of trucks carrying troops, carrying ammunition,
carrying all-important oil, hauling guns, big and small.
The bridge over a stream or a canal at Leuze has been
blown up, but German engineers have already constructed an emergency one over which we go.

Leuze is jammed with vehicles and troops. Blocks of

houses have been smashed to smithereens. Some still
smoulder. We stop for half an hour on a pleasant little
square, surrounded by a church, a school, and the City
Hall or some government building. The school is a Red
Cross station. I meander over to it. The ambulances
are lined up, waiting to unload the wounded, seven or
eight of them, waiting. Even with the wounded there
is the same machine-like, impersonal organization. No
excitement, no tension. Even the wounded seem to play
their part in this gigantic businesslike machine. They
do not moan. They do not murmur. Nor complain.

We get a bite to eat while we wait — a piece of brown
bread with some sort of canned fish ragout spread over
it. Then off to the front. Before we start, the army
officer in charge warns of the danger. Warns that we
must follow his orders promptly. Explains how to dive
for a near-by field and lie flat on your belly if the Allied
planes come over or if the French artillery opens fire.
Our party is a little tense now as we go forward. We
proceed north, parallel with the front, and back of it
about five miles to Renaix, hurry through the town, and
then north towards the Scheldt River, where they're
fighting. Infantry on foot, almost the first we've seen
— on foot — are deploying down various paths towards
the river. Heavy artillery — and this is amazing to see
— six-inch guns, pulled by caterpillar trucks, and on
rubber tires, are being hauled up a hillside at forty miles
an hour. (Is this one of the German military secrets,
such big guns being hauled so fast?) Finally we stop.
A battery of six-inch guns, concealed under trees in an
orchard at the right of the road, is pounding away.
Now we have a view over the valley of the Scheldt and
can see the slopes on the other side. The artillery
thunders, and a second later you see the smoke from the
shells on the far slopes. An officer explains they're

bombarding the roads behind the enemy lines. You
can follow the winding roads on the other side by the
smoke of each exploding shell. We pile out of our cars,
but immediately someone orders us back. Someone explains we're too exposed. Enemy planes or artillery
could get us here. So we cut back, and then turn due
west and climb a hill beyond the artillery positions, so
that they are now behind us, firing over our heads. This
is an artillery observation post in the woods at the sum-
mit of the hill. We sit on a slope and look through the
trees towards the front line.

But it's disappointing. You see so little, actually.
You cannot make out the infantry, or what they're doing. An officer explains they're fighting along the river
there below. The Allies still hold both banks, but are
retreating across the Scheldt. The only evidence you
have of infantry fighting is that the German artillery
barrage advances. Then stops. Then starts again much
nearer to us. You conclude that the other side has
counter-attacked, and the German attack, behind its
own artillery barrage, must start all over again. An
amateur officer from the Wilhelmstrasse insists he can
follow the infantry. I grab my glasses. The infantry
is invisible.

From the smoke of the exploding shells on the slopes
across the Scheldt you can see that the Germans are
giving the enemy's rear lines of communication a terrific pounding. Through field-glasses you see how the
Germans shoot up the road, following all the windings.
After a while there is a great cloud of smoke spreading
over the far side. So far we haven't heard much of the
German artillery as a factor in their amazing progress.
The work of the Stuka bombers took most of our attention. But it's obvious that this German motorized
artillery, brought up to position right behind the ad-

vancing tanks at forty miles per hour, is a tremendous
factor. The Allies probably had not reckoned that artillery could move so fast. Around us now the Germans
are firing with six-inch guns and 105's. The noise is
not so deafening as I expected. Perhaps one's ears get
used to it.

A young soldier comes up and attempts to plant some
propaganda on us. Remarks offhand that last night
the British counter-attacked, got back as far as the
woods where we are, and carried off all the civilians.
Most of us are not impressed. I conclude that if they
did counter-attack and came back for an evening, most
of the civilians probably went back with them of their
own accord, so as not to fall into German hands. Even
the Italians with us laugh.

I note that over the front all afternoon hover two
or three reconnaissance planes, German, obviously directing artillery fire. They cruise above the battlefield
unmolested. But there are no planes directing Allied
artillery fire, which seems to be aimed exclusively against
the German forward positions, at no time against German artillery, which is strange. The lack of observation planes alone puts the Allies in a hole. In fact we
do not see an Allied plane all day long. Once or twice
we get an alarm, but no planes show up. How England
and France are paying now for the criminal neglect of
their aviation!

As the afternoon wears away to the pounding of the
guns, artillery units near us get orders to take up new
positions forward. The advance, you suppose, is going
ahead according to schedule. Immediately from all
around us in the woods, men and motors, which we have
not even seen, limber up, the men toss off some of the
tree-limbs which have so completely camouflaged them,
and get off. We take a last look at the Scheldt Valley,

at the smoke rising from the bursting shells on the other
side of the river. Probably it all has meaning for these
German officers around us. Each whistling shell has a
certain errand. Each gun and truck rushing down the
road is going to some place assigned to it. Each of the
thousands upon thousands. The whole chaos (to me)
of the battlefield is in reality a picture of a well-oiled
machine of destruction in action.

We drive back to Brussels. German dive-bombers fly
past us, going up to do a little late-afternoon work.
At Brussels German fighters and bombers demonstrate
over the city. This is the German idea of how to impress
the population. . . .

It is midnight before we reach Aachen. At Maastricht the Germans are expecting British bombers. A
quarter of a mile from the repaired bridge, a soldier
stops us. All lights must be put out. We drive along
in the moonlight — it's almost full moon tonight; lovely
— across the bridge. A quarter of a mile away, a soldier
stops us; says we can put on our dim lights. Efficiency.

Most of the boys in the party have looted Brussels
for the second time, and are worried that the Germans
(who still keep up a customs shed at the old Dutch-
German border!) will take away their booty. But they
do not.

Too late to broadcast, so I write a story to be phoned
to Berlin, cabled to New York, and there read over the
air. I've hardly sat down to write when the British come
over Aachen. I leave my room, which is on the next to
the top floor (having moved out of the attic), and write
my piece in the dining-room on the ground floor. The
anti-aircraft of all calibres keeps thundering away.
Now and then you feel the concussion of a bomb and
hear it exploding. Our little hotel is a hundred yards
from the station. The British are obviously trying to

get the station and the railroad yards. You hear the roar of their big planes; occasionally the whirr of German night chasers. . . .

My call comes through about one twenty a.m. I can hardly make myself heard for the sound of the guns and the bombs.

While writing my story, I keep notes on the air-raid.

12.20 a.m.	Sound of anti-aircraft.
12.40	Air-raid sirens sound off.
12.45	Big anti-aircraft gun near by thunders suddenly.
12.50	Sound of cannon from German chasers.
1.00	Light anti-aircraft around station blazes away.
1.15	Still going on.

It went on for four hours, until just after four a.m. But after my call to Berlin, being a little sleepy, I went up to bed and fell immediately to sleep.

BERLIN, *May* 24

Two weeks ago today Hitler unloosed his *Blitzkrieg* in the west. Since then this has happened: Holland overrun; four fifths of Belgium occupied; the French army hurled back towards Paris; and an Allied army believed to number a million men, and including the élite of the Franco-British forces, trapped and encircled on the Channel.

You have to see the German army in action to believe it. Here are some of the things, so far as I could see, that make it good:

It has absolute air superiority. It seems incredible, but at the front I did not see a single Allied plane during the day-time. Stuka dive-bombers are softening the

Allied defence positions, making them ripe for an easy attack. Also, they're wrecking Allied communications in the rear, bombing roads filled with trucks, tanks, and guns, wiping out strategic railroad stations and junctions. Furthermore, reconnaissance planes are giving the German command a perfect picture of what is going on. Against this, the Allies have no eyes; few of their reconnaissance planes get over. Also, Allied bombers have completely failed to disturb German lines of communications by *day-time* attacks. One of the sights that overwhelms you at the front is the vast scale on which the Germans bring up men, guns, and supplies unhindered. Because of the thorough manner in which the Belgians and French destroyed their railroad bridges, the German command decided to use exclusively motor transport. All day long at the front, driving along at forty or fifty miles an hour, you pass unending mechanized columns. They stretch clear across Belgium, unbroken. And they move fast — thirty or forty miles an hour. You wonder how they are kept fed with gasoline and oil. But they are. Gas supplies come forward with everything else. Every driver knows where he can tank up when he runs short.

What magnificent targets these endless columns would make if the Allies had any planes!

And what a magnificent machine that keeps them running so smoothly. In fact that is the chief impression you get from watching the German army at work. It is a gigantic, impersonal war machine, run as coolly and efficiently, say, as our automobile industry in Detroit. Directly behind the front, with the guns pounding daylight out of your ears and the airplanes roaring overhead, and thousands of motorized vehicles thundering by on the dusty roads, officers and men alike remain cool and business-like. Absolutely no excitement, no tension. An officer directing artillery fire stops for half an hour to explain to you what he is up to. General von Reichenau, directing a huge army in a crucial battle, halts for an hour to explain to amateurs his particular job.

Morale of the German troops fantastically good. I remember a company of engineers which was about to go down to the Scheldt River to lay a pontoon bridge under enemy fire. The men were reclining on the edge of the wood reading the day's edition of the army daily paper, the *Western Front.* I've never seen men going into a battle from which some were sure never to come out alive so — well, so nonchalantly.

The contention of the BBC that these flying German columns — such as the one that broke through to the sea at Abbeville — are weak forces which cannot possibly hold what they get, is a myth. The Germans thrust not only with tanks and a few motorized infantry, but with *everything.* Light and heavy motorized artillery goes right up behind the tanks and infantry.

BERLIN, *May 25*

German military circles here tonight put it flatly. They said the fate of the great Allied army bottled up in Flanders is sealed.

BERLIN, *May 26*

Calais has fallen. Britain is now cut off from the Continent.

BERLIN, *May* 28

King Leopold has quit on the Allies. At dawn
the Belgian army, which with the British and French
has been caught in an ever narrowing pocket for a week
in Flanders and Artois, laid down its arms. Leopold
during the night had sent an emissary to the German
lines asking for an armistice. The Germans demanded
unconditional surrender. Leopold accepted. This
leaves the British and French in a nice hole. High
Command says it makes their position "hopeless."
Picked up a broadcast by Reynaud this morning accusing Leopold of having betrayed the Allies. Churchill, according to BBC, was more careful. Said, in a
short statement to Commons, he would not pass judgment.

Great jubilation in the press here over the capitulation of the Belgians. After eighteen days, the Berlin
papers remind us. It took the Germans just eighteen
days to liquidate the Poles. They'll probably have the
rest of the Allied army in their pocket before the week-
end. Churchill, according to the BBC, warned the
House to expect bad news soon.

For the first time, communiqués today kept pouring out of the "Führer's Headquarters." All of them
sounded as if they'd been dictated by Hitler himself.
For example this typical attempt to sound generous:
"DNB. Führer's Headquarters, May 28. The Führer
has ordered that the King of the Belgians and his army
be given treatment worthy of the brave, fighting soldiers which they proved to be. As the King of the Belgians expressed no personal wishes for himself, he will
be given a castle in Belgium until his final living-place
is decided upon."

Decided upon by whom?

Nazi propaganda is doing its best to show that Leopold did the decent, sensible thing. Thus the wording of a special communiqué which the German radio tells its listeners will " fill the German nation with pride and joy ":

" From the headquarters of the Führer it is announced: Impressed by the destructive effect of the German army, the King of the Belgians has decided to put an end to further senseless resistance and to ask for an armistice. He has met the German demands for unconditional capitulation. The Belgian army has today laid down its arms and therewith ceased to exist. In this hour we think of our brave soldiers. . . . The entire German nation looks with a feeling of deep gratitude and unbounded pride upon the troops . . . which forced this capitulation. . . . The King of the Belgians, in order to put an end to the further shedding of blood and to the completely pointless devastation of his country, reached his decision to lay down arms, against the wishes of the majority of his Cabinet. This Cabinet, which is mainly responsible for the catastrophe which has broken over Belgium, seems to be willing even now to continue to follow its English and French employers."

The headlines tonight: "CHURCHILL AND REYNAUD INSULT KING LEOPOLD! — THE COWARDS IN LONDON AND PARIS ORDER THE CONTINUATION OF THE SUICIDE IN FLANDERS." The German radio said tonight: " Leopold acted like a soldier and a human being."

I saw at the front last week the terrible punishment the Belgian army was taking; saw all of Belgium, outside of Brussels, laid waste by the German artillery and Stukas. You can sympathize with Leopold in a sense for wanting to quit. But the French and British say he did it without consulting them, thus betraying them and leaving them in a terrible situation, with no chance of extricating their armies from the trap. The three armies together had a small chance of fighting their way out. With half a million excellent Belgian troops out of the picture, the fate of the French and British armies, it would seem, is sealed.

A nice, civilized war, this. Göring announces tonight that as a result of information reaching him that the French are mistreating captured German airmen, all French flyers captured by the Germans will be immediately put in *chains*. Further, Göring proclaims that if he hears of a German flyer being shot by the French, he will order *five* French prisoners shot. Further still, if he hears of a German flyer being shot " while parachuting," he will order *fifty* French prisoners shot.

Allies, as far as we know, are shooting parachutists who fail to surrender, because these boys were largely responsible for the fall of Holland and play hell behind the lines. Probably ordinary German flyers parachuting from shot-down planes have been mistaken for the dreaded parachutists. Göring's order, however, is obviously part of Hitler's technique of conquering by sowing terror. B., who was in Rotterdam last week, says the town was largely destroyed *after* it had surrendered. German excuse is that surrender came after the Stukas had left the ground and they could not be recalled in time! This sounds flimsy, as they all carry radios and are in constant touch with the ground.

Göring added that the above rule of shooting five to one or fifty to one would not apply to the English, " as they have not as yet given grounds for such reprisals."

The Propaganda Ministry tonight showed us a full-length news-reel, with sound effects, of the destruction in Belgium and France. Town after town, city after city, going up in flames. Close-ups of the crackling flames devouring the houses, shooting out of the windows, roofs and walls tumbling in, where a few days ago men and women were leading peaceful, if not too happy, lives.

The German commentator's enthusiasm for the destruction seemed to grow as one burning town after another was shown. He had a cruel, rasping voice and by the end seemed to be talking in a whirl of sadism. "Look at the destruction, the houses going up in flames," he cried. "This is what happens to those who oppose Germany's might!"

And is Europe soon to be ruled and dominated by such a people — by such sadism?

BERLIN, May 29

Boss of one of the big American broadcasting chains (not Columbia) cables the German Broadcasting Company today: "PLEASE ARRANGE BROADCAST BY KING LEOPOLD."

Lille, Bruges, Ostend captured! Ypres stormed! Dunkirk bombarded! Fate of encircled Allied armies sealed! . . . the incredible headlines went on today without a let-up. Tonight still another phase of this gigantic battle, without precedent in history, appeared — at least in Berlin — to be drawing to a conclusion.

The German High Command told the story in these words at the beginning of its communiqué today: " The fate of the French army in Artois is sealed. Its resistance south of Lille has collapsed. The English army which has been compressed into the territory around Dixmude, Armentières, Bailleul, Bergues, west of Dun·

kirk, is also going to its destruction before our con-
centric attack."

And then this evening the German command announced that in rapid attacks designed to crush the
British army Ypres and Kemmel had been stormed.

In reality, the Germans tell us, the French and British armies since yesterday have been isolated, the one
from the other, and each trapped in a tiny pocket.
The smaller pocket, which is in the form of a square, the
sides of which are about twelve miles long, lies south of
Lille — between there and Douai. In that small square
is what is left of three French armies, and tonight the
Germans are battering them from four sides. The
larger pocket runs roughly in a semicircle around the
port of Dunkirk, reaching inland for some twenty-five
miles. Here the British are trapped.

What next, then, if the British and French armies either surrender or are annihilated, as the Germans say
they will be in their two pockets? The first invasion of
England since 1066? England's bases on the Continent, barring a last-minute miracle, are gone. The lowlands, just across the Channel and the narrow southern
part of the North Sea, which it has always been a cardinal part of British policy to defend, are in enemy hands.
And the French Channel ports which linked Britain with
its French ally are lost.

Most people here think Hitler will try now to conquer
England. Perhaps. I'm not so sure. Maybe he'll try
to finish France first.

One weird aspect of yesterday's fighting: When the
Germans yesterday took French positions east of Kas-
sel, they actually rushed the French fortifications along
the Franco-Belgian border from *behind*, from the *reverse side*.

Prince Wilhelm of Prussia, killed in action on the western front, was buried with military honours in Potsdam today. If things had gone smoothly for Germany after 1914, he probably would have been the German emperor. Present at the funeral were the Crown Prince and Princess, Mackensen and a lot of World War officers in their quaint spike helmets. The former Kaiser sent a wreath.

More on the nerve war: An official statement tonight says that for every German civilian killed and every stone damaged in Germany during the night raids of the British, revenge will be taken many times over.

BERLIN, *May* 30

Our Memorial Day. I remembered it when one of the consuls phoned and reminded me of a month-old golfing date. How many killed in the Civil War?

A German dropped in today. He said: " How many *years* will the war last? " The question surprised me in the light of the news. Last week three Germans in the Wilhelmstrasse bet me the Germans would be in London in three weeks — that is, two weeks from now.

This German also mentioned a matter that's been bothering me: German losses and the effect on the people of not being allowed to know by Hitler what the losses are and who is killed. (Hitler will not permit the publication of casualty lists.) He said people are comparing *that* situation with the one in 1914–18, when every day the papers published the names of those lost, and every few months, he said, a résumé of the total casualties up to date in killed and wounded. But today no German has the slightest idea of what the western offensive has cost in German lives. He doesn't even know what the Norwegian campaign cost. The last figures he had were on the Polish campaign, and even then he was skeptical of those Hitler gave.

The great battle in Flanders and Artois neared its end today. It's a terrific German victory. Yesterday, according to the German High Command, the British made a great bid to rescue what is left of the BEF by sea. Sent over fifty transports to fetch their troops along the coast around Dunkirk. Germans say they sent over two flying corps to bomb them. Claim they sank sixteen transports and three " warships," which no doubt is exaggerated, and hit and damaged, or set on fire, twenty-one transports and ten warships, which probably is an even greater exaggeration. British sent out hundreds of planes to protect their fleet. The Germans claim they shot down 68 British planes. The British claim they shot down 70 German planes.

What is left of the three French armies cut off in Flanders and Artois is being gradually annihilated, one gathers from the German reports. Today the Germans say they captured the commander of the 1st French Army, General Prieux. They'd already got General Giroud, commander of one of the other two armies, the day he took over. The French apparently are entirely surrounded. The British still have the sea open and are undoubtedly getting as many men out as possible. London yesterday said the British were fighting " the greatest rear-guard action in history." But they've been fighting too many of these.

Much talk here that Hitler is getting ready to bomb the hell out of London and Paris. A press and radio campaign to prepare his own people for it is already under way. Today the attack was mostly against the

French. The *Völkische Beobachter* called them "bastardized, negroized, decadent," and accused them of torturing German airmen whom they've captured. It said that soon the French will be made to pay for all of this. The papers are full of talk of revenge for this and that.

The German Ambassador to Belgium gave us a harangue at the press conference today on how he was mistreated by the French on his way out to Switzerland. As a German told me afterwards, the Germans seem incapable of apprehending that the hate against them in France and Belgium is due to the fact that Germany invaded these countries — Belgium without the slightest excuse or justification — and laid waste their towns and cities, and killed thousands of civilians with their bombings and bombardments. Just another example of that supreme German characteristic of being unable to see for a second the other fellow's point of view. Same with the wrath here at the way their airmen are treated. The other side is tough with airmen coming down in parachutes because it knows Hitler has conquered Holland by landing parachutists behind the lines. But the Germans think that the other side should not defend itself against these men dropping from the skies. If it does, if it shoots them, then Germany will massacre prisoners already in her hands.

BERLIN, *May* 31

Italy seems to be drawing near to the day of decision — to go in on Germany's side. Today Alfieri, the Italian Ambassador, saw Hitler at his headquarters.

It was three weeks ago today that Hitler hurled his armies into Holland, Belgium, Luxemburg, and France

in a desperate effort to knock out the Allies in one blow.
So far, after three weeks, he has had nothing but success. What it has cost him in lives and material, we do
not know yet. This is what he's accomplished in three
weeks:

1. Overrun Holland; forced Dutch army to surrender.

2. Overrun Belgium; forced Belgian army to surrender.

3. Advanced far south of the extension of the Maginot Line on a front extending over two hundred miles
from Montmédy to Dunkirk.

4. Knocked out the 1st, 7th, and 9th French Armies,
which were cut off when one German army broke
through to the sea.

5. Knocked out the BEF, which also is surrounded.
Some of the men, at least, of the BEF, are getting away
on ships from Dunkirk. But as an army it's finished.
It cannot take away its guns and supplies and tanks.

6. Obtained the Dutch, Belgian, and French Channel coasts as a jumping-off place for an invasion of
England.

7. Occupied the important coal mines and industrial
centres of Belgium and northern France.

I said in my broadcast tonight: " The Germans have
certainly won a terrific first round. But there has been
no knockout blow — yet. The fight goes on."

Some of my friends thought that was being a bit optimistic — from the Allied point of view. Maybe. But
I'm not so sure.

First American ambulance driver to be captured by
the Germans is one Mr. Garibaldi Hill. The Germans
have offered to release him at once. Only they can't find
him.

Word from our people in Brussels today that there is food in Belgium for only fifty days.

Ran into one of our consuls from Hamburg. He says the British have been bombing it at night severely. Trying to hit, for one thing, the oil tanks. He claims they're dry. It seems that the Germans took all the anti-aircraft guns from Hamburg for use at the front. Hence the British came over without trouble and were able to fly low enough to do some accurate bombing. The population got so jittery that the authorities had to bring some of the guns back.

BERLIN, *June* 1

Though the public is no more aroused about the great victories up on the Channel than they have been about anything else in this war, the newspaper headlines today do their best to stir up interest. Typical is the *B.Z. am Mittag* today: "CATASTROPHE BEFORE THE DOORS OF PARIS AND LONDON — FIVE ARMIES CUT OFF AND DESTROYED — ENGLAND'S EXPEDITIONARY CORPS NO LONGER EXISTS — FRANCE'S 1ST, 7TH, AND 9TH ARMIES ANNIHILATED!"

The mass of the German army which liquidated the Allied forces in Flanders is now ready for new assignments. There are two courses open to the German High Command. It can strike across the Channel against England or roll the French back on Paris and attempt to knock France out of the war. From what I gather in military circles here, there seems to be no doubt that the German command has already chosen the second course and indeed moved most of its troops into position facing what is left of the French along the rivers

Somme and Aisne. General Weygand has now had ten days to organize his armies along this line, but the fact that he has not felt himself strong enough to attempt an offensive northward from the Somme against the fairly thin German line — a move which if pushed home would have saved the Franco-British-Belgian armies in Flanders — has convinced the German generals, if they needed convincing, that they can crack his forces fairly easily and quickly break through to Paris and to the Norman and Breton ports.

I learn from a High Command officer that God at last has given the British a break. They have had two days of fog and mist around Dunkirk and as a result the Luftwaffe has been unable to do much bombing of the transports busily engaged in taking off British troops. Today the weather cleared and Göring's bombers went back to work over Dunkirk beach. Says the High Command tonight in a special communiqué: " The rest of the defeated British Expeditionary Force tried today to escape on small craft of all kinds to the transports and warships lying off shore near Dunkirk. The German air force frustrated this attempt through continuous attacks, especially with Junker dive-bombers, on the British ships. According to the reports received so far, three warships and eight transports, totalling 40,000 tons, were sunk, and four warships and fourteen transports set on fire and damaged. Forty English fighter planes protecting the ships were shot down."

No mention of the German air losses, so I assume they were larger than the British — otherwise Göring would have mentioned them. The Junker-87 dive-bomber is a set-up for any British fighter.

The Germans claim today that the battleship *Nelson*, flagship of the British Home Fleet, has been sunk with the loss of 700 of her crew of 1,350. So far as I can make out, the only source for this is an alleged dispatch from the A.P. in New York. But a naval officer tonight insisted it was true. He said the ship was sunk on May 11.

BERLIN, *June* 2

Those British Tommies at Dunkirk are still fighting like bulldogs. The German High Command admits it.

Its official war communiqué today: " In hard fighting, the strip of coast on both sides of Dunkirk which yesterday also was stubbornly defended by the British, was further narrowed. Nieuport and the coast to the northwest are in German hands. Adinkerke, west of Furnes, and Ghyvelde, six and a quarter miles east of Dunkirk, have been taken." Six and a quarter miles — that's getting close.

In the air the Germans again make mighty claims. The official communiqué: " All together, four warships and eleven transports, with a total tonnage of 54,000 tons, were sunk by our bombers. Fourteen warships, including two cruisers, two light cruisers, an anti-aircraft cruiser, six destroyers, and two torpedo boats, as well as thirty-eight transports, with a total tonnage of 160,000, were damaged by bombs. Numberless small boats, tugs, rafts were capsized. . . ." [1]

Despite the lack of popular enthusiasm for this collossal German victory in Flanders, I gather quite a few Germans are beginning to feel that the deprivations which Hitler has forced on them for five years have not been without reason. Said my room waiter this morn-

[1] A fair example of Göring's exaggerations. When I visited the beach of Dunkirk two and a half months later, I found the wrecks of only two freighters, two destroyers, and one torpedo boat.

ing: " Perhaps the English and French now wish they had had less butter and more cannon."

And yet the picture this capital presents at this great moment in German history still confounds me. Last evening, just before dark, I strolled down the Kurfürstendamm. It was jammed with people meandering along pleasantly. The great sidewalk cafés on this broad, tree-lined avenue were filled with thousands, chatting quietly over their *ersatz* coffee or their ice-cream. I even noticed several smartly dressed women. Today, being the Sabbath and a warm and sunny June day, tens of thousands of people, mostly in family groups, betook themselves to the woods or the lakes on the outskirts of the city. The Tiergarten, I noticed, also was thronged. Everyone had that lazy, idle, happy-go-lucky Sunday holiday air.

One reason for this peculiar state of things, I suppose, is that the war has not been brought home to the people of Berlin. They read about it, or on the radio even hear the pounding of the big guns. But that's all. Paris and London may feel in danger. Berlin doesn't. The last air-raid alarm I can recall here was early last September. And then nothing happened.

BERLIN, *June* 3

BBC just announced that the Germans bombed Paris this afternoon. Maybe the Allies will drop a few on Berlin tonight.

Donald Heath, our chargé d'affaires, was called to the Wilhelmstrasse this noon and handed a copy of a press release in which the German government stated it had information from confidential sources that the British secret service planned to sink three American liners — the *President Roosevelt* and *Manhattan* now en route to New York with American citizens, and the *Washington* en route to Bordeaux to bring back a further batch of American refugees. The Germans informed the American government through this press release — a curious diplomatic procedure — that strict orders have been dispatched to all German naval commanders instructing them not to molest any of the three American ships.

An official statement in the release said : " The Reich government expects the American government to take all necessary measures to frustrate such a crime as the British contemplate perpetrating."

The German " theory " is that if the ships are sunk the Americans will blame the Germans. Something very suspicious about this. What is to prevent the Germans from torpedoing these American vessels themselves and then crying to the skies that the British did it and that Berlin had even gone out of its way to warn Washington beforehand that the British would do it. Submarine periscopes are very difficult to identify.

Berlin, *June* 4

The great battle of Flanders and Artois is over. The German army today entered Dunkirk and the remaining Allied troops — about forty thousand — surrendered. The German High Command in an official communiqué says the battle will go down in history " as the greatest battle of destruction of all time." German losses for the western offensive, as given out tonight, are said to be : dead — 10,252 ; missing — 8,467 ; wounded — 42,523 ; planes lost — 432. All of which is very surprising. Only three days ago the military people tipped us that the losses would soon be given out, and that they were approximately 35,000 to 40,000 dead; 150,000 to 160,000 wounded. But most Germans will believe any figures they are given.

The communiqué speaks of Allied losses: 1,200,000 prisoners, counting the Belgians and the Dutch. And a whole navy destroyed, including five cruisers and seven destroyers sunk, and ten cruisers and twenty-four destroyers damaged. It also claims the German navy did not lose a single vessel.

Paris says 50 killed, 150 injured in yesterday's German air-raid. BBC says the Parisians are demanding revenge. But no planes came over here last night; none so far tonight. . . .

I'm worried about Tess and Baby. She called this afternoon, said she'd at last got passage on the *Washington*, but that it would not call at Genoa. She must get it at Bordeaux. But she's advised not to cross France with the French in their present panicky mood. The railroad near Lyon which she must take has been bombed twice this week by the Germans. And she would still prefer to stay on.

BERLIN, *June* 6

The church bells rang, and all the flags were out today, by order of Hitler, to celebrate the victory in Flanders. There is no real elation over the victory discernible in the people here. No emotion of any kind. In grandiose proclamations to the army and the people, Hitler announced that today a new offensive was being launched in the west. So far no details are available here, but the BBC says the offensive is on a two-hundred-kilometre front from Abbeville to Soissons, with the biggest German pressure along the Somme-Aisne Canal.

I've heard here that the Allies have been bombing Munich and Frankfurt the last few nights. But Berlin is never told of these enemy air-raids. No one here feels the war as yet.

Berlin, *June* 7

The Germans are keeping very mum about their new offensive on the Somme. High Command simply states that the so-called Weygand line has been broken through on the entire front. Strange, though, that no details are given; no place names at all. No special war communiqués tonight. Can it be that the drive isn't going so well?

Our Ambassador to Belgium, Cudahy, arrived here today. He confirms what I was told a few days ago, that the Belgians have food for not more than fifty days.

I took the day off from the war yesterday. I walked for hours in the Grunewald, swam in the Havel, and found a neat little restaurant in the woods which produced a surprisingly good beefsteak. After lunch I walked, sun-bathed, swam some more.

Berlin, *June* 8

Still no news here of the offensive, although it's at the end of its fourth day. The High Command merely states that it is continuing successfully, but gives no details, no place names. One almost dares to think . . .

Berlin, *June* 9

The High Command broke its reserve about the great offensive with a bang this afternoon. It says the French south of the Somme and in the Oise district

have been beaten all along the line. It talks about the
German troops driving towards the lower Seine, which
is a hell of a way forward from the Somme, where they
started four days ago. BBC at six tonight confirmed
this. Weygand issues another order of the day to his
men to hold. But there is something desperate in it.

The Germans also announce: " This morning on a
further part of the front in France a new offensive has
started." Weygand reveals it's on a front from Reims
to the Argonne. The Germans are now hurling themselves forward on a two-hundred-mile front from the
sea to the Argonne. No drive in World War I was on
this scale!

The High Command also states that Germany's only
two battleships, the *Gneisenau* and the *Scharnhorst,*
have put to sea and have gone to the relief of the German forces driven out of Narvik a couple of weeks ago.
Hand it to the Germans for their daring, their sense
of surprise. How could the British fleet allow two battleships to get up to Narvik? High Command says the
two have already sunk the British aircraft-carrier
Glorious, the 21,000-ton transport *Orama,* and an oil
tanker of 9,100 tons. Another instance of the Germans
taking a chance — taking the initiative. The Allies
seem to take neither.

BERLIN, *June* 10

Italy is in the war.

She has stabbed France in the back at the moment
when the Germans are at the gates of Paris, and France
appears to be down.

At six o'clock this evening, just as people here were
tuning in on their radios to hear the latest news of the
German army's onslaught on Paris, the announcer said:

" In one hour the Duce will address the Italian people and the world. All German stations will broadcast his speech."

An hour later they did — with a German radio commentator conveniently at hand (he'd been sent to Rome last Saturday, June 8, for the job) at the Piazza Venezia to describe the tumult.

We got wind of it early in the afternoon when we were convoked for a special press conference at the Foreign Office at seven p.m., to hear Ribbentrop make a declaration. At four thirty p.m., at the Propaganda Ministry, we were shown the English propaganda film *The Lion Has Wings*. Even making allowances for the fact that it was turned out last fall, I thought it very bad. Supercilious. Silly. At the six p.m. press conference we were given another dose of the weekly German news-reel. Again the ruined towns, the dead humans, the putrefying horses' carcasses. One shot showed the charred remains of a British pilot amid the wreckage of his burnt plane. Most Germans there seemed to get a sadistic pleasure from these pictures of death and destruction. A few I know, however, didn't. A few react still like human beings.

I went over to the Foreign Office about seven and soon found myself crowding into the Hall of whatever-it-is. Designed to hold about fifty people, five hundred had already jammed their way in. It was a hot day, the windows were sealed tight, and hot Klieg lights were burning so that Ribbentrop could be properly photographed. In one corner of the room the most screeching radio I ever heard was screaming out Mussolini's speech at the Piazza Venezia in Rome. I caught just enough of it to learn that he was announcing Italy's decision to enter the war on the side of Germany. The combination of this tin-pan racket and the foul, hot air,

and the photographers scrapping and most of the newspapermen standing there sweating, and of some other
things, was enough for me. S. and I pushed our way
out before Ribbentrop arrived. I went back to Joe's
room, tuned in on the radio, and got from Rome a rather
comical English translation of the Duce's words.

About the same time there was a comedy act in front
of the Italian Embassy, which Ralph described to me.
Two or three thousand Italian Fascists, residents of
Berlin, shouted themselves hoarse in the little street that
runs off the Tiergarten past the Italian Embassy. The
Germans had rigged up loud-speakers, so that the mob
could hear the Duce's words. Later Ribbentrop and
Alfieri, the new Italian Ambassador, appeared on the
balcony, grinned, and made brief inane speeches, Ralph
reported.

In the meantime the German army closes in on Paris.
It looks dark for the Allies tonight. Roosevelt is broadcasting at one fifteen a.m. tonight.

BERLIN, *June* 11

Roosevelt came through very clearly on the
radio last night. He promised immediate material help
for the Allies. Scorched Mussolini for his treachery.
Not a word about the speech in press or radio here.

The Wilhelmstrasse keeps making the point that
American aid will come too late. A man just back from
seeing Hitler tells me the Führer is sure that France will
be finished by June 15 — that is, in four days — and
Great Britain by August 15 at the latest! He says
Hitler is acting as if he had the world at his feet, but
that some of the generals, although highly pleased with
the military successes, are a little apprehensive of the
future under such a wild and fanatical man.

Word here is that the French government has left
Paris. The Germans tonight are roughly about as near
Paris as they were on September 1, 1914. This led the
High Command to point out to us today that the German position is much better than it was then. First,
because their right wing is stronger, and has maintained
its advance *west* of Paris, whereas in 1914 it wheeled
east of Paris. Second, there is no real British army to
help the French. Third, there is no eastern front, so
that, not as in 1914, the entire German army can now
be hurled against Paris. (In 1914, two army corps
were hurriedly withdrawn from France to stop the Russians in the east. How Paris and London are now paying for their short-sighted anti-Russian policy! Before
Munich, even *after* Munich, even a year ago this June,
they could have lined up the Russians against Germany.)

After my twelve forty-six broadcast tonight we were
sitting in D.'s room at the *Rundfunk* when we picked
up a broadcast from New York saying that the liner
Washington, a day out from Lisbon en route for Gal-
way, Ireland, and packed with American refugees,
mostly women and children, had been halted by an unknown submarine just at dawn and given *ten* minutes
to lower boats before being sent to the bottom. Tess
and child had booked on that voyage of the *Washington,* but had been unable to get to Bordeaux in time
after the liner had cancelled its scheduled stop at Genoa.
Finally at zero hour, after the ten minutes had elapsed,
the U-boat commander signalled: "Sorry. Mistake.
Proceed." A German naval officer, himself a U-boat
commander in the last war, happened to be listening
with me. He became quite angry. "A British submarine! No doubt of it!" he exclaimed. "Those British
will stop at nothing!" The captain added angrily,

when I suggested that maybe it might have been a
German U-boat: "Impossible. Why, a German commander who did such a thing would be court-martialled
and shot."

BERLIN, *June* 12

It *was* a German submarine that stopped the
Washington, after all.

This was officially admitted in Berlin after the Wilhelmstrasse had kept silent all day. The Germans blame
it on the State Department or our Embassy for it.
They claim that our Embassy neglected to inform the
German government that the *Washington* was proceed-
ing to Ireland from Lisbon.

If the government didn't know it, the German press
and radio certainly did. They've announced it for days.

I went over to our Embassy to check this, but they
seemed a little troubled and asked us to let the State
Department answer, which was reasonable enough. It
would have been a hell of a slip-up if they hadn't informed the Germans.

The official statement here also gives another curious
explanation. It says the "error" came about because
the German U-boat commander mistook the *Washington* for a Greek (!) steamer which he had stopped before and told to change its course. When the American
boat appeared on the horizon, he thought, says the official statement, it was the Greek boat disobeying his
instructions, and that's why he stopped it.

One might ask: (1) Have the Greeks a single vessel
anywhere near the size of the *Washington,* which is a
24,000-ton liner? The answer: No. (2) Why did a
German submarine commander order the passengers
and crew to their boats before he had properly identi-

fied the steamer? (3) If the commander thought it was
his Greek steamer, why did he wait ten minutes after
the *Washington* had signalled that it was an American
ship? These points are not taken up in the official statement. In my broadcast the censors allowed me to mention only the first point. Their view was that the last
two questions were unfair.

In view of the suspicious German warning of June 3,
in which Berlin claimed to have knowledge that the
British intended to torpedo the *Washington*, I'm convinced that Berlin itself gave orders to sink that ship.
It then intended to launch a terrific propaganda campaign charging that the British did the deed and pointing out that the German government had already
warned Washington on June 3 of what would happen.
I think Ribbentrop naïvely believed he could thus poison
Anglo-American relations and put a damper on our
sending supplies to Britain. German naval men tell me
that the U-boat held up the *Washington* just at dawn.
Washington dispatches say the ship was somewhat behind schedule. It is highly possible, then, that the German submarine commander planned to torpedo the ship
while it was still too dark for his craft to be identified.
But the *Washington* did not arrive on the scene until
dawn, a couple of hours later than expected, and the
commander refrained from launching his torpedo only
out of fear that in the prevailing light his U-boat could
be recognized as German. It was not submerged and
therefore was easily recognizable.

I had a nasty scare this afternoon. I was listening to
the three fifteen BBC broadcast when the announcer
suddenly reported that Geneva had been bombed last
night, that bombs had fallen in a residential suburb,
and that there had been killed and wounded. For a

moment I was floored. Our home is in one of the few residential suburbs.

It took hours to get through to Geneva with an urgent call. But about eight I heard Tess's voice. The bombs *did* fall in our district, she said, shook the house, and hit a hotel down the street where we formerly lived, killing five or six and injuring a score more. They had two air-raid alarms and she took the baby to the cellar. I told her she and the child must come to Germany, much as we both hate the idea. It's the safest place now. They're cut off from any possibility of getting home.

The *B.Z. am Mittag* plays up the farewell broadcast of the CBS man from Paris Monday night, probably Eric Sevareid. It quotes him as concluding: " If in the next days anyone talks to America from Paris, it won't be under the control of the French government." I suppose I'm nominated. It's my job. It will be the saddest assignment of my life.

Though the German High Command does not mention it, the truth is that the Germans are at the gates of Paris tonight. Thank God, the city will not be destroyed. Wisely the French are declaring it an open city and will not defend it. There was some question as to whether the Germans would recognize it as an open city, but about midnight it became plain that they would.

The taking of Paris will be a terrific blow to the French and the Allies. To the east of Paris, too, the Germans appear to have broken through to Châlons.

BERLIN, *June* 14

Paris has fallen. The hooked-cross flag of Hitler flutters from the Eiffel Tower there by the Seine in that Paris which I knew so intimately and loved.

This morning German troops entered the city. We got the news on the radio at one p.m., after loud fanfares had blazed away for a quarter of an hour, calling the faithful to hear the news. The news was a war communiqué from the Supreme Command. It said: " The complete collapse of the entire French front from the Channel to the Maginot Line at Montmédy destroyed the original intention of the French leaders to defend the capital of France. Paris therefore has been declared an open city. The victorious troops are just beginning to march into Paris."

I was having lunch in the courtyard of my hotel. Most of the guests crowded around the loud-speaker in the bar to hear the news. They returned to their tables with wide smiles on their faces, but there was no undue excitement and everyone resumed eating.

In fact, Berlin has taken the news of the capture of Paris as phlegmatically as it has taken everything else in this war. Later I went to Halensee for a swim, it being warm and I feeling the need of a little relaxation. It was crowded, but I overheard no one discussing the news. Out of five hundred people, three bought extras when the newsboys rushed in, shouting the news.

It would be wrong, though, to conclude that the taking of Paris has not stirred something very deep in the hearts of most Germans. It was always a wish dream of millions here. And it helps wipe out the bitter memories of 1918 which have lain so long — twenty-two years — in the German soul.

Poor Paris! I weep for her. For so many years it was my home — and I loved it as you love a woman. Said the *Völkische Beobachter* this morning: " Paris was a city of frivolity and corruption, of democracy and capitalism, where Jews had entry to the court, and

niggers to the salons. That Paris will never rise again."
But the High Command promises that its soldiers will
behave — will be " as different as night is from day,
compared to the conduct of the French soldiers in the
Rhine and Ruhr."

The High Command also said today: " The second
phase of the campaign is over with the capture of Paris.
The third phase has begun. It is the pursuit and final
destruction of the enemy."

I walked into a door in the *Herald Tribune* office
tonight. First time since the black-out that it has been
closed. Cut my nose considerably, but got it patched up
at a near-by first-aid station and recovered sufficiently
to go out and do my midnight broadcast.

Tomorrow, probably, I shall leave for Paris. I do
not want to go. I do not want to see the heavy-heeled
German boots tramping down the streets I loved.

BERLIN, *June* 15

Leaving for Paris today.

NEAR MAGDEBURG, *June* 15 (*later*)

Spending the night in a hostelry along the
Autobahn. Very good and modern, and better food
than in Berlin. Our car broke down six miles out of
Berlin on the way to Potsdam. This held us up two
hours waiting for a new car. I fear we shall not get to
Paris tomorrow. At ten p.m. in the restaurant of the
road-house we heard the news. Verdun taken! The
Verdun that cost the Germans six hundred thousand
dead the last time they *tried* to take it. And this time
they take it in one day. Granted that the French army

is in a fix; that the fall of Paris has demoralized it still further. Still you ask: What has happened to the French? Germans also claim Maginot Line broken through.

Maubeuge, *June* 16

Got up at three a.m., started at four a.m. from the little road-house for Aachen. In the Ruhr there was little evidence of the British night bombings. We arrived at Aachen at eleven a.m. Thence through Limburg to Liége and Namur. Surprised to see so little destruction along this route. It's quite unlike the road from Aachen to Brussels, where most of the towns lie in ruins. We drove all afternoon up the valley of the Meuse. Amazingly little evidence of the war. Dinner at Charleroi. Bitter faces in the streets. No bread in the town, and water only for drinking. But we got some meat and salad in a little *bistro*.

I bought the local journal, the *Journal de Charleroi*. It publishes both the German *and* French war communiqués. An order in the paper said the German troops and the Belgian gendarmerie would fire without warning into any lighted windows. Another notice from the German *Feldkommandantur* had to do with stopping any monkey business with carrier pigeons. Another signed by the chief army physician ordered all local doctors to report. Anyone unjustifiably absent, said the order, would be punished. " No excuses will be accepted," it added.

Maubeuge itself has been terribly destroyed. The main part of the town is reduced to broken stone, twisted girders, and ashes. One of the German officers tells us what happened. German tanks tried to get through the town. French anti-tank guns concealed in houses got

the first five or six. The Germans had to retreat. Word
was sent back to the Stukas. They came over and did
their job with their usual deadly efficiency. Underneath the church, the commandant tells us, was the
town's biggest air-raid shelter. One of the bombs hit
it square on. Result: five hundred civilians lie buried
under the debris. Buried air-tight, though, because on
this warm, starlit summer evening there is no smell.

One of the soldiers from South Germany later whispers to me: "Yeah, it was the Prussians who destroyed
the town." He, a common German soldier, is disgusted
with the destruction. "Always the poor people who
get it," he says.

The local commandant, a German businessman called
up from the reserve, receives us in one of the few houses
in town still standing. A few facts from him: Ten thousand out of twenty-four thousand residents of Maubeuge either have returned or rode out the bombing
and bombardment. The German army, and, since a few
days, German relief workers, help to keep them from
starving. They bring bread from Germany. But yesterday, the old boy says, he uncovered some wheat and
is getting it ground into flour. "One business," he
says, "apparently didn't close up shop at any time, during the battle or since. The local *bordel*. I finally closed
it, but the Madame came in to see me and was very put
out. ' Business as usual, why not? ' she said." Yesterday, he reveals, the High Command ordered the opening of all houses of prostitution in the part of France
occupied by German troops. "I must send for the
Madame. She will be pleased to hear it," he chuckles.

We consume several bottles of pretty fair *vin rouge*
and nibble biscuits, and the commandant talks on en-
thusiastically about his problem. Obviously he enjoys
his job, and he is certainly not the old sadistic Prussian

master of the story-books. On the whole, a very human
fellow. Homesick, I gather. Hoping the war won't last
much longer. Somehow it's worse, he thinks, than what
he went through the four years of the World War in
this very district. But perhaps that is because it's so
recent, and the old memories blurred. Anyway, he talks
of his dog and his wife and family.

We finally take our leave. An orderly shows us our
quarters, in an abandoned house with atrocious pseudo-
Oriental furnishings, which, we soon establish from the
wall-hangings and papers lying around, was occupied
by one of the leading local bankers. French bourgeois
taste at its very lowest. I take to myself one of the
family bedrooms. The mattress is still on the old-
fashioned double bed. The banker's clothes hang neatly
in the *armoire*. Even the long-tailed black coat — you
can see him, fat and important, strolling through the
streets to church on Sundays in it — is there. Obviously he has left in a great hurry. No time to pack his
wardrobe. Downstairs we noticed the breakfast dishes
on the dining-room table. A meal never finished.

What a break in his comfortable bourgeois life this
must have been, this hasty flight before the town was
blown up! Here in this house — until last month —
solidity, a certain comfort, respectability; the odds and
ends collected for a house during a lifetime. This house
one's life, such as it is. Then boom! The Stukas. The
shells. And that life, like the houses all around, blown
to bits; the solidity, the respectability, the hopes, gone
in a jiffy. And you and your wife and maybe your children along the roads now, hungry, craving for a drink
of water — like an animal, or at best — and who would
have dreamed it a month ago! — like a caveman.

Three soldiers take us for a stroll through the debris
of the town as dusk falls. Just inside the town gates

a frowsy-looking woman is digging in a pile of bricks. The soldiers shout for her to beat it. It is after the curfew hour. She continues digging. One of the men, grasping his rifle, steps over to chase her away. We hear her shout: " *Coucher?* " She asks him to go to bed with her. By God, all is not destroyed here. The soldier laughs and sort of pushes her on her way. Apparently she is living in a cellar near by — like a rat. We continue through the town and pretty soon we see her over the shambles of what was once an alley. She shouts: " *Coucher?* " and then runs. We walk through the town, pausing before what is left of the church. It is hard to grasp that under those charred bricks and rubble five hundred women and children lie buried. There is so much debris that their grave has been perfectly sealed. There is not a whiff of the familiar, nauseating, sweet smell.

Back to our banker's house as darkness comes. Outside, the army trucks roll by all night long. Once during the night I hear some anti-aircraft going into action down the road. Up at dawn, feeling not too bad, and off towards Paris.

Paris, *June* 17

It was no fun for me. When we drove into Paris, down the familiar streets, I had an ache in the pit of my stomach and I wished I had not come. My German companions were in high spirits at the sight of the city.

We came in about noon, and it was one of those lovely June days which Paris always has in this month and which, if there had been peace, would have been spent by the people going to the races at Longchamp or the tennis at Roland Garros, or idling along the boulevards under the trees, or on the cool terraces of a café.

First shock: the streets are utterly deserted, the stores closed, the shutters down tight over all the windows. It was the emptiness that got you. Coming from Le Bourget (remembering, sentimentally, that night I raced afoot all the way into town from there to write the story of Lindbergh's landing), we drove down the rue Lafayette. German army cars and motorcycles speeding, screaming down the street. But on the sidewalks not a human being. The various corner cafés along the street which I knew so well. They had taken in the tables and drawn the shutters. And had fled — the *patrons,* the *garçons,* the customers. Our two cars roared down the rue Lafayette, honking at every street we crossed, until I asked our driver to desist.

There, on the corner, the *Petit Journal* building in which I had worked for the Chicago *Tribune* when I first came to Paris in 1925. Across from it, the Trois Portes café — how many pleasant hours idled there when Paris, to me, was beautiful and gorgeous; and my home!

We turned left down the rue Pelletier to the Grand Boulevard. I noticed the Petit Riche was closed. The boulevard too was deserted except for a few German soldiers, staring into the windows of the few shops that did not have their shutters down. The Place de l'Opéra now. For the first time in my life, no traffic tie-up here, no French cops shouting meaninglessly at cars hopelessly blocked. The façade of the Opera House was hidden behind stacked sandbags. The Café de la Paix seemed to be just reopening. A lone *garçon* was bringing out some tables and chairs. German soldiers stood on the terrace grabbing them. Then we turned at the Madeleine, its façade also covered with sandbags, and raced down the rue Royale. Larue's and Weber's, I

noted, were closed. Now before us, the familiar view.
The Place de la Concorde, the Seine, the Chambre des
Députés, over which a giant Swastika flag flies, and in
the distance the golden dome of the Invalides. Past the
Ministry of the Marine, guarded by a big German tank,
into the Concorde. We drew up in front of the Hôtel
Crillon, now German Headquarters. Our officer went
in to inquire about quarters. I, to the displeasure of the
German officials with us, stepped over to pay a call at
the American Embassy next door. Bullitt, Murphy —
everyone I knew — were out to lunch. I left a note for
Bullitt.

We got rooms in the Scribe, where I had often stayed
in the civilized days. To my surprise and pleasure, Demaree Bess and Walter Kerr, who had stayed on in
Paris after almost all of their colleagues had left, were
in the lobby. They came up to my room and we had a
talk. Walter seemed more nervous than ever, but just
as likable. Demaree was his old stolid self. He and
Dorothy had been in the Élysées Park Hotel on the
Rond-Point. The day before the city fell, the *patron* of
the hotel had come panting to them and begged them
to flee too; at any rate, he was scooting and closing the
hotel. They persuaded him to turn the hotel over to
them! . . . I inquired about my friends. Most of them
had left Paris.

Demaree says the panic in Paris was indescribable.
Everyone lost his head. The government gave no lead.
People were told to scoot, and at least three million out
of the five million in the city ran, ran without baggage,
literally ran on their feet towards the south. It seems
the Parisians actually believed the Germans would rape
the women and do worse to the men. They had heard
fantastic tales of what happened when the Germans occupied a city. The ones who stayed are all the more

amazed at the very correct behaviour of the troops —
so far.

The inhabitants are bitter at their government, which
in the last days, from all I hear, completely collapsed.
It even forgot to tell the people until too late that Paris
would not be defended. The French police and fire departments remained. A curious sight to see the *agents*,
minus their pistols, directing traffic, which consists exclusively of German army vehicles, or patrolling the
streets. I have a feeling that what we're seeing here
in Paris is the complete breakdown of French society
— a collapse of the army, of government, of the morale
of the people. It is almost too tremendous to believe.

Paris, *June* 18

Marshal Pétain has asked for an armistice!
The Parisians, already dazed by all that has happened,
can scarcely believe it. Nor can the rest of us. That
the French army must give up is clear. But most of us
expected it to surrender, as did the Dutch and Belgian
armies, with the government going, as Reynaud had
boasted it would, to Africa, where France, with its navy
and African armies, can hold out for a long time.

The inhabitants got the news of Pétain's action by
loud-speaker, conveniently provided by the Germans in
nearly every square in town. I stood in a throng of
French men and women on the Place de la Concorde
when the news first came. They were almost struck
dead. Before the Hôtel Crillon — where Woodrow Wilson stayed during the Peace Conference when the terms
for Germany were being drawn up — cars raced up
and unloaded gold-braided officers. There was much
peering through monocles, heel-clicking, saluting. In
the Place there, that square without equal in Europe,

where you can see from one spot the Madeleine, the
Louvre, Notre-Dame in the distance down the Seine,
the Chamber of Deputies, the golden dome of the Invalides, where Napoleon is buried, then the Eiffel Tower,
on which floats today a huge Swastika, and finally, up
the Champs-Élysées, the Arc de Triomphe — the people in the Place de la Concorde did not notice the bustle
in front of German Headquarters at the Crillon. They
stared at the ground, then at each other. They said:
" Pétain surrendering! What does it mean? *Comment? Pourquoi?* " And no one appeared to have the
heart for an answer.

This evening Paris is weird and, to me, unrecogniz-
able. There's a curfew at nine p.m. — an hour before
dark. The black-out is still enforced. The streets tonight are dark and deserted. The Paris of gay lights,
the laughter, the music, the women in the streets —
when was that? And what is this?

I noticed today some open fraternizing between German troops and the inhabitants. Most of the soldiers
seem to be Austrian, are well mannered; and quite a
few speak French. Most of the German troops act like
naïve tourists, and this has proved a pleasant surprise
to the Parisians. It seems funny, but every German
soldier carries a camera. I saw them by the thousands
today, photographing Notre-Dame, the Arc de Triomphe, the Invalides. Thousands of German soldiers
congregate all day long at the Tomb of the Unknown
Soldier, where the flame still burns under the Arc. They
bare their blond heads and stand there gazing.

Two newspapers appeared yesterday in Paris, *La
Victoire* (as life's irony would have it) and *Le Matin.*
I saw Bueno-Varilla, publisher of the *Matin*, at the Em-
bassy yesterday. I'm told he's anxious to please the

Germans and see that his paper gets off to a favourable
start. It has already begun to attack England, to blame
England for France's predicament! *La Victoire*, run
by a crank, urges Parisians no longer to refer to the
Germans as " *Boches.*" Its editorial yesterday ended:
" *Vive Paris! Vive la France!* "

The German army moved into Bess's hotel yesterday,
but they valiantly held on to their floor.

PARIS, *June* 19

The armistice is to be signed at Compiègne!
In the same *wagon-lit* coach of Marshal Foch that witnessed the signing of that other armistice on November 11, 1918 in Compiègne Forest. The French don't
know it yet. The Germans are keeping it secret. But
through somebody's mistake I found out today.

At four thirty p.m. the military rushed me out to
Compiègne. That was the mistake. They shouldn't
have. But orders got mixed up, and before they could
get unentangled I was there. Yesterday Hitler and
Mussolini met at Munich to draw up the armistice terms
for France. Driving out, I recalled that yesterday I
had asked a German Foreign Office official, half jokingly, if Hitler (as rumour had it) would insist on the
armistice being signed at Compiègne. He did not like
my question and replied coolly: " Certainly not."

But when we arrived on the scene at six p.m., German
army engineers were feverishly engaged in tearing out
the wall of the museum where Foch's private car in
which the 1918 armistice was signed had been preserved.
The building itself was donated by one Arthur Henry
Fleming of Pasadena, California. Before we left, the
engineers, working with pneumatic drills, had demolished the wall and hauled the car out from its shelter.

The plan is, the Nazis tell me, to place the car in exactly the same spot it occupied in the little clearing in Compiègne Forest that morning at five a.m. on November 11, 1918, and make the French sign *this* armistice here. . . . We talked over technical details for broadcasting the story with various German officers and officials. It will make a spectacular broadcast, but a tragic one for Americans. Some colonel showed me through the armistice car. Place cards on the table showed where each had sat at that historic meeting in 1918.

Returning to Paris towards evening, we stopped on the road that winds over the wooded hills between Compiègne and Senlis. A small French column had been bombed there on the road. Scattered along a quarter of a mile were twenty hastily dug graves. The dead horses, buried very shallow, still stunk. A " 75 " stood near the road with the other leavings, which from the look of them — blankets, coats, shoes, socks, guns, ammunition, etc. — had been abandoned in great haste. I looked at the date of the cannon. 1918! Here the French defended the most important road to the capital with World War guns!

It is still a mystery to me how this campaign has been won so easily by Hitler. Admitted, the French fought in the towns. But even in the towns not many of the millions of men available could have fought. There was not room. But they did not fight in the fields, as in all other wars. The grain twenty yards from the main roads has not been touched by the tramping feet of soldiers or their tens of thousands of motorized vehicles. I do not mean to say that at many places the French did not fight valiantly. Undoubtedly they did, But there was no *organized*, well-thought-out defence

as in the last war. From all I've seen, the French let
the Germans dictate a new kind of warfare. This was
fought largely along the main roads; rarely on a line
running across the country. And on the roads the Germans had everything in their favour: utter superiority
in tanks and planes, the main implements for road
fighting. An Austrian soldier told me last night that
it was unbelievably simple. They went down the roads
with tanks, with artillery support in the rear. Seldom
did they meet any serious resistance. Dug-outs or posts
here and there would fire. Usually the heavily armoured
German tanks paid no attention, just continued down
the road. Infantry units on trucks behind, with light
artillery, would liquidate the pillboxes and the machine-
gun nests. Once in a while, if resistance was a little
strong, they'd phone or radio or signal back for the
artillery. If the big guns didn't silence it, an order went
back for the Stukas, which invariably did. So it went,
he said, day after day.

I keep asking myself: If the French were making a
serious defence, why are the main roads never blown
up? Why so many strategic bridges left untouched?
Here and there along the roads, a tank barrier, that is,
a few logs or stones or debris — but nothing really
serious for the tanks. No real tank-*traps*, such as the
Swiss built by the thousands.

This has been a war of machines down the main highways, and the French do not appear to have been ready
for it, to have understood it, or to have had anything
ready to stop it. This is incredible.

General Glaise von Horstenau (an Austrian who
betrayed Schuschnigg shamelessly and has now been
named by Hitler one of the chief official historians of
this war) put it another way last night. His idea is
that Germany caught the Allies at one of the rare mo-

ments in military history when, for a few weeks or
months or years, offensive weapons are superior to those
of defence. He explains that this fantastic campaign
probably could have taken place only in this summer
of 1940. Had it been delayed until next year, the Allies
would have had the defensive weapons — anti-tank
guns, anti-aircraft guns, and fighter airplanes — to
have offset the offensive arms of Germany. There then
would have ensued, he thinks, the kind of stalemate
which developed on the western front from 1914 to
1918, when the powers of offence and defence were about
equal.

Another thing: I do not think the losses on either
side have been large. You see so few graves.

PARIS, *June* 20

The men who went down to Orléans and Blois
yesterday tell a horrible tale. Along the road they saw
what they estimated to be 200,000 refugees — people
of all classes, rich and poor, lying along the roadside
or by the edge of the forests, starving — without food,
without water, no shelter, nothing.

They are just a few of the millions who fled Paris
and the other cities and towns before the German in-
vaders. They fled, tearing in fright along the roads
with their belongings on their backs or on bikes or in
baby-carriages, and their children atop them. Soon the
roads were clogged. Troops also were trying to use
them. Soon the Germans came over, bombing the roads.
Soon there were dead and dying. And no food, no
water, no shelter, no care. Bullitt estimates there are
seven million refugees between here and Bordeaux. Almost all face starvation unless something is done at
once. The German army is helping a little, but not

much. It has had to carry most of its own food into
France from Germany. The Red Cross is doing what
it can, but is wholly inadequate.

A human catastrophe, such as even China has not experienced. (And how many Frenchmen or other Europeans softened their hearts when a flood or a famine
or a war snuffed out a million Chinese?)

Lunch with Bullitt, at his residence. He is still
stunned by what has happened. Though Hitler, Ribbentrop, and Goebbels hate him almost as much as they
loathe Roosevelt, he reported that the German military
authorities had shown him every courtesy. The Nazis
had made the three American representatives of the
three American press associations pledge not to see
Bullitt or even call at the American Embassy (a pledge
they scrupulously kept, though Fred Oechsner had the
courage to phone the Embassy and pay his respects).
I feel under no obligation not to act as a free American
citizen here, despite Nazi pressure, and gladly accepted
the invitation of the Ambassador, whom I've known for
many years. Most talkative guest at lunch was M.
Henry-Haye,[1] senator, and mayor of Versailles. He is
one of the few politicians who stuck to his post. His
bitterness at the British during the luncheon talk was
only matched by his bitterness at the Germans. I
couldn't tell which he blamed most for the French collapse; he sputtered away at both. He was in a great
state of emotion. Yesterday, he related, a young German officer had brushed into his mayoralty office at Versailles and summarily ordered him to have his car repaired. If the car wasn't ready in an hour, said the
German, M. Henry-Haye would be arrested. This was
too much for the senator-mayor.

[1] Later named by Marshal Pétain French Ambassador in Washington.

" You are speaking, sir," he said he told the German,
" to a French senator and the mayor of Versailles. I
shall report your conduct immediately to your military
superiors in Paris."

Whereupon, though his gasoline supply was short, he
sped off to Paris to make good his word.

" *Oh, les Boches!* " he kept muttering, a word which,
I must say, we all tossed across the table with some fre-
quency.

PARIS, *June* 21

On the exact spot in the little clearing in the
Forest of Compiègne where at five a.m. on November
11, 1918 the armistice which ended the World War was
signed, Adolf Hitler today handed *his* armistice terms
to France. To make German revenge complete, the
meeting of the German and French plenipotentiaries
took place in Marshal Foch's private car, in which Foch
laid down the armistice terms to Germany twenty-two
years ago. Even the same table in the rickety old
wagon-lit car was used. And through the windows we
saw Hitler occupying the very seat on which Foch had
sat at that table when he dictated the other armistice.

The humiliation of France, of the French, was complete. And yet in the preamble to the armistice terms
Hitler told the French that he had not chosen this spot
at Compiègne out of revenge; merely to right an old
wrong. From the demeanour of the French delegates I
gathered that they did not appreciate the difference.

The German terms we do not know yet. The preamble says the general basis for them is: (1) to prevent
a resumption of the fighting; (2) to offer Germany
complete guarantees for her continuation of the war
against Britain; (3) to create the foundations for a

peace, the basis of which is to be the reparation of an injustice inflicted upon Germany by force. The third point seems to mean: revenge for the defeat of 1918.

Kerker for NBC and I for CBS in a joint half-hour broadcast early this evening described today's amazing scene as best we could. It made, I think, a good broadcast.

The armistice negotiations began at three fifteen p.m. A warm June sun beat down on the great elm and pine trees, and cast pleasant shadows on the wooded avenues as Hitler, with the German plenipotentiaries at his side, appeared. He alighted from his car in front of the French monument to Alsace-Lorraine which stands at the end of an avenue about two hundred yards from the clearing where the armistice car waits on exactly the same spot it occupied twenty-two years ago.

The Alsace-Lorraine statue, I noted, was covered with German war flags so that you could not see its sculptured work nor read its inscription. But I had seen it some years before — the large sword representing the sword of the Allies, and its point sticking into a large, limp eagle, representing the old Empire of the Kaiser. And the inscription underneath in French saying: "TO THE HEROIC SOLDIERS OF FRANCE . . . DEFENDERS OF THE COUNTRY AND OF RIGHT . . . GLORIOUS LIBERATORS OF ALSACE–LOR-RAINE."

Through my glasses I saw the Führer stop, glance at the monument, observe the Reich flags with their big Swastikas in the centre. Then he strode slowly towards us, towards the little clearing in the woods. I observed his face. It was grave, solemn, yet brimming with revenge. There was also in it, as in his springy step, a note of the triumphant conqueror, the defier of the world. There was something else, difficult to describe, in his expression, a sort of scornful, inner joy at being present at this great reversal of fate — a reversal he himself had wrought.

Now he reaches the little opening in the woods. He pauses and looks slowly around. The clearing is in the form of a circle some two hundred yards in diameter and laid out like a park. Cypress trees line it all round — and behind them, the great elms and oaks of the forest. This has been one of France's national shrines for twenty-two years. From a discreet position on the perimeter of the circle we watch.

Hitler pauses, and gazes slowly around. In a group just behind him are the other German plenipotentiaries: Göring, grasping his field-marshal's baton in one hand. He wears the sky-blue uniform of the air force. All the Germans are in uniform, Hitler in a double-breasted grey uniform, with the Iron Cross hanging from his left breast pocket. Next to Göring are the two German army chiefs — General Keitel, chief of the Supreme Command, and General von Brauchitsch, commander-in-chief of the German army. Both are just approaching sixty, but look younger, especially Keitel, who has a dapper appearance with his cap slightly cocked on one side.

Then there is Erich Raeder, Grand Admiral of the German Fleet, in his blue naval uniform and the invariable upturned collar which German naval officers usually wear. There are two non-military men in Hitler's suite — his Foreign Minister, Joachim von Ribbentrop, in the field-grey uniform of the Foreign Office; and Rudolf Hess, Hitler's deputy, in a grey party uniform.

The time is now three eighteen p.m. Hitler's personal flag is run up on a small standard in the centre of the opening.

Also in the centre is a great granite block which stands some three feet above the ground. Hitler, followed by the others, walks slowly over to it, steps up, and reads the inscription engraved in great high letters on that block. It says: "HERE ON THE ELEVENTH OF NOVEMBER 1918 SUCCUMBED THE CRIMINAL PRIDE OF THE GERMAN EMPIRE . . . VANQUISHED BY THE FREE PEOPLES WHICH IT TRIED TO ENSLAVE."

Hitler reads it and Göring reads it. They all read it, standing there in the June sun and the silence. I look for the expression on Hitler's face. I am but fifty yards from him and see him through my glasses as though he were directly in front of me. I have seen that face many times at the great moments of his life. But today! It is afire with scorn, anger, hate, revenge, triumph. He steps off the monument and contrives to make even this gesture a masterpiece of contempt. He glances back at it, contemptuous, angry — angry, you almost feel, because he cannot wipe out the awful, provoking lettering with one sweep of his high Prussian boot. He glances slowly around the clearing, and now, as his eyes meet ours, you grasp the depth of his hatred. But there is triumph there too — revengeful, triumphant hate. Suddenly, as though his face were not giving quite complete expression to his feelings, he throws his whole body into harmony with his mood. He swiftly snaps his hands on his hips, arches his shoulders, plants his feet wide apart. It is a magnificent gesture of defiance, of burning contempt for this place now and all that it has stood for in the twenty-two years since it witnessed the humbling of the German Empire.

Finally Hitler leads his party over to another granite stone, a smaller one fifty yards to one side. Here it was that the railroad car in which the German plenipoten-

tiaries stayed during the 1918 armistice was placed —
from November 8 to 11. Hitler merely glances at the
inscription, which reads: "The German Plenipotentiaries." The stone itself, I notice, is set between a pair
of rusty old railroad tracks, the ones on which the German car stood twenty-two years ago. Off to one side
along the edge of the clearing is a large statue in white
stone of Marshal Foch as he looked when he stepped out
of the armistice car on the morning of November 11,
1918. Hitler skips it; does not appear to see it.

It is now three twenty-three p.m. and the Germans
stride over to the armistice car. For a moment or two
they stand in the sunlight outside the car, chatting.
Then Hitler steps up into the car, followed by the
others. We can see nicely through the car windows.
Hitler takes the place occupied by Marshal Foch when
the 1918 armistice terms were signed. The others
spread themselves around him. Four chairs on the opposite side of the table from Hitler remain empty. The
French have not yet appeared. But we do not wait long.
Exactly at three thirty p.m. they alight from a car.
They have flown up from Bordeaux to a near-by landing field. They too glance at the Alsace-Lorraine memorial, but it's a swift glance. Then they walk down the
avenue flanked by three German officers. We see them
now as they come into the sunlight of the clearing.

General Huntziger, wearing a bleached khaki uniform, Air General Bergeret and Vice-Admiral Le Luc,
both in dark blue uniforms, and then, almost buried in
the uniforms, M. Noël, French Ambassador to Poland.
The German guard of honour, drawn up at the entrance
to the clearing, snaps to attention for the French as they
pass, but it does not present arms.

It is a grave hour in the life of France. The Frenchmen keep their eyes straight ahead. Their faces are

solemn, drawn. They are the picture of tragic dignity.

They walk stiffly to the car, where they are met by two German officers, Lieutenant-General Tippelskirch, Quartermaster General, and Colonel Thomas, chief of the Führer's headquarters. The Germans salute. The French salute. The atmosphere is what Europeans call " correct." There are salutes, but no handshakes.

Now we get our picture through the dusty windows of that old *wagon-lit* car. Hitler and the other German leaders rise as the French enter the drawing-room. Hitler gives the Nazi salute, the arm raised. Ribbentrop and Hess do the same. I cannot see M. Noël to notice whether he salutes or not.

Hitler, as far as we can see through the windows, does not say a word to the French or to anybody else. He nods to General Keitel at his side. We see General Keitel adjusting his papers. Then he starts to read. He is reading the preamble to the German armistice terms. The French sit there with marble-like faces and listen intently. Hitler and Göring glance at the green table-top.

The reading of the preamble lasts but a few minutes. Hitler, we soon observe, has no intention of remaining very long, of listening to the reading of the armistice terms themselves. At three forty-two p.m., twelve minutes after the French arrive, we see Hitler stand up, salute stiffly, and then stride out of the drawing-room, followed by Göring, Brauchitsch, Raeder, Hess, and Ribbentrop. The French, like figures of stone, remain at the green-topped table. General Keitel remains with them. He starts to read them the detailed conditions of the armistice.

Hitler and his aides stride down the avenue towards the Alsace-Lorraine monument, where their cars are waiting. As they pass the guard of honour, the German band strikes up the two national anthems, *Deutschland, Deutschland über Alles* and the *Horst Wessel* song. The whole ceremony in which Hitler has reached a new pinnacle in his meteoric career and Germany avenged the 1918 defeat is over in a quarter of an hour.

P A R I S , *June 22* (*midnight*)

       Too tired to write of today. Here is what I broadcast:

" The armistice has been signed. The armistice between France and Germany was signed at exactly six fifty p.m., German summer time — that is, one hour and twenty-five minutes ago. . . . It was signed here in the same old railroad coach in the middle of Compiègne Forest where the armistice of November 11, 1918 was made. . . . Now the armistice, though signed by the French and the Germans, does not go into effect yet. We've been informed that the French delegation is leaving by special plane for Italy. When it gets there, Italy will lay down armistice terms for ceasing *its* war with France. . . . As soon as the French and Italians sign, the news will be flashed to the Germans. They will immediately inform the French government at Bordeaux. And then, six hours after this, the fighting stops, the guns cease fire, the airplanes come down, the blood-letting of war is at an end. That is, between Germany and Italy on the one hand, and France on the other. The war with Britain, of course, goes on. . . .

" The negotiations for this armistice have gone much faster than anyone expected. There has been a good deal of telephoning and telegraphing between here and Bordeaux by the French. One of the little wonders of this war was a telegraph line to Bordeaux which went right through both the front lines where they're still fighting.

" As a matter of fact, late last night the Germans and French succeeded in establishing *telephone* contact between the plenipotentiaries here at Compiègne and the French government at Bordeaux. A few minutes ago I listened to a recording of the first conversation as they were establishing the first communication. It's an interesting record, if a minor one, for history.

" The Germans got the telephone line going as far as the Loire River at Tours. There German army engineers strung a line over a bridge across the river, where it was hooked up, strangely and miraculously enough, with the French telephone central, which carried it on to Bordeaux. We could hear the German telephonist here in Compiègne say: ' Hello, Bordeaux. Hello, the French government in Bordeaux!' He said it in both French and German. It sounded uncanny, and it must have been, too, to the French when he said in French: ' *Ici la centrale de l'armée allemande à Compiègne.* Here's the headquarters of the German army at Compiègne, calling the French government at Bordeaux.' The line was very good, and we could hear the telephonist in Bordeaux very clearly. The line was then turned over to the French government and their delegates here.

" And so the negotiations went on last night and today for the ending of the war. Occasionally the French delegation would return to the car from their tent for further talks with General Keitel. About midnight last night the talks were broken off and the French delegates, though cots had been provided for them in their tent, were driven by the Germans into Paris, some fifty miles away, where they spent the night. The city must have seemed strange to them.

" The French delegates returned to Compiègne Forest this morning. About ten thirty a.m. we saw them filing into Marshal Foch's old Pullman coach. They remained for an hour and then General Keitel arrived. Through the windows we could see them talking and going over various papers. At one thirty p.m. there was a recess so that the French could contact their government in Bordeaux for the last time.

" And then came the big moment. At six fifty p.m. the gentlemen in the car started affixing their signatures to Germany's armistice conditions. General Keitel signed for Germany; General Huntziger for France.

" It was all over in a few moments."

And now to depart from my broadcast to set down a scene which I gave to Kerker for his part of the transmission. I know that the Germans have hidden microphones in the armistice car. I seek out a sound-truck in the woods. No one stops me and so I pause to listen. It is just before the armistice is signed. I hear General Huntziger's voice, strained, quivering. I note down his exact words in French. They come out slowly, with great effort, one at a time. He says: " I declare the French government has ordered me to sign these terms of armistice. I desire to read a personal declaration. Forced by the fate of arms to cease the struggle in which we were engaged on the side of the Allies, France sees imposed on her very hard conditions. France has the right to expect in the future negotiations that Germany show a spirit which will permit the two great neighbouring countries to live and work peacefully."

Then I hear the scratching of pens, a few muffled remarks from the French. Later someone, watching through the window, tells me Admiral Le Luc fights back the tears as the document is signed. Then the deep voice of Keitel: " I request all members of the

German and French delegations to rise in order to fulfil a duty which the brave German and French soldiers have merited. Let us honour by rising from our seats all those who have bled for their fatherland and all those who have died for their country." There is a minute of silence as they all stand.

As I finished speaking into the microphone, a drop of rain fell on my forehead. Down the road, through the woods, I could see the refugees, slowly, tiredly, filing by — on weary feet, on bicycles, on carts, a few on trucks, an endless line. They were exhausted and dazed, those walking were footsore, and they did not know yet that an armistice had been signed and that the fighting would be over very soon now.

I walked out to the clearing. The sky was overcast and rain was coming on. An army of German engineers, shouting lustily, had already started to move the armistice car.

" Where to? " I asked.

" To Berlin," they said.

PARIS, *June* 23

It seems we had something of a scoop yesterday. We beat the world with the announcement that the armistice had been signed, not to mention a detailed description of it. Some of those who helped us get it are catching hell. I had no idea we'd had a scoop until this morning when Walter Kerr told me he had picked up some American broadcast last night. For two or three hours, he says, we were the only ones with the news. Some of our commentators, he says, appeared to grow a little nervous as the hours ticked by and there was no confirmation. They were probably thinking of the premature U.P. story on the armistice on November 7, 1918.

I got my first night's sleep in a week, and felt a little better. Breakfasted at noon at the Café de la Paix with Joe [Harsch] and Walter on café crème and brioches, and the sun on the terrace was warm and soothing. At one we went down the street to Philippe's, where we had a nice lunch, the first decent one since arriving.

Then Joe and I made a little " Sentimental Journey." On foot, because there are no cars, buses, or taxis. We walked down through the Place Vendôme and thought of Napoleon. Pushed on through the Tuileries. It made my heart feel a little better to see so many children about. They were playing on the seesaws. The merry-go-round was turning with its load of children, until an irate *agent* for some reason (to curry favour with the Germans?) closed it down.

It was an exquisite June day, and we stopped to admire the view (my millionth, surely!) up the Tuileries to the Champs-Élysées, with the silhouette of the Arc de Triomphe on the horizon. It was as good as ever. Then through the Louvre and across the Seine. The fishermen were dangling their lines from the bank, as always. I thought: " Surely this will go on to the end of Paris, to the end of time . . . men fishing in the Seine." I stopped, as I have always stopped a thousand times, to see if — after all these years — I might witness one man at last having at least a bite. But though they jerked their lines out continually, no one caught a fish. I have never seen a fish caught in the Seine.

Then down the Seine to Notre-Dame. The sandbags had been removed from the central portal. We stopped

to observe it. Inside the Cathedral the light was too
strong, with the original rose window and the two tran-
sept windows out. But from up the river as we had approached, the view of the façade, the Gothic in all its
glory, was superb. We went round behind. The grace
of the flying buttresses that support the upper part of
the nave!

Then I turned guide for Joe. Took him to the near-by
Church of Saint-Julien-le-Pauvre, the oldest in Paris,
then down the little street past the Hôtel Du Caveau,
in whose cellars we had had some nights in my younger
days. I showed him, a little farther down, the *bordel*
across the eighteen-foot-wide street from the police station. Apparently the whores had all fled, like almost all
of the good people of France. Then up past the Cluny,
which was closed, stopping at the statue of Montaigne
with its eloquent quotation about Paris being the " glory
of France." We stopped for a beer at the Balzar, next
to the Sorbonne, a pub where I had spent so many
nights in my first years in Paris after 1925. Then, since
this was a " Sentimental Journey," naked and un-
ashamed, we hit up the Boulevard Saint-Michel, then
up the rue de Vaugirard to the Hôtel de Lisbonne, where
I had lived for two years when I first came to Paris. The
Lisbonne looked as dirty and dilapidated as ever. But,
according to the sign, they'd added a bath. No such
sign of civilization when I lived there.

Then the Panthéon, from the Boulevard Saint-
Michel, and then through the Luxembourg Gardens, as
lovely as ever, and crowded with children, as ever, which
cheered me up again, and the statues of the Queens of
France around the central pond, and at the pond the
kids sailing their boats, and the Palace off to one side,
and a pretty girl sitting under the statue of the Queen
so-and-so who reigned, I noticed, as we took our eyes

off the beautiful thing, in 1100 and something.

And then Montparnasse, with apéritifs on the side-walk of the Rotonde, and the Dôme across the street as jammed with crackpots as ever, and in front of us a large table full of middle-aged French women of the bourgeoisie, apparently recovering from their daze, because their anger was rising at the way the little *gamins* (*elles sont françaises, après tout!*) were picking up the German soldiers.

And then a walk back, with a drink at the Deux Magots across from Saint-Germain-des-Prés, whose solid tower seemed more comforting today than ever before, and down the rue Bonaparte past the bookshops, the art shops, so civilized, past the house where Tess and I had lived in 1934. Across the Seine again, and Joe wanted to stroll in the gardens of the Palais Royal, which we did, and they were as peaceful as ever before, and as still, except for the German planes roaring overhead.

And thence to our hotel, filled with German soldiers, and outside, on the boulevard, a long column of German artillery roaring by.

BERLIN, *June 26*

Returned from Paris. We left there at seven a.m. and drove through the " battlefields " (more accurately, the destroyed towns where what fighting there was in this war took place) to Brussels. The German officers and officials said they wanted to have one last square meal before returning to the *Vaterland*, so I took them around to the Taverne Royale. We stuffed on hors d'œuvres, steak, mountains of vegetables, and fresh strawberries and cream, washing it all down with two bottles of quite good Château Margaux.

En route to Brussels we passed through Compiègne, Noyon, Valenciennes, and Mons — all well smashed up. But except in the towns I could see no evidence of any serious fighting. Abandoned Allies' tanks and trucks here and there, but no sign along the roads that the French had offered serious resistance. The French and Belgians in the towns still seemed numbed, but not particularly resentful, as one might have expected. As elsewhere, they acted extremely civil to the German troops.

An attaché of the German Embassy in Brussels accompanied us as far as Louvain, and the reason soon became evident. In Louvain we were driven straight to the charred remains of the library. As we stepped out of our cars, it just *happened* that a priest came up on a bicycle and greeted us. It just happened that he seemed to be on good terms with the German Embassy official. The two of them then related the story the propagandists had given me some weeks before on the same spot — namely, that the British had fired the library of Louvain University before their retreat.

I admit there are some points that bother me. None of the near-by buildings, some of which are only fifty feet from the library, suffered any damage at all. Even their windows are intact. The Germans and the Belgian priest kept harping on this as proof that no German bombs could have hit the library. On the other hand, I notice two small shell-holes in the tower, which still stands. And incendiary bombs dropped on the library wouldn't have disturbed the adjacent buildings. True, if many had been dropped, some would have missed the target and set the near-by houses on fire.

The priest, who said he was one of the librarians, explained that the priceless manuscripts were kept in fireproof vaults in the basement. He then claimed that the British had started the fire in the basement and had ac-

tually set fires going in the fire-proof vaults. He and
the Germans kept emphasizing that it was obvious from
the looks of the charred remains, girders and all,
that the fire had been started from the basement. But
this wasn't obvious to me.

Approaching the German border towards sundown,
we avoided the Maastricht-Aachen road because the
German Embassy in Brussels had told our Germans
that the Reich customs people there would be very strict
with us; and our two cars were loaded down with booty
purchased with marks forced on the French at the
thievish rate of twenty francs to one mark. The German officers and officials had raided Paris, buying suits,
Scotch woollens for making suits, handbags, silk stockings, perfumes, underwear, etc. We drove around for
hours trying to find a lonely customs post. The nearer
to the border we approached, the more nervous the Germans became. An officer of the High Command — one
of the most decent Germans I know — kept pointing out
to me how embarrassing it would be for him, in uniform,
to be caught red-handed bringing in so much booty.
He said his fellow officers had been abusing their opportunities so scandalously that Hitler himself a few
days before had issued a blunt order to the customs
guards to seize everything found on returning officers
or men. I finally offered to take the blame, if it came
to a showdown, and explain to the customs people that
the booty was all mine.

The little valley east of Liége was green and cool in
the late afternoon, and there was little trace of the war
except for one destroyed village and the blown-up
bridges of the main railroad line to Aachen. Finally
we arrived at the German border. Our chauffeur, a
private, who had certainly bought his share of the booty
in Paris, became so nervous he almost ran down and

killed the customs officer. But our High Command officer spoke convincingly and fast, and we got through with our plunder.

Arrived in Aachen just in time to catch the night train to Berlin. Stiff and cold from fatigue and lack of sleep, I slumped into my upper berth and fell immediately into a heavy slumber. This was about ten p.m. About eleven thirty I was awakened by a furious shrieking of the sirens. By the noise, I could tell we were in a station (Duisburg, I later learned). The siren had hardly stopped before the train got off with a tremendous jerk and gathered speed so rapidly I thought some of the curves would surely derail us. I was now fully awakened and not a little scared — to be perfectly honest. Above the noise of the train, I could hear the British bombers flying low, then diving still lower, and obviously trying to get us. (Kerker said next morning he *saw* them from the car window.) Apparently the British in the end gave our train up as small fry, which it was. I felt no bomb explosions, at least. The sound of the British planes died away. Our engineer slowed down the train to a reasonable speed. I went back to sleep.

BERLIN, *June* 27

To sum up:

Make some reservations. That it is too early to know all. That you didn't see all, by any means. And all that.

But from what I've seen in Belgium and France and from talks I've had with Germans and French in both countries, and with French, Belgian, and British prisoners along the roads, it seems fairly clear to me that:

France did not fight.

If she did, there is little evidence of it. Not only I, but several of my friends have driven from the German

border to Paris and back, along all the main roads.
None of us saw any evidence of serious fighting.

The fields of France are undisturbed. There was
no fighting on any sustained line. The German army
hurled itself forward along the roads. Even on the
roads there is little sign that the French did any more
than harry their enemy. And even this was done only
in the towns and villages. But it was only harrying, de-
laying. There was no attempt to come to a halt on a line
and strike back in a well-organized counter-attack.

But since the Germans chose to fight the war on the
roads, why didn't the French stop them? Roads make
ideal targets for artillery. And yet I have not seen one
yard of road in northern France which shows the effects
of artillery fire. Driving to Paris over the area where
the second German offensive began, an officer from the
High Command who had missed the campaign kept
mumbling that he could not understand it, that up there
on that height, dominating the road and providing wonderful artillery cover with its dense woods, the French
must have had the sense to plant a few guns. Just a few
would have made the road impassable, he kept repeating, and he would order us to stop while he studied the
situation. But there had been no guns on those wooded
heights and there were no shell-holes on or near the road.
The Germans had passed along here with their mighty
army, hardly firing a shot.

The French blew up many bridges. But they also left
many strategic ones standing, especially over the Meuse,
a great natural defence because of the deepness, the
steepness of the valley, and its wooded cover. More than
one French soldier I talked to thought it was downright
treachery.

At no point in France and at only two or three in
Belgium did I see a road properly mined, or, for that

matter, mined at all. In the villages and towns the French had hastily thrown up tank-barriers, usually of blocks of stone and rubbish. But the Germans brushed them aside in minutes. A huge crater left by an exploded mine could not have been brushed aside in a few minutes.

D. B. in Paris, having seen the war from the other side, concludes that there was treachery in the French army from top to bottom — the fascists at the top, the Communists at the bottom. And from German and French sources alike I heard many stories of how the Communists had received their orders from their party not to fight, and didn't. . . .

Many French prisoners say they never saw a battle. When one seemed imminent, orders came to retreat. It was this constant order to retreat before a battle had been joined, or at least before it had been fought out, that broke the Belgian resistance.

The Germans themselves say that in one tank battle they were attacked by a large fleet of French tanks after they had themselves run out of ammunition. The German commander ordered a retreat. After the German tanks had retired some distance to the rear, with the French following them only very cautiously, the Germans received orders to turn about and simulate an attack, firing automatic pistols or anything they had out of their tanks, and executing complicated manœuvres. This they did, and the French, seeing an armada of tanks descend upon them, though these were without ammunition, turned and fled.

One German tank officer I talked to in Compiègne said: " French tanks in some ways were superior to ours. They had heavier armour. And at times — for a few hours, say — the French tank corps fought bravely and well. But soon we got a definite feeling that their heart

wasn't in it. When we learned that, and acted on the
belief, it was all over." A month before, I would have
thought such talk rank Nazi propaganda. Now I believe it.

Another mystery: After the Germans broke through
the Franco-Belgian border from Maubeuge to Sedan,
they tell that they continued right on across northern
France to the sea hardly firing a shot. When they got
to the sea, Boulogne and Calais were defended mostly
by the British. The whole French army seemed paralysed, unable to provide the least action, the slightest
counter-thrust.

True, the Germans had air superiority. True, the
British didn't provide the air power they could and
should have provided. Yet even that does not explain
the French debacle. From what one can see, the effectiveness of the air force in this war has been over-empha-
sized. One read of the great mass air attacks on the
Allied columns along the roads. But you look in vain
for the evidence of it on the roads. There are no bomb
craters. True, the German technique was first to machine-gun the troops and then, when they'd scattered
to the side of the road, to bomb the *sides* (thus sparing
the road when they wanted to use it later). But you
also see little evidence of this. A crater here and there
along the roadside or in a near-by field — but not
enough to destroy an army. The most deadly work of
the German air force was at Dunkirk, where the British
stopped the Germans dead for ten days.

On the whole, then, while the French here and there
fought valiantly and even stubbornly, their army seems
to have been paralysed as soon as the Germans made
their first break-through. Then it collapsed, almost
without a fight. In the first place the French, as though
drugged, had no will to fight, even when their soil was

invaded by their most hated enemy. There was a complete collapse of French society and of the French soul. Secondly, there was either treachery or criminal negligence in the High Command and among the high officers in the field. Among large masses of troops Communist propaganda had won the day. And its message was: " Don't fight." Never were the masses so betrayed.

Two other considerations:

First, the quality of the Allied and German commanding officers. Only a few weeks ago General Sir Edmund Ironside, chief of the British Imperial General Staff, was boasting to American correspondents in London of the great advantage he had in possessing several generals in France who had been division commanders in the World War, whereas all the German generals were younger men who had never commanded more than a company in the last war. Sir Edmund thought the World War experience of his older generals would tell in the end.

It was an idle boast and no doubt the general regrets it now in the light of what has happened. True, the commanding officers of the German army are, for the most part, mere youngsters compared to the French generals we have seen. The latter strike you as civilized, intellectual, frail, ailing old men who stopped thinking new thoughts twenty years ago and have taken no physical exercise in the last ten years. The German generals are a complete contrast. More than one not yet forty, most of them in the forties, a few at the very top in their fifties. And they have the characteristics of youth — dash, daring, imagination, initiative, and physical prowess. General von Reichenau, commander of a whole army in Poland, was first to cross the Vistula River. He swam it. The commander of the few hundred German parachutists at Rotterdam was a general, who took his chances with the lieutenants and privates, and was in fact severely wounded. All the big German tank attacks were *led* in person by commanding generals. They did not sit in the safety of a dug-out ten miles behind the lines and direct by radio. They sat in their tanks in the thick of the fray and directed by radio and signalling from where they could see how the battle was going.

And as was to be expected from youth, these young generals did not hesitate at times to adopt innovations, to do the unorthodox thing, to take chances.

The great trouble with the Allied command — especially the French — was that it was dominated by old men who made the fatal mistake of thinking that this war would be fought on the same general lines as the last war. The rigidity of their military thinking was fixed somewhere between 1914 and 1918, and the matrix of their minds was never broken. I think this helps to explain why, when confronted by the Germans with a new type of war, the French were unable to adjust themselves to countering it.

It wasn't that these tired old men had to adapt themselves to a revolutionary kind of warfare overnight. One of the mysteries of the campaign in the west is that the Allied command seems never to have bothered to learn the lesson of the Polish campaign. For in Poland the German army revealed the tactics it would use in the lowlands and France — parachutists and Stukas to disrupt communications in the rear, and swift, needle-like thrusts with *Panzer* divisions down the main roads through the enemy lines, pushing them ever deeper and then closing them like great steel claws, avoiding frontal attack, giving no opportunity for frontal defence along a line, striking far into the enemy's rear before he could organize for a stand. Eight months elapsed between the

Polish campaign and the offensive in the west, and yet there is little evidence that the generals of Britain and France used this precious time to organize a new system of defence to cope with the tactics they watched the Germans use in Poland. Probably they greatly underestimated the fight the Polish army put up; probably they thought it had been merely a badly armed rabble, and that against a first-rate army like the French, entrenched behind its Maginot Line, the new style of warfare would beat its head in vain. Had the Maginot Line really extended from Sedan to the sea, this attitude might have been justified. But as the Allies knew, and as the Germans remembered, the Maginot Line proper stopped some miles to the east of Sedan.

The second consideration is the fantastically good morale of the German army. Few people who have not seen it in action realize how different this army is from the one the Kaiser sent hurtling into Belgium and France in 1914. I remember my surprise at Kiel last Christmas to find an entirely new *esprit* in the German navy. This *esprit* was based on a camaraderie between officers and men. The same is true of the German army. It is hard to explain. The old Prussian goose-step, the heel-clicking, the " *Jawohl* " of the private when answering an officer, are still there. But the great gulf between officers and men is gone in this war. There is a sort of equalitarianism. I felt it from the first day I came in contact with the army at the front. The German officer no longer represents — or at least is conscious of representing — a class or caste. And the men in the ranks feel this. They feel like members of one great family. Even the salute has a new meaning. German privates salute each other, thus making the gesture more of a comradely greeting than the mere recognition of superior rank. In cafés, restaurants, dining-cars, officers and men off duty sit at the same table and converse as men to men. This would have been unthinkable in the last war and is probably unusual in the armies of the West, including our own. In the field, officers and men usually eat from the same soup kitchen. At Compiègne I had my lunch with a youthful captain who lined up with the men to get his rations from a mobile " soup cannon." In Paris I recall a colonel who was treating a dozen privates to an excellent lunch in a little Basque restaurant off the avenue de l'Opéra. When lunch was over, he drew, with all the care of a loving father, a plan for them to visit the sights of Paris. The respect of these ordinary soldiers for their colonel would be hard to exaggerate. Yet it was not for his rank, but for the man. Hitler himself has drawn up detailed instructions for German officers about taking an interest in the personal problems of their men. One of the most efficient units in the German army at the front is its post office which brings letters and packages from home to the men, regardless of where they are, and which attends to the dispatch of letters and packages from the men home in record time. There are few German soldiers who have not dispatched in the last days silk stockings and perfume home to their families through the free facilities of the army post office.

One reason for the excellent morale of the troops is their realization that they and not the civilians back home are receiving the best treatment the nation can afford. They get the pick of the food and clothing available. In the winter the homes of Germany may not be heated, but the barracks are. The civilians in the safe jobs may not see oranges and coffee and fresh vegetables, but the troops see them every day. Last Christmas it was the soldiers who sent food packages home to their families, and not the reverse. Hitler once said that as a private of the last war he would see to it that the men in the new army benefited by the lessons he had learned. And in this one case, at least, he seems to have kept his promise.

BERLIN, *June* 28

A word about something the Germans will shoot me for if the Gestapo or the Military Intelligence ever find these notes. (I hide them about my hotel room here, but even an amateur detective could find them easily enough.)

I have been shocked at the way the German army in Belgium and France has been abusing the Red Cross sign.

The other day when we were within forty miles of Paris, we stopped at a big army gasoline dump to refuel our cars. Forty or fifty army oil trucks were drawn up under the trees of an orchard. Several of them were plastered with huge Red-Cross signs. Many of the ordinary trucks with canvas tops which were being used to carry drums of oil had red crosses on their sides and roofs and indeed looked like Red Cross ambulances. A German officer apparently noticed me taking in this shameless misuse of the Red Cross sign. He hurriedly bundled us into our cars and got us off.

This may explain why the Luftwaffe has not respected the mark of the Red Cross on the Allied side. Göring probably figures that the Allies are doing just what he does. This may explain something the correspondents who went into Dunkirk the other day told me. The thing that shocked them most there was the sight of the charred remains of a long line of British and French Red Cross ambulances drawn up on the quay. They had been about to unload the wounded on

some ships, it was evident, and then the Stukas had come
over and bombed them with explosive and incendiary
bombs. The burnt bodies of the wounded still lay in the
ambulances. No German pilot, the correspondents observed, could have failed to see the large Red Cross
marks on the top of the ambulances.

I noticed too in Belgium and France many German staff officers riding up and down in cars marked
with the Red Cross.

Today was the twenty-first anniversary of the signing of the Treaty of Versailles. And the world it created appeared to be gasping its swan-song today as
German troops reached the Spanish border, and Soviet
troops marched into Bessarabia and Bukovina. In
Paris last week I learned on good authority that Hitler
planned a further humiliation of France by holding a
victory parade before the Palace of Versailles on this
twenty-first anniversary day. He would make a speech
from the Hall of Mirrors, where it was signed, proclaiming its official end. For some reason it was called off.
It is to be held, instead, in Berlin, I hear.

Official comment on Russia's grabbing Bessarabia
and Bukovina from Rumania today was: " Rumania
has chosen the reasonable way."

The nomination of Willkie gets three lines in the
Berlin press today. It refers to him as " *General-Direktor* " Willkie.

One or two American representatives of American
press associations spoke so strongly to Dr. Boehmer,
the Propaganda Ministry press chief, about our radio
scoop on the armistice at Compiègne that he assured
them I had not been allowed to use a German transmitter but must have got my story out over " some French

˚station." Actually we used a German transmitter and one located just outside of Berlin at Zeesen, as Dr. Boehmer no doubt knows.

As a matter of fact, the Germans did a superb technical job on our two armistice broadcasts. By a superhuman effort, army communication engineers had laid down in a couple of days a radio-cable line from Brussels to the Compiègne Forest. Earlier in the campaign they₉ had linked up the Belgian capital with Cologne, the nearest German point on the Reich net of radio-cable lines. How necessary it was to have a radio-cable and not just a mere overhead telephone line was shown the first day at Compiègne. Whereas the voices of Kerker and myself came into New York, we were informed, as clear as a bell, the American newspaper correspondents, telephoning their stories only as far as Berlin over an ordinary overhead telephone wire, complained that even by shouting at the top of their voices they could scarcely make themselves understood in Berlin.

Given a perfect cable line over Brussels and Cologne to Zeesen, nine tenths of our troubles were over. The German Broadcasting System provided us with microphones, which they set up within fifty feet of the armistice car, and with an amplifier truck. That was all we needed. Also, in Berlin the RRG had a man calling New York constantly over the shortwave to inform them when we would be on the air. Paul White cables that on the first day they only picked us up one minute before we started talking, which gave very little time to cut off the program then on the air and switch to us.

Our scoop, like all scoops, was due largely to a combination of lucky circumstances. In the first place, we did not know until the next day that the official communiqué on the signing of the armistice had had to be

approved by Hitler before it was released in Berlin. As
Hitler was some distance away, this took several hours.
We had supposed that the DNB had released the communiqué in Berlin as soon as it was flashed from Compiègne at six fifty p.m., the second the armistice was
signed. We did not go on the air until eight-fifteen, an
hour and twenty-five minutes later.

In fact we were held up forty-five minutes because the
RRG quite naturally was using the cable line to clear
its own German broadcast to Berlin. Fortunately for
us, this German account was not rebroadcast simultane-
ously, but recorded in Berlin and held until the High
Command could okay it. This, fortunately for us, took
several hours.

Now, the day before, the High Command had forced
us to go through the same process. That is, we had had
to broadcast our description of the first day to Berlin,
where it was recorded and played off to the army censors, and we had only gone on the air directly to New
York after the military in Berlin had given us the go-
ahead. But on the second day I saw an opportunity of
taking advantage of the excitement of the Germans over
the signing of the armistice, and by much bludgeoning
and with the co-operation of three Germans — Hada-
mowsky, head of the German radio, Diettrich, head of
the shortwave, and a certain colonel of the German High
Command — we dispensed with the recording and went
on the air direct to New York. We were not supposed
to. Later the three above-mentioned gentlemen swore
we were not supposed to be on the air. The important
thing was that in the excitement I had got them to give
the all-important order merely to throw a switch in a
Berlin control room which put us on the air, direct to
New York. When Hitler, the High Command, and Dr.
Goebbels learned that we had given the American peo-

ple a detailed thirty-minute description of the signing of the armistice several hours before the signing was
even officially announced in Berlin and several hours
more before the German radio gave it to their own people, they were furious. My three German friends faced
court-martial or worse and spent some very uncomfortable days before the matter finally blew over.

The curious thing is that the German army alone in
this country understands the position of American radio
as a purveyor of news and news analysis in the United
States. Dr. Goebbels and his foreign press chief, Dr.
Boehmer, have never appreciated it, and it was only at
the insistence of the army that Kerker and I were taken
to Compiègne at all. Boehmer, who is definitely anti-
radio, actually rushed Lochner, Huss, and Oechsner,
the three American agency correspondents, from Compiègne to Berlin by air the morning of the day the armistice was signed so that from the German capital they
could be first with the news. As it turned out, this was
a strategic error and there was not a single press correspondent at Compiègne the day the armistice was made.

Though a couple of the American news correspondents have often complained to the Nazis about taking
me to the front, on the ground that instantaneous radio
communication puts them at a disadvantage, since they
must file their stories by the slower method of telephone
and cable relays, I have tried to iron out this absurd
competitive idea by agreeing to hold up my ordinary
broadcasts until their stories could get through to New
York. Since NBC and CBS subscribe to all the press
associations, there is no danger of radio ever being
scooped by the press. And I feel we are doing different
jobs which, after all, merely complement each other.
There should be no insane rivalry between American
press and radio over here.

GENEVA, *July* 4

Here for a week's rest. The smell of the dead horses and the dead soldiers in Belgium and France seems a part of another world you lived in a long time ago. The excited cries of Eileen when I take her in swimming for the first time of her life at the proud age of two and a half, the soft voice of Tess reading a fairy-tale to Eileen before she goes to bed — these become realities again and are good.

Everyone here is full of talk about the " new Europe," a theme that brings shudders to most people. The Swiss, who mobilized more men per capita than any other country in the world, are demobilizing partially. They see their situation as pretty hopeless, surrounded as they are by the victorious totalitarians, from whom henceforth they must beg facilities for bringing in their food and other supplies. None have any illusions about the kind of treatment they will get from the dictators. The papers are full of advice: Prepare for a hard life. Gone, the high living standard. The freedom of the individual. Decency in public life.

Probably, too, the Swiss do not realize what the dictators really have in store for them. And now that France has completely collapsed and the Germans and Italians surround Switzerland, a military struggle in self-defence is hopeless.

Mont Blanc from the quay today was magnificent, its snow pink in the afternoon sun. Later went to a 4th of July celebration at the consul's. Nice home in the country and restful, with the cows grazing in the pastures around it. Talked too much.

People are talking about the action of the British yesterday in sinking three French battleships in Oran to save them from falling into the hands of the Germans.

The French, who have sunk to a depth below your imagination, say they will break relations with Britain.
They say they trusted Hitler's word not to use the
French fleet against Britain. Pitiful. And yet there
will be great bitterness throughout France. The En-
tente Cordiale is dead.

We had dinner along the lake, on the Alpine side, under a thick old chestnut tree, its branches extending
over the water. The Juras were bluer — a deep smoky
blue — than I've ever seen them. They looked lonely
and proud, and now the Germans were occupying them.
I left the party and went over to the rail to gaze at
the scene as the sun was setting. The overwhelming
blue of the Juras had cast its colour on Lake Geneva,
which was like glass, neatly placed amongst the green
hills and the trees. The lights started to sparkle across
the lake.

GENEVA, *July* 5

Avenol, Secretary-General of the League,
apparently thinks he'll have a job in Hitler's United
States of Europe. Yesterday he fired all the British
secretaries and packed them off on a bus to France,
where they'll probably be arrested by the Germans or
the French.

Tonight in the sunset the great white marble of the
League building showed through the trees. It had a
noble look, and the League has stood in the minds of
many as a noble hope. But it has not tried to fulfil it.
Tonight it was a shell, the building, the institution, the
hope — dead.

B e r l i n , *July* 8

Tomorrow France, which until a few weeks
ago was regarded as the last stronghold of denıocracy
on the Continent, will shed its democracy and join the
ranks of the totalitarian states. Laval, whom Hitler
has picked to do his dirty work in France — the notorious Otto Abetz is the main go-between — will have
the French Chamber and Senate meet and vote themselves out of existence, handing over all power to Marshal Pétain, behind whom Laval will pull the strings
as Hitler's puppet dictator. The Nazis are laughing.

The armistice car arrived here today.

B e r l i n , *July* 9

The Nazis are still laughing. Said the organ
of the Foreign Office, *Dienst aus Deutschland,* in commenting on Vichy's scrapping the French Parliament
today: " The change of the former regime in France
to an authoritarian form of government will not influence in any way the political liquidation of the war.
The fact is that Germany does not consider the Franco-
German accounts as settled yet. Later they will be settled with historical realism . . . not only on the basis
of the two decades since Versailles, but they will also
take into account much earlier times."

Alfred Rosenberg told us at a press conference this
evening that Sweden would have to join the rest of
Scandinavia and come under the benevolent protection
of the Reich. Emissaries of Goebbels and Ribbentrop
who were in the room dashed out to inform their bosses
of Rosenberg's blunt remarks and were back before he
had finished speaking, he being very long-winded. They
passed notes to Dr. Boehmer, who was presiding. As

soon as Rosenberg sat down, Boehmer popped up and announced excitedly that Rosenberg was speaking only for himself and not for the German government.

BERLIN, *July* 10

Hans came in to see me. He had just driven from Irun, on the Franco-Spanish border, to Berlin. He said he could not get over the looks of Verdun, which he visited yesterday. Not a house there has been scratched, he said. Yet in the World War, when it was never taken, not a house remained standing. There you have the difference between 1914–18 and 1940.

BERLIN, *July* (*undated*)

Ralph Barnes, correspondent of the *Herald Tribune* (and one of my oldest friends), who came here from London just before the big offensive, left Berlin today, by request. With him went Russell Hill, assistant to Ralph and to me. They were thrown out because of a story of Ralph's that Russo-German relations were not so friendly now as of old. The Wilhelmstrasse is very touchy on the subject, but I think the real reason is the Nazi hate of the *Herald Tribune's* editorial policy and its insistence on maintaining fearlessly independent correspondents here — the only New York paper that does. Though Russell had nothing to do with the story, the Nazis could not forgive him for his steadfast refusal to knuckle down to them, and so took this opportunity to get rid of him too. Ralph and I had a farewell walk in the Tiergarten this afternoon, he naturally depressed and not quite realizing that his going was a proof that he had more integrity than any of us who are allowed to stay.[1]

[1] Within less than four months he was killed in a British bomber returning from a raid on the Italian lines in Albania.

BERLIN, *July* 15

The German press today informed its readers
that German troops of all arms " now stand ready for
the attack on Britain. The date of the attack will be
decided by the Führer alone." One hears the High Command is not keen about it, but that Hitler insists.

BERLIN, *July* 17

Three hundred S.S. men in Berlin have
started learning Swahili. Swahili is the lingua franca
of the former German colony in East Africa.

BERLIN, *July* 18

For the first time since 1871, German troops
staged a victory parade through the Brandenburg
Gate today. They comprised a division conscripted
from Berlin. Stores and factories closed, by order, and
the whole town turned out to cheer. Nothing pleases
the Berliners — a naïve and simple people on the whole
— more than a good military parade. And nothing more
than an afternoon off from their dull jobs and their
dismal homes. I mingled among the crowds in the Pariserplatz. A holiday spirit ruled completely. Nothing
martial about the mass of the people here. They were
just out for a good time. Looking at them, I wondered
if any of them understood what was going on in Europe,
if they had an inkling that their joy, that this victorious
parade of the goose-steppers, was based on a great tragedy for millions of others whom these troops and the
leaders of these people had enslaved. Not one in a thousand, I wager, gave the matter a thought. It was somewhat sultry, and scores of women in the Platz fainted.
An efficient Red Cross outfit hauled them from the pave-

ment on stretchers to a near-by first-aid station.

The troops were tanned and hard-looking, and goose-stepped past like automatons. One officer's horse, obviously unused to victory parades, provided a brief comedy. Kicking wildly, he backed into the reviewing stand, just missing Dr. Goebbels.

The last time German troops paraded through the Brandenburger Tor after a war was on a dismal cold day of December 16, 1918. That was the day the Prussian Guard came home. Memories are short.

Hitler will speak in the Reichstag tomorrow, we hear. But we're threatened with expulsion if we say it to America. Himmler is afraid the British bombers will come over. There is some speculation whether it will be, as on the grey morning of September 1, an occasion to announce a new *Blitzkrieg* — this time against Britain — or an offer of peace. My hotel filled with big generals arriving for the show.

BERLIN, *July* 19

It is not to be a *Blitzkrieg* against Britain. At least not yet. In the Reichstag tonight, Hitler " offered " peace. He said he saw no reason why this war should go on. But of course it's peace with Hitler sitting astride the Continent as its conqueror. Leaving the fantastic show in the Reichstag — and it was the most colourful of all I've ever seen — I wondered what the British would make of it. As to the Germans, there's no doubt. As a manœuvre calculated to rally them for the fight against Britain, it was a masterpiece. For the German people will now say: " Hitler offers England peace, and no strings attached. He says he sees no reason why this war should go on. If it does, why, it's England's fault."

I wondered a little what answer the British would make, and I had hardly arrived at the *Rundfunk* to prepare my talk when I picked up the BBC in German.[1] And there was the answer already! It was a great big No. The more I thought of it, the less I was surprised. Peace for Britain with Germany absolute master of the Continent *is* impossible. Also: the British must have some reason to believe they can successfully defend their island and in the end bring Hitler down. For Hitler has given them an easy way out to save at least some pieces for themselves. Only a year and a half ago at Munich I saw them grasping at such a straw. The BBC No was very emphatic. The announcer heaped ridicule on Hitler's every utterance. Officers from the High Command and officials from various ministries sitting around the room could not believe their ears. One of them shouted at me: " Can you make it out? Can you understand those British fools? To turn down peace now? " I merely grunted. " They're crazy," he said.

Hitler put his peace " offer " very eloquently, at least for Germans. He said: " In this hour I feel it my duty before my own conscience to appeal once more to reason and common sense. I can see no reason why this war must go on."

There was no applause, no cheering, no stamping of heavy boots. There was silence. And it was tense. For

[1] It is only fair to state that the officials of the German State Broadcasting Company, who treated me with the greatest courtesy throughout the war, never objected to my listening to what the enemy had to say on the BBC. They usually put a radio set at my disposal for this purpose. Foreign correspondents were exempted from the decree prohibiting listening to foreign radio stations as long as they did not pass on what they heard to Germans. Radio provided the only means we in Berlin had of learning what was going on in the outside world. Sale of foreign newspapers except those from Italy or the occupied cities was forbidden. Occasionally a few American newspapers and periodicals got through in the mails, but they were from two to six months old by the time they arrived.

in their hearts the Germans long for peace now. Hitler
went on in the silence: " I am grieved to think of the sacrifices which it will claim. I should like to avert them,
also for my own people."

The Hitler we saw in the Reichstag tonight was the
conqueror, and conscious of it, and yet so wonderful an
actor, so magnificent a handler of the German mind,
that he mixed superbly the full confidence of the conqueror with the humbleness which always goes down so
well with the masses when they know a man is on top.
His voice was lower tonight; he rarely shouted as he
usually does; and he did not once cry out hysterically as
I've seen him do so often from this rostrum. His oratori-
cal form was at its best. I've often sat in the gallery of
the Kroll Opera House at these Reichstag sessions
watching the man as he spoke and considering what a
superb actor he was, as indeed are all good orators.
I've often admired the way he uses his hands, which are
somewhat feminine and quite artistic. Tonight he used
those hands beautifully, seemed to express himself almost as much with his hands — and the sway of his
body — as he did with his words and the use of his
voice. I noticed too his gift for using his face and eyes
(cocking his eyes) and the turn of his head for irony, of
which there was considerable in tonight's speech, especially when he referred to Mr. Churchill.

I noticed again, too, that he can tell a lie with as
straight a face as any man. Probably some of the lies
are not lies to him because he believes fanatically the
words he is saying, as for instance his false recapitula-
tion of the last twenty-two years and his constant reiter-
ation that Germany was never really defeated in the last
war, only betrayed. But tonight he could also say with
the ring of utter sincerity that all the night bombings
of the British in recent weeks had caused no military

damage whatsoever. One wonders what is in his mind
when he tells a tall one like that. Joe [Harsch], watching him speak for the first time, was impressed. He
said he couldn't keep his eyes off his hands; thought the
hand work brilliant.

Under one roof I have never seen so many gold-
braided generals before. Massed together, their chests
heaving with crosses and other decorations, they filled a
third of the first balcony. Part of the show was for
them. Suddenly pausing in the middle of his speech,
Hitler became the Napoleon, creating with the flick of
his hand (in this case the Nazi salute) twelve field-marshals, and since Göring already was one, creating a special honour for him — Reichsmarshal. It was amusing
to watch Göring. Sitting up on the dais of the Speaker
in all his bulk, he acted like a happy child playing with
his toys on Christmas morning. (Only how deadly that
some of the toys he plays with, besides the electric train
in the attic of Karin Hall, happen to be Stuka bombers!)
Throughout Hitler's speech Göring leaned over his desk
chewing his pencil, and scribbling out in large, scrawly
letters the text of his remarks which he would make after
Hitler finished. He chewed on his pencil and frowned
and scribbled like a schoolboy over a composition that
has got to be in by the time class is ended. But always
he kept one ear cocked on the Leader's words, and at
appropriate moments he would put down his pencil and
applaud heartily, his face a smile of approval from one
ear to the other. He had two big moments, and he reacted to them with the happy naturalness of a big child.
Once when Hitler named two of his air-force generals
field-marshals, he beamed like a proud big brother, smiling his approval and his happiness up to the generals in
the balcony and clapping his hands with Gargantuan
gestures, pointing his big paws at the new field-marshals

as at a boxer in the ring when he's introduced. The climax was when Hitler named him Reichsmarshal. Hitler turned around and handed him a box with whatever insignia a Reichsmarshal wears. Göring took the box, and his boyish pride and satisfaction was almost touching, old murderer that he is. He could not deny himself a sneaking glance under the cover of the lid. Then he went back to his pencil-chewing and his speech. I considered his popularity — second only to Hitler's in the country — and concluded that it is just because, on occasions like this, he's so human, so completely the big, good-natured boy. (But also the boy who in June 1934 could dispatch men to the firing squad by the hundreds.)

Count Ciano, who was rushed up from Rome to put the seal of Axis authority on Hitler's " offer " of peace to Britain, was the clown of the evening. In his grey and black Fascist militia uniform, he sat in the first row of the diplomatic box, and jumped up constantly like a jack-in-the-box every time Hitler paused for breath, to give the Fascist salute. He had a text of the speech in his hand, but it was probably in Italian, so that he was not following Hitler's words. Without the slightest pretext he would hop to his heels and expand in a salute. Could not help noticing how high-strung Ciano is. He kept working his *jaws*. And he was not chewing gum.

Saddest figure to me in the Assembly — I do not count the wooden automatons who as " deputies " sat below on the main floor — was General Halder, chief of the German General Staff. Most people think that he is the brains of the German army, that it was he who made the final plans for the Polish campaign and the great offensive in the west and executed them in such an astonishingly successful manner. But he has never kowtowed to Hitler. It is widely reported that he has on occasions talked very sharply to the Great Man. And that, as a result, Hitler hates him. At any rate, he was not made a field-marshal tonight, but merely promoted one grade. (After the Polish campaign Hitler also skipped over him in bestowing honours, but the army kicked so hard that Hitler had belatedly to make amends.) I watched him tonight, his classically intellectual face, and he seemed to be hiding a weariness, a sadness, as he warmly congratulated his younger generals who were now raised over him as field-marshals.

Alexander Kirk, our chargé, was there too. The Nazis put him in the back row with the small fellows, but he didn't seem to mind. He sat there all evening, his face like a sphinx, breaking only occasionally into an ironic smile when some of his diplomatic colleagues from the Balkans popped up to give the new slave salute. Quisling, a pig-eyed little man, crouched in a corner seat in the first balcony, drinking the amazing scene in.

BERLIN, *July* 20

No official British reaction to Hitler's " peace offer," but Goebbels had the local press tonight break the news gently to the German people that apparently the Britons aren't having any. The Germans I talk to simply cannot understand it. They want peace. They don't want another winter like the last one. They have nothing against Britain, despite all the provocative propaganda. (Like a drug too often given, it is losing what little force it had.) They think they're on top. They think they can lick Britain too, if it comes to a showdown. But they would prefer peace.

Roosevelt has been renominated at Chicago for a third term. This is a blow to Hitler which the Wilhelmstrasse scarcely hid today. Goebbels gave orders to the Berlin press not to comment, but he did allow the **DNB** to publish a brief dispatch from its Washington correspondent stating that the methods by which Roosevelt's nomination was achieved " have been sharply condemned by all eyewitnesses."

Hitler will now hope that Roosevelt is defeated in the election by Willkie. The point is that Hitler fears Roosevelt. He is just beginning to comprehend that Roosevelt's support of Great Britain is one of the prime reasons why the British decline to accept his kind of peace. As Rudolf Kircher, editor of the *Frankfurter Zeitung,* will be allowed to put it tomorrow: " Roosevelt is the father of English illusions about this war. It may be that Roosevelt's shabby tactics are too much for the Americans, it may be that he will not be re-elected, it may be that, if he is re-elected, he will stick closely to the non-intervention program of his party. But it is also clear that while he may not intervene with his fleet or his army, he will intervene with speeches, with intrigues, and with a powerful propaganda which he will put at the disposal of the English."

BERLIN, *July* 21

Holland is beginning to feel the Nazi yoke. Mass arrests, we hear.

BERLIN, *July* 22

Hitler has given Mussolini a birthday present. It's an anti-aircraft armoured train.

Halifax broadcast Britain's answer to Hitler's " peace proposal." It was an emphatic No. A poor speech though, I thought while listening to it at the *Rundfunk*

— for America. He sounded awfully pious. He appealed too much to God. I remember him in India as a very religious man. But God's been pretty good to Hitler so far. . . .

BERLIN, *July 23*

The die seems cast, as the papers put it this evening. Halifax's speech has jolted official circles. There were angry Nazi faces at the noon press conference. Said the spokesman with a snarl: " Lord Halifax has refused to accept the peace offer of the Führer. Gentlemen, there will be war."

The press campaign to whip up the people for the war on Britain started with a bang this morning. Every paper in Berlin carried practically the same headline: "CHURCHILL'S ANSWER — COWARDLY MUR- DERING OF A DEFENCELESS POPULATION!"

The story is that since Hitler's Reichstag " appeal for peace " the British have answered by increasing their night attacks — on helpless women and children. Details not previously given us as to the extent of the British bombings are suddenly hauled out. Bombings of Bremen, Hamburg, Paderborn (where there's a big tank works), Hagen, and Bochum (all teeming with military objectives). But according to Goebbels's lies — only women and children have been hit. Afraid the German people will swallow this. They are very depressed that Britain will not have peace. But they now pin their hopes on a quick victory which will be over by fall and therefore save them from another war winter.

BERLIN, *July 25*

Today we get the first glimpse of how Hitler intends to break up France. A special German governor named Weyer has been appointed for the five French departments which comprise Brittany, and a Breton " National Committee " formed and made to proclaim a new Breton national state.

Today in Alsace French signs were removed and German substituted.

From Dr. Walther Funk, president of the Reichsbank and Minister of Economics, who showed up at our evening press conference, we also received a first glimpse into Hitler's " new order." Funk, a shifty-looking little man who, they say, drinks too much, but who is not unintelligent and not devoid of humour, admitted quite frankly that the purpose of the " new order " was to make Germany a richer land. He put it this way : " It must guarantee Germany a maximum of economic security and a maximum also of goods consumption. This is the goal of the new European economy." Later the censor cut this part out of my report.

Funk also said that gold would be abandoned as the basis of the new European currency, and the now worthless Reichsmark substituted. Gold would also lose most of its importance, he claimed, as a means of international payment. Thus America's great gold supply would lose most of its value. The Reichsbank, he went on, would act as clearing house for the new European system. In other words, any trade, say, that America might want to carry on with a European country would have to be done through Berlin. On the other hand Funk belligerently attacked what he called America's " intervention " in Germany's trade with South America. " Either we will trade directly with the sovereign South American states or we won't trade at all," he shouted. Just one more example of the Germans wanting one standard for themselves and a worse one for others.

Funk's enmity to Dr. Schacht, whom he chased out

of the Reichsbank and the economics ministry, cropped
out when we asked him about the widespread reports
that Schacht, too, had worked out a plan for the " new
order." " I haven't heard of it," he snapped. Then on
second thought: " Oh, I did read something in the foreign press about it, but I only believe half of what I
read in the papers." Then seriously: " The Führer entrusted *me* with the economic plans for the ' new order.' "

BERLIN, *July* 28

More about the " new order." Dr. Alfred
Pietzsch, president of the Reich Economic Chamber,
says the Continent under the " new order " will have a
population of 320,000,000 people and cover 1,500,000
square miles of space. It will grow annually 160,000,-
000 tons of potatoes and 120,000,000 tons of grain
and will be practically self-supporting in foods. Dr.
Pietzsch admits something which most Nazis won't.
He says the Hitler-dominated Continent will be far from
self-sufficient in raw materials. For example, it will
grow little wool and practically no cotton. At the present time, he says, the Continent imports annually a bil-
lion and a half dollars' worth of raw materials.

Himmler announced today that a Polish farm la-
bourer had been hanged for sleeping with a German
woman. No race pollution is to be permitted.

Another American correspondent kicked out today.
He is Captain Corpening of the Chicago *Tribune*, said
to be a confidential man of Colonel McCormick's. He
arrived yesterday from Switzerland and broke a story
about Germany's peace terms to Britain which he thinks
have been sent to London through Sweden. The Propaganda Ministry attempted to pin the story on the *Tribune's* regular correspondent, Sigrid Schultz, whom they

would like to toss out because of her independence and
knowledge of things behind the scenes, but finally decided to expel only the captain.

BERLIN, *July* 31

The news-reels today show German army engineers blowing up the French armistice monuments at
Compiègne. They dynamited all but the one of Marshal Foch. Last month in Paris a German official invited
me to Compiègne to see the dynamiting, but when I expressed amazement that the Germans would do such a
barbaric thing he withdrew the invitation.

I remarked in my broadcast tonight that the German
people at the moment were certainly benefiting by the
amount of vegetables, eggs, and bacon which the Dutch
and Danes were sending in. The censors said I could
not mention the subject.

BERLIN, *August* 1

Goebbels made the German radio today falsify
a statement by Secretary of War Stimson. It quoted
Stimson as saying: " Britain will be overpowered in a
short time and the British fleet will pass under enemy
control." This is part of a new propaganda campaign
to convince the German people that even the United
States has given up hope of saving Britain.

Everyone impatient to know when the invasion of
Britain will begin. I have taken two new bets offered
by Nazis in the Wilhelmstrasse. First, that the Swastika will be flying over Trafalgar Square by August 15.
Second, by September 7. The Nazis say General Milch,
right-hand man of Göring, has tipped the latter date as
a dead certainty.

BERLIN, *August* 3

Sir Lancelot Oliphant, British Ambassador to Belgium, who is being held a captive by the Nazis at a Gestapo training school between here and Potsdam, is sore. The other night they had an air-raid out there and he said he'd be damned if he'd take refuge in the cellar when his own people came over to bomb. The S.S. guards thereupon removed him forcibly to the cellar. Sir Lancelot raised such a howl that the matter went to Hitler. The Führer's decision is that he may damned well stay where he pleases when his own folks come over, but that he must sign a paper absolving the Germans of any responsibility.

Great excitement at our noon press conference at the Foreign Office yesterday. The official spokesman was droning away as usual when suddenly all the anti-aircraft guns on the roofs of the Chancellery and Air Ministry down the street started blazing away. He stopped abruptly. Just as all present were getting ready to run for shelter the firing stopped. Seems a German student flyer entered the forbidden air zone over Berlin without giving the proper signal.

BERLIN, *August* 4

I flew to Hamburg yesterday in a weird old transport plane which the German army had been using previously to transport captive horses from Paris to Berlin. There were no seats, so we sat on the floor, which vibrated considerably. The German authorities had phoned that they were inviting me and two others to fly to Hamburg, where we could see anything we wanted. The British, they said, had just announced that Hamburg had been " pulverized " by the RAF bombings.

When I got to the airport there were twenty others

who had been invited, and when we arrived at Hamburg
I soon saw that the Germans had no intention of showing me " anything " I wanted to see. For two hours
before leaving I had studied the map of Hamburg and
made a list of certain military objectives such as oil-
storage tanks, airplane factories, shipbuilding yards,
and one secret airfield. After we had been taken around
on a conducted tour for a couple of hours and shown
among other things how one British bomb had wiped out
a wing of an institute for epileptics, I presented my list
to those in charge of the party.

" Certainly," they answered. " We will show you all."
Whereupon they rushed us in a bus through the docks
at thirty-five miles an hour. The docks certainly weren't
pulverized, but it was impossible to see whether there
had not been hits here and there. Afterwards we climbed
to the top of the St. Michaelis tower, three hundred feet
high, from where we had a panoramic view of the port.
Even with field-glasses, I must admit, I couldn't see anything. The oil tanks were too far away for accurate
observation. But the docks and one Blohm & Voss ship-
yard near by seemed intact. In one part of the river a
couple of small boats had been sunk, their masts still
visible above the water. Soon it was getting dark, and
we were rushed back to the plane.

Ruminating on the vibrating floor of the plane returning to Berlin I was depressed. Even if the Germans
hadn't kept their promise to show me the things I asked
for, it was plain from what little we saw that slight damage had been done. I had expected that after two months
of almost nightly bombings the RAF would have accomplished much more. The port, though it undoubtedly
had been hit here and there, had not really been affected
by the bombings. The two all-important bridges over
the Elbe in the middle of the harbour had not been

touched — the nearest bomb had landed two hundred yards away. Germany's two great passenger ships, the *Bremen* and *Europa*, lay in the distance, tied up at Finkenwerder and apparently untouched. Several troop trains were unloading their men in the harbour, part of the force for the invasion of Britain, I suppose. The talk was that they would be crowded on to the two big liners.

The point was that a square mile or more in the centre of Rotterdam had been utterly wiped out in one half-hour of bombing by German Stukas. Why had not the British, then, in two months of bombing wiped out the Hamburg harbour works and the Blohm & Voss shipping yards, which were busy constructing naval vessels, especially submarines? The important targets were largely concentrated on two islands in the Elbe — objectives which at night you could hardly miss if you followed the river up from the sea. It was depressing, too, to think that perhaps British propaganda had exaggerated the effects of their raids in other places in Germany.

The chief complaint of the people in Hamburg with whom I talked was not the damage caused, but the fact that the British raids robbed them of their sleep.

Strolled in the Tiergarten this afternoon, it being warm and the sun out brightly. At six different spots a crowd had gathered to watch someone feed the squirrels. Even soldiers on leave stopped to watch. And these squirrel-feeders are the ones who have stormed through Norway to Narvik and through Holland, Belgium, and France to the sea.

BERLIN, *August 5*

Despite all the talk about the invasion of Britain being launched within the next few days, the military people here tell me that the Luftwaffe must do a great deal more work before there is any question of an attempt at landing troops. Göring said as much in an article in the *Völkische Beobachter* yesterday signed " Arminius," which is Latin for Hermann, his first name. He explained that the first job of an air force is to gain complete superiority in the air by destroying the other fellow's planes, airfields, hangars, oil stores, and anti-aircraft nests. That over, he said, the second phase begins with the air force able to devote most of its energies to supporting the land army. This was the German strategy in Poland and in the west.

My question is: Why hasn't the Luftwaffe attacked Britain on a bigger scale, then? Is it because Hitler still hopes to force Churchill to accept peace? Or because the generals of the land army still don't want to attempt the invasion? Or because the RAF is too strong to risk the Luftwaffe in one big blow?

French coal mines are working again. They were not destroyed by the French this time as in 1914. A photograph in one of the papers shows French miners unloading coal at a pit. Watching over them is a steel-helmeted German soldier with a bayonet. Their Moscow-dominated Communist Party and their unions told them not to work and not to fight when France was free. Now they must work under German bayonets.

A big conference in the Chancellery tonight between Hitler and the High Command. My spies noticed Keitel, von Brauchitsch, Jodl, Göring, Raeder, and all the other big military shots going in. They are to decide about the invasion of Britain. The censors won't let us mention the business.

BERLIN, *August* 8

The Wilhelmstrasse told us today that Germany declines all responsibility for any food shortages which may occur in the territories occupied by the German army. The Germans are hoping that America will feed the people in the occupied lands. They would like to see Hoover do the job.

BERLIN, *August* 10

French sailors loyal to de Gaulle will be treated as pirates and shown no mercy if captured, the Foreign Office announced officially today.

BERLIN, *August* 11

For some days now workmen have been busy erecting new stands in the Pariserplatz outside my hotel. Today they painted them and installed two huge golden eagles. At each end they also are building gigantic replicas of the Iron Cross. Now the talk in party circles is that Hitler is so certain of the end of the war — either by conquest of Britain or by a " negotiated " peace with Britain — that he has ordered these stands to be ready before the end of the month for the big victory parade through the Brandenburger Tor.

Funk, speaking at Königsberg this morning, warmly praised Lindbergh for having remarked: " If the rich become too rich and the poor too poor, then something must be done."

" That's just what I said some time ago," remarked Funk.

LATER. — Today has seen along the coast of England the greatest air battle of the war. German fig-

ures of British losses have been rising all evening. First
the Luftwaffe announced 73 British planes shot down
against 14 German; then 79 to 14; finally at midnight
89 to 17. Actually, when I counted up the German figures as given out from time to time during the afternoon
and evening, they totalled 111 for British losses. The
Luftwaffe is lying so fast it isn't consistent even by its
own account.

B**ERLIN**, *August* 13

Today was the third big day of Germany's
massive air attack on Britain. Yesterday's score as
given by the Luftwaffe was 71 to 17. Tonight's score
for the third day is given as 69 to 13. On each day the
British figures, as given out from London, have been just
about the reverse. I suspect London's figures are more
truthful. Tomorrow I'm flying to the Channel with
half a dozen other correspondents. We don't know
whether we're being taken up to see Hitler launch his
invasion of Britain or merely to watch the air attacks.

I**N A** G**ERMAN ARMY TRANSPORT PLANE BETWEEN**
B**ERLIN AND** G**HENT**, *August* 14

Last night we had our first air-raid alarm for
a long time. It came at two a.m. just after I'd returned
from broadcasting. Tess, who has been in Berlin for a
few days, and I stayed up to see the fireworks, but there
were none.

We take off at Staachen at ten forty-five a.m., flying
low at about five hundred feet so as to be easily recognizable by German anti-aircraft crews. They shoot
down altogether too many of their own planes. . . .
Now Antwerp to the north and the pilot is coming down.

. . . One bad moment. Two fighters dive on us from
out of the clouds and we think they may be Spitfires.
(The other day they got a German general flying from
Paris to Brussels.) But they're Messerschmitts and veer
off. Now the pilot is trying to find his field — no small
job because of the way the fields here are camouflaged. . . .

GHENT, BELGIUM, *August* 14

   The camouflage of this field worth noting.
From the air I noticed it looked just like any other place
in the landscape, with paths cutting across it irregularly
as though it were farm land. Each war plane on the
ground has its own temporary hangar made of mats
plastered with grass. Tent poles support the mats.
Along the back and both sides of this tent of mats, sandbags are piled to protect the plane from splinters. So
skilfully are these hangars constructed that I doubt if
you could distinguish one from above a thousand feet.
The field itself is not large, but the Germans are feverishly enlarging it. Gangs of Belgian workers are busy
tearing down adjacent buildings — villas of the local
gentry. An example, incidentally, of how Belgians are
made to aid Germany's war on Belgium's ally, Britain.
One neat way the Germans hide their planes, I notice,
is to build pockets — little clearings — some distance
away from the field. Narrow lanes from the main airfield
lead to them. Along the sides of these pockets are rows
of planes hidden under the trees. From the air it would
be hard to spot these pockets and you might bomb the
airfield heavily without touching any of these planes.
  Ghent has a certain romantic interest for me because
I remember my grade-school histories' telling of the signing of the peace treaty concluding our War of 1812 on

Christmas Eve here. A Flemish town would be a pictur-
esque place around Christmas Eve, if we can believe the
early Flemish painters. Here were the American and
British delegates leisurely coming to an agreement to
end a war which neither side wanted. Christmas was in
the air, snow in the narrow, winding streets, skaters on
the canals, and there was much hearty eating and drinking. Christmas Eve was an appropriate moment to conclude the peace. But there was no radio, no cable line
across the Atlantic then, and America only learned of
the peace three months later. In the meantime Jackson
had fought at New Orleans.

We sit around in the gaudy salon of a sugar mer-
chant's villa which the German flyers have taken over.
We are waiting for cars to take us to the " front."
Someone forgot to order them in advance. Dr. Froelich,
from the Propaganda Ministry, whom we call " the
oaf," a big, lumbering, slow-thinking, good-natured
German with a Harvard degree and an American wife,
can never bring himself to make a decision. We wait
and the German flyers serve drinks from the sugar mer-
chant's fine cellar. The cars do not come, so we take a
bus in to see the town. Ghent is not so romantic as I
had imagined. It is a grey, bleak, lowlands industrial
town. Many German soldiers in the street, buying up
the last wares in the shops with their paper marks. We
drop in and chat with a local shopkeeper. He says the
soldiers behave themselves fairly well, but are looting
the town by their purchases. When present stocks are
gone, they cannot be replaced.

OSTEND, BELGIUM, *August* 14

Our cars finally came at seven p.m. and we
made off for Ostend, skirting round Bruges, a fairy-

tale town in which I had spent my first night on the
Continent exactly fifteen years ago. Driving into
Ostend, I kept my eyes open for the barges and ships
that are to take the German army of invasion over to
England, but we saw very few craft of any kind. None
in the harbour, and only a few barges in the canals behind the town. The Germans selected for us a hotel
called the Piccadilly.

LATER. *August 15, 6 a.m.* — Sat up all night.
When the Germans had gone to bed, the proprietor and
his wife and his exceedingly attractive black-haired,
black-eyed daughter of about seventeen brought out
some fine vintages and we made an evening of it. Some
local Belgians joined us and we (Fred Oechsner, Dick
Boyer, and I) had much good talk. It was touching how
the Belgians kept hoping the British bombers would
come over. They did not seem to mind if the British
bumped them off if only the RAF got the Germans too.
One Belgian woman, whose bitterness was very pleasant
to me, explained that most of the damage in Ostend, the
majority of whose houses are pretty well smashed up,
was the work of German artillery, which kept on firing
into the town long after the British had left. Some time
before dawn we went for a walk along the beach. There
was a slight mist which softened the moonlight and made
even the battered ruins of the houses along the sea-front
take on a pattern of some beauty. The smell of the salt
water and the pounding of the waves made you feel good.
The Belgians kept cursing the British for not coming
over.

CALAIS, *August 15* (*noon*)

Driving down along the coast, I was struck
by the *defensive* measures of the Germans. A line of

trenches, dug-outs, and machine-gun nests, strongly manned, stretched along the sand dunes a hundred yards from the water's edge all the way down to Dunkirk. There were many anti-aircraft guns and about a quarter of a mile to the rear countless batteries of artillery. I had not thought before of the possibility of the British doing any attacking. We do not see any evidence at any place along the coast of German preparations for an invasion. No large concentrations of troops or tanks or barges. But of course they may be there, and we just didn't see them.

About ten miles from Dunkirk, we suddenly come upon the sickly sweet smell of dead horse and human flesh. Apparently they have not yet had time to fish the bodies out of the numerous canals. Dunkirk itself has been cleaned up, and those who were there two months ago scarcely recognize it. The sentry does not allow us into the part of town around the main port, possibly because we might learn something of the invasion forces. In and around Dunkirk, acres of ground are covered with the trucks and *matériel de guerre* left by the British Expeditionary Force. German mechanics are at work trying to get the trucks, at least, to run. Others are stripping off the rubber tires, which are of a quality unknown in Germany. In the town long lines of French civilians stand before the soup kitchens for a hand-out of food. Surprising that there are still civilians in this town after the murderous bombing and shelling it got. We all underestimate the power of human beings to endure.

We drive to the beach from which a quarter of a million British troops made their get-away. What surprises me after the German boasts about all the transports and other ships they sank off that beach (in one day, we were told in Berlin, the Luftwaffe had sunk *fifty*

ships) is that along a twenty-mile stretch you see the
wrecks of only two freighters. Besides these there are
the remains of two destroyers, one of which, I believe,
was bombed long before the withdrawal from Dunkirk,
and a torpedo boat. Five small vessels in all. And any
boat sunk within a great distance of the beach would be
visible because of the shallowness of the water here.
When a bomb does hit a ship, though, it pretty well fin-
ishes it. The destroyer nearest us — about two hundred yards off shore — had received a direct hit just in
front of the bridge. A huge chunk some twenty feet
wide had been torn off the craft down to the water-line.

LATER. — While we are still at lunch here in
Calais, we hear the first wave of German bombers roaring
over to England. They fly so high you can hardly see
them — at least twelve thousand feet. I count twenty-
three bombers, and above them is a swarm of Messerschmitt fighters. The weather is clearing. It's going to
be a nice day—for the pilots. About three p.m. we set off
in cars along the coast to Cap Gris-Nez. Passing
through the harbour, I note that here too there is no
concentration of ships, barges, or even the little motor
torpedo-boats. Only three of the latter tied up at a
quay. Can it be that the Germans have been bluffing
about their invasion of Britain? We drive out along the
coast road. Now the German planes are humming over,
there a squadron of twenty-seven bombers, here fifty
Messerschmitt fighters coming in to meet them. They
all turn and swing out to sea towards Dover, flying very
high. It is soon evident that the British do not come
out — at least very far — to meet them. We watch for
the British over the Channel. Not a single Spitfire
shows.

We speed on up the coast towards Cap Gris-Nez,

where Gertrude Ederle and later a fat Egyptian and a host of others used to camp out in the days — how long ago they seem! — when the world was interested in boys and girls swimming the Channel. The air is now full of the sight and roar of planes, bombers and fighters, all German. A swarm of Heinkel bombers (we have not seen a single Stuka yet) limp back from the direction of Dover. Three or four are having a hard time of it, and one, nearly out of control, just manages to make a piece of land back of the cliffs. Messerschmitt 109's and 110's — the latter twin-motored — dash about at 350 miles per hour like a lot of nervous hens protecting their young. They remain in the air until all the bombers are safely down, then climb and make off for England. We have stopped our cars to watch. One of our officers swears the Heinkel was hit by a Spitfire and that the British fighter was brought down, but this is his imagination, for he saw no more than did we. This sort of thing will happen all afternoon. We resume our drive. Peasants sit on binders cutting the brown-ripe wheat. We crane our necks excitedly to watch the murderous machines in the sky. The peasants do not crane their necks, do not look up. They watch the wheat. You could think: who's being civilized now? We pass a big railroad naval gun which has been firing on Dover. It is neatly camouflaged by netting on which the Germans have tied sheaves of grain. All along the coast gangs of French labourers have been put to work by the Germans, building artillery emplacements. Finally we turn towards the sea down the road that leads to Cap Gris-Nez. Many new gun emplacements here and searchlights, all perfectly camouflaged by nets. How much more attention the Germans seem to pay to the art of camouflage than the Allies! Soldiers are busy camouflaging the entire defence works at Cap Gris-Nez, which the French,

incidentally, have left intact and never bothered to
screen. Gangs of men are digging up sod from a near-
by pasture and putting it over the gravel around the
gun emplacements and the look-out pits. It makes a
lot of difference because the white gravel makes an easily
distinguished landmark against the green fields.

We spend the rest of the afternoon idling on the grass
at the edge of the cliff at Cap Gris-Nez. The German
bombers and fighters keep thundering over towards
Dover. Through field-glasses you can see plainly the
Dover cliffs and occasionally even spot an English
sausage balloon protecting the harbour. The German
bombers, I note, go over in good formation very high,
usually about fifteen thousand feet, and return much
lower and in bad formation or singly. We keep on the
watch for a dog-fight, or for a formation of Spitfires to
light on the returning German bombers. It's a vain
watch. We do not see a British plane all afternoon.
Over the Channel today the Germans have absolute supremacy. Hugging our side of the coast are German
patrol boats, mostly small torpedo craft. They would
make easy targets for British planes if any ever ventured over. The sea is as calm as glass, and German
seaplanes with big red crosses painted on their wings
keep lighting and taking off. Their job is to pick up
airmen shot down in the Channel. About six p.m. we
see sixty big bombers — Heinkels and Junker-82's —
protected by a hundred Messerschmitts, winging high
overhead towards Dover. In three or four minutes we
can hear plainly the British anti-aircraft guns around
Dover going into action against them. Judging by the
deep roar, the British have a number of heavy *flak* guns.
There is another kind of thud, deeper, and one of our
officers thinks this comes from the bombs falling. In an
hour what looks to us like the same bombing squadron

returns. We can count only eighteen bombers of the
original sixty. Have the British accounted for the rest?
It is difficult to tell, because we know the Germans often
have orders to return to different fields from those they
started from. One reason for doing this apparently is
to ensure that the German flyers will not know what
their losses are.

Boyer and I keep hoping some Spitfires will show up.
But now the sun is turning low. The sea is like glass.
The skies quiet. The afternoon on the cliff has seemed
more like a bucolic picnic than a day on the front line of
the air war. The same unequal struggle that we saw
in Belgium and northern France. Not a British plane
over, not a bomb dropped. The little Jap sneaks up to
the gun emplacements to snap some photographs until
a sentinel grabs him. The rest of us rouse ourselves
lazily from the grass and hurl pebbles over the cliff into
the sea. It is time to return to Calais and sup. One of
our officers comes running down from the gun emplace-
ment and says excitedly that three Spitfires have been
shot down this afternoon over the French coast. This is
surprising. We ask to be shown.

The first Spitfire they show us on the way back has
been there so long that German mechanics have had time
to remove the Rolls-Royce motor and the instrument
board. It is already rusting. We point this out. Our
officer offers to show us another. It is near the beach of
a little village half-way back to Calais. The motor is
still on and the instrument board, but a young lieutenant
from a near-by anti-aircraft battery takes me aside and
ventures the interesting information that this particular Spitfire was shot down weeks ago and that only this
very afternoon had he succeeded in dragging it out of
the sea at low tide. When our officer offers to show us

his third Spitfire, we say we are hungry and suggest we
return to Calais.

LATER. — The thing I'll never forget about
these coastal towns in Belgium and France is the way
the Belgians and French pray every night for the British bombers to come over, though often when their pray-
ers are answered it means their death and often they
cheer the bomb which kills them. It is three a.m. now and
the German *flak* has been firing at top speed since eleven
thirty p.m. when we heard the first thud of a British
bomb tonight down by the harbour. Fortunately the
British seem to be aiming accurately at the harbour and
nothing has fallen near enough to us here in the town to
cause much worry. There is no air-raid alarm. The
sound of the anti-aircraft and the bursting of the bombs
is your only signal. No one goes to the cellar. When
the Germans have cleared out, we sit in the back room
with the French proprietor, his family, and two waiters and drink *vin rouge* to each new British bomb that
crashes. To bed now, and fear there are bugs in this
room.

CALAIS, *August* 16

There were bugs. At breakfast everyone
scratching and complaining he got no sleep. You can
sleep through the night bombings but not the night attacks by fleas and bedbugs. We eat a hasty breakfast
and are off for Boulogne at eight thirty a.m.

BOULOGNE, *August* 16

How wonderfully the Germans have camouflaged their temporary airfields! We drove by at least

three between Calais and Boulogne. They have established them not in pastures, as I had expected, but in
wheat-fields. The shocks of wheat are left in the field,
with only narrow lanes left free across the field for the
planes to take off from and land on. Each plane is
hidden under a hangar made of rope netting over which
sheaves of wheat have been tied. As at Ghent, the sides
and back of each hangar are protected by sandbags. In
one big wheat-field there must have been a hundred of
these little hangars. Workshops and oil dumps were
also housed under the same kind of netting. The
" pocket " system which I saw at Ghent is also used.
The planes, when they have landed, taxi down a lane
or a road to a near-by " pocket " that may be some distance from the field proper. Here the planes are either
hidden under netting or backed up into a wood.

Our officers and officials have been careful to see that
we do not talk with any returning German pilots. But I
talked to a number of navy and army men in charge of
the coastal guns yesterday and this morning and was
surprised that they all thought the war would be over in
a few weeks. One naval captain in charge of a big gun
at Cap Blanc-Nez, half-way between Calais and Cap
Gris-Nez, took me this morning into his little dug-out,
scooped out of the side of the slope, to show me how he
had fixed it up. It was very cozy. He had slung a ham-
mock between the two walls and had a little table
crowded with German books and magazines. He was a
straw-blond, clean-cut young man from near Hamburg,
and extremely intelligent. I had taken a liking to him
the day before.

" You've got a nice little place here," I said.
" Only — "

" Only what? " he laughed.

" Well, I know Normandy in winter, and from the

end of October until April it's damned cold here and it rains every day. Your dug-out is all right now, captain, but it won't be so comfortable over the winter."

He looked at me in complete amazement.

" Why, I haven't the slightest intention of spending the winter here," he said, deadly serious now. " Why, the war will be over long before then. You were kidding, I think, isn't it? "

" No, I wasn't kidding," I said, a little taken back by his dead certainty. " Do you mean you think the invasion will be completed and England conquered before Christmas, captain? "

" I shall be home with my family this Christmas," he said.

We have lunch here at Boulogne, the food fair, a bottle of Château Margaux, 1929, excellent. After lunch our party goes out to loot a little more with the marks. In a perfume shop I pick up a conversation with an engaging little French sales-girl after I've convinced her by my accent that I'm an American. She says the Germans have cleaned out the town of silk stockings, underwear, soap, perfume, coffee, tea, chocolate, tobacco, and cognac. But she is mainly interested in food. " How will we find enough to eat this winter? " she asks.

About four p.m. we start back for Brussels, driving some distance inland through Saint-Omer, Lille, Tournai.

BRUSSELS, *August* 16

In a couple of fields along the way this afternoon, we saw what looked under the camouflage like barges and pontoons loaded with artillery and tanks. But there was certainly not enough to begin an invasion of England with. However, two or three German officers in our party keep emphasizing what we saw and hinting that there is much more that we didn't see. Maybe. But I'm suspicious. I think the Germans want us to launch a scare story about an imminent invasion of Britain.

LATER. 2 *a.m.* — To bed now, and the German anti-aircraft guns still pounding away at the British bombers. The noise started shortly after midnight. Can't hear or feel any bombs. Suspect the British are after the airport.

BRUSSELS, *August* 17

A little annoyed at not getting back to Berlin today. I feel depressed in these occupied cities. And the Germans won't let me broadcast from here.

I went out to call on Mme X, a Russian-born Belgian woman, whom I've known for twelve years. She has just been through a frightful ordeal, but you would never have suspected it from her talk. She was as charming and vivacious and beautiful as ever. When the Germans approached Brussels, she set off in her car with her two young children. Somewhere near Dunkirk she got caught between the Allied and German armies. She took refuge in a peasant's house and for several days lived through the nightmare of incessant artillery bombardment and bombing. Fortunately there was enough food in the house so that they did not starve. The children, she said, behaved beautifully. When it was over, she related simply, she found enough gasoline in the barn to get back to Brussels. The banks were closed and she had no money, but the German army, seizing her car, paid her a few thousand francs in cash, so that she could buy food.

Her chief worry, she said, was about Pierre, her hus-

band, but even that had turned out better than she had
expected. Though a veteran of the last war and a member of Parliament, he had volunteered the first day of
the war and gone off to fight. She had heard nothing
from him until last week when word had come that he
had been captured.

" He's alive," she said softly. " I've been lucky. We
both might easily have been killed. But we're both alive.
And the children. I have been fortunate."

Pierre, she had heard, had been put to work on a potato farm near Hamburg.

" But Hitler announced a month ago he was releasing
all Belgian prisoners," I said.

" One must be patient," she said. " He is alive. He
is on a farm. He cannot be starving. I can wait."

From my talks with Belgians and French in the last
few days it is encouraging that they both place their
last desperate hopes on the British holding out. For
they now realize that if Hitler wins they are doomed to
become a slave people. Despite the stiff prison sentences
being meted out by the Nazis to anyone caught listening to a foreign radio station, they all keep their sets
tuned in to London, their hopes ebbing and flowing with
the news they get from the BBC. They have all asked
me desperately : " Will the British hold out? Have they
a chance? Will America help? " The fact that all the
newspapers in occupied territory are forced to publish
only German propaganda often throws them into fits of
depression, for Goebbels feeds them daily with the most
fantastic lies.

On the Channel the Germans would not let us talk
with the German pilots, but this afternoon Boyer and I,
sitting lazily on the terrace of a café, struck up a conversation with a young German air officer.

He says he's a Messerschmitt pilot who took part in
the big attack on London yesterday and the day before.
(The planes we saw going over from Calais then were
London-bound.) He does not appear to be a boastful
young man, like some pilots I've met.

He says quietly: " It's a matter of another couple of
weeks, you know, until we finish with the RAF. In a
fortnight the British won't have any more planes. At
first, about ten days ago, they gave us plenty of trouble.
But this week their resistance has been growing less and
less. Yesterday, for example, I saw practically no British fighters in the air. Perhaps ten in all, which we
promptly shot down. For the most part we cruised to
our objectives and back again without hindrance. The
British, gentlemen, are through. I am already making
plans to go to South America and get into the airplane
business. It has been a pleasant war."

We ask him about the British planes.

" The Spitfires are as good as our Messerschmitts,"
he says. " The Hurricanes are not so good and the De-
fiants are terrible."

He gets up, explaining he must see a comrade in the
hospital who was wounded yesterday and rushed here
for an operation. Dick Boyer and I are impressed and
depressed. Dick has just arrived over here and does not
know the Germans very well.

" I shall write a story about what he said," Dick remarks. " He seemed absolutely sincere."

" That he did. But let's wait. Flyers, you know,
have large horizons."

LATER. — Dick and Fred Oechsner and I are
having a night-cap in the bar of the Atlantis about midnight when there is a dull thud outside.

" A bomb, close," the Belgian waiter thinks.

We go outside, but do not see anything. When Dick comes in later, he reports it pulverized a house in the next block and killed everyone in it. Out towards the airfield we can hear the *flak* pounding.

ABOARD A GERMAN ARMY TRANSPORT PLANE, BRUS-
   SELS TO BERLIN, *August* 18

The morning papers of Brussels interesting. The Belgian paper has this headline over the story of the bomb we heard last night: "L'IGNOBLE CRIME ANGLAIS CONTRE BRUXELLES!" The Germans make the Belgians print such headlines. But I'm more interested in the High Command communiqué in the German-language paper, the *Brüsseler Zeitung*. It reports that in Friday's air battles over Britain the English lost 83 planes and the Germans 31. What was that our sincere little Messerschmitt pilot told us about seeing practically no British planes on Friday and that there was no opposition from the RAF?

At the Brussels airport I note that we have been taken to the field in a roundabout way, so that we approach it some distance from the main hangars. But our plane is not yet ready and there are a dozen German army officers scrapping as to which two of them shall be taken on our plane back to Berlin, and I take advantage of the commotion to stroll over towards the hangars. Two of them have been freshly bombed, and behind them are large piles of wrecked German planes. The British attacks, then, were not so harmless.

To note down the contents of a poster I saw placarded all over Brussels yesterday: " In the village of Savanthem near Brussels, an act of sabotage has been committed. I have taken fifty hostages. In addition, until further notice there will be a curfew at eight p.m. Also all cinemas and all other kinds of pleasure centres will be closed until further notice."

It is signed by the German commandant. It is good news. It shows the Belgians are resisting. Noon now and coming into Berlin.

BERLIN, *August* 20

An air-raid alarm last night, the second in a week, though we have not had a half-dozen since the war began a year ago, and the Berlin population, unlike that of northern and western Germany, has been utterly spared the slightest inconvenience from the war.

The sirens sounded forty-five seconds before I was due to broadcast. I was sitting in the studio with a German announcer (who I notice lately follows a copy of my script to see that I don't cheat). We heard the alarm, but saw no reason for not going on with our work. A frightened English lad, one Clark, seventeen-year-old son of a former BBC official, who with his mother has turned traitor and is working for the Nazis, pounded on the studio window and shouted: " *Flieger Alarm!* " The German with me fortunately was not frightened and motioned him away. Our broadcast then began. Afterwards I was a little surprised at the excitement in the control room, since the people in Belgium and France take a nightly pounding without thinking much about it. Part of the excitement, it developed, was due to the fact that the broadcaster of the news in Spanish had made for the air-raid shelter at the first sound of the sirens and missed his broadcast, which was to have begun as soon as I finished mine. When I returned to the radio offices from the studios, one of the office boys, who at night becomes an all important air-raid warden, tried to hustle me down to the cellar, but I refused. We listened to the anti-aircraft guns from a balcony and watched the searchlights, but they couldn't pick up the British planes which kept over the factory districts to the north.

BERLIN, *August* 24

The Germans now admit serious sabotage in Holland. General Christiansen, the German military commander there, warns that if it continues, fines will be assessed against Dutch communities and hostages taken. The nature of the sabotage may be judged by the general's admonition to the Dutch about " failing to report the landing of enemy flyers on Dutch soil." He adds: " People in Holland who give shelter to enemy soldiers will be severely punished, even by death." This seems to confirm some private reports I've had that the British are landing agents by parachute at night.

The Germans deny they're taking food from the occupied countries, but I see in a Dutch paper an official statement by the German authorities to the effect that between May 15 and July 31, 150,000,000 pounds of foodstuffs and fresh vegetables have been sent from Holland to the Reich.

New clothing cards here this week. They give 150 points instead of 100, as last year, but it's a typical Nazi swindle. You get more total points, but you also have to give more points for each item of clothing. For something you could formerly buy for 60 points, this year you must pay 80 points, and so on. An overcoat takes 120 of the 150 points. One point actually entitles you to sixteen grams' worth of clothing material, the card to about five pounds a year.

The Foreign Office has turned down America's request for safe conduct for American ships to evacuate children under sixteen from the war zones.

BERLIN, *August* 26

    We had our first big air-raid of the war last night. The sirens sounded at twelve twenty a.m. and the all-clear came at three twenty-three a.m. For the first time British bombers came directly over the city, and they dropped bombs. The concentration of anti-aircraft fire was the greatest I've ever witnessed. It provided a magnificent, a terrible sight. And it was strangely ineffective. Not a plane was brought down; not one was even picked up by the searchlights, which flashed back and forth frantically across the skies throughout the night.

The Berliners are stunned. They did not think it could happen. When this war began, Göring assured them it couldn't. He boasted that no enemy planes could ever break through the outer and inner rings of the capital's anti-aircraft defence. The Berliners are a naïve and simple people. They believed him. Their disillusionment today therefore is all the greater. You have to see their faces to measure it. Göring made matters worse by informing the population only three days ago that they need not go to their cellars when the sirens sounded, but only when they heard the *flak* going off near by. The implication was that it would never go off. That made people sure that the British bombers, though they might penetrate to the suburbs, would never be able to get over the city proper. And then last night the guns all over the city suddenly began pounding and you could hear the British motors humming directly overhead, and from all reports there was a pell-mell,

frightened rush to the cellars by the five million people
who live in this town.

I was at the *Rundfunk* writing my broadcast when
the sirens sounded, and almost immediately the bark of
the *flak* began. Oddly enough, a few minutes before, I
had had an argument with the censor from the Propaganda Ministry as to whether it was possible to bomb
Berlin. London had just been bombed. It was natural,
I said, that the British should try to retaliate. He
laughed. It was impossible, he said. There were too
many anti-aircraft guns around Berlin.

I found it hard to concentrate on my script. The gun-
fire near the *Rundfunk* was particularly heavy and the
window of my room rattled each time a battery fired or a
bomb exploded. To add to the confusion, the air-wardens, in their fire-fighting overalls, kept racing through
the building ordering everyone to the shelters. The
wardens at the German radio are mostly porters and
office boys and it was soon evident that they were making
the most of their temporary authority. Most of the
Germans on duty, however, appeared to lose little time
in getting to the cellar.

I was scheduled to speak at one a.m. As I've explained
before in these notes, to get to the studio to broadcast
we have to leave the building where we write our scripts
and have them censored, and dash some two hundred
yards through a blacked-out vacant lot to the sheds
where the microphones are. As I stepped out of the
building at five minutes to one, the light guns protecting
the radio station began to fire away wildly. At this moment I heard a softer but much more ominous sound. It
was like hail falling on a tin roof. You could hear it
dropping through the trees and on the roofs of the sheds.
It was shrapnel from the anti-aircraft guns. For the
first time in my life I wished I had a steel helmet. There

had always been something repellent to me about a German helmet, something symbolic of brute Germanic force. At the front I had refused to put one on. Now I rather thought I could overcome my prejudice. I hesitated in the shelter of the doorway. In two or three minutes now my broadcast would begin. I made a dash for it, running blindly, frightenedly down the path, stumbling down the wooden stairway where the terrace was. Sigrid had lent me her flashlight. I switched it on. A guard in the doorway yelled to put it out. As he shouted, I crashed into the corner of a shed and sprawled into the sand. The sound of the shrapnel falling all around egged me on. One last dash and I made the studio door.

" You're crazy," snapped the S.S. guard who had taken shelter from the splinters in the doorway. " Where's your pass? "

" I've got a broadcast in just one minute," I panted.

" I don't care. Where's your pass? "

I finally found it. In the studio cell the engineer requested me to speak very close to the microphone. He did not say why, but the reason was obvious. The closer to the mike I spoke, the less " outside " noise would be picked up. But I wanted the guns to be heard in America. The censors had allowed me to pronounce only one sentence about the raid, merely stating that one was on.

Actually when I spoke there seemed to be a most unfortunate lull in the firing. Only in the distance, through the studio doors, could I hear a faint rumble. Apparently the guns were more audible in America than in my studio, because a few minutes later I picked up the rest of our program by shortwave to hear Elmer Davis remark in New York that the sound of guns or bombs during my broadcast was most realistic. This pleased me greatly, but I noticed deep frowns on the faces of the German officials who also caught Mr. Davis's comment.

Sigrid, who spoke for Mutual a half-hour later, pluckily braved the shrapnel which seemed to be falling even thicker than before, though several of us tried to dissuade her from going to the studio. As it was, in trying to dodge one hail of splinters, she stumbled and fell, receiving an ugly gash in the leg. She went on with her broadcast, though in great pain. But luck was not with her. The same transmitter which had functioned perfectly for CBS and NBC only a few minutes before suddenly broke down and her talk did not get through to America.

Until almost dawn we watched the spectacle from a balcony. There was a low ceiling of clouds, and the German searchlight batteries tried vainly to pick up the British bombers. The beams of light would flash on for a few seconds, search the skies wildly, and then go off. The British were cruising as they wished over the heart of the city and flying quite low, judging by the sound of their motors. The German *flak* was firing wildly, completely by sound. It was easy, from the firing, to follow a plane across the city as one battery after another picked up the sound of the motors and fired blindly into the sky. Most of the noise came from the north, where the armament factories are.

Today the bombing is the one topic of conversation among Berliners. It's especially amusing therefore to see that Goebbels has permitted the local newspapers to publish only a six-line communiqué about it, to the effect that enemy planes flew over the capital, dropped a few incendiary bombs on two suburbs, and damaged one wooden hut in a garden. There is not a line about the explosive bombs which we all plainly heard. Nor is there a word about the three streets in Berlin which have been roped off all day today to prevent the curious from seeing what a bomb can do to a house. It will be interest-

ing to watch the reaction of the Berliners to the efforts
of the authorities to hush up the extent of the raid. It's
the first time they've been able to compare what actually happened with what Dr. Goebbels reported. The
British also dropped a few leaflets last night, telling the
populace that " the war which Hitler started will go on,
and it will last as long as Hitler does." That's good
propaganda, but unfortunately few people were able
to find the leaflets, there being only a handful dropped.

BERLIN, *August* 29

The British came over in force again last night
and for the first time killed Germans in the capital of the
Reich. The official account is ten persons killed and
twenty-nine wounded in Berlin. At the Kottbuserstrasse
out towards Tempelhof (which the British probably
were aiming at) and not far from the Görlitzer railroad
station (which they might have been aiming at) two
hundred-pound bombs landed in the street, tore off the
leg of an air-raid warden standing at the entrance to
his house, and killed four men and two women, who, un-
wisely, were watching the fireworks from a doorway.

I think the populace of Berlin is more affected by the
fact that the British planes have been able to penetrate
to the centre of Berlin without trouble than they are by
the first casualties. For the first time the war has been
brought home to them. If the British keep this up, it
will have a tremendous effect upon the morale of the
people here.

Goebbels today suddenly changed his tactics. His orders after the first big bombing were to play the story
down in the press. Today he orders the newspapers to
cry out at the " brutality " of the British fliers in attacking the defenceless women and children of Berlin.

One must keep in mind that the people here have not yet been told of the murderous bombings of London by the Luftwaffe. The invariable headline today about last night's raid is: "COWARDLY BRITISH ATTACK." And the little *Doktor* makes the papers drum into the people that German planes attack only military objectives in Britain, whereas the " British pirates " attack " on the personal orders of Churchill " only non-military objectives. No doubt the German people will fall for this lie too. One paper achieves a nice degree of hysteria: it says the RAF has been ordered " to massacre the population of Berlin."

It's obvious from what we've seen here the last few nights — and Göring must have known it — that there is no defence against the night bombers. Neither on Sunday nor last night did the anti-aircraft defences of Berlin, which are probably the best in the world, even spot a single British plane in the beam of a searchlight, let alone bring one down. The official communiqué, hesitating to tell the local people that any planes were brought down last night over the city when thousands of them probably saw that none were, announced today that one bomber was shot down on its way *to* Berlin and another after it *left* Berlin.

I had my own troubles at the radio last night. First, the censors announced that we could no longer mention a raid while it was on. (In London Ed Murrow not only mentions it, but describes it.) Secondly, I got into somewhat of a row with the German radio officials. As soon as I had finished my broadcast, they ordered me to the cellar. I tried to explain that I had come here as a war correspondent and that in ordering me to the cellar they were preventing me from exercising my profession. We exchanged some rather sharp words. Lord Haw-Haw, I notice, is the only other person around here ex-

cept the very plucky girl secretaries who does not rush
to the shelter after the siren sounds. I have avoided him
for a year, but have been thinking lately it might be
wise to get acquainted with the traitor. In the air-raids
he has shown guts.

BERLIN, *August* 31

Laid up with the flu for a bit. When the maid
came in last night just before the bombing started, I
asked: " Will the British come over tonight? "

" For certain," she sighed resignedly. All her confidence, all the confidence that five million Berliners had
that the capital was safe from air attack, is gone.

" Why do they do it? " she asked.

" Because you bomb London," I said.

" Yes, but we hit military objectives, while the British, they bomb our homes." She was a good advertisement for the effectiveness of Goebbels's propaganda.

" Maybe you bomb their homes too," I said.

" Our papers say not," she argued. She said the
German people wanted peace. " Why didn't the British
accept the Führer's offer? " she wanted to know. This
woman comes from a worker's family. Her husband is
a worker, probably an ex-Communist or Socialist. And
yet she has fallen a complete victim to the official propaganda.

The British gave us a good strafing last night and
even German officials admitted that the damage was
greater than ever before. A German friend dropped in
to tell me the great Siemens works had been hit. The
Börsen Zeitung headlines tonight: "BRITISH AIR PI-
RATES OVER BERLIN."

I've turned down the Propaganda Ministry's offer to
take me along with other correspondents on a conducted

tour each morning after a raid to see the damage. I
know the German military authorities have no intention
of showing us any military objectives that may be hit.
To make an honest check-up would take several hours of
motoring over the vast area of Berlin.

BERLIN, *September* 1

I was in my bath at midnight last night and
did not hear the sirens sound the alarm. First I knew
of the raid was when the guns started to thunder. I
dozed off to sleep, still having the flu with me, but was
awakened during the night by the thud and shock of two
bomb explosions very near the hotel.

Today the High Command announces officially that
the British fliers last night were "hindered" from
dropping their bombs by the splendid work of the capital's anti-aircraft guns, and that the only bombs dropped
therefore fell outside the city limits.

This is strange because the Tiergarten was roped off
today and this evening the press admits that several
"bomb craters" were discovered in the park after last
night's raid. I staggered off to the *Rundfunk* tonight
to do an anniversary broadcast. The military censor,
a very decent chap, was puzzled about the conflicting
German reports of the bombing.

"My instructions are you can't contradict the communiqués of the High Command," he said.

"But the German press contradicts them," I argued.
"I heard the bombs fall in the Tiergarten, and the Berlin papers admit that some did."

He was a good sport and let me read the contradictory
reports.

The main effect of a week of constant British night
bombings has been to spread great disillusionment

among the people here and sow doubt in their minds. One said to me today: " I'll never believe another thing they say. If they've lied about the raids in the rest of Germany as they have about the ones on Berlin, then it must have been pretty bad there."

Actually, the British bombings have not been very deadly. The British are using too few planes — fifteen or twenty a night — and they have to come too far to carry really effective, heavy loads of bombs. Main effect is a moral one, and if the British are smart they'll keep them up every night. Tonight another attack began just before I broadcast, but it was not much of a show.

A year ago today the great "counter-attack" against Poland began. In this year German arms have achieved victories never equalled even in the brilliant military history of this aggressive, militaristic nation. And yet the war is not yet over, or won. And it was on this aspect that people's minds were concentrated today, if I am any judge. They long for peace. And they want it before the winter comes.

BERLIN, *September* 2

I learned today that the Germans you see removing time bombs are for the most part prisoners from concentration camps. If they live through the experience, they are promised release. As a matter of fact it probably is an easy choice for them. Even death is a welcome release from the tortures of the Gestapo. And there's always the chance that the bomb won't go off. Some of the bombs that fell in the Tiergarten, it's now revealed, were time bombs.

For some time now our censors have not allowed us

to use the word " Nazi " on the air. They say it has a bad sound in America. One must say " National Socialist " or avoid the term altogether, as I do. The word " invasion " in reference to what happened in Scandinavia and the west, and what is planned for England, is also taboo.

Studying the German figures on air losses over Britain, which are manifestly untrue, I find that nearly every day they run 4 to 1 in favour of the Luftwaffe. This ratio must have a magic attraction to someone in the Air Ministry.

BERLIN, *September 4-5* (3 *a.m.*)

Hitler made a surprise speech here this afternoon, the occasion being the opening of the *Winterhilfe* — winter relief — campaign. Like the *Volkswagen,* the cheap " people's car " on which German workers are paying millions of marks a month in instalments though the factory which is supposed to make them is actually manufacturing only arms, the *Winterhilfe* is one of the scandals of the Nazi regime, though not one German in a million realizes it. It is obvious that in a country without unemployment not much " winter relief " is necessary. Yet the Nazis go on wringing several hundred million marks each winter out of the people for " winter charity " and actually use most of the money for armaments or party funds.

Hitler's appearance today was kept a secret until the last minute, the Propaganda Ministry rushing off the correspondents from the afternoon press conference to the Sportpalast. What is Himmler afraid of, since British bombers cannot come over during daylight? Is he afraid of an " incident "?

The session was another beautiful example of how

Hitler takes advantage of the gullibility of his people. He told them, for instance, that while the German air force attacked Britain by day, the cowardly RAF comes over only at night. He did not explain *why* this is so — that the Germans can get over England by day because it is only twenty-five miles from German bases and they can thus protect their bombers with fighters, whereas Germany is too far from Britain to enable the British to protect their bombers with fighters.

Hitler said with lovely hypocrisy: " I waited three months without answering the British night bombings in the hope they would stop this mischief. But Herr Churchill saw in this a sign of weakness. You will understand that we are now answering, night for night. And when the British air force drops two or three or four thousand kilograms of bombs, then we will in one night drop 150- 230- 300- or 400,000 kilograms."

At this point he had to stop because of the hysterical applause of the audience, which consisted mostly of German women nurses and social workers.

" When they declare," continued Hitler, " that they will increase their attacks on our cities, then we will raze *their* cities to the ground." Here the young nurses and social workers were quite beside themselves and applauded phrenetically. When they had recovered, he said:

" We will stop the handiwork of these air pirates, so help us God." At this the young German women hopped to their feet and, their breasts heaving, screamed their approval.

" The hour will come," Hitler went on, " when one of us will break, and it will not be National Socialist Germany." At this juncture the raving maidens kept their heads sufficiently to break their wild shouts of joy with a chorus of: " Never! Never!"

Though grim and dripping with hate most of the evening, Hitler had his humorous, jaunty moments. His listeners found it very funny when he said: " In England they're filled with curiosity and keep asking: 'Why doesn't he come?' Be calm. Be calm. He's coming! He's coming!" And the man squeezed every ounce of humour and sarcasm out of his voice. The speech was not broadcast direct, but recorded and rebroadcast two hours after he had finished.

LATER. — The British came over again to-night, arriving punctually at fifteen minutes before midnight, which is their usual time. The fact that the searchlights rarely pick up a plane has given rise to whispers among the people of Berlin that the British planes are coated with an invisible paint. Tonight the bombers cruised over the city at intervals for two hours. The *flak* guns thundered away like mad, but without effect. Another bomb dropped in the Tiergarten and killed a policeman.

BERLIN, *September* 5

Very annoyed still that the German radio officials refuse to let me view the nightly air-raids. They come each night when I am at the *Rundfunk*. Nor can we mention them if they occur during our talk. To-night when I arrived for my broadcast I found that the RRG had installed a lip microphone for us to speak in. In order to make your voice heard you have to hold your lips to it. But the sounds of the anti-aircraft guns firing outside do not register. That is why they installed it. But they have put it in the same building, so that we no longer have to race through a hail of falling shrapnel to get to a microphone.

The United States is to turn over fifty destroyers to the British in return for naval and air bases in British possessions off our eastern coast. The Germans say it is a breach of neutrality, as it is, but they're not going to do anything about it, not even protest. They're hoping that our isolationists and our Lindberghs will keep us out of the war and they intend to refrain from doing anything to jeopardize their position.

BERLIN, *September* 7

Last night we had the biggest and most effective bombing of the war. The Germans have brought in several more batteries of *flak* during the past few days, and last night they put up a terrific barrage, but failed to hit a single plane.

The British were aiming better last night. When I returned from the *Rundfunk* shortly after three a.m., the sky over the north-central part of Berlin was lit up by two great fires. The biggest was in the freight house of the Lehrter railroad station. Another railroad station at the Schussendorfstrasse also was hit. A rubber factory, I'm told, was set afire.

Despite this the High Command said in its communiqué today: " The enemy again attacked the German capital last night, causing some damage to persons and property as a result of his indiscriminate throwing of bombs on non-military targets in the middle of the city. The German air force, as reprisal, has therefore begun to attack London with strong forces."

Not a hint here — and the German people do not know it — that the Germans have been dropping bombs in the very centre of London for the last two weeks. My censors warned me today not to go into this matter. I apparently have some German listeners, who can pick up my talk from the German transmitter that shortwaves it to New York. Since it's a German transmitter, there is no penalty.

The statement of the High Command, obviously forced upon it by Hitler himself — he often takes a hand in writing the official army communiqués — deliberately perpetrates the lie that Germany has only decided to bomb London as a result of the British *first* bombing Berlin. And the German people will fall for this, as they fall for almost everything they're told nowadays. Certainly never before in modern times — since the press, and later the radio, made it theoretically possible for the mass of mankind to learn what was going on in the world — have a great people been so misled, so unscrupulously lied to, as the Germans under this regime.

And so tonight the High Command, which all good Germans believe tells only the gospel truth, issued a special communiqué saying that as reprisal for the British raids on Berlin, London was attacked with strong forces for the *first* time today. As a result of this reprisal attack, it says, " one great cloud of smoke tonight stretches from the middle of London to the mouth of the Thames."

To give American radio listeners an idea of the kind of propaganda (though I couldn't label it as such) which the German people are being subjected to now, I read in my broadcast tonight the following quotation from today's Berlin newspaper, the *Börsen Zeitung:* " While the attack of the German air force is made on purely military objectives — this fact is recognized by both the British press and radio — the RAF knows nothing better to do than continually to attack nonmilitary objectives in Germany. A perfect example of this was the criminal attack on the middle of Berlin last

night. In this attack only lodging-houses were hit; not
a single military objective."

The German people have no inkling — because the
Nazi press and radio have carefully suppressed the
story — that in August alone more than one thousand
English civilians were killed by the Luftwaffe's attacks
on British " military objectives."

Another type of lying here: The official statement of
last night's bombing of Berlin says that the first two
waves of British planes were turned back by the capital's defences, and that only a few planes of the third
wave were able to slip through. Now, every Berliner
knows that from the minute the alarm was sounded last
night, British planes were heard overhead. There were
several waves and each time you heard the hum of the
motors. Yet I fear the majority will believe the official
explanation.

The *Börsen Zeitung* even went so far last night as to
tell its innocent readers that all military objectives in
Germany were so well protected by anti-aircraft guns
that it was quite impossible for the British planes to
bomb them. Therefore the British went after unpro-
tected civilian houses. How many Germans will ask
then, why, with an admitted concentration of guns in
and around Berlin such as no other area in the world
has ever seen — why has not a single plane yet been
brought down?

And personally I'm getting a little tired of the censorship restrictions on our telling even a modicum of
truth about this air war to America. I shall not stand
for it much longer.

BERLIN, *September* 8

All Sunday morning papers carry the same headline: "BIG ATTACK ON LONDON AS REPRISAL."

BERLIN, *September* 9

A typical Nazi trick was played on me today. The three censors fought with me so long over the script of my two p.m. broadcast, which they charged was unduly ironic about the " reprisal " bombings of London, which it was, that by the time they had finally okayed it, there was no time for me to go on the air. My five minutes of air time was over.

There was no objection to this, since the censors have a perfect right to hold up a script they don't like, just as I have the right not to talk if I think they've censored the true sense out of my talk. But this evening I learn from Paul White in New York, through channels which permit me to receive cables from him without the Germans knowing their contents, that the short-wave director of the German Broadcasting Company cabled him today an explanation of why I did not broadcast at two p.m. The cable read: " Regret Shirer arrived too late today to broadcast."

The British bombers failed to come over last night or the night before. Official explanation to the German people: The British planes tried to get through both nights to Berlin, but were turned back. Whenever the British choose not to bomb Berlin henceforth, I hear, Goebbels has ordered the people to be told that they tried to but were repulsed by the capital's magnificent defences.

Whenever the British come over Germany now, most

of the German radio stations hurriedly go off the air so as not to serve as radio beacons for the British pilots. The German radio announced tonight that its broadcasts, already greatly curtailed in the last fortnight on " military grounds," will be further curtailed. " This is no time," said the announcement, " to explain further the reasons for this."

BERLIN, *September* 10

A light raid last night, though a few houses were demolished. Commenting on the bombing, the *Lokal Anzeiger* says: " The fliers of His Britannic Majesty have given a heavy blow to the laws governing an honourable and manly conduct of war."

At the Propaganda Ministry today we were shown one of Britain's " secret weapons," a new sort of incendiary weapon. It looks like a large calling card — about two inches square — and is made of a celluloid substance. Two celluloid sheets are pasted together and between them is a tablet of phosphorus. The British drop them in a dampened condition. When they dry, after a few minutes of sun, or ten minutes of dry, daytime air, they ignite and cause a small flame that burns for two or three minutes. Actually, they were first used by the Irish Republicans, who dropped them in letter-boxes to burn the mail in England. The Germans admit they have set fire to fields of grain and hay as well as a few forests. Probably the British, who started dropping them in August, hoped to burn up a considerable acreage of grain. Unfortunately, we had a very wet August and few of them got dry enough to ignite.

BERLIN, *September* 11

Last night the severest bombing yet. And the German papers are beside themselves. The *Börsen Zeitung* calls our pilot visitors of last evening " barbarians " and bannerlines: "CRIME OF BRITISH ON BERLIN." According to the Nazis, only five persons were killed, but for the first time the British dropped a considerable number of fire bombs and there were quite a few small fires. Three incendiaries fell in the yard of the Adlon, five in the garden of the Embassy next door, and a half-dozen more in the garden of Dr. Goebbels just behind the Embassy. The office of the Minister of Munitions between the Adlon and the Embassy also was hit. All the incendiaries were put out before they did any damage. Actually the British were aiming at the Potsdamer Bahnhof, and they had bad luck. They took almost a perfect run for it, their first bombs hitting the Reichstag and then falling in a direct line towards the Potsdamer station on the Brandenburger Tor, the Embassy, and in the gardens behind. But the last one was about three hundred yards short of the station.

Today the BBC claims that the Potsdamer station was hit, but this is untrue and at least three Germans today who heard the BBC told me they felt a little disillusioned at the British radio's lack of veracity. The point is that it is bad propaganda for the British to broadcast in German to the people here that a main station has been set on fire when it hasn't been touched.

I almost met a quick end last night. Racing home from the *Rundfunk* after the all-clear at fifty miles an hour in my car, I suddenly skidded into some debris and came to a stop twenty feet from a fresh bomb crater on the East-West Axis about a hundred and fifty yards from the Brandenburger Tor. In the black-out you could not see it, and the air-wardens had not yet discovered it. A splinter from the bomb that made this crater hurtled two hundred yards through the air to the American Embassy and crashed through the double window of the office of Donald Heath, our First Secretary. It cut a neat hole in the two windows, continued directly over Don's desk, and penetrated four inches into the wall on the far side of the room. Don was supposed to have had night duty last night and would have been sitting at his desk at the time, but for some reason Chargé d'Affaires Kirk had told him to go home and himself had done the night trick.

BERLIN, *September* 12

Off to Geneva for a few days so that I can talk some matters over with New York on the telephone without being overheard by the Nazis. The Germans want Hartrich, my assistant, to leave, and I'm against it.

The rumour is that the big invasion hop against England is planned for the night of September 15, when there will be a full moon and the proper tide in the Channel. I'll chance this trip anyway.

GENEVA, *September* 16

The news coming over the near-by border of France is that the Germans have attempted a landing in Britain, but that it has been repulsed with heavy German losses. Must take this report with a grain of salt.

Lunch with John Winant, head of the International Labour Office, who strives valiantly to keep his institu-

tion, and what it stands for, from going under after the
blow the war has given it. More than any other American in public life whom I know, he understands the
social forces and changes that have been at work in the
last decade both at home and in Europe, and that are
now in new ferment as a result of the war. We talked
about the job to be done after the war if Britain wins
and if the mistakes of 1919 are not to be repeated. He
spoke of his own ideas about reconstruction and how
war economy could be replaced by a peace economy
without the maladjustment, the great unemployment
and deflation and depression that followed the last war.
Personally I cannot look that far ahead. I cannot see
beyond Hitler's defeat. To accomplish that first is such
a gigantic task and so overwhelmingly important that
all else seems secondary, though undoubtedly it is a
good thing that some are taking a longer view.

Winant is a likable, gaunt, awkward, Lincolnesque
sort of man and was a good enough politician and execu-
tive to be re-elected Governor of New Hampshire a
couple of times. I think he would make a good president to succeed Roosevelt in 1944 if the latter gets his
third term.

BERLIN, *September* 18

Somewhere near Frankfurt on the train from
Basel last night the porter shouted: " *Flieger-Alarm!* "
and there was a distant sound of gun-fire, but nothing
hit us. We arrived at the Potsdamer Bahnhof right
on time and I observed again that the station had not
been hit despite the claims of the BBC. I noticed several lightly wounded soldiers, mostly airmen, getting
off a special car which had been attached to our train.
From their bandages, their wounds looked like burns.

I noticed also the longest Red Cross train I've ever
seen. It stretched from the station for half a mile to
beyond the bridge over the Landwehr Canal. Orderlies
were swabbing it out, the wounded having been unloaded, probably, during the night. The Germans usually unload their hospital trains after dark so that the
populace will not be unduly disturbed by one of the
grimmer sides of glorious war. I wondered where so
many wounded could have come from, as the armies in
the west stopped fighting three months ago. As there
were only a few porters I had to wait some time on the
platform and picked up a conversation with a railway
workman. He said most of the men taken from the hospital train were suffering from burns.

Can it be that the tales I heard in Geneva had some
truth in them after all? The stories there were that
either in attempted German raids with sizable landing-
parties on the English coast or in rehearsals with boats
and barges off the French coast the British had given
the Germans a bad pummelling. The reports reaching
Switzerland from France were that many German
barges and ships had been destroyed and a considerable
number of German troops drowned; also that the British used a new type of wireless-directed torpedo (a Swiss
invention, the Swiss said) which spread ignited oil on
the water and burned the barges. Those cases of burns
at the station this morning bear looking into.

Ribbentrop suddenly went off to Rome tonight.
Many guesses as to why. Mine: to break the news to
Mussolini that there will be no attempt at invading
Britain this fall. This will put Il Duce in a hole, as he
has already started an offensive on Egypt and advanced
a hundred miles over the desert to Sidi-el-Barrani. But
this Italian effort, it seems, was originally planned only

to distract attention from the German invasion of Britain. It begins to look now (though I still think Hitler *may* try to attack England) as though the war will shift to the Mediterranean this winter, with the Axis powers trying to deliver the British Empire a knockout blow by capturing Egypt, the Suez Canal, and Palestine. Napoleon did this once, and the blow did not fell the British Empire. (Also, Napoleon planned to attack Britain, gathered his ships and barges just where Hitler has gathered his, but never dared to launch the attack.) But the Axis seizure of Suez might knock out the British Empire now. The reason Franco's handyman, Serrano Suñer, is here in Berlin is that Hitler wants him either to take Gibraltar himself or to let the German army come in from France to do the job. Much talk here, I find, of Germany and Italy dividing up Africa between themselves, giving Spain a larger slice if Franco plays ball.

Only one air-raid here since I left, and the five million people in Berlin have caught up on their sleep and are full of breezy confidence again. They really think the British planes can't get through. Churchill is making a mistake in not sending more planes over Berlin. A mere half-dozen bombers per night would do the job — that is, would force the people to their cellars in the middle of the night and rob them of their sleep. Morale tumbled noticeably in Berlin when the British visited us almost every evening. I heard many complaints about the drop in efficiency of the armament workers and even government employees because of the loss of sleep and increased nervousness. The British haven't enough planes to devastate Berlin, but they have enough — five or six for Berlin each night — to ruin the morale of the country's most important centre of population. Can it be that the British hope to get the Germans to stop their terrible bombing of London by laying off Berlin? This would be a very silly calculation.

BERLIN, *September* 19

Having saved a little extra gasoline from my ration of thirty-seven gallons a month, I drove out to Siemensstadt with Joe Harsch and Ed Hartrich this afternoon to see if there had been any damage by bombing to the Siemens Electrical Works, one of the most important war industrial plants in Germany. I was also curious to see what mood the workers were in. We drove slowly around the plant, but could find no trace of any damage. The thousands of workers filing out after the afternoon shift seemed well fed and quite contented. Some of them looked downright prosperous and lit up cigars as they came out. During the fortnight that the British came over practically every night, the strain of working a full ten-hour shift after a night without sleep had begun to affect them, several Germans had told me. But today they looked disgustingly fit.

Returning to town somewhat disheartened by our findings, we noticed a large crowd standing on a bridge which spanned a railroad line. We thought there had been an accident. But we found the people staring silently at a long Red Cross train unloading wounded. This is getting interesting. Only during the fortnight in September when the Poles were being crushed and a month this spring when the west was being annihilated have we seen so many hospital trains in Berlin. A diplomat told me this morning his Legation had checked two other big hospital trains unloading wounded in the

Charlottenburg railroad yards yesterday. This makes four long trains of wounded in the last two days that I know have arrived here.

Not since the war started has the German press been so indignant against the British as today. According to it, the British last night bombed the Bodelschwingh hospital for mentally deficient children at Bethel in western Germany, killing nine youngsters, wounding twelve.

The same newspapers which have now begun to chronicle with glee the "reprisal" attacks on the centre of London town and which, to show the success of the "reprisals," published British figures telling of the thousands of civilians, including hundreds of children, killed by German bombs, today are filled with righteous indignation against the British for allegedly doing the same thing to Germans. Some of the headlines tonight: *Nachtausgabe:* "NIGHT CRIME OF BRITISH AGAINST 21 GERMAN CHILDREN—THIS BLOODY ACT CRIES FOR REVENGE." *Deutsche Allgemeine Zeitung:* "MURDER OF CHILDREN AT BETHEL; REVOLTING CRIME." *B.Z. am Mittag:* "ASSAS-SINS' MURDER IS NO LONGER WAR, HERR WINSTON CHURCHILL!—THE BRITISH ISLAND OF MURDERERS WILL HAVE TO TAKE THE CON-SEQUENCES OF ITS MALICIOUS BOMBINGS."

Editorial comment is in a similar vein. The *Börsen Zeitung* writes: "They wished, on the orders of Church-ill, simply to murder. . . . Albion has shown herself to be a murder-hungry beast which the German sword will liquidate in the interest not only of the German people but of the whole civilized world. . . . The sa-distic threats of the British apostles of hate will end in the smoke of their cities."

This paper in the very same editorial points out how

stores in the west of London as well as a subway station there have been hit by German bombs.

The *Diplo*, written and edited in the Foreign Office, says pontifically tonight: " It is a fact that Germany is waging war with clean weapons and in a chivalrous manner." (And London bombed indiscriminately nearly every night now, the British fighter defence having stopped the Luftwaffe's day-time attacks.)

One must keep in mind that the newspapers here do not reflect public opinion. This hysterical indignation is artificially created from above. No doubt the real reason for it is to justify in the minds of the German people what the Luftwaffe is doing to London.

Censorship of our broadcasts is growing daily more impossible. I had a royal scrap with one Nazi censor tonight. He wouldn't let me read the newspaper headlines quoted above. He said it gave America a " wrong impression." He said I was too ironic, even in my selection of headlines.

BERLIN, *September* 20

Another beautiful example today of Nazi hypocrisy. I wrote in both my broadcasts today that the German press and radio were making the most of a New York report that the British censor had decided to forbid foreign correspondents in London to mention air-raids while they were on. The German Propaganda Ministry jumped on this dispatch and through its short-wave and foreign-press services tried to tell the world that henceforth America was going to be deprived of trustworthy news from London. I pointed out, incidentally, that the Nazis had clamped the same kind of censorship on us some time ago. My censors would not hear of my saying any such thing.

I ask myself why I stay on here. For the first eight
months of the war our censorship was fairly reasonable
— more so than Sevareid and Grandin had to put up
with in Paris. But since the war became grim and
serious — since the invasion of Scandinavia — it has
become increasingly worse. For the last few months
I've been trying to get by on my wits, such as they are;
to indicate a truth or an official lie by the tone and
inflexion of the voice, by a pause held longer than is
natural, by the use of an Americanism which most Germans, who've learned their English in England, will
not fully grasp, and by drawing from a word, a phrase,
a sentence, a paragraph, or their juxtaposition, all the
benefit I can. But the Nazis are on to me. For some
time now my two chief censors from the Propaganda
Ministry have been gentlemen who understand American as well as I, Professor Lessing, who long held a
post in an American university, and Herr Krauss, for
twenty years a partner in a Wall Street bank. I cannot fool them very often. Personally, both are decent,
intelligent Germans, as is Captain Erich Kunsti, former
Program Director of the Austrian Broadcasting System and now my principal military censor. But they
must do what they're told. And the Foreign Office and
Propaganda Ministry keep receiving reports from the
United States — not only from the Embassy at Washington, but from their well-organized intelligence service throughout our country — that I'm getting by with
murder (which I'm not) and must be sat upon. Dr.
Kurt Sell, the Nazi man in Washington whose duty,
among other things, is to report to Berlin on what we
send, has several times reported unfavourab'y on the
nature of my broadcasts. I haven't the slightest interest in remaining here unless I can continue to give
a fairly accurate report. And each day my broadcasts

are forced by the censorship to be less accurate. Tonight I noticed for the first time that one of the young
Germans who do my modulating (call New York on
the transmitter until time for me to speak) and follow
my script to see that I read it as written and censored
was *scanning* a copy of my broadcast as I spoke, making funny little lines under the syllables as we used to
do in school while learning to scan poetry. He was trying to note down, I take it, which words I emphasized,
which I spoke with undue sarcasm, and so on. I was
so fascinated by this discovery that I stopped in the
middle of my talk to watch him.

BERLIN, *September* 21

X came up to my room in the Adlon today,
and after we had disconnected my telephone and made
sure that no one was listening through the crack of
the door to the next room, he told me a weird story. He
says the Gestapo is now systematically bumping off the
mentally deficient people of the Reich. The Nazis call
them " mercy deaths." He relates that Pastor Bodelschwingh, who runs a large hospital for various kinds
of feeble-minded children at Bethel, was ordered arrested a few days ago because he refused to deliver up
some of his more serious mental cases to the secret
police. Shortly after this, his hospital is bombed. By
the " British." Must look into this story.

BERLIN, *September* 22

We know that Himmler has hanged, without
trial, at least one Pole for having had sexual relations
with a German woman. We know too that at least half
a dozen German women have been given long prison sen-

tences for having bestowed favours upon Polish prisoners or farm labourers. Several Germans have told me of placards prominently displayed in the provincial towns warning Germans not to have anything to do with Polish labourers and to treat them rough. Last week every household in Berlin received a leaflet from the local office of the " Bund of Germans Abroad " warning the people not to fraternize with the Poles now working as labourers or prisoners in Germany. A few choice extracts from this document:

" German people, never forget that the atrocities of the Poles compelled the Führer to protect our German people by armed force! . . . The servility of the Poles to their German employers merely hides their cunning; their friendly behaviour hides their deceit. . . . Remember, there is no community whatever between Germans and Poles! Be careful that no relationship shall result because of the common religious faith! . . . . Our farmers may think each Pole who greets them with a ' Jesus Christ be praised! ' is a decent fellow and may answer: ' For ever and ever, amen! '

" Germans! The Pole must never be your comrade! He is inferior to each German comrade on his farm or in his factory. Be just, as Germans have always been, but never forget that you are a member of the master race! "

I note that Poles working in Germany now have been forced to wear an arm-band or an emblem sewn on the front of their coat marked with a large " P " in purple on a yellow background. In German-occupied Poland, Jews wear a similar emblem marked with a " J."

LATER. — Ribbentrop is back from Rome, and the press hints that the " final phase " of the war has been decided upon. Rudolf Kircher, editor of the

Frankfurter Zeitung, writes from Rome that the military situation is so rosy for the Axis that Ribbentrop and the Duce actually spent most of their time planning the " new order " in Europe and Africa. This may make the German people feel a little better, but most Germans I speak to are beginning for the first time to wonder why the invasion of Britain hasn't come off. They're still confident the war will be over by Christmas. But then, until a fortnight ago they were sure it would be over before winter, which will be on us within a month. I have won all my bets with Nazi officials and newspapermen about the date of the Swastika appearing in Trafalgar Square and shall — or should — receive from them enough champagne to keep me all winter. Today when I suggested to some of them another little bet so they could win back some of their champagne, they did not think it was funny. Neither would they bet.

German correspondents in Rome today reported that Italy is displeased with Greece and that the British are violating the neutrality of Greek waters as they once did those of Norway. This sounds bad. I suppose Greece will be next.

BERLIN, *September* 23

After a week's absence the British bombers came over last night and kept the populace in their cellars for two hours and twenty minutes in the middle of the night. This was a little shock for most people, for they had been told all week that for several nights the British had been trying to get through but had always been turned back by the anti-aircraft defences. The local papers again rage against the " British criminals " for having bombed us last night. The *Nacht-*

ausgabe bannerlines: "NEW NIGHT ACT OF THE
PIRATES." The same paper editorializes: "Winston
Churchill again yesterday gave British airmen the
order to drop their bombs on the German civilian population and thus continue their murder of German men,
women, and children." The *Börsen Zeitung* holds that
"last night Churchill continued the series of his
criminal blows against the German civil population.
Frankly, Churchill belongs to that category of criminals who in their stupid brutality are unteachable."

While this line of nonsense is of course dictated to
the German press by Goebbels, it does indicate, I think,
that the Germans can't take night bombing as the
British are taking it. If London was only more on its
toes it would realize this. RAF strategy, I gather, is
to concentrate on Germany's war industries and supply-
depots. But while they've no doubt hit some interesting
targets, like the Leuna works, where coal is made into
oil (they've hit Leuna, but not knocked it out), it is
certain that they have not succeeded in crippling Germany's war industrial production to any appreciable
extent, nor have they blown up many stores. What
they must do is to keep the German people in their
damp, cold cellars at night, prevent them from sleeping,
and wear down their nerves. Those nerves already are
very thin after seven years of belt-tightening Nazi
mobilization for Total War.

Last night an old German acquaintance dropped in
on me. He's in the Luftwaffe now and for the last three
weeks has been a member of the crew of a night bomber
which has been working on London. He had some interesting details.

1. He was impressed by the size of London. He said
they've been pounding away on it for three weeks and
he is amazed that so much of it is left! He said they

were often told before taking off that they would find
their target by a whole square mile of the city on fire.
When they got there they could find no square mile on
fire; only a fire here and there.

2. He relates that they approach London at a height
of from 15,000 to 16,000 feet, dive to about 10,000 feet,
and release their bombs at this height — too high for
accurate night bombing. They don't dare to go below
7,000 feet, he says, on account of the barrage balloons.
He describes the anti-aircraft fire over London as
" pretty hot."

3. German night bomber crews, he says, are tired.
They are being overworked. The Luftwaffe figured
that they would destroy the RAF during daylight operations as they had destroyed the Polish, Dutch, Belgian, and French air forces and neglected to train
enough men for night work. Present crews, he divulged,
are flying four nights out of seven a week. Unlike Dr.
Goebbels, whose propaganda machine drums it into the
people that British airmen are cowards when they're
not brutes, my friend says quite frankly that the German pilots have the highest admiration for their British adversaries — for their skill and their bravery.
They're particularly fond of one British fighter-pilot,
he relates, who roars into a fight with a cigarette stuck
at a smart angle between his lips. If this man is ever
shot down on the German side, the German airmen have
sworn to hide him and not to hand him over as a prisoner
of war.

4. He confirms that the British bombers are pounding hell out of the French and Belgian coasts at night.
And often they swoop down in the night and machine-
gun the German bomber bases just as the German
planes are taking off or alighting.

5. Göring *did* fly over London, he asserts. This news

was given the foreign press here, but withheld from
the German papers, which made us suspicious of it.

6. He relates that the British have built a number
of dummy airfields and littered them with wooden
planes, but the Germans have most of them spotted by
now.

7. He confirms that the German bombers usually
return from a flight over Britain to different bases,
rarely to the one they have taken off from. He says
the bombers start from widely scattered fields in France,
Belgium, and Holland, but always on a strict time-table
so as to avoid collisions in the darkness. The exact
course back from London is always prescribed in advance, so that planes entering over the area will not
crash into those leaving. He has an interesting explanation of the big beating the Germans took in a daylight
attack on London a week ago Sunday when, according
to the British, 185 German planes were shot down,
mostly bombers. He says that the German time schedule
went wrong, that the German fighters which were to
protect the bombers arrived at a prearranged rendez-
vous off the English coast, but found no bombers there.
After waiting twenty-five minutes they had to fly home
because their gas was getting low. The bombers eventually arrived, coming over the North Sea, but there was
no fighter escort for them, and the British chasers
mowed them down.

8. He said the German night bombers go over in
squadrons of seven. He also insisted that each Luftwaffe base reports its correct losses and that any doctor-
ing of figures is done either at headquarters or in Berlin.

He confirms that the Luftwaffe has failed so far to
gain air supremacy over Britain, though when I was
on the Channel five weeks ago the Germans said this
would be a matter of but a fortnight.

It's a fact that since about a fortnight the Germans have given up large-scale day attacks on England and have gone over largely to night bombing. This in itself is an admission of defeat.

BERLIN, *September* 24

The British really went to work on Berlin last night. They bombed heavily and with excellent aim for exactly four hours. They hit some important factories in the north of the city, one big gas works, and the railroad yards north of the Stettiner and Lehrter stations.

But we couldn't tell the story. The authorities said no damage of military importance was done and the Propaganda Ministry, suddenly very nervous over last night's destruction, warned all of us correspondents that we could only report what the military said. Goebbels's Ministry even cancelled its usual post-raid conducted tour of the city, giving as an excuse that there was so much to see and so little time to see it in.

The German press and radio have never been made to lie quite so completely about a raid as today. Even the stolid Berliners, judging by their talk, appear to be stirred at the lies of their own newspapers. Said the official account: " In spite of violent anti-aircraft fire a few British bombers succeeded in reaching the northern and eastern suburbs of Berlin last night and dropped a number of bombs. The position of the bombs, far away from all military or industrial objectives, provides fresh evidence of the fact that the British airmen deliberately attack residential quarters. There was no damage of military importance."

Even the High Command, in whose veracity many Germans still believe, repeated the lie later in its daily

war communiqué. The hundreds of thousands of com-
muters from the northern suburbs who had to get off
their trains today three times and be conveyed by bus
over three stretches of one main railway line where
British bombs had blown up the tracks were somewhat
surprised by what they read in their papers.

The British just missed twice blowing up the elevated
Stadtbahn railroad running east-west through the centre of Berlin. In both places the bomb missed the tracks
by a few yards, damaging adjacent houses. This line
not only carries the bulk of the suburban electric traffic, but a large number of passenger trains. It's the
most important line within the city limits. The debris
from buildings which were hit held up traffic last night,
but today the line was running.

Serrano Suñer, Franco's brother-in-law and Minister of Interior, returned from a visit to the western
front just in time to experience his first British bombing attack. This may have been helpful. We correspondents kept imagining Suñer returning to Madrid,
and Franco, who is under tremendous pressure from
Berlin and Rome now to hop on the Axis band-wagon,
asking him about those British attacks on Berlin, and
Suñer replying: "What attacks? I saw no attacks. I
was in Berlin ten days. The British couldn't get over
even once. The British are finished, generalissimo, and
now is the time for Spain to get in on the Axis spoils."

Goebbels and most of the other luminaries of the
Nazi Party were dining Suñer at the Adlon last night
when the bombing began. The banquet was brought to
an abrupt close before the dessert had been served and
all present made for the Adlon's spacious air-raid cellar
next to the barber-shop. When I returned at four a.m.
from the radio, they were just leaving.

I learn Ciano is coming here Thursday. A deal is

on between Berlin and Rome to finish the war in Africa this winter and divide up the Dark Continent. But they must be sure of Spain first and are insisting that Franco either take Gibraltar or let the Germans take it.

Berlin pleased tonight that the French, who have practically turned over Indo-China to the Japs without a blow and daily make new concessions to the Axis without a murmur, today opened fire on de Gaulle and the British, who want to have Dakar.

Last night's bombing reminds me that the best air-raid shelter in Berlin belongs to Adolf Hitler. Experts doubt that he could ever be killed in it. It is deep, protected by iron girders and an enormous amount of reinforced concrete, and is provided with its own ventilating and lighting plant, a private movie and an operating room. Were British bombs to blow the Chancellery to smithereens, cutting off all apparent escape from the cellar, the Führer and his associates could emerge safely by simply walking through one of the tunnels that run from his shelter to points several hundred yards away. Hitler's cellar also is fitted out with spacious sleeping-quarters, an important consideration, but one utterly neglected in most shelters, since the loss of sleep is hurting the German people far more than British bombs.

If Hitler has the best air-raid cellar in Berlin, the Jews have the worst. In many cases they have none at all. Where facilities permit, the Jews have their own special *Luftschutzkeller*, usually a small basement room next to the main part of the cellar, where the " Aryans " gather. But in many Berlin cellars there is only one room. It is for the " Aryans." The Jews must take refuge on the ground floor, usually in the hall leading from the door of the flat to the elevator or stairs. This is fairly safe if a bomb hits the roof, since the chances are that it will not penetrate to the ground floor. But

experience so far has shown that it is the most dangerous
place to be in the entire building if a bomb lands in
the street outside. Here where the Jews are hovering,
the force of the explosion is felt most; here in the entry-
way where the Jews are, you get most of the bomb splinters.

BERLIN, *September 25*

Dr. Boehmer, the Propaganda Ministry foreign-press chief, who is a typical Nazi except that he
is intelligent and has travelled widely, especially in
America, is peeved from time to time over our " lack
of appreciation " of such Nazi favours as giving the
correspondents extra food. If the way to a correspondent's heart is through his stomach, then Dr. Goebbels
certainly tries hard. In the first place he classifies us
as " heavy labourers," which means we get double rations of meat, bread, and butter. Every other Thursday, after our press conference, we line up for a fortnight's extra food cards. Moreover, Dr. Goebbels not
only permits us, but actually encourages us to import
each week, against a liberal payment in dollar exchange,
a food packet from Denmark. This latter is a life-saver.
It enables me to have bacon and eggs at breakfast four
or five times a week. Ordinarily I do not eat bacon and
eggs for breakfast, but on the short war rations now
available, I find it fortifies one for the entire day. I
also got in enough coffee from Holland before the western campaign to provide me for the next six months.
In a word, we correspondents are hardly affected by the
war-time rationing. We have plenty to eat. And the
Germans see to it that we do have enough, not because
they like us, but because — quite rightly, I suppose —
they think we'll be more kindly disposed to them if we

operate on full stomachs, we being human beings after
all.

Moreover, the Propaganda Ministry and the Foreign
Office, which fight each other over many things, have
set up a fierce rivalry to see which one can establish
the best dining club for the foreign press. Ribbentrop's
establishment, the Ausland Presse Club, off the Kurfürstendamm, is at the moment more sumptuous than Goebbels's Ausland Club on the Leipzigerplatz. But the
Doktor, I hear, has just appropriated several million
marks to modernize *his* club and make it more gaudy
than Ribbentrop's. I used to eat a couple of nights a
week at the Ausland Club, it being conveniently located
for me, and the prospect of a real beefsteak and real
coffee proving a great temptation. Moreover, it was
a place to chew the rag with the Nazis and see what was
in their minds, if anything. Since the wanton aggression against Holland and Belgium I have not gone
there, being unable any more to stomach Nazi officials
with my dinner.

If we eat well, that is not to say that the German
people do. But reports abroad about the people here
starving are greatly exaggerated. They are not starving. After a year of the blockade they are getting
enough bread, potatoes, and cabbage to keep them going for a long time. Adults get a pound of meat a week
and a quarter of a pound of butter. Americans could
hardly subsist on this diet. But Germans, whose bodies
have become accustomed for a century to large amounts
of potatoes, cabbage, and bread, seem to do very well
on it. The meat and fat ration, though considerably
under what they are used to, is enough to keep them
tolerably fit.

The shortage of fruit is acute and last winter's severe
cold has ruined the German fruit crop. We saw no

oranges or bananas last winter and are not likely to
see any this winter. The occupation of Denmark and
Holland helped temporarily to augment the stocks of
vegetables and dairy products, but Germany's inability
to furnish fodder to these countries will shortly make
them liabilities in the matter of food. There's no doubt
that the Germans looted all the available food in Scandinavia, Holland, Belgium, and France, though it's
true they paid for it — in paper marks which cost
them nothing. Only Mr. Herbert Hoover's representative here doubts that.

The important thing is that Britain will not win the
war, say, in the next two or three years by starving the
German people. And Hitler, who is never sentimental
about non-Germans, will see to it that every one of the
hundred million people in the occupied lands dies of
hunger before one German does. Of that the world may
be sure.

BERLIN, *September 26*

We had the longest air-raid of the war last
night, from eleven p.m. to four o'clock this morning. If
you had a job to get to at seven or eight a.m., as hundreds of thousands of people had, you got very little
sleep. The British ought to do this every night. No
matter if not much is destroyed. The damage last night
was not great. But the psychological effect was tremendous.

No one expected the British so early, and thousands
were caught in subways, on the Stadtbahn, in buses
and street-cars. They hastily made for the nearest public shelter and spent most of the night there. The first
result of the early arrival of the British last night —
theoretically they can arrive at ten p.m., two hours

after dark — is that all the theatres today announce
a new opening hour: six p.m., instead of seven thirty
or eight p.m. And the Ministry of Education sends out
word that in case of air-raids lasting after midnight,
grade schools will remain closed the following morning
in order to allow the children to catch up on their sleep.

It burns me up that I cannot mention a raid that is
going on during my broadcast. Last night the anti-
aircraft guns protecting the *Rundfunk* made such a
roar while I was broadcasting that I couldn't hear my
own words. The lip microphone we are now forced to
use at night prevented the sound of the guns from ac-
companying my words to America, which is a pity.
Noticed last night too that instead of having someone
talk to New York from the studio below to keep our
transmitter modulated for the five minutes before I began to talk, the RRG substituted loud band music.
This was done to drown out the sound of the guns.

The *B.Z. am Mittag* begins its account of last night's
attack: " The greatest war-monger of all times, Winston Churchill, dispatched his murderers to Berlin
again last night. . . ."

As soon as I had finished my broadcast at one a.m.,
the Nazi air-wardens forced me into the air-raid cellar.
I tried to read Carl Crow's excellent book *Four Hundred Million Customers*, but the light was poor. I became awfully bored. Finally Lord Haw-Haw and his
wife suggested we steal out. We dodged past the guards
and found an unfrequented underground tunnel, where
we proceeded to dispose of a litre of schnaps which
" Lady " Haw-Haw had brought. Haw-Haw can drink
as straight as any man, and if you can get over your
initial revulsion at his being a traitor, you find him an
amusing and even intelligent fellow. When the bottle
was finished we felt too free to go back to the cellar.

Haw-Haw found a secret stairway and we went up to his room, opened the blinds, and watched the fireworks. To the south of the city the guns were hammering away, lighting up the sky.

Sitting there in the black of the room, I had a long talk with the man. Haw-Haw, whose real name is William Joyce, but who in Germany goes by the name of Froehlich (which in German means " Joyful "), denies that he is a traitor. He argues that he has renounced his British nationality and become a German citizen, and that he is no more a traitor than thousands of British and Americans who renounced their citizenship to become comrades in the Soviet Union, or than those Germans who gave up their nationality after 1848 and fled to the United States. This doesn't satisfy me, but it does him. He kept talking about " we " and " us " and I asked him which people he meant.

" We Germans, of course," he snapped.

He's a heavily built man of about five feet nine inches, with Irish eyes that twinkle and a face scarred not by duelling in a German university but in Fascist brawls on the pavements of English towns. He speaks a fair German. I should say he has two complexes which have landed him in his present notorious position. He has a titanic hatred for Jews and an equally titanic one for capitalists. These two hatreds have been the mainsprings of his adult life. Had it not been for his hysteria about Jews, he might easily have become a successful Communist agitator. Strange as it may seem, he thinks the Nazi movement is a proletarian one which will free the world from the bonds of the " plutocratic capitalists." He sees himself primarily as a liberator of the working class.

(Haw-Haw's colleague, Jack Trevor, an English actor, who also does anti-British broadcasts for Dr.

Goebbels, has no interest in the proletariat. His one burning passion is hatred of the Jews. Last winter it used to be a common sight to see him stand in the snow, with a mighty blizzard blowing, and rave to an S.S. guard outside the studio door about the urgent necessity of liquidating all Jews everywhere. The guard, who undoubtedly had no special love for the Jews, but whose only thought was how much longer he must stand guard on an unholy wintry night, would stamp his freezing feet in the snow, turn his head from the biting wind, and mutter: " *Ja. Ja. Ja. Ja,*" probably wondering what freaks Englishmen are.)

Haw-Haw's story, as I've pieced it together from our conversations and from his little booklet, *Twilight over England,* just published in Berlin (and which he gave me after I had presented him with an English book I had smuggled in entitled *The Life and Death of Lord Haw-Haw*), is this:

He was born in New York in 1906 of Irish parents who, he says, lost what money they had in Ireland " by reason of their devotion to the British crown." He studied literature, history, and psychology at the University of London and in 1923, the year of Hitler's ill-fated Munich *Putsch,* joined the British Fascists. He says he earned his living thereafter as a tutor. In 1933 he entered Sir Oswald Mosley's British Union of Fascists and became one of its chief speakers and writers. For three years he was Mosley's propaganda chief. He claims he left Mosley's movement in 1937 " owing to differences on matters pertaining to organization." He teamed up with John Beckett, a former Socialist M.P., and started the National Socialist League, but within a few months Beckett left it because he thought Joyce's methods " too extreme."

Of these days Joyce writes: " We lived National Socialism. . . . We were all poor enough to know the horrors of freedom in democracy. One of our members was driven mad by eighteen months of unemployment and starvation. I lived for months with real friends who loved England and could not get enough to eat from her."

Twice during the year that preceded the war he was arrested on charges of assault and disturbing the peace. Then came the war clouds.

" For me," he writes, " the decision was easy to make. To me it was clear on the morning of August 25 that the greatest struggle in history was doomed to take place. It might have been a very worthy course to stay in England and incessantly work for peace. But I had one traditionally acquired or inherited prejudice. . . . England was going to war. I felt that if, for perfect reasons of conscience, I could not fight for her, I must give her up for ever."

He did. On August 25 he and his wife, " who had to leave without even being able to say farewell to her parents," set out for Germany to take part in what he calls the " sacred struggle to free the world."

Any mind which sees Hitler's cold-blooded tramping down of the free peoples of Europe as a sacred struggle to free the world speaks for itself. Haw-Haw's book is a hodge-podge of Nazi nonsense about England, studded with obvious truths about its blacker and meaner side which the whole world knows.

Haw-Haw's extremely nasal voice was at first considered by Propaganda Ministry officials as wholly unfit for broadcasting. A Nazi radio engineer who had studied in England first saw its possibilities and he was given a trial. On the radio this hard-fisted, scar-faced young Fascist rabble-rouser sounds like a decadent old English blue-blood aristocrat of the type familiar on our stage. Ed Murrow told me last winter that check-ups showed that Haw-Haw commanded at least half of the English radio audience when he was on the air. But that was when the English were bored by the " phony " war and found the war and Joyce amusing. I think he himself realizes that he has lost most of his hold on the English people. Of late he has also begun to chafe at the inane things which Goebbels makes him say.

There is a third English traitor to note here. He is Baillie Stewart, a former captain of the Seaforth Highlanders, who a few years ago was sentenced to imprisonment in the Tower for betraying military secrets to a foreign power. The girl who led him to this was a German siren, and after his release he followed her here. He did some broadcasts at first, but his Scottish nature was too unbending for the Nazi officials of the Propaganda Ministry and the German Broadcasting Company. He is now off the air and working as a translator in the Foreign Office.

While on the subject, I might as well note down the three Americans who are doing Nazi propaganda for the German radio.

Fred Kaltenbach of Waterloo, Iowa, is probably the best of the lot, actually believing in National Socialism with a sincere fanaticism and continually fighting the Nazi Party hacks when they don't agree with him. He is not a bad radio speaker. I avoid all three and have seen Kaltenbach only once. That was at Compiègne when he was having one of his periodic feuds with the Nazi radio authorities. They gave orders that he was not to be taken from Paris to Compiègne, but he stole a ride with some army officers and " gate-crashed " the ceremony. He was continually being arrested by the military and ejected from the grounds, but he came

back each time. Most Nazis find him a bit " too American " for their taste, but Kaltenbach would die for
Nazism.

The second American speaker is one Edward Leopold Delaney, who goes here by the name of E. D.
Ward. He's a disappointed actor who used to have occasional employment with road companies in the United
States. He has a diseased hatred for Jews, but otherwise is a mild fellow and broadcasts the cruder type of
Nazi propaganda without questioning.

The third person is Miss Constance Drexel, who
many years ago wrote for the Philadelphia *Public
Ledger.* The Nazis hire her, so far as I can find out,
principally because she's the only woman in town who
will sell her American accent to them. Bizarre: she
constantly pesters me for a job. One American network
hired her at the beginning of the war, but dropped her
almost at once.

For their other foreign-language broadcasts the
Nazis have a strange assortment of hired Balkanites,
Dutch, Scandinavians, Spaniards, Arabs, and Hindus.
Once in a great while one of these speakers turns out
to be "unreliable." Such a one was the Yugoslav
speaker who began his broadcast the other night:
" Ladies and gentlemen, what you are about to hear
from Berlin tonight is a lot of nonsense, a pack of lies,
and if you have any sense, you will turn your dials."
He got no further, for there are " checkers " sitting listening at the Propaganda Ministry at the other end
of town. The last seen of the fellow was when the S.S.
guards carted him off to jail.

The Norwegian people were brusquely informed last
night in a broadcast by the Nazi Commissar in Oslo,
Gauleiter Terboven, of the hard row that lies ahead

of them. Announced the *Gauleiter:* (1) The Norwegian
Royal House has no more political importance and will
never return to Norway. (2) The same goes for
the Nygaardsvold government which emigrated. (3)
Therefore any activity in favour of the Royal House
or the government which fled is prohibited. (4) In accordance with a decree of Hitler, a commissarial council
is named to take over the business of the government.
(5) The old political parties are dissolved immediately.
(6) Any combinations for the purpose of political activity of any kind will not be tolerated.

Thus is Norway, all that is decent and democratic in
Norway, destroyed — for the time being. And Germany shows so plainly how unfit she is to rule over anybody else. There was a short time, when the Reich first
took over Norway — the same is true of Holland —
when Germany might have succeeded in winning over
the goodwill of the people there, who saw it was hopeless to struggle against the overwhelming military
power of Hitler. But the Germans did everything possible to forfeit goodwill, and in a few weeks the sentiment changed. Now in all the occupied countries the
German rulers are bitterly hated. No decent Norwegian or Dutchman will have anything to do with them.

The *Gauleiter's* broadcast was a fine example of German tactlessness. He told the Norwegian people that
he had tried in vain to negotiate with the old political
parties, but they had held out for power and had not
" heeded " his warnings; so he had had to liquidate
them. In conclusion, he told the Norwegians that it
had now become clear that the way of the Quisling
movement had always been the only possible one for
Norway, and that this party would be the only one tolerated by the Germans in the future. Thus, in effect,
he told the Norwegians that a miserable little traitor,

detested by ninety-nine and a half per cent of the population, was not only right, but henceforth would have
the only say — so far as any Norwegian will have any
say, which is little enough — about the future of their
country.

You don't have to be profound to conclude that the
rule of brute force now exercised by the Germans over
the occupied territories can never last very long. For
despite complete military and police power, which the
Germans admittedly have, you cannot for ever rule over
foreign European peoples who hate and detest you.
The success of Hitler's " new order " in Europe is therefore doomed even before it is set up. The Nazis, of
course, who have never troubled to study European
history but are guided by a primitive Germanic tribal
urge of conquest with no thought for the possible consequences, think that they are well on their way to installing a European " new order " which will be dominated by Germany for the greater good of Germany for
all time. Their long-term plan is not only to keep the
subjected European peoples permanently disarmed so
that they cannot revolt against their German masters,
but to make them so dependent on Germany economically that they cannot exist without Berlin's benevolent
will. Thus those heavy and highly technical industries
which still function in the slave lands will be concentrated in Germany. The slave peoples will produce the
raw materials to feed them, and the food to feed the
German masters. They will be largely agricultural and
mining communities — much as the Balkan lands fulfil
that role for western Europe today. And they will be
utterly dependent upon Germany.

The subjected peoples of Europe will be saved, of
course, if Britain holds out and ultimately wins this
war. But even if Germany should win the war it will

lose its struggle to organize Europe. The German, I am profoundly convinced after mingling with him now for many years, is incapable of organizing Europe. His lack of balance, his bullying sadism when he is on top, his constitutional inability to grasp even faintly what is in the minds and hearts of other peoples, his instinctive feeling that relations between two peoples can only be on the basis of master and slave and never on the basis of let-live equality — these characteristics of the German make him and his nation unfit for the leadership in Europe they have always sought and make it certain that, however he may try, he will in the long run fail.

Ciano arrives here tomorrow from Rome. Most people think it is for the announcement that Spain is entering the war on the side of the Axis. Suñer is here for the ceremony, if it comes off.

BERLIN, *September* 27

　　　　　Hitler and Mussolini have pulled another surprise.

At one p.m. today in the Chancellery, Japan, Germany, and Italy signed a military alliance directed against the United States. I was caught way off base thinking that Ciano had come to pipe Spain into the war. Suñer was not even present at the theatrical performance the fascists of Europe and Asia staged today.

I came to my senses this morning when I noticed the schoolchildren who had been marched to the Wilhelmstrasse to cheer — waving Japanese flags. As I had a broadcast at two p.m. and the correspondents were convoked at the Chancellery for " an important announcement " at one p.m., I asked Hartrich to cover the actual ceremony. At the *Rundfunk* I followed it by radio.

Core of the pact is Article III. It reads: " Germany, Italy, and Japan undertake to assist one another with all political, economic, and military means when one of the three contracting parties is attacked by a power at present not involved in the European war or in the Sino-Japanese conflict."

There are two great powers not yet involved in either of those wars: Russia and the United States. But Article III does not refer to Russia; Article V refers to Russia. Article V says: " Germany, Italy, and Japan affirm that the aforesaid terms do not in any way affect the political status which exists at present between each of the three contracting parties and Soviet Russia."

The Soviet Union is out. That leaves the U.S.A. in. There was no attempt to disguise this obvious fact in Nazi circles tonight, though, as expected, my censors tried to stop me from saying so and I had to use all my wits in getting the thing across in my broadcasts. Though it would have been more honest and accurate to say bluntly that Nazi circles did not disguise the fact that the alliance was directed against the United States, I had to water it down to this beautiful opening sentence: " There is no attempt in informed circles here tonight to disguise the fact that the military alliance signed in Berlin today . . . *has one great country in mind.* That country is the United States." Then to clinch the argument I had to resort to a nebulous analysis of the text of the treaty and the German interpretation thereof, which the censors, after some sour remarks, finally passed.

Now, why did Hitler, instigator of this alliance, hurriedly rig it up just at this time? My theory is this: Ribbentrop journeyed suddenly to Rome a fortnight ago to break the news to Mussolini that the expected

land invasion of Britain, which Hitler in a speech only
a few days previously at the Sportpalast had promised
the German people would certainly take place soon,
could not be carried out as planned. Mussolini had already started an invasion of Egypt to coincide with
the attack on Britain and to divide the Empire's forces,
but not to do much more than that this fall. We
know that Ribbentrop stayed longer in Rome than he
planned. The Duce, no doubt, was disturbed at Hitler's
abandoning the all-out attack on Britain which he was
confident would end the war — and Italy had only entered the war when she did because she thought it was
almost over. What was the Axis to do? The obvious
thing seemed to devote the winter to attacking the
heart of the British Empire in Egypt, conquer that
country, take the Suez Canal, then grab Palestine,
Iraq, where badly needed oil was at hand, and possibly
continue down the Euphrates and take the Persian oil
region, or at least its export base at the head of the Persian Gulf. Germany could supply thousands of airplanes and tanks and some complete *Panzer* divisions
which had been assembled for the attack on Britain. If
necessary, Yugoslavia and Greece could be occupied
(Italy to get Dalmatia permanently), and southern
Greece used as a starting-place for German planes
against Egypt and the British Mediterranean fleet.

To ensure the complete and timely success of the
campaign, Spain must be brought in and made to take
Gibraltar immediately, thus destroying Britain's position in the western Mediterranean. Serrano Suñer,
Franco's brother-in-law, Minister of Interior and leader
of the Falangists, was in Berlin. He personally seemed
favourable. Only Franco, that ingrate, hesitated. The
British, Franco apparently thought, were not yet
beaten, and . . .

There was that other factor, the United States.

Until recently, that factor had not been taken much into account in Berlin. Last fall Göring had scoffed to us of the possibility of American aid to the Allies playing a role in this war. All through the summer, as the German army smashed through the west, Berlin was confident that the war would be over by fall, and that therefore American aid, which could only become really effective next spring, was of no concern to Germany. That view seems to have been sincerely held here until very recently. In the last two or three weeks something has gone wrong with the plans to invade Britain. They may or may not be off, but probably are. At any rate it dawned on Berlin a few days ago that Britain might not be defeated after all this fall, might still be fighting next spring, and that then American aid to Britain, especially in planes, would begin to make itself felt rather seriously. Something must be done after all about the United States. What? Something to scare her and to set the American isolationists loose again with a new cry about the danger of war.

In Japan a few weeks ago a new government under Prince Konoye came to power proclaiming a " new life " and a " new order " in eastern Asia. The Prince was a man the Germans could deal with. Herr Stahmer, a confidential man of Ribbentrop's who used to be employed in working on the British appeasers, was dispatched to look over the ground. There follows now a military alliance designed to threaten America and keep her out of the war. If I am any judge of American character, no one at home with the exception of the Wheelers, Nyes, and Lindberghs will be the least bit frightened by this. The effect will be just the opposite from what Hitler and Ribbentrop, who never fail to misjudge Anglo-Saxon character, expect.

Then too, this tripartite pact is a thing the Axis powers and especially Germany can ballyhoo to the skies, thus taking people's minds off the fact that the promised invasion of England isn't coming off and that the war — which every German confidently expected since midsummer would be over in a month or two — isn't going to end before winter comes, after all.

The ballyhoo today has already been terrific, pushing all other news completely off the front page. The German people are told that the pact is of world-shaking importance and will shortly bring final " world peace." The ceremony of signing, as described by Hartrich, who was present, was carried through with typical Axis talent for the theatrical. In the first place, the surprise of the event itself. Then the showy setting. When Ribbentrop, Ciano, and Japanese Ambassador M. Kurusu, a bewildered little man, entered the gala hall of the Chancellery, Klieg lights blazed away as the scene was recorded for history. Brightly coloured uniforms all over the place. The entire staffs of the Italian and Japanese embassies present. (No other diplomats attended. The Russian Ambassador was invited, but replied he would be out of town this noon.) The three men sit themselves at a gilded table. Ribbentrop rises and motions one of his slaves, Dr. Schmidt, to read the text of the pact. Then they sign while the cameras grind away. Then comes the climactic moment, or so the Nazis think. Three loud knocks on the giant door are heard. There is a tense hush in the great hall. The Japanese hold their breath. The door swings slowly open, and in strides Hitler. Ribbentrop bobs up and formally notifies him that the pact has been signed. The Great Khan nods approvingly, but does not deign to speak. Hitler majestically takes a seat in the middle of the table, while the two foreign min-

isters and the Japanese Ambassador scramble for chairs.
When they have got adjusted, they pop up, one after
another, and deliver prepared addresses which the radio
broadcasts round the world.

To add: Article I of the pact states that Japan rec-
ognizes the leadership of Germany and Italy in the
creation of a new order in Europe. Article II says:
" Germany and Italy recognize the leadership of Japan
in the creation of a new order in the greater east Asiatic
territory."

Neither of the two sides can lend the slightest economic or military help to the other so long as they are
separated by the British navy. What Japan gets out
of it is not clear, since if we should go to war with her
neither Germany nor Italy could harm us until they had
conquered the British navy. And should we get involved in war with Berlin and Rome, Japan is bound to
declare war on us, though her own interests might dictate not doing so. However, she could no doubt find
an excuse for forgetting the treaty in that case.

One thing is clear: Hitler would not have promul-
gated the tripartite pact if he thought the war was
coming to an end before winter. There would have been
no need of it.

BERLIN, *September* 30

A two-hour alarm last night, but we heard
nothing. Apparently the British were attacking Brandenburg, to the west of the capital. Though damage
from British bombing is still negligible, the authorities,
I learn, have ordered the evacuation of all children
under fourteen from Berlin. Agricultural Minister
Darré today claimed that food supplies for the winter
have now been secured. He estimates the potato crop

at sixty million tons. The grain crop is two million tons less than last year, but will be sufficient. Rations for meat, fats, and bread will remain the same throughout the winter.

BERLIN, *October* 3

Tipped off that Hitler and Mussolini are to pull a surprise meeting at the Brenner tomorrow. Hitler has already quit Berlin amidst the usual secrecy. We are not allowed to report it, as Hitler's movements are considered military secrets. (Himmler keeps the Führer's standard flying above the Chancellery nowadays even when the great man is absent, so that no one will know.) I did manage to slip in a concluding sentence in my broadcast tonight about a " news development of special interest " being scheduled for tomorrow.

BERLIN, *October* 4

The meeting in the Brenner took place shortly before noon today. The official communiqué gave no information on the talk except that Keitel was present. The Foreign Office warned us not to speculate.

It would be reasonable to conclude, I think, that there must have been differences between the two Axis powers so fundamental that Hitler deemed it advisable to see the Duce personally. For in the last month Ribbentrop has been to Rome, and Ciano has been here, so that there has been no lack of contact between the nominal directors of foreign policy. The best guess here is that Mussolini is sore because the Germans apparently have abandoned the idea of invading Britain this fall, leaving him holding the bag with his offensive in the Egyptian desert, where his army, now seventy-five or a hundred miles within the desert, must transport all its own water overland. Obviously Ribbentrop failed to appease the Italians, so it was necessary for Hitler to do it. It would be wishful thinking, though, to conclude that today's meeting was only negative. Obviously future war plans were gone over and perhaps a decision made to tackle the British Empire seriously at its waistline, by a drive on Egypt and the Suez Canal. It may be that Germany agreed to establish military bases in the Balkans to help this drive. One German plan much talked about here is an offensive through Turkey to the Near East.

BERLIN, *October 5*

The German newspapers make amusing reading today with their reports of the Brenner meeting. They rave for columns about its world-shaking importance, but offer not the slightest information to their readers as to why. They give no information whatsoever. But in the present totalitarian atmosphere, where words have lost all meaning, anything becomes true merely because the controlled press says so. I received one trustworthy report today that the Brenner meeting was rather stormy, with Mussolini doing some real lusty shouting. The Italians here put out a story, probably apocryphal, but indicative of Italo-German amity. They say the Duce asked the Führer yesterday why he had given up his plan to invade Britain. Hitler swallowed and then dodged an answer by posing a question of his own:

" Why haven't you, Duce, been able to take a little place like Malta? I am very disappointed about that."

The Italians here say Mussolini screwed up his face and said: " Führer, don't forget that Malta is an island too."

The fifth week of Germany's great air offensive against Britain began today. And the Germans are in a great state of mind because the British won't admit they're licked. They cannot repress their rage against Churchill for still holding out hopes of victory to his people, instead of lying down and surrendering, as have all of Hitler's opponents up to date. The Germans cannot understand a people with character and guts.

BERLIN, *October* 7

A characteristic Nazi journalistic fake. The press quotes Knickerbocker, whom it dubs " the American world liar," as having told Portuguese journalists in Lisbon that he fled London because it was no longer possible to live there. Knowing Knick, I know this is pure invention.

BERLIN, *October* 8

Lunch with the Greek Minister and Mme Rangabe. Their daughter, Elmina, whom we used to see a lot with Martha Dodd and who has a dark, Balkan beauty, was present. The Minister very glum, his valuables packed, and fearing Italian invasion any day. He clings to a slim hope that Hitler will save Greece because of what he calls the Führer's " admiration for the glories of Athens."

Though I do not broadcast to America until a quarter to two in the morning, I have to be at the *Rundfunk* at ten p.m., since it is theoretically possible for the British bombers to be over the city by then. When they do come, the Germans halt all transportation, not even permitting you to walk in the streets. That means that if I am caught elsewhere by an alarm, there is no broadcast. Last night I was helping celebrate the departure for home of " Butch " Leverich, Second Secretary of Embassy, at a party given by the Heaths when ten o'clock came. It was a great temptation to stay on. All present were certain the British would not come over. I left, however, got hopelessly lost in the black-out somewhere south of the Wittenbergplatz, but eventually got my bearings and steered my Ford through the inky night to the *Rundfunk*. As I turned off the motor, the sirens screamed, and before I could reach the building, the anti-aircraft shrapnel was falling all around like hail. The British attack lasted until four a.m., and was the most intensive yet. Once again the railroad tracks north of the Lehrter and Stettiner stations were torn up by bombs. One young German woman I know owes her life to the fact that she missed her suburban train by about twenty feet. She caught a second one fifteen minutes later, but it did not run very far. The first had been hit square on by a British bomb and blown to pieces, fifteen passengers perishing!

The German press harps so much on the Luftwaffe attacks on Britain being reprisals for the sort of thing we received last night that the public is already nauseated by the term — and Germans take a lot of nauseating. The story around town is that the average Berliner when he buys his ten-pfennig evening paper now says to the newsboy: " Give me ten pfennigs' worth of reprisals." It's interesting, by the way, how few people buy the evening newspapers. Get on a subway or a bus during the evening rush hour. Not one German in ten is reading a newspaper. Slow-thinking and long-suffering though they are, they are beginning to be aware, I think, that their newspapers give them little news, and that little so doctored by propaganda that it is difficult to recognize. Radio news is no better and of late I have noticed more than one German shut off a news broadcast after the first couple of minutes with that expressive Berlin exclamation: " Oh, *Quatsch!* " which is stronger than " Oh, nonsense! " " Rubbish " is probably a better translation.

BERLIN, *October* 15

I have pretty well made up my mind about some personal matters. For some time I've been getting information from military circles that Hitler is making ready to go into Spain in order to get Gibraltar — whether Franco, who is helpless, likes it or not. That will cut off the last avenue of escape for my family in Geneva. The only way you can get to America now from Europe is through Switzerland, unoccupied France, Spain, and Portugal to Lisbon, the one remaining port on the Continent from which you can get a boat or a plane to New York. If things come to the worst, I can always get out by way of Russia and Siberia, but that is no adventure for a child of two. This winter the Germans, to show their power to discipline the sturdy, democratic Swiss, are refusing to send Switzerland even the small amount of coal necessary for the Swiss people to heat their homes. The Germans are also allowing very little food into Switzerland, for the same shabby reason. Life in Switzerland this winter will be hard. Though Tess would rather stay, she has agreed to go home at the end of the month.

I shall follow in December. I think my usefulness here is about over. Until recently, despite the censorship, I think I've been able to do an honest job of reporting from Germany. But it has become increasingly difficult and at present it has become almost impossible. The new instructions of both the military and the po-

litical censors are that they cannot allow me to say anything which might create an unfavourable impression
for Nazi Germany in the United States. Moreover, the
new restrictions about reporting air attacks force you
either to give a completely false picture of them or to
omit mention of them altogether. I usually do the latter,
but it is almost as dishonest as the former. In short, you
can no longer report the war or conditions in Germany
as they are. You cannot call the Nazis " Nazis " or an
invasion an " invasion." You are reduced to re-broad-
casting the official communiqués, which are lies, and
which any automaton can do. Even the more intelligent
and decent of my censors ask me, in confidence, why I
stay. I have not the slightest interest in remaining under these circumstances. With my deep, burning hatred
of all that Nazism stands for, it has never been pleasant
working and living here. But that was secondary as
long as there was a job to do. No one's personal life in
Europe counts any more, and I have had none since
the war began. But now there is not even a job to do —
not from here.

ZÜRICH, *October* 18

A wonderful thing, that relief you always feel
the minute you get out of Germany. Flew down from
Berlin this afternoon. From Munich to Zürich we had
a Douglas plane flown by Swiss pilots, and off to the left
the whole time the gorgeous panorama of the Alps, the
peaks and high ranges already deep in snow. When the
sun started to set, the snow turned pink, a magnificent
shade. A half-hour out of Munich two Germ n fighter
planes pursued us, the rooky pilots using us to practise
diving on. Three or four times, swooping down on us,
they nearly touched our wings. I began to perspire,

but there was nothing to do about it. They had parachutes; we didn't.

Soon a thick cloud belt began to blanket the country under us, and I worried a bit about getting down
through it to the Zürich airport, surrounded as it is by
high hills. Finally we plunged into the clouds. We
soon appeared to be lost, for the pilot, after circling
about for five minutes, climbed above the clouds again
and turned back towards Munich. Then another
plunge, this time a deep one, and suddenly it was dark
and the thought that we were probably going to make
an emergency landing in Germany depressed me, for
a few minutes before, I had felt free of the Reich at last.
Now we were diving at a steep angle. The pilot signalled to adjust the safety belt. I gripped the seat hard.
And then out of the darkness the red fog light of a land-
ing-field, and the familiar roof-tops, and the city lights
sparkling — this could be no city of blacked-out Germany, this could only be Zürich — and in a minute we
were on hard ground. The pilot had made a perfect
blind landing in the fog.

I sit here in the Bahnhof waiting for my Geneva train,
the Dôle red wine good, the free people of Switzerland
bustling through the hall a sight worth seeing, feeling a
release and yet sad at the farewell that must be said in
Geneva next week, and the realization that still another
home we tried to make will be broken up.

GENEVA, *October* 23

Tess and Eileen got off at dawn this morning
on a Swiss bus that will take them in two days and nights
of hard driving across unoccupied France to Barcelona,
from where they can get a train to Madrid and Lisbon,
and from Lisbon a boat for home. There are no trains

across France yet. By bus is the only way, and I suppose we were lucky, because there are more than a thousand refugees here waiting to get on the two buses that ply once a week to Spain. They could carry little luggage, and we must store our belongings here for the duration. The American Express would not dispatch its bus today because of word that floods in the Pyrenees had washed out the roads between France and Spain, but our company said it hoped to get through, a hope I share. Tess carried food and water for herself and child, as there are no provisions to be had en route in France. The child was happy with excitement as the bus pulled away and I was glad she was too young to notice or feel the tragedy in that car-load of human beings, most of whom were German Jews, who were nervous and jittery almost to a point of hysteria, for they were afraid that the French might take them off and turn them over to Himmler's tortures, or that the Spaniards would not let them through.[1] If they could get to Lisbon they would be safe, but Lisbon was far.

Betty Sargent tells me Robert Dell has died in America — that grand old man of liberal English journalism whose love of justice, decency, peace, democracy, life, good talk, good food, good wine, and beautiful women was scarcely equalled by that of any man I know. I shall miss him.

BERN, *October* 24

A sad, gloomy trip with Joe [Harsch] up from Geneva this afternoon. I gazed heavy-hearted through the window of the train at the Swiss, Lake Geneva, the mountains, Mont Blanc, the green hills and the marble palace of the League that perished.

[1] Most of them were turned back at the Spanish frontier.

MUNICH, *October* 25

Blind-landed in a thick fog and the authorities would not let us continue our flight to Berlin because of the lack of visibility. Am taking the night train. All the restaurants, cafés, and beer-halls here packed tonight with lusty Bavarians. Notice they've completely stopped saying: " *Heil Hitler.*"

BERLIN, *October* 27

Ed Hartrich off in a couple of days for home and I shall leave early in December. Harry Flannery is arriving from St. Louis to take over.

BERLIN, *October* 28

Today we've had a classic example of how a Fascist dictatorship suppresses news it feels might too easily shock its people. This morning the Italian army marched into Greece. This morning, too, Hitler popped up in Florence and saw Mussolini about this latest act of Fascist aggression. The Berlin newspapers have great headlines about the meeting in Florence. But they do not carry a single line about the Italian invasion of Greece. My spies report that Goebbels has asked for a couple of days to prepare German public opinion for the news.

No word from Tess since she left Geneva. With the present chaos in unoccupied France and Spain, anything can happen.

BERLIN, *October* 29

Twenty-four hours after Italy's wanton aggression against Greece, the German people are still deprived of the news by their rulers. Not a line in the morning papers or the noon papers. But Goebbels is carefully preparing his public for the news. This morning he had the press publish the text of the outrageous Italian ultimatum to the Greek government. It was almost an exact copy of the ultimatums which the Germans sent to Denmark and Norway, and later to Holland and Belgium. But the German public may have wondered what happened after the ultimatum, since it expired yesterday morning.

Later. — The news was finally served the German people in the p.m. editions in the form of the text of today's Italian war communiqué. That was all. But there were nauseating editorials in the local press condemning Greece for not having understood the " new order " and for having plotted with the British against Italy. The moral cesspool in which German editors now splash was fairly well illustrated by their offerings today. After several years of it I still find it exasperating. Also today, the usual Goebbels fakes. For example, one saying that the Greeks disdained even to answer the ultimatum, though the truth is that they did. They rejected it.

There is certainly no enthusiasm among the people here for the latest gangster step of the Axis. German military people, always contemptuous of the Italians, tell me Greece will be no walk-away for Mussolini's legions. The mountainous terrain is difficult for motorized units to operate in and moreover, they say, the Greeks have the best mountain artillery in Europe. General Metaxas, the Premier, and quite a few Greek officers have been trained at Potsdam, the Germans tell me.

BERLIN, *October* 31

The story is that Hitler rushed from France,
where he had seen Franco and Pétain (the Führer
greatly impressed by the French marshal, but not by
Franco, say the party boys), to Florence to stop Mussolini from going into Greece. He arrived four hours too
late, and by the time he saw Mussolini there was no
turning back. The fact is that Hitler thinks he can
take the Balkans without a fight. He does not want a
war there for two reasons: first, it disrupts the already
inadequate transportation facilities which are needed
now to bring food and raw materials from the Balkans
to Germany; secondly, it forces him to spread still further his forces, which now must hold a line stretching
for more than a thousand miles from Narvik to Hen-
daye in the west, and on the east the long frontier with
Russia, where he keeps a minimum of thirty-five divisions and one whole air fleet. Hitler is reported furious
at his junior Axis partner for jumping the gun.

With winter upon us, it is now obvious that there
will be no German attempt to invade Britain this fall.
Why has the invasion not been attempted? What has
happened to the grand lines of Hitler's strategy? Why
no final victory, no triumphant peace, by now? We
know that at the beginning of last June he felt certain
of them by summer's end. His certainty inspired the
armed forces and the entire German people with the
same sure feeling. He and they had no doubts about it.
Were not the stands erected and painted, and decorated
with shining Swastika eagles and black-and-silver iron
crosses for the great Victory Parade through the Brandenburger Tor? Early last August they were ready.

What, in truth, went wrong?

We do not yet know the entire answer. Some things we can piece together.

In the first place, Hitler hesitated and his hesitation may well prove to have been a blunder as colossal as the indecision of the German High Command before Paris in 1914, marking a turning-point in the war that none of us can yet grasp, though it is manifestly too early yet to say so. The French army was liquidated by June 18, when Pétain asked for an armistice. Many who followed the German army into France expected Hitler to turn immediately and strike at Britain while the iron was hot, while the magic spell of invincibility was still woven round him and his magnificent military machine. The British, Hitler knew, were reeling from the titanic blows just struck them. They had lost their ally, France. They were just receiving home the demoralized remnants of their Continental expeditionary force, whose costly, irreplaceable arms and equipment had been abandoned on the beach of Dunkirk. They had no longer a great organized, equipped land army. Their shore defences were pitiful. Their all-powerful navy could not fight in great force in the narrow waters of the English Channel, over which Göring's bombers and Messerschmitts, operating from bases in sight of the sea, now had control.

This was the situation when Hitler strode into the little clearing of Compiègne Forest on June 21 to dictate a harsh armistice to France. I recall now — though the fact did not make any impression on me at the time — that at Compiègne there seemed to be no hurry on the part of the German military to finish with Britain. Piecing together today — long after the event — stray bits of conversation picked up here and there in Compiègne and Paris, I think the word had come down from Hitler that an invasion of Britain, though it must be

quickly and thoroughly prepared, would never be necessary. Churchill would accept the kind of peace which
the little Austrian was mulling over in his mind. It
would be a Nazi peace, it would bar Great Britain from
the continent of Europe at long last; it might be merely
an armistice, a breathing-spell during which Germany
could consolidate such overwhelming strength on the
mainland that Britain in the end would have to bow to
the Nazi conqueror without a fight — but it would be
a face-saving peace for Churchill. And he would accept
it. I believe Hitler really thought he would. And his
certainty delayed and slackened the work which was
necessary to prepare a devastating invasion force — the
construction and concentration of barges, pontoons,
shipping, and a thousand kinds of equipment.

[LATER. *1941.* — The breathing-spell might also be
used to settle accounts with Russia. Some observers in
Berlin were convinced at the end of June that Hitler
was sincerely anxious to conclude peace with Britain
(on his own terms, of course) so that he could turn on
the Soviet Union — always his long-term objective.
Hitler, they believed, felt sure the British would understand this. Had not Chamberlain's policy been to en-
courage the German military machine to turn east
against Russia? The fact that during the last days of
June and throughout the first three weeks of July one
German division after another was recalled from France
and hurriedly transported to what the Germans usually
referred to as the " Russian front " would seem to bear
this out. But it is by no means certain. Russia, Hitler
believed, was weak. Russia could wait. What was important was getting Great Britain out of the way. Yet
his mind seemed full of puzzling contradictions. He

realized very clearly that German hegemony on the Continent, not to mention a foothold in Africa, could never
be safely maintained as long as Britain held command
of the seas and possessed a growing air force. But Hitler must have known that Britain, battered and groggy
though she was by what had happened in France and
the Low Countries, would never accept a peace which
would rob her of her sea power or curtail her increasing
strength in the air. Yet this was the only kind of peace
he could afford to offer her. The evidence seems con-
clusive, however, that he was confident that Churchill
preferred this manner of peace to facing a German invasion.]

It may well be that Hitler expected Churchill to
make the first move for peace. Didn't an Englishman
know when he was beaten? Hitler would be patient and
wait and let the realization sink into his thick British
head.

He waited a month. All through the last lovely week
of June and the first three weeks of July he waited. In
Berlin we heard rumours that contact had been made
between Berlin and London at Stockholm and that
peace was being talked, but we never had any confirmation of them and in all probability there was nothing to
them.

On July 19 Hitler spoke out in the Reichstag. He
publicly offered Britain peace, though concealing his
terms. But the very fact that he devoted most of the
session to promoting his leading generals to be field-
marshals, as though the victorious war were in truth
over, indicated that he still felt certain that Churchill
would bid for peace.

The Luftwaffe had been established on the North Sea

and the Channel for more than a month, but German planes had refrained from any serious attacks on the land of Britain. Hitler was holding it back.

I think the prompt and sweeping reaction in England to his " offer of peace " came as a shock to him. He was not prepared for such a quick and unequivocal rejection. I think he hesitated until the end of July — twelve days — before he accepted that rejection as Churchill's final answer. By then a month and a half of precious time had been largely lost.

There is reason to believe that most of the generals of the High Command, especially General von Brauchitsch, commander-in-chief of the army, and General Halder, chief of the General Staff, maintained grave doubts as to the chances of success of an invasion of Britain by a land army, particularly by the end of July, when the British, they knew, had to some extent recovered from the blows of May and June. The naval problem involved seems to have baffled them, for one thing. And though Göring, it is reliably reported, assured them he could knock out the RAF in a fortnight, as he had destroyed the Polish air force in three days, they seem to have had some doubts on this score too — doubts that in the end proved fully justified.

Throughout July the Germans had been gathering barges and pontoons in the canals, rivers, and harbours along the French, Belgian, and Dutch coasts and assembling shipping at Bremen, Hamburg, Kiel, and various ports in Denmark and Norway. A common sight on the new highways in western Germany was that of Diesel-motored barges taken from as far away as the Danube being hauled on rollers towards the west coast. Workshops and garages all over the Reich were put to work on small armoured, self-propelling pontoons which could carry a tank or a heavy gun or a company of

troops in a calm sea, but not in a rough one, over the
Channel. Behind Calais and Boulogne on August 16 I
saw a few of them.

On the night of August 5, as noted elsewhere in this
journal, Hitler had a long conference in the Chancellery
with his chief military advisers. Present were Göring,
Admiral von Raeder, Brauchitsch, Keitel, and General
Jodl, the last a member of Hitler's own separate military staff and extremely influential in the army since
the beginning of the offensive in the west. It is likely
that Hitler at this meeting made his decision to attempt
the invasion as soon as possible and went over the final
plans with the chiefs of the three armed forces.

What were those plans? Probably we shall never
know. But from what little has leaked out, I think we
can deduce the grand lines of the strategy decided upon.
It was cautious and it was classical. A great air offensive against the British air force would be launched on
or about August 13. The RAF would be wiped out by
September 1. And then with complete mastery of the
air over the Channel so as to prevent the British navy
from concentrating, and over England to smash the
defending British artillery, the invasion would be
launched. The main force would cross the Channel in
barges, pontoons, and small boats. Other ships, protected by planes, would set out from Bremen, Hamburg,
and the Norwegian ports to make landings in Scotland,
but this would be only a secondary move and one that
would depend upon the action of the British navy in
these waters. Another small expedition of ships from
Brest would take Ireland. And of course there would be
parachute action on a large scale to demoralize the
English and the Irish in the rear.

The army would not move until the Royal Air Force
had been annihilated. On this being accomplished de-

pended the whole setting-in-action of the plans for actual invasion. Göring promised its speedy accomplish-
ment. But like many a German before him, he made a
grave miscalculation about British character and therefore British strategy. Göring, I think it is now clear,
based his confidence on a very simple calculation. He
had four times as many planes as the British. No matter how good English planes and pilots were — and he
had a healthy respect for both — he had only to attack
in superior numbers, and even if he lost as many planes
as the enemy, in the end he would still have a substantial
air fleet, and the British would have none. And there
was little likelihood of losing as many as your opponent
if you always attacked with more planes than he had.

What Göring and all the other Germans were incapable of grasping was that the British were prepared to
see their cities bombed and destroyed before they would
risk *all* of their planes in a few great air battles to defend them. To the British this was mere common sense
and the only tactic that could save them. To the German military mind it was incomprehensible. It is primarily due to this error of judgment, so typically German, I'm convinced, that the plan to invade Britain this
year had to be abandoned.

To destroy the British air force Göring had to get it
off the ground. But try as he did — and when I was
on the Channel in the middle of August he was sending
as many as a thousand planes a day across the Channel
to lure the British into the air — he never succeeded.
The British kept most of their planes in reserve. Their
cities, for a while, suffered as a result. But the RAF
remained intact. And as long as it did, the German land
army massed on the coast would not move.

Why, many Germans here have asked, could not the
Luftwaffe destroy the RAF on the ground? The air

forces of Poland, Holland, Belgium, and France had
largely been wiped out by the Germans demolishing
their planes on the airfields before they had a chance
to take off. The Luftwaffe's own answer is undoubtedly
true. German airmen tell me that the British simply
scattered their planes on a thousand far-flung fields. No
air force in the world, with any opposition at all, could
hunt them out in sufficient numbers to destroy any sizable portion of Britain's available planes.

There is another aspect of Göring's failure which is
not so clear to us here in Berlin. He tried for a month —
from the middle of August to the middle of September
— to destroy the air arm of Britain's defence. This attempt was made in daylight attacks, for you cannot destroy a nation's air force at night. But by the third
week of September the great daylight raids had ceased.
I note that in my broadcast of the night of September 23
I wrote: " It now seems clear from a perusal of the
German reports that Germany's big air attacks on Britain — unlike a month ago — now take place at night,
not during the day. The High Command today calls
the day flights ' armed reconnaissance '; the night raids
' reprisal attacks.' " The military censor did not like the
paragraph and only allowed me to use it after I had
softened it down by writing that the large-scale attacks
of the Luftwaffe " are recently more at night," which
was bad English but did not prevent the idea from being
put across.

At first thought there seems to be some contradiction between our belief here that the British preferred to
see their cities bombed rather than risk too many of
their planes in the air at any one time to drive off the
Germans — between that and the fact that in the short
space of a month the RAF obviously took such a toll
of German planes that Göring had to abandon his

grandiose daylight attacks. And this contradiction has bothered most of the neutral air attachés here, who, like the rest of us, have access to only the German side of the picture.

Probably it is no contradiction at all. From what German airmen themselves have told me, I think the truth is that while the British never risked more than a small portion of their available fighters on any one day, they did send up enough to destroy more German bombers per day than Göring could afford to lose. For he was using them in large mass formations, more as a snare to get the British fighters off the ground so that his Messerschmitts could wipe out Britain's fighter defence than for mere bombing. And here British air tactics played an important role. The Germans tell me that the British fighter squadrons had strict orders to avoid combat with German fighters whenever possible. Instead they were instructed to dart in on the bombers, knock off as many of the cumbersome machines as they could, and then steal away before the German fighters could engage them. These tactics led many a German Messerschmitt pilot to complain that the British Spitfire and Hurricane pilots were cowards, that they fled whenever they saw a German fighter. I suspect now the German pilots understand that the British were not being cowardly but merely smart. Knowing they were outnumbered, that the German aim was to destroy their entire fighter force and that Britain was lost when her last fighters were destroyed, the British adopted the only strategy which would save them. They went after the German bombers, which are set-ups for a pursuit ship, and avoided the Messerschmitts. After all, the Messerschmitts carried no bombs which could destroy England. On at least three separate days, during the latter part of August and the first days of September,

British fighters shot down some 175 to 200 German planes, mostly bombers, and crippled probably half as many more. These were blows which made the Luftwaffe momentarily groggy and which it could not indefinitely sustain despite its numerical superiority, because the British were losing only a third or a fourth as many planes, though, to be sure, they were mostly fighters.

There was another factor. As most of the air battles took place over England, the British were saving at least half of the pilots whose machines were shot down. They were able to bail out and come down safely by parachute. But every time a German plane was shot down, its occupants, though they might save their lives with parachutes, were lost to the Luftwaffe for the duration of the war. In the case of bombers, this meant a loss of four highly trained men with each plane brought down.

And so the first fortnight in September came and went, and still the Germans could not destroy the British air force and, as a consequence, wrest complete superiority in the air over England. And the great Nazi land army waited, cooling its heels behind the cliffs at Boulogne and Calais and along the canals behind the sea. It was not left entirely unmolested. At night, as I have described from personal experience earlier in this journal, the British bombers came over, blasting away at the ports and the canals and the beaches where the barges were being assembled and loaded. The German High Command has maintained absolute silence about this little chapter in the war. What losses in men and materials were sustained by these insistent British air attacks is not known. I can get no authoritative information on the subject. But from what I saw of these bombings myself and from what I've been told by Ger-

man airmen, I think it is highly improbable that the
German army was ever able to assemble in the ports
of Boulogne, Calais, Dunkirk, and Ostend, or on the
beaches, enough barges or ships to launch an invasion in
the force that would have been necessary. Whether it
ever seriously attempted to do so is also doubtful.

The stories emanating from France that an actual
full-fledged invasion of Britain was attempted on or
around the middle of September and repulsed by the
British also seem to be without foundation on the basis
of what we know here. In the first place, the British,
whose morale probably was none too high at this time,
would certainly have let the news out if they had actually repulsed an all-out German attempt to invade England. Publication of the news not only would have had
an electrifying effect on British public opinion and that
of the rest of Europe but would have been of immeasur-
able value in rallying help from America. Washington
in August, I'm told, had almost given Britain up as lost
and was in a state of jitters for fear the British navy
would fall into Hitler's hands and thus place the American eastern seaboard in great danger. Also, the British
would have had little trouble through short-wave broadcasts in German and the dropping of pamphlets in letting the German people know that Hitler's great bid
for the conquest of Britain had failed. The psychological effect in Germany would have been crushing.

What probably happened, so far as we can learn here,
is that the Germans early in September attempted a
fairly extensive invasion rehearsal. They put barges
and ships to sea, the weather turned against them, light
British naval forces and planes caught them, set a number of barges on fire, and caused a considerable number
of casualties. The unusual number of hospital trains
full of men suffering from burns would bear out this

version, though we have no other concrete information
to go on.

Perhaps the British have already put out information
that makes this account of why the invasion attempt
never came off superfluous. I note it down as the sum of
our information here in Berlin, which is little enough.
The only time the Germans give out information is
when they are winning, or have won. They have not
mentioned their submarine losses, for instance, for
nearly a year.

BERLIN, *November 5*

If all goes well, I shall leave here a month
from today, flying all the way to New York — by Lufthansa plane from here to Lisbon, by Clipper from
there to New York. The very prospect of leaving here
takes a terrible load off your heart and mind. I feel
swell. It will be my first Christmas at home in sixteen
years, my other brief visits having all been during the
summer or fall. Went to a Philharmonic concert this
evening. A Bach concerto for three pianos and orchestra, with the conductor, Furtwängler, and Wilhelm
Kemp and some other noted pianist at the pianos, was
very good indeed. Afterwards played my accordion —
sacrilege after the Philharmonic and Bach! — but a
gruff-voiced man occupying the next room did not appreciate my efforts and knocked on the wall until I betook myself, with accordion, to the bathroom. He is
probably one of those Rhineland industrialists who
come up here to get some sleep, since in western Germany they are visited by the RAF nearly every night.
The hotel is full of them and they are very cranky.

B ERLIN, *November* 6

Roosevelt has been re-elected for a third term! It is a resounding slap for Hitler and Ribbentrop and the whole Nazi regime. For despite Willkie's almost outdoing the President in his promises to work for Britain's victory, the Nazis ardently wished the Republican candidate to win. Nazi bigwigs made no secret of this in private, though Goebbels made the press ignore the election so as not to give the Democrats the advantage of saying that the Nazis were for Willkie.

Last week at least three officials in the Wilhelmstrasse phoned me excitedly to ask if the Gallup Poll could be trusted. They had just had a cable from Washington, they said, that the poll showed Willkie having a fifty-fifty chance. The news made them exceedingly happy.

Because Roosevelt is one of the few real leaders produced by the democracies since the war (look at France; look at Britain until Churchill took over!) and because he can be tough, Hitler has always had a healthy respect for him and even a certain fear. (He admires Stalin for his toughness.) Part of Hitler's success has been due to the luck of having mediocre men like Daladier and Chamberlain in charge of the destinies of the democracies. I'm told that since the abandonment for this fall of the invasion of Britain Hitler has more and more envisaged Roosevelt as the strongest enemy in his path to world power, or even to victory in Europe. And there is no doubt that he and his henchmen put great hope in the defeat of the President. Even if Willkie turned out to be a bitter enemy of Berlin, the Nazis figured that, were he elected, there would be a two months' interim at Washington during which nothing would be done to help the Allies. There would be more months of indecision, they calculated, before Willkie, inexperienced in politics and world affairs, could hit his stride. This could only profit Nazi Germany.

But now the Nazis face Roosevelt for another four years — face the man whom Hitler has told a number of people is more responsible for keeping up Britain's resistance to him than any other factor in the war except Winston Churchill. No wonder there were long faces in the Wilhelmstrasse tonight when it became certain that Roosevelt had won.

BERLIN, *November* 8

The British tonight, we hear, are giving Munich a bad pounding. It is the anniversary of the beerhouse *Putsch* and therefore a timely evening to bomb. That *Putsch* was hatched on the evening of November 8, 1923 at the Bürgerbräukeller in Munich, and all the anniversary celebrations have always been held there. A year ago tonight a bomb went off in the place a few minutes after Hitler and *all* the Nazi leaders had left, but it killed several lesser fry. Tonight Hitler took no chance on Himmler's planting another bomb on him. He held his speech in another beer cellar, the Löwenbräu. As with all his speeches since the British began to come over, he began it before dark so that the meeting was over before the RAF bombers arrived. His address today raised a problem for American broadcasters. Neither CBS nor NBC permit recordings to be broadcast on their networks. When the German Broadcasting Company called me up this afternoon to offer Hitler's speech to CBS, I was a little suspicious at the time given for the broadcast — eight p.m. I didn't think the Führer would dare speak so late — since theoretically, now that the long nights are upon us, the British could be in Munich by nine p.m. or so. So I asked whether it

was a recording they were offering us. A high official
of the RRG would not say. He said it was a military
secret.

" Nor," he added, " may you cable your New York
office whether you suspect it is a recording or not. If
you cable, you must merely say that we offer a Hitler
broadcast to America."

I have means of contacting Paul White in New York
very quickly without using the German commercial radio
service, which first submits my messages to the censor.
As a matter of fact, it was not necessary this evening.
Before I could get in touch with New York, word came
that there would be no broadcast of Hitler at all this
evening. His speech would be broadcast only tomorrow.
The British bombing has stopped the broadcast. Later
in the evening I learned that the Germans knew all the
time they were offering me a recorded broadcast of the
speech at eight p.m., since the original talk had been
made at five p.m. Must take this up with New York.

Amusing to note of late, on the desks of the German
officials I have business with, copies of cables which I
have received from, or sent to, my New York office. I
of course have known for some time that they saw all
my outgoing and incoming messages and have had no
end of fun sending absurd messages to New York criti-
cizing these officials by name or concocting something
that would keep them guessing. Fortunately Paul
White has a sense of humour and has sent appropriate
answers.

BERLIN, *November* 9

To record a few of the jokes which the Germans
are telling these days:

The chief of the Air-Raid Protection in Berlin re-

cently advised the people to go to bed early and try to
snatch two or three hours of sleep before the bombings
start. Some take the advice, most do not. The Berliners
say that those who take the advice arrive in the cellar
after an alarm and greet their neighbours with a " Good
morning." This means they have been to sleep. Others
arrive and say: " Good evening! " This means they
haven't yet been to sleep. A few arrive and say: " *Heil
Hitler!* " This means they have always been asleep.

Another: An airplane carrying Hitler, Göring, and
Goebbels crashes. All three are killed. Who is saved?

Answer: The German people.

A man from Cologne tells me what he claims is a true
story. He says there are so many different uniforms to
be seen in the streets there now that one can't keep track
of them. Thus it was that a British flying-officer who
had to bail out near Cologne walked into the city on a
Sunday afternoon to give himself up. He expected that
the police or some of the soldiers on the street would arrest him immediately. Instead they clicked their heels
and saluted him. He had a ten-mark note with him, as,
my friends say, all British pilots flying over Germany
do, and decided to try his luck at a movie. He asked for
a two-mark seat. The cashier gave him back nine marks
in change, explaining politely that men in uniform got
in for half-price. Finally, the movie over, he walked the
streets of Cologne until midnight before he could find
a police station and give himself up. He told the police
how difficult it was for a British flyer in full uniform
to get himself arrested in the heart of a German city.
The police would not believe him. But they summoned
the cashier of the movie house just to see.

" Did you sell this man a ticket to a performance this
evening? " they asked her.

" Certainly," she piped back; " for half-price, like

all men in uniform." Then proudly, espying the initials
RAF on his uniform: " It isn't every day I can welcome
a *Reichs Arbeits Führer*. Me, I know what RAF stands
for."

Molotov is coming to Berlin. For more than a year
— ever since Ribbentrop flew to Moscow in August 1939
and signed the pact which brought the two arch-enemies
of this earth together — we've had rumours that the
number-two Bolshevik would repay the visit. Once during the summer I know for a fact that a lot of old Soviet
red flags were dusted off and assembled in the Chancellery for a Molotov visit that failed to come off because,
for one thing, Moscow insisted on sending a regiment of
GPU plain-clothes men, and Himmler would agree to
only a company of them. Then Hitler and Ribbentrop
exerted all the pressure they could to force Stalin to
send Molotov here just before the American elections.
For some reason they thought that if ballyhooed properly, it would scare the American people and result in
the defeat of Roosevelt. Stalin apparently understood
the reason and declined. But tonight it's official. Molotov is coming next week. The timing of the visit is still
good. It will help make up for the slap of Roosevelt's
election, which the German people faintly realize was
not good news for Hitler, and also for the waning prestige of the Axis caused by the failure of the Italians to
make any progress in Greece.

BERLIN, *November* 11

        Armistice Day, which in a way now seems like
a great irony. There was no mention of it in the German press. In Belgium and France the German military authorities forebade its celebration. Roosevelt's

Armistice Day speech was completely suppressed here. We broadcast from coast to coast every utterance of Hitler, but the German people are not permitted to know a word of what Roosevelt speaks. This is one of the weaknesses of democracy, I think, though some people think it is one of its strengths.

This evening I went to see Harald Kreuzberg dance. He's getting a little old now and is not quite so nimble or graceful, though still very good. The hall was packed.

BERLIN, *November* 12

A dark, drizzling day, and Molotov arrived, his reception being extremely stiff and formal. Driving up the Linden to the Soviet Embassy, he looked to me like a plugging, provincial schoolmaster. But to have survived in the cut-throat competition of the Kremlin he must have something. The Germans talk glibly of letting Moscow have that old Russian dream, the Bosporus and the Dardanelles, while they will take the rest of the Balkans, Rumania, Yugoslavia, and Bulgaria. If the Italians can take Greece, which is beginning to look doubtful, they can have it.

When I went to our Embassy today to get a tin of coffee from my stores, which I keep there, the box, containing a half-year's supply, was gone. It had just disappeared. If I were not leaving shortly, this would be a blow. Coffee, ever since it became impossible to buy it in Germany, has assumed a weird importance in one's life. The same with tobacco. Some times the Embassy takes pity on me, but for the most part I smoke German pipe tobacco. Of late it has made foul smoking.

BERLIN, *November* 14

We thought the British would come over last
night when Ribbentrop and Göring were fêting Molotov at a formal state banquet. The Wilhelmstrasse was
very nervous at the prospect, for they did not like the
idea of adjourning to the cellar with their honoured
Russian guests. Instead, the British came over this evening — shortly before nine p.m., the earliest yet —
while Molotov was host to the Germans at the Soviet
Embassy. Molotov, we hear, declined to go to the cellar and watched the fireworks from a darkened window.
The British were careful not to drop anything near by.

According to the German radio and the Warsaw *Zeitung*, Mr. Hoover's American representative here has
offered his congratulations to Dr. Frank, the tough little
Nazi Governor of Poland, on the anniversary of his year
in office. He congratulates him for what he has done
for the Poles!

My information is that there will be no Polish race
left when Dr. Frank and his Nazi thugs get through
with them. They can't kill them all, of course, but they
can enslave them all.

BERLIN, *November* (*undated*)

A pleasant dinner and evening at X's in Dah-
lem. Two well-known German figures present, one a
high Nazi official, and they spent the evening telling
jokes on the regime, especially on Goebbels, whom they
both appeared to loathe. About ten p.m. the British
came and we went up on the balcony to watch the fireworks, which were considerable. Once there came the
familiar whistle of a bomb just before it lands near you.
Automatically we all dived through the open door into

a pitch-dark bedroom, landing in a heap on the floor.
The bomb shook the house, but we got no splinters.
Pitiful how few planes the British can spare for this
Berlin job. There were not more than a dozen of them
tonight. They have done comparatively little damage
here so far.

BERLIN, *November* 20

Today was *Busstag,* some sort of German
Protestant holiday. Feeling low, I went to a candle-
light concert in the Charlottenburg castle and heard
a string quartet play Bach nobly. I am definitely getting away from here by plane to Lisbon on December 5
if I can get all the necessary papers in time. The Foreign Office, the police, the secret police, and so on must
approve my exit visa before I can leave. And getting
Spanish and Portuguese visas is proving no easy job.
Harry Flannery has arrived from St. Louis to take
over.

BERLIN, *November* 23

Was having a most excellent dinner and some
fine table-talk at Diplomat G.'s about eight forty-five
this evening when the butler called me away to the
phone. It was one of the girls at the *Rundfunk* saying
that the British bombers were about ten minutes away
and that I had better hurry if I wanted to broadcast
this evening. I dashed out to my car. An aid-warden
who also had the advance notice tried to stop me from
driving away, but I brushed past him. I was not familiar with the blacked-out streets in this neighbourhood and twice almost drove at great speed into the
Landwehr Canal. I reached the Knie, about two miles

from the *Rundfunk*, when the sirens sounded. To stop, obey the law, put my lights out, park, and go to a shelter, as the law insisted? That meant no broadcast. Better to have remained at the dinner and enjoyed an evening for a change. I had never missed a broadcast because of air-raids. I decided to disobey the law. I left my hooded lights on and stepped on the gas. One policeman after another along the Kaiserdamm popped out waving a little red lamp. I raced by them, at fifty miles an hour. It was a stupid thing to do, because several times I just brushed other cars which had stopped in the darkness and put out their lights, as the law prescribes. You could not see them. By a miracle I did not smash into any of them, but about three blocks from the *Rundfunk* I decided my luck had been good enough, pulled up my car, and sprinted to the radio before the police could snatch me into a public shelter.

I hear from party circles that Julius Streicher, the sadistic, Jew-baiting czar of Franconia and notorious editor of the anti-Semitic weekly *Stürmer*, has been arrested on orders of Hitler. No tears will be shed within or without the party, for he was loathed by nearly all. I shall always remember him swaggering through the streets of Nuremberg, where he was absolute boss, brandishing the riding whip which he always carried. He has been arrested, say party people, pending investigation of certain financial matters. If Hitler cared much, he could make some additional investigations. He could look into the little matter of how it came about that so many party leaders acquired great country estates and castles.

BERLIN, *November* 25

     I have at last got to the bottom of these "mercy killings." [1] It's an evil tale.

The Gestapo, with the knowledge and approval of the German government, is systematically putting to death the mentally deficient population of the Reich. How many have been executed probably only Himmler and a handful of Nazi chieftains know. A conservative and trustworthy German tells me he estimates the number at a hundred thousand. I think that figure is too high. But certain it is that the figure runs into the thousands and is going up every day.

The origin of this peculiar Nazi practice goes back to last summer after the fall of France, when certain radical Nazis put the idea up to Hitler. At first it was planned to have the Führer issue a decree of law authorizing the putting to death of certain persons found mentally deficient. But it was decided that this might be misunderstood if it leaked out and be personally embarrassing to Hitler. In the end Hitler simply wrote a letter to the secret-police administration and the health authorities authorizing the *Gnadenstoss* (coup de grâce) in certain instances where persons were proved to be suffering from incurable mental or nervous diseases. Philipp Bouhler, state secretary in the Chancellery, is said to have acted as intermediary between Hitler and the Nazi extremists in working out this solution.

At this point Bethel, already mentioned in these notes, creeps into the story. Dr. Friedrich von Bodelschwingh is a Protestant pastor, beloved by Catholics and Protestants alike in western Germany. At Bethel, as I have noted down previously, is his asylum for mentally deficient children. Germans tell me it is a model institution

[1] See entry for September 21.

of its kind, known all over the civilized world. Late last summer, it seems, Pastor von Bodelschwingh was asked to deliver up certain of his worst cases to the authorities. Apparently he got wind of what was in store for them. He refused. The authorities insisted. Pastor von Bodelschwingh hurried to Berlin to protest. He got in touch with a famous Berlin surgeon, a personal friend of Hitler's. The surgeon, refusing to believe the story, rushed to the Chancellery. The Führer said nothing could be done. The two men then went to Franz Gürtner, Minister of Justice. Gürtner seemed more troubled at the fact that the killings were being carried out without benefit of a written law than that they were being carried out. However, he did agree to complain to Hitler about the matter.

Pastor von Bodelschwingh returned to Bethel. The local *Gauleiter* ordered him to turn over some of his inmates. Again he refused. Berlin then ordered his arrest. This time the *Gauleiter* protested. The pastor was the most popular man in his province. To arrest him in the middle of war would stir up a whole world of unnecessary trouble. He himself declined to arrest the man. Let the Gestapo take the responsibility; he wouldn't. This was just before the night of September 18. The bombing of the Bethel asylum followed. Now I understand why a few people wondered as to *who* dropped the bombs.

Of late some of my spies in the provinces have called my attention to some rather peculiar death notices in the provincial newspapers. (In Germany the custom among all classes is to insert a small paid advertisement in the newspapers when a death occurs, giving the date and cause of death, age of the deceased, and time and place of burial.) But these notices have a strange ring to them, and the place of death is always given as one of three spots: (1) Grafeneck, a lonely castle situated near Münzingen, sixty miles southeast of Stuttgart; (2) Hartheim, near Linz on the Danube; (3) the Sonnenstein Public Medical and Nursing Institute at Pirna, near Dresden.

Now, these are the very three places named to me by Germans as the chief headquarters for the " mercy killings."

I am also informed that the relatives of the unfortunate victims, when they get the ashes back — they are never given the bodies — receive a stern warning from the secret police not to demand explanations and not to " spread false rumours." These provincial death notices therefore take on more meaning than they might otherwise. I will note down here some typical ones, changing the names, dates, and places, for obvious reasons.

Leipziger Neueste Nachrichten, October 26: "JOHANN DIETTRICH, FRONT SOLDIER 1914–1918, HOLDER OF SEVERAL WAR DECORATIONS, BORN JUNE 1, 1881, DECEASED SEPTEMBER 23, 1940. AFTER WEEKS OF UNCERTAINTY, I RECEIVED THE UNBELIEVABLE NEWS OF HIS SUDDEN DEATH AND CREMATION AT GRAFENECK IN WÜRTTEMBERG."

From the same paper in October: "AFTER WEEKS OF UNCERTAINTY, THE INTERMENT OF MY BELOVED SON, HANS, WHO DIED SUDDENLY ON SEPTEMBER 17 AT PIRNA, WILL TAKE PLACE ON OCTOBER 10."

Again: "WE HAVE RECEIVED THE UNBELIEVABLE NEWS THAT MY MOST BELOVED SON, THE ENGINEER RUDOLF MÜLLER, DIED SUDDENLY

AND UNEXPECTEDLY NEAR LINZ–ON–THE–
DANUBE. THE CREMATION TOOK PLACE
THERE."

Another: "AFTER THE CREMATION HAD TAKEN
PLACE WE RECEIVED FROM GRAFENECK THE
SAD NEWS OF THE SUDDEN DEATH OF OUR
BELOVED SON AND BROTHER, OSKAR RIED.
INTERMENT OF THE URN WILL TAKE PLACE
PRIVATELY AT X CEMETERY UPON ITS RECEIPT."

And: "AFTER WEEKS OF ANXIOUS UNCER–
TAINTY WE RECEIVED THE SHOCKING NEWS ON
SEPTEMBER 18 THAT OUR BELOVED MARIANNE
DIED OF GRIPPE ON SEPTEMBER 15 AT PIRNA.
THE CREMATION TOOK PLACE THERE. NOW
THAT THE URN HAS BEEN RECEIVED, THE
BURIAL WILL TAKE PLACE PRIVATELY ON HOME
SOIL."

This last notice is signed October 5, indicating that
the authorities delayed three weeks in delivering the
ashes. Twenty-four such advertisements, I'm informed,
appeared in the Leipzig papers the first fortnight of
last month.

I am struck in the second from the last of these notices by the expression: " *After* the cremation had
taken place, we received the sad news of the sudden
death. . . ." Struck too by the expression used in the
first two: " after weeks of uncertainty " came " sudden
death "; and by the use of the words: " unbelievable
news."

No wonder that to Germans used to reading between
the lines of their heavily censored newspapers, these
notices have sounded highly suspicious. Does sudden
death come naturally after " weeks of uncertainty "?
And why are the bodies cremated first and the relatives
told of the deaths later? Why are they cremated at all?

Why aren't the bodies shipped home, as is usually done?

A few days ago I saw the form letter which the families of the victims receive. It reads:

"We regret to inform you that your ——, who was recently transferred to our institution by ministerial order, unexpectedly died on —— of ——. All our medical efforts were unfortunately without avail.

"In view of the nature of his serious, incurable ailment, his death, which saved him from a lifelong institutional sojourn, is to be regarded merely as a release.

"Because of the danger of contagion existing here, we were forced by order of the police to have the deceased cremated at once."

This is hardly a reassuring letter, even for the most gullible of Germans, and some of them, upon its receipt, have journeyed down to the lonely castle at Grafeneck, it seems, to make a few inquiries. They have found the castle guarded by black-coated S.S. men who denied them entrance. Newly painted signs on all roads and paths leading into the desolate grounds warned: " *Seuchengefahr!* " (" Keep away! Danger of Pestilence! ") Frightened peasants near by have told them how the S.S. suddenly took over and threw a cordon around the estate. They told of seeing trucks thundering into the castle grounds — but only at night. Grafeneck, they said, had never been used as a hospital before.

Other relatives, I'm told, have demanded details from the establishment at Hartheim, near Linz. They have been told to desist, and that if they talk, severe punishment will be meted out. Some of them obviously have taken their courage in their hands to publish these death notices, no doubt hoping to attract public attention to the murderous business. The Gestapo, I hear, has now forbidden publication of such notices, just as Hitler, after the heavy naval losses in Norway, forbade the relatives of drowned sailors to publish notices.

X, a German, told me yesterday that relatives are rushing to get their kin out of private asylums and out of the clutches of the authorities. He says the Gestapo is doing to death persons who are merely suffering temporary derangement or just plain nervous breakdown.

What is still unclear to me is the motive for these murders. Germans themselves advance three:

1. That they are being carried out to save food.

2. That they are done for the purpose of experimenting with new poison gases and death rays.

3. That they are simply the result of the extreme Nazis deciding to carry out their eugenic and sociological ideas.

The first motive is obviously absurd, since the death of 100,000 persons will not save much food for a nation of 80,000,000. Besides, there is no acute food shortage in Germany. The second motive is possible, though I doubt it. Poison gases may have been used in putting these unfortunates out of the way, but if so, the experimentation was only incidental. Many Germans I have talked to think that some new gas which disfigures the body has been used, and that this is the reason why the remains of the victims have been cremated. But I can get no real evidence of this.

The third motive seems most likely to me. For years a group of radical Nazi sociologists who were instrumental in putting through the Reich's sterilization laws have pressed for a national policy of eliminating the mentally unfit. They say they have disciples among many sociologists in other lands, and perhaps they have. Paragraph two of the form letter sent the relatives plainly bears the stamp of this sociological thinking: " In view of the nature of his serious, incurable ailment, his death, which saved him from a lifelong institutional sojourn, is to be regarded merely as a release."

Some suggest a fourth motive. They say the Nazis calculate that for every three or four institutional cases, there must be one healthy German to look after them. This takes several thousand good Germans away from more profitable employment. If the insane are killed off, it is further argued by the Nazis, there will be plenty of hospital space for the war wounded should the war be prolonged and large casualties occur.

It's a Nazi, messy business.[1]

BERLIN, *November 27*

Flannery, though he has just arrived, must leave for Paris. The Nazis pledge us to secrecy about a big story they claim will break there next week. In radio, we must be there beforehand, if possible, to make our technical arrangements. But I shall depart from this city on December 5, anyway. Many stories about increasing sabotage in Holland. The Germans are furious at the number of their men, in both the army and police, who are being shoved into the numerous Dutch canals on these dark nights and drowned. X tells me a funny one. He says the British intelligence in Holland is working fine. Both sides in this war have built a number of dummy airdromes and strewn them with wooden planes. X says the Germans recently completed a very large one near Amsterdam. They lined up more than

[1] On December 6, 1940 the Vatican condemned the "mercy killings." Responding to the question whether it is illicit for authorities to order the killing of those who, although they have committed no crime worthy of death, nevertheless are considered no longer useful to society or the state because of physical or mental deficiencies, the Sacred Congregation of the Holy Office held that "such killings are contrary to both natural and divine law." It is doubtful if the mass of German Catholics, even if they learned of this statement from Rome, which is improbable, understood what it referred to. Only a minority in Germany know of the "mercy deaths."

a hundred dummy planes made of wood on the field and waited for the British to come over and bomb them. Next morning the British did come. They let loose with a lot of bombs. The bombs were made of wood.

Berlin, *December* 1

This being Sunday, with no noon broadcast, a word or two summing up some things before I leave.

A year and a half of the blockade has pinched Germany, but it has neither brought the German people to the verge of starvation nor seriously hampered the Nazi war machine. The people in this country still eat fairly well. The diet is not fancy and Americans could hardly subsist on it, but Germans, whose bodies in the last century became accustomed to large amounts of potatoes, cabbage, and bread, are still doing pretty well — on potatoes, cabbage, and bread. What they lack are enough meats, fats, butter, and fruit. The present ration of a pound of meat and a quarter of a pound of butter or margarine a week is not so much as they were used to in peace-time, but it will probably keep them fairly fit for some time to come. The shortage of fruit, rich in vitamins, is acute. Last winter's severe cold ruined the German fruit crop. At the moment apples are the only fruit on the market and they are being reserved for the young, the sick, and pregnant women. Last winter we never saw an orange or banana, nor have any appeared this winter. In the meantime vitamin pills of poor quality are being rationed to troops and children. It is true the German people have no coffee, tea, chocolate, fruit. They get one egg a week and too little meat and fat. But they have almost everything else and they are not going to starve in any measurable future.

If it is to be a long war, the clothing problem will become serious. Germany must import all of its cotton and almost all of its wool, and the present system of clothing rations is based on the theory that on the whole the German people must get along with what they now possess on their backs and in their closets until the war is over and the blockade lifted. The shortage of textiles is felt not only by civilians but also in the army, which is hard put to it to find enough overcoats for all its troops this winter. Hitler has already had to put his Labour Service men into stolen Czech uniforms. The so-called *Organisation Todt*, comprising several hundred thousand men who perform the jobs usually done by our army labour battalions, has no uniforms at all for its men. When I saw them at the front last summer, they were wearing tattered civilian clothes. The Germans are striving desperately to make up for their shortage of raw materials by developing *ersatz* textiles, especially those made of cellulose. But I don't think you can clothe eighty million people with wood products yet.

As to the raw materials necessary for the prosecution of the war, the situation is this: Germany has plenty of iron. And from Yugoslavia and France she gets enough bauxite to provide her with all the aluminum she needs for her vast aircraft production. There is a serious shortage of copper and tin, but she is probably getting enough from the Balkans and Russia to keep her out of desperate straits.

As to oil, General Schell, the czar of the oil business, says he is not worried. If he were, of course, he wouldn't admit it. But certain facts must be kept in mind:

1. The German air force is absolutely independent of imported stocks of oil. All German airplane engines are designed and manufactured to operate on synthetic

gasoline which Germany manufactures herself from her own coal. Her present supply of this — some four million tons a year — is more than adequate for the needs of the Luftwaffe. The British could endanger this supply by bombing the oil refineries where coal is made into gasoline. This they are trying to do. They've hit the great Leuna works near Leipzig and another refinery at Stettin. But their attacks have been too weak to put the refineries out of action or even seriously affect their output.

2. Germany is now obtaining practically the complete output of the Rumanian oil fields and, on paper at least, is getting one million tons a year from Russia, though I doubt if the Soviets have actually delivered that much since the war began.

3. When the war started, Germany had large stocks of oil on hand, and she obtained quite a windfall in Norway, Holland, and Belgium.

4. Civilian consumption of oil has been reduced to almost nothing. No private cars and practically no delivery trucks are allowed to operate. And oil is prohibited for heating purposes.

My guess is that Germany has enough oil or will get enough to satisfy her military requirements for at least two more years.

As to British air attacks on Germany, their value so far has been principally psychological, bringing the war home to the weary civilian population, wearing their already frayed nerves still thinner and robbing them of sleep. The actual physical damage wrought by bombs after six months of night attacks has on the whole not been very great. Its exact extent, of course, we do not know. Probably only Hitler, Göring, and the High Command know, and they do not tell. But I think we have a fair idea. In general, the damage has been greatest in the Ruhr, where German heavy industry is concentrated. Were this region to be really devastated by air attacks, Germany could not continue the war. But so far it has received only pin-pricks. I'm afraid the truth is that Germany's actual war production has not yet been seriously curtailed by the RAF attacks. Probably the most serious result in the Ruhr has not been the actual physical damage to plant or transportation, but something else. Two things: First, millions of working hours have been lost by the workers' being forced to spend part of their evenings in shelters. Second, the efficiency of the workers has been reduced by loss of sleep.

Next to the Ruhr, the German ports of Hamburg and Bremen and the naval bases at Wilhelmshaven and Kiel have received the severest bombing. But they have not yet been put out of business. Undoubtedly the most savage British bombing has been reserved for the German-occupied Channel ports. There the RAF has a short haul and can carry bigger bombs and more of them. There is little left of the docks at Ostend, Dunkirk, Calais, and Boulogne.

Berlin itself has suffered comparatively little damage from the night raids. I suppose a stranger arriving here for the first time could walk for hours through the business and residential sections without seeing a damaged building. Probably not more than five hundred dwellings have been hit and, since the British use small bombs, most of them have been repaired and reoccupied within a month. Most of the British attacks have been on the factories which skirt the city. Some of them of course have been hit, but, with the exception of two or three small plants, none of them have been seriously crippled, so far as we know. The great Siemens electrical works on the northwestern fringe of Berlin has been

hit, a machine shop here, a storage room there, damaged.
But it is extremely doubtful if its armament production
has been lowered by more than five per cent on any one
day. When I drove around it recently, its great machines were humming and no damage at all was visible
from the outside.

For some reason the British have greatly reduced
their air attacks on Berlin during the last six weeks.
This is a great mistake. For when they came over
nearly every night, the morale of this nerve centre which
keeps Germany together slumped noticeably. The Germans, I'm convinced, simply cannot take the kind of
pounding which the Luftwaffe is meting out to the British in London. Admittedly the British can't give it to
them, yet; but they can certainly send over a handful
of planes five or six nights a week to keep the Berliners
in their cellars. The effect of this on morale would be
great.

Why hasn't there been more damage done to Germany by the RAF? Because the British have attacked
with too few planes and their bomb loads have been too
light. Neutral air attachés differ in their estimates of
the number of British planes employed in the bombing
of Berlin, but the best opinion is that the maximum
number on any one night is thirty planes, with the average number being about fifteen. The total number of
British planes over Germany on a good night varies
from sixty to eighty.

The British bomb loads are too light because the
RAF planes have to fly a distance that necessitates
most of the load being made up of gasoline and oil. For
the Berlin run they must make a round trip of 1,100
miles. The American-built Flying Fortresses could
carry the big destructive bombs to Berlin and get safely
back to England. But so far we haven't heard or seen

any of them. As it is, the British flyers — certainly the
world's bravest men — have a very narrow margin of
time to find their objectives in Berlin. Probably not
more than fifteen minutes. The Luftwaffe people say
that some of their planes never get back, being forced
down by lack of fuel in the North Sea.

How many airplanes has Germany? I don't know.
I doubt if twenty persons in the world know. But I do
know something about German airplane production.
At the moment it varies between 1,500 and 1,600 planes
a month. Maximum German production capacity is
3,000 planes a month. That is, Göring could force production up to that figure if he had all the supplies he
needed and ordered all available plants to be run at full
capacity twenty-four hours a day, seven days a week.
Incidentally, Germany has not added a square foot of
aviation plant since the war began. At the moment
Göring, Milch, and Udet are searching desperately for
a new type of fighter plane — something that will be
definitely superior to the new Spitfires and the Airaco-
bras which Britain is ordering from America.

After a year and a half of actual total war German
morale is still good. Let us admit the fact. There is
no popular enthusiasm for the war. There never was.
And after eight years of deprivation caused by Nazi
preparation for war, the people are weary and fatigued.
They crave peace. They are disappointed, depressed,
disillusioned that peace did not come this fall, as promised. Yet as the war goes into its second long, dark
winter, public morale is fairly high. How explain the
contradiction? Keep in mind three things:

First, that the millennium-old longing of Germans for
political unification has been fulfilled. Hitler achieved

it, where all others in the past — the Habsburgs, the
Hohenzollerns, Bismarck — failed. Few people outside
this country realize how this unification has knitted the
German nation together, given the people self-confi-
dence and a sense of historical mission, and made them
forget their personal dislike of the Nazi regime, its
leaders, and the barbaric things it has done. Also —
coupled with the rebirth of the army and air force and
the totalitarian reorganization of industry, trade, and
agriculture on a scale never before realized in this world
— it makes the German feel strong. For most Germans
this is an end in itself, for to be strong in their scheme
of life is to be all. It is the emergence of the primitive,
tribal instinct of the early German pagans of the vast
forests of the North to whom brute strength was not
only the means but the end of life. It is this primitive
racial instinct of " blood and soil " which the Nazis have
reawakened in the German soul more successfully than
any of their modern predecessors and which has shown
that the influence of Christianity and western civilization on German life and culture was only a thin veneer.

Second, morale is good because the German people
feel they have this summer revenged the terrible defeat
of 1918 and have achieved a string of military victories
which has at last ensured their place in the sun — domination today of Europe, tomorrow perhaps of the world.
And German character is such that the German must
either dominate or be dominated. He understands no
other relation between human beings on this earth. The
golden mean of the Greeks which the Western world has
achieved to some extent is a concept beyond his compre-
hension. Moreover, the great mass of workers, peasants,
and petty tradesmen — as well as the big industrialists
— are conscious that if Hitler succeeds with his New

Order, as they are confident now he will, it will mean
more of the milk and honey of this world for them. That
it will of necessity be obtained at the expense of other
peoples — Czechs, Poles, Scandinavians, French —
does not bother the German in the least. On this he has
no moral scruples whatsoever.

Third, one of the prime springs which push the German people along in full support of a war for which they
have no enthusiasm, and which they would end tomorrow
if they could, is their growing fear of the consequences
of defeat. Slowly but surely they are beginning to realize the frightful magnitude of the seeds of wrath which
their high-booted troops and Gestapo men have sown
in Europe since the conquest of Austria. They are beginning to see that a victory with the Nazi regime, however much many of them may dislike it, is better than
another German defeat, which this time, if it ever comes
about, will make Versailles seem like a peace of sweet
reason and destroy not only the nation but the Germans
as a people. More than one German of late has confided
to me his fears. If Germany loses, they see the embittered peoples of Europe whom they have brutally enslaved, whose cities they have ruthlessly destroyed, whose
women and children, many of them, in such places as
Warsaw, Rotterdam, and London, they have cold-
bloodedly slain, storming in angry, revengeful hordes
over their beautiful, orderly land, dynamiting it to destruction, and leaving those whom they do not butcher
to starve and die in an utter wasteland.

No, these people, ground down and cheated though
they may be by the most unscrupulous gang of rulers
modern Europe has yet seen, will go a long, long way
in this war. Only a dawning realization some day that
they can't win coupled with Allied assurances that to

give up the struggle will not mean their destruction will make them falter before one side or the other is destroyed.

We who have been so close to this German scene, who have seen with our own eyes the tramping Nazi boots over Europe and heard with our own ears Hitler's hysterical tirades of hate, have found it difficult to keep a sense of historical perspective. I suppose the reasons why Germany has embarked on a career of unbridled conquest do go deeper than the mere fact, all-important though it is, that a small band of unprincipled, tough gangsters have seized control of this land, corrupted its whole people, and driven it on its present course. The roots go deeper, I admit, though whether the plant would have flowered as it has without Hitler, I seriously doubt.

One root is the strange, contradictory character of the German people. It is not correct to say, as many of our liberals at home have said, that Nazism is a form of rule and life unnatural to the German people and forced upon them against their wish by a few fanatic derelicts of the last war. It is true that the Nazi Party never polled a majority vote in Germany in a free election, though it came very close. But for the last three or four years the Nazi regime has expressed something very deep in the German nature and in that respect it has been representative of the people it rules. The Germans as a people lack the balance achieved, say, by the Greeks, the Romans, the French, the British, and the Americans. They are continually torn by inner contradictions which make them uncertain, unsatisfied, frustrated, and which force them from one extreme to the other. The Weimar Republic was so extreme in its liberal democracy that the Germans couldn't work it. And now they have

turned to the extremes of tyranny because democracy
and liberalism forced them to live as individuals, to
think and make decisions as free men, and in the chaos
of the twentieth century this was too much of a strain
for them. Almost joyfully, almost masochistically, they
have turned to an authoritarianism which releases them
from the strain of individual decision and choice and
thought and allows them what to a German is a luxury
— letting someone else make the decisions and take the
risks, in return for which they gladly give their own
obedience. The average German craves security. He
likes to live in a groove. And he will give up his independence and freedom — at least at this stage of his
development — if his rulers provide this.

The German has two characters. As an individual he
will give his rationed bread to feed the squirrels in the
Tiergarten on a Sunday morning. He can be a kind and
considerate person. But as a unit in the Germanic mass
he can persecute Jews, torture and murder his fellow
men in a concentration camp, massacre women and children by bombing and bombardment, overrun without
the slightest justification the lands of other peoples, cut
them down if they protest, and enslave them.

It must also be noted down that Hitler's frenzy for
bloody conquest is by no means exclusive to him in Germany. The urge to expansion, the hunger for land and
space, for what the Germans call *Lebensraum*, has lain
long in the soul of the people. Some of Germany's best
minds have expressed it in their writings. Fichte, He-
gel, Nietzsche, and Treitschke fired the German people
with it in the last century. But our century has not
lacked for successors, though they are little known outside this country. Karl Haushofer has poured books
from the presses dinning into the ears of the Germans
the maxim that if their nation is to be great and lasting,

it must have more *Lebensraum*. Books of his such as *Macht und Erde* (*Power and Earth*) and *Weltpolitik von Heute* (*World Politics of Today*) have profoundly influenced not only the Nazi leaders but a great mass of people. So has Hans Grimm's *Volk ohne Raum* (*People without Space*), a novel which has sold nearly a half-million copies in this country despite its length of some thousand pages. And so has Moeller van den Bruck's *The Third Reich,* written eleven years before Hitler founded the Third Reich.

All these writings emphasized that Germany was entitled by the laws of history and nature to a space more adequate to its mission in life. That this space would have to be taken from others, mostly from Slavs who had settled on it when the Germans themselves were little more than rough tribesmen, made no difference. It is this basic feeling in almost all Germans that the " lesser breed " of Europeans are not entitled to absolute rights of their own, to a piece of land to till and live on, to the very towns and cities they have built up with their own sweat and toil, if a German covets them, which is in part responsible for the present state of Europe.

It is the evil genius of Adolf Hitler that has aroused this basic feeling and given it tangible expression. It is due to this remarkable and terrifying man alone that the German dream now stands such a fair chance of coming true. First Germans and then the world grossly underestimated him. It was an appalling error, as first the Germans and now the world are finding out. Today, so far as the vast majority of his fellow countrymen are concerned, he has reached a pinnacle never before achieved by a German ruler. He has become — even before his death — a myth, a legend, almost a god, with that quality of divinity which the Japanese people

ascribe to their Emperor. To many Germans he is a
figure remote, unreal, hardly human. For them he has
become infallible. They say, as many peoples down
through history have said of their respective gods:
" He is always right."

Notwithstanding many reports to the contrary which
float abroad, he is the sole and absolute boss of Germany
today, brooking no interference from anyone and
rarely asking and almost never heeding suggestions
from his intimidated lieutenants. The men around him
are all loyal, all afraid, and none of them are his friends.
He has no friends, and since the murder of Röhm in the
1934 purge there has not been a single one of his followers who addressed him with the familiar *Du*. Göring,
Goebbels, Hess, and all the others address him in only
one way: " *Mein Führer*." He leads a lonely, closely
guarded life, and since the beginning of the war his
very whereabouts are carefully kept from the public
and the outside world by Himmler.

Nowadays he rarely dines with his chief aides, preferring the easier company of his party cronies of the
early " fighting " days, men like Wilhelm Brückner, his
adjutant, Hess, his first private secretary — the only
man in the world he fully trusts — and Max Amann,
his top sergeant during the World War, whom he has
made czar of the highly remunerative Nazi publishing
house, the Eher Verlag.[1] The really big shots in the
Nazi world, Göring, Goebbels, Ribbentrop, Ley, and the
heads of the armed services, see Hitler either at appoint-
ments during the day, or after dinner in the evening,
when he often invites them to see a private showing of a
film. Hitler has a passion for movies — including the

---

[1] Amann is also president of the Reich Press Chamber, in which
capacity he rules the newspapers of Germany. Through the Eher
Verlag and subsidiary holding companies, Amann has also gained
financial control of most of the large newspapers in the country.

products of Hollywood. (Two of his favourites were
It Happened One Night and *Gone with the Wind*.)

Hermann Göring is very definitely the Number Two
man in Germany and the only Nazi who could carry on
the present regime were Hitler to pass on. The fat,
bemedalled Reichsmarschall enjoys a popularity among
the masses second only to Hitler's — but for opposite
reasons. Where Hitler is distant, legendary, nebulous,
an enigma as a human being, Göring is a salty, earthy,
lusty man of flesh and blood. The Germans like him because they understand him. He has the faults and vir-
tues of the average man, and the people admire him for
both. He has a child's love for uniforms and medals.
So have they. He has a passion for good food and drink
in Gargantuan quantities. They too. He loves display
— palaces, marble halls, great banqueting rooms, gay
costumes, servants in livery. They love them too. And
despite the efforts of Goebbels to stir up popular criti-
cism of his rival, they display no envy, no resentment
of the fantastic, mediæval — and very expensive —
personal life he leads. It is the sort of life they would
lead themselves, perhaps, if they had the chance.

No other henchman of Hitler has the popularity or
the strength or the ability to keep the Nazi regime in
power.

Hitler always hoped that his protégé Hess might be
his successor and in his will has named him to take over
after Göring. But Hess lacks the strength, the ambi-
tion, the driving force and imagination for the job of
top man. Goebbels, who used to be Number Three, has
lost ground since the war, partly because he has been
swept aside by the military and the secret police, partly
because he has bungled his propaganda job at crucial
moments, as when he ordered the press and radio to

celebrate the victory of the *Graf Spee* the day before
it was scuttled.

Goebbels's place as the third man in Germany has
been taken by Heinrich Himmler, the mild-mannered
little fellow who looks like a harmless country school-
teacher, but whose ruthlessness, brutality, and organizing talents have landed him in a key position in the
Third Reich. He's important because he has whipped
the Gestapo into an organization which now watches
over almost every department of life in the country and
which keeps for Hitler and the politicians a watchful
eye on the army itself. Himmler, alone among Hitler's
lieutenants, has power of life and death over all citizens
of Germany and the occupied lands, and it is a rare day
when he does not take advantage of it. The evidence you
find buried daily in the back pages of the newspapers
in the little notices which read: " S.S. Chief Himmler
announces that Hans Schmidt, a German (or Ladislav
Kotowski, a Pole), has been shot while offering resistance to the police."

There are two other " big men " around Hitler,
Joachim von Ribbentrop and Dr. Robert Ley. Ribbentrop, a vain and pompous man, thoroughly disliked in
the party and by the public, is still in favour with the
Führer because he guessed right about England and
France (Göring guessed wrong and as a result suffered
a temporary eclipse) at Munich. The fact that he
guessed wrong in September 1939, when he assured
Hitler the British wouldn't fight, has not affected, for
some reason, his standing at the Chancellery. Hitler
recently has taken to calling him a " second Bismarck,"
though men like Göring, who despises him, can't understand why.

Dr. Robert Ley is boss of the Nazi party machine and

of German Labour, a tough, brawling, hard-drink-ing, able administrator, fanatically loyal to his chief.

These men — Göring, Himmler, Hess, Ribbentrop, and Ley — comprise the " Big Five " around Hitler. They are called in for consultation. All but Göring give their advice very carefully and with some timidity. In every case the decision is always Hitler's.

There are lesser men in the hierarchy, some Nazi chiefs who have been given big jobs, some men who hold their posts because Hitler thinks they are competent technicians. The most important are: Walther Darré, an able and enterprising Minister of Agriculture, Bern-hard Rust, who as Minister of Education has revolu-tionized and degraded the schools of Germany, Wilhelm Frick, a lifelong civil servant who owes his present po-sition as Minister of Interior to his betrayal of the Bavarian government, of which he was a permanent official, Dr. Walther Funk, who ousted Dr. Schacht to become president of the Reichsbank and Minister of Economics, and Dr. Todt, a brilliant and imaginative engineer who built Hitler's great network of super-highways and the fortifications of the Westwall.

Alfred Rosenberg, Hitler's mentor in early party days and formerly one of the chief men in the party, has entirely lost out and today has no importance in the party or the country. He was too much of a dreamer to be practical, and in the jungle struggle with the more ruthless men who make up the Nazi firmament he failed miserably. Since the Nazi alliance with Moscow in August 1939, which he alone opposed, he has been little heard of. To assuage his feelings Hitler has given him a magnificent title: *Beauftragter des Führers zur Überwachung der Nationalsozialistischen Bewegung* (Commissioner of the Leader for the Supervision of the

National Socialist Movement). He has also managed
to hold on as editor of Hitler's daily newspaper, *Völkische Beobachter*, though he has little to say about its
policy.

Julius Streicher, once a sinister power in the country,
the man who terrorized his *Gau* of Franconia with a
horsewhip, has also, as previously noted, passed out
of the picture because he couldn't keep his finances
straight.

If Hitler makes the political decisions, be it noted
that he also calls the tune in the army. General von
Brauchitsch, the able but not brilliant commander-in-
chief of the army, occasionally speaks up, though not
often. Keitel is little more than liaison man between
Hitler and the General Staff. General Halder, chief
of the General Staff, is probably the most brainy man
in the army, but is allowed no credit by Hitler, who encourages talk that he himself personally directs both the
tactics and the strategy of the great campaigns. General von Reichenau has told me personally that this is
true, but I doubt it. On the other hand Hitler no doubt
makes the major decisions of where the next blow will
fall and when. One of his chief military advisers, very
powerful in the army — though completely unknown
to the German public — is General Alfred Jodl, chief
of Hitler's own military staff.

There is one final question to be tackled in these
rambling conclusions: does Hitler contemplate war with
the United States? I have argued this question many
hours with many Germans and not a few Americans here
and have pondered it long and carefully. I am firmly
convinced that he does contemplate it and that if he
wins in Europe and Africa he will in the end launch it

unless we are prepared to give up our way of life and adapt ourselves to a subservient place in his totalitarian scheme of things.

For to Hitler there will not be room in this small world for two great systems of life, government, and trade.[1] For this reason I think he also will attack Russia, probably before he tackles the Americas.

It is not only a question of conflict between the totalitarian and democratic ways of life, but also between Pan-German imperialism, whose aim is world domination, and the fundamental urge of most of the other nations on the earth to live as they please — that is, free and independent.

And just as Hitler's Germany can never dominate the continent of Europe as long as Britain holds out, neither can it master the world as long as the United States stands unafraid in its path. It is a long-term, fundamental conflict of dynamic forces. The clash is as inevitable as that of two planets hurtling inexorably through the heavens towards each other.

As a matter of fact, it may come sooner than almost all Americans at home imagine. An officer of the High Command somewhat shocked me the other day while we were discussing the matter. He said: " You think Roosevelt can pick the moment most advantageous to America and Britain for coming into the war. Did you ever stop to think that Hitler, a master at timing, may choose the moment for war with America — a moment which he thinks will give him the advantage? "

I must admit I never did.

As far as I can learn, Hitler and the High Command

---

[1] He publicly admitted it in a speech on December 10, 1940. Contrasting the totalitarian and democratic worlds, he said: " We can never be reconciled with this world. . . . One of these worlds must break asunder. . . . These are two worlds, and I believe one of these worlds must crack up."

do not contemplate any such move within the next few months. They still hold that they can bring Britain to her knees before American aid becomes really effective. They talk now of winning the war by the middle of next summer, at the latest. But there are a few in high places who argue that if Hitler actually declares war (he hasn't *declared* any wars yet) against America, he can reap decided advantages. First, it would be the signal for widespread sabotage by thousands of Nazi agents from coast to coast, which would not only demoralize the United States but greatly reduce its shipments to Britain. Second, in case of an actual declaration of war, they argue, our army and especially our navy, alarmed at what Japan might do (according to the tripartite pact it would have to go to war against us), would hold all war supplies at home, supplies that otherwise would go to Britain. Third, they believe that there would be a great increase in American internal strife, with the isolationists blaming Roosevelt for the state of things, as they blamed him for the Three-Power pact. The third point obviously is false thinking, as a war declaration by Germany would destroy American isolationist sentiment in America in ten seconds.

The Lindberghs and their friends laugh at the idea of Germany ever being able to attack the United States. The Germans welcome their laughter and hope more Americans will laugh, just as they encouraged the British friends of the Lindberghs to laugh off the very idea that Germany would ever turn on Britain.

How would Germany ever attack the United States? I have no authoritative information of German military plans. But I have heard Germans suggest the following possibilities:

If they got all or part of the British navy or have time to build in Europe's shipyards (whose total capac-

ity is far beyond ours) a fairly strong navy, they would
attempt to destroy in the Atlantic that part of our
fleet which was not engaging the Japanese in the Pacific. This done, they could move an army and air force
in stages across the North Atlantic, basing first on Ice-
land, then Greenland, then Labrador, then Newfound-
land and thence down the Atlantic seaboard. As the
bases were moved westward, the air armada would penetrate farther, first towards and then into the United
States. This sounds fantastic, perhaps, but at the present time we have no great air force to oppose such a
move.

Most Germans talk more convincingly of a move
across the South Atlantic. They assume that Germany
will have the French port of Dakar from which to jump
off for South America. They assume too that the main
United States fleet will be engaged in the Pacific. From
Dakar to Brazil is a much shorter distance than from
Hampton Roads to Brazil. A German naval force
based on the African port could feasibly operate in
Brazilian waters, but these waters are almost too far
for an American fleet to be effective in. Transports
could get there from Dakar before transports from
America arrived. Fifth-column action by the hundreds
of thousands of Germans in Brazil and Argentina would
paralyse any defence which those countries might try
to put up. South America could thus, think these Germans, be taken fairly easily. And once in South America, they argue, the battle is won.

BERLIN, *December* 2

Only three more days!

BERLIN, *December* 3

A round of farewell parties which I would just as soon avoid, but can't. An amusing incident at one of them when a Foreign Office official, more decent than most, got rather in his cups and said he had long wanted to show me something. Whereupon he took out a card showing he was a member of the secret police! I must say I hadn't suspected him, though I knew some of his colleagues were members.

The Foreign Office still holding up my passport and exit visa, which worries me. Did my last broadcast from Berlin tonight and fear I swallowed a couple of times.

Before I went on the air Flannery called from Paris. He was quite excited about a big story he said would break day after tomorrow there. He evidently had a German official at his back, for I could not get out of him a hint as to what was up. The rumour here is that Hitler is to offer France some sort of a semi-permanent peace settlement, install Laval in power in Vichy, making Pétain a mere figurehead, in return for France's joining the Axis and entering the fight against Britain.

BERLIN, *December* 4

Got my passport and official permission to leave. Nothing to do now but pack. Wally [Deuel], who is as anxious to get away as I am, left today. He was to go by plane, but the weather was bad and the Germans, who've lost three big passenger planes in the last three weeks — a good friend of mine was killed on one of them — sent him as far as Stuttgart by train. Hope I have better luck. I must leave all my books and most of my clothes here, as baggage accommodation on

the plane is limited. Ed Murrow promises to meet me
at Lisbon. My last night in a black-out. After tonight
the lights . . . and civilization!

In a plane, Berlin–Stuttgart, *December* 5

It was still dark and a blizzard was blowing
when I left the Adlon for the airport at Tempelhof this
morning. There was some question whether we would
take off, but at nine thirty a.m., a few minutes ago, we
finally did. I don't like this weather to fly in. . . .

Dresden Airport. Later. — We've just
had a rather close call. We were about two thirds of
the way to Stuttgart when our big Junkers thirty-two-
passenger plane suddenly began to ice up. Through
the window I could see ice forming on the wing and the
two starboard motors. The stewardess, though she tried
to hide it bravely, got frightened, and when a stewardess on a plane gets frightened, so do I. Perspiration
began to pour down the forehead of a Lufthansa official
sitting opposite me. He looked very worried. Clumps
of ice breaking off from the motors hurled against the
side of the cabin with a terrifying crack. The pilot,
hardly able to control the plane, tried to climb, but
the ice was too heavy. Finally he turned back and
dived and slipped from 2,500 metres to 1,000 metres
(roughly, from 8,200 to 3,200 feet).

" Can't go lower or we'll hit a mountain," the Lufthansa man explained to me.

" So, so . . ." I said.

" Can't use the radio because the blizzard blots it
out," he continued.

" Perhaps we could land some place," I suggested.

"Not around here," he said. "Ground visibility is zero."

"So, so . . ." I said.

The plane tossed and dipped. Pretty soon, by the dial, I saw we were dropping below 1,000 metres. The weight of the ice was getting too much. The next fifteen minutes were an age. And then out of the mist and snow we dived towards a road. It was a two-lane *Autobahn.* We flew along fifty feet above it, but sometimes when we hit a flurry of snow or a fog spot, the pilot, momentarily blinded, zoomed up, afraid of grazing the trees or a hill. And then at eleven thirty we were skimming into an airport. It turned out to be Dresden, which is as far from Stuttgart as Berlin, if not farther. It was nice to feel one's feet on the ground. The two pilots, when they stepped out of their cabin, looked very shaky. Over lunch here I overheard one telling the airport superintendent that he had had to fight like hell to keep his machine in the air. Weird: we had no more stepped into the lunchroom here than the noon news broadcast was switched on and the first item of news told of an American plane cracking up near the Chicago airport with several fatal casualties. It's just an unlucky day, I guess.

In a plane, Stuttgart—Lyon—Marseille—Barcelona, *December* 6

A slight *Katzenjammer* . . . last night the excitement at leaving Germany, the close shave in the plane, the nice bars in Stuttgart. . . . Hallet Johnson, counsellor of our Legation in Stockholm, shows up in the plane. He says I've been sleeping for an hour — ever since we left Stuttgart — and that this is his first flight and that we've been flying blind through the clouds and . . . We refuel at Lyon. The German air force is in control of the field, though this is in unoccupied France. On one side of the field a large number of dismantled French war planes piled up; on the other side a hundred French planes lined up, in perfect condition — some of those planes the French never used to fight with. . . . A German Foreign Office official with the face of a crow looks at the junked planes and sneers: " *La Belle France!* And how we've destroyed her! For three hundred years, at least! " . . . Nearing Barcelona we skirt the coast, and suddenly off the starboard side I see our little Spanish village, Lloret de Mar, the houses white in the afternoon sun against the green hills. A long time. . . .

LATER. BARCELONA. — Fascism has brought chaos and starvation here. This is not the happy, carefree Barcelona I used to know. On the Paseo, on the Ramblas, on the Plaza de Cataluña, gaunt, hungry, bitter faces moving silently about. At the Ritz Hotel, which we reach on a rickety farm wagon from the air station, because there is no oil for cars, I run into a couple of friends.

" God, what has happened here? " I ask. " I know the civil war left things in bad shape. But this . . ."

" There is no food," they reply. " There is no organization. The jails are jammed and overflowing. If we told you about the filth, the overcrowding, the lack of food in them, you would not believe us. But no one really eats any more. We merely keep alive."

At the airport the Spanish officials keep us cooped up in a tiny room all afternoon, though we are only a few. They, too, seem paralysed — incapable of the least bit of organizing. The chief officer of police has not

washed his hands for a week. His main preoccupation
is our money. We count over and over for him our silver,
our paper money, our travel cheques. Finally, as darkness falls, he lets us go.

Wally comes in on a German plane from Stuttgart
about an hour after we have arrived. He has a tale to
tell of leaving Germany. His plane had not gone from
Berlin to Stuttgart and he had made the journey by
train, thus losing a day. That made his exit visa run
out before he could leave German soil. No official in
Stuttgart at first would take the responsibility of issuing a new one. He must return to Berlin for that. To
return to Berlin meant that he would have to begin all
over again — wait for a new exit visa, wait for new
visas for Spain and Portugal, wait months for a place
in the plane from Berlin to Lisbon and more months
for a place on the plane or boat from Lisbon to America.
He saw his return to America postponed indefinitely,
perhaps until the end of the war. At the last minute the
secret police finally allowed him to depart.

ESTORIL, NEAR LISBON, *December* 7

Lisbon and light and freedom and sanity at
last! We flew from Barcelona to Madrid against a hun-
dred-kilometre-an-hour gale. The pilot of the slow old
Junkers-52 thought for a while he would have to turn
back because of lack of fuel, but he finally made it. We
bumped the whole way over the mountains, most of
which we cleared by only a few feet. Air pockets so
bad that two passengers hit the ceiling, one of them
being knocked out by the blow.

The chaos at the Madrid airport was even worse than
at Barcelona. Franco's officers ran madly round in
circles. The authorities decided that because of the gale

no planes could take off. Then they decided one of three scheduled flights could be made to Lisbon. They told me I could go, then that I couldn't go, then that I must catch the four p.m. train, then that the train had left. All the while shouting officials and passengers milling about the place. There was a restaurant, but it had no food. In the end they called the passengers for the Lisbon plane. Only a group of Spanish officials and the German diplomat would be allowed to go. I asked for my baggage. No one knew where it was. Then an official came tearing up to me and tugged me towards a plane. No opportunity to ask about baggage or where the plane was going. In a minute we were off, flying over the ruins of the University Cité, and then down the Tagus Valley until dusk, when Lisbon came into view. At the airport the Portuguese authorities held me up a couple of hours because I could not show a ticket for New York, but finally they let me go. In Lisbon the hotels were full, no rooms to be had — the city full of refugees — but here I have found one. A good dinner tonight with some local wines and a stroll through town to stare at the lights and now to bed, feeling a great load slipping off. Ed [Murrow] arrives tomorrow from London and we shall have a mighty reunion.

Estoril, *December* 8

Unable to sleep — a sudden toothache, the first in my life, and now I shall pay for my neglect though it was impossible to do anything in Germany, where the shortage of gold and other metals has reduced dentists to plugging teeth with a tin alloy. But there was a glorious southern sun and I spent the morning tramping through the municipal garden, delighted that so many flowers were still in bloom, and then along the beach, where great blue rollers were coming in from the sea, breaking furiously into foam on the sun-strewn sands. The tranquillity, the peacefulness, the soft rhythm of the sea were tremendous. They were too much, they demanded an adjustment that could not be made in a morning. I fled, hailed a taxi, and went into Lisbon to wait for Ed's plane. The suspicious Britishers at the air-line would not say when the London plane was coming in or whether it was coming, apparently for fear the information in some miraculous way would get to the Germans, who would shoot it down. I waited until dark and then returned to Estoril.

LATER. — Ed finally arrived and it was grand. Since ten p.m. we have been talking a year of the war out of our systems and now at five a.m. to bed, pleasantly exhausted. Considering the bombings he has taken and the killing pace of his job, Ed looked better than I had expected — in fact, right fit.

ESTORIL, *December* 9

We lolled in the sun on the beach. Ed says the bombing of Britain has been severe, but not so bad as the Germans have boasted. Besides London — Coventry, Bristol, Southampton, and Birmingham have taken terrible poundings, but it has been the centre of these cities — the churches, the public buildings, the private dwellings — that has been hardest hit. The curtailment of war industrial output, Ed thinks, has been due not so much to physical damage of actual factory plant, but to the disorganization of the cities where the workers live and where electric power, water, and gas facilities are concentrated. The British argue, he says, that the Luftwaffe in its night attacks does not aim at factories, but has two other main objectives: first, to strike terror in the civilian population; second, to knock out essential public services and thus paralyse the great cities. I think this is correct.

Ed has good tidings about British morale, about which we in Berlin were a little doubtful. He says it's superb.

Estoril, *December* 10

Pat Kelly, the genial and able local manager of Pan American Airways, confides that I have small chance of getting home for Christmas if I wait for a Clipper. The service is stalled because of ground swells at Horta, which prevent the big ships from taking off. He advises taking the boat. Since this will be my first Christmas at home in sixteen years, if I make it, I went in this afternoon to the offices of the Export Lines to book on the *Excambion*, leaving Friday. The office was jammed with a mob of refugees — jittery, desperate, tragic victims of Hitler's fury — begging for a place — any place — on the next ship. But as one of the company officials explained to me, there are three thousand of them in Lisbon and the boats only carry one hundred and fifty passengers and there is only one boat a week. He promised me a place on the *Excambion*, sailing Friday the 13th, though it may only be a mattress in the writing room.

Tonight Ed and I did the Casino. The gaming rooms were full of a weird assortment of human beings, German and British spies, male and female, wealthy refugees who had mysteriously managed to get a lot of money out and were throwing it about freely, other refugees who were obviously broke and were trying to

win their passage money in a few desperate gambles
with the fickle roulette wheel, and the usual international
sharpsters you find at such places. Neither Ed nor I
had any luck at roulette and we adjourned to the ballroom, where the same kind of people were trying to
drown whatever feelings they had in drink and jazz.

ESTORIL, *December* 11

A visit to a Lisbon *dentista*. He gave me some
herbs to boil for my ulcerated tooth, which has made
sleep impossible since I arrived.

Ed depressed at a wire from London this afternoon
telling him that his new office was bombed and demolished by the Germans last night. Fortunately no one
was killed. His old office was destroyed by a German
bomb a couple of months ago.

ESTORIL, *December* 12

We sat up until four o'clock this morning
batting out a joint broadcast scheduled for tonight.
We feel rather pleased with it.

LATER. — No broadcast. The talk was set
for two a.m. this night and we sent the script over to the
local radio at eight p.m. so the Portuguese censors
would have plenty of time. At midnight the censor telephoned and said very politely that he had only been
able to translate two of the ten pages, but that he found
it very interesting and no doubt would be able to finish
it by next week, and we could broadcast then. We argued until almost air-time, but it was obvious that the
Portuguese had no intention of risking wounding the

feelings of either the British or the Germans. We got New York to postpone the show until four a.m., but by three thirty we had made no progress whatsoever, and finally, defeated, we went to bed.

ABOARD THE *Excambion, December* 13 (*midnight*)

All day both of us depressed at leaving, for we have worked together very closely, Ed and I, during the last three turbulent years over here and a bond grew that was very real, a kind you make only a few times in your life, and somehow, absurdly no doubt, sentimentally perhaps, we had a presentiment that the fortunes of war, maybe just a little bomb, would make this reunion the last.

We paced up and down the dock in the darkening light of dusk, waiting for the ship to go. There was a little open-air bar for the stevedores on the dock with a tough, frowzy Portuguese blonde behind it. She kept chattering and pouring the drinks. Soon it was dark and they began pulling the gangway in. I climbed aboard and Ed disappeared into the night.

A full moon was out over the Tagus, and all the million lights of Lisbon and more across the broad river on the hills sparkled brightly as the ship slid down to sea. For how long? Beyond Lisbon over almost all of Europe the lights were out. This little fringe on the southwest corner of the Continent kept them burning. Civilization, such as it was, had not yet been stamped out here by a Nazi boot. But next week? Next month? The month after? Would not Hitler's hordes take this too and extinguish the last lights?

Five other American correspondents going home from the war, from England, from Germany, from France,

sat in the ship's little bar over "old-fashioneds."
It was a very good way of cushioning your farewell. I
joined them. I had one. But alcohol is not always
enough. I felt restless, excited. I went up on deck. For
a time I stood against the rail watching the lights recede
on a Europe in which I had spent all fifteen of my adult
years, which had given me all of my experience and what
little knowledge I had. It had been a long time, but they
had been happy years, personally, and for all people
in Europe they had had meaning and borne hope until
the war came and the Nazi blight and the hatred and the
fraud and the political gangsterism and the murder and
the massacre and the incredible intolerance and all the
suffering and the starving and cold and the thud of a
bomb blowing the people in a house to pieces, the thud
of all the bombs blasting man's hope and decency.

INDEX

William Craig

THE FALL OF JAPAN

General Hideki Tojo, known as The Razor, had worked long and hard to extend Japanese power. He succeeded brilliantly: By August of 1942, Japan ruled the Pacific. Here, for the first time, is the full story of how Tojo's achievement was undone in the final phase of World War II—the exciting, tumultuous weeks that sank the Japanese Empire in a sea of fire and fury. "William Craig has described the most violent, shock-filled, and melancholy chapter in human history. . . . He has a vivid imagination, a sense of pace, a clean style, an intense feeling for people, diligence in research, and, most astonishing of all, exactitude and perspective in dealing with military operations, bureaucratic tangles, and technical problems. . . . *The Fall of Japan* is virtually faultless"—*The New York Times Book Review*. "Popular contemporary history at its best"—*Atlantic*.